Toward a Psychology of Art

Rudolf Arnheim TOWARD A

PSYCHOLOGY OF ART

COLLECTED ESSAYS

University of California Press, Berkeley and Los Angeles 1972

University of California Press
Berkeley and Los Angeles, California

© 1966 by The Regents of the University of California

Third Printing 1972
First Paperback Edition 1972

Picasso's Nightfishing at Antibes © 1966, SPADEM,
by French Reproduction Rights, Inc.

ISBN: 0-520-00038-2 (cloth)
      0-520-02161-4 (paper)
Library of Congress Catalog Card Number: 66-10692

Designed by Jane Hart

Manufactured in the United States of America

To Mary

BECAUSE SHE SEES WHILE I PUZZLE

CONTENTS

1 INTRODUCTION

I. Keynotes
7 FORM AND THE CONSUMER

17 AGENDA FOR THE PSYCHOLOGY OF ART

II. The Sense of Sight
27 PERCEPTUAL ABSTRACTION AND ART

51 THE GESTALT THEORY OF EXPRESSION

74 PERCEPTUAL AND AESTHETIC ASPECTS
OF THE MOVEMENT RESPONSE

90 PERCEPTUAL ANALYSIS OF A RORSCHACH CARD

102 A REVIEW OF PROPORTION

III. The Visible World
123 ORDER AND COMPLEXITY IN LANDSCAPE DESIGN

136 THE MYTH OF THE BLEATING LAMB

151 ART HISTORY AND THE PARTIAL GOD

162 ACCIDENT AND THE NECESSITY OF ART

181 MELANCHOLY UNSHAPED

192 FROM FUNCTION TO EXPRESSION

IV. Symbols

215 ARTISTIC SYMBOLS—FREUDIAN AND OTHERWISE

222 PERCEPTUAL ANALYSIS OF A SYMBOL OF INTERACTION

245 FOUR ANALYSES:
   THE HOLES OF HENRY MOORE
   A NOTE ON MONSTERS
   PICASSO'S "NIGHTFISHING AT ANTIBES"
   CONCERNING THE DANCE

266 ABSTRACT LANGUAGE AND THE METAPHOR

V. Generalities

285 ON INSPIRATION

292 CONTEMPLATION AND CREATIVITY

302 EMOTION AND FEELING IN PSYCHOLOGY AND ART

320 THE ROBIN AND THE SAINT

VI. To Teachers and Artists

337 WHAT KIND OF PSYCHOLOGY?

343 IS MODERN ART NECESSARY?

353 THE FORM WE SEEK

363 INDEX

INTRODUCTION

A pyramid of science is under construction. The ambition of the builders is eventually to "cover" all things, mental and physical, human and
natural, animate and inanimate, by a few rules. The pyramid will look
sharp enough at the peak, but toward the base it will vanish inevitably
in a fog of stimulating ignorance like one of those mountains that dissolve
in the emptiness of untouched silk in Chinese brush paintings. For as
the base broadens to encompass an ever greater refinement of species,
those few sturdy rules will intertwine in endless complexity and form
patterns so intricate as to appear untouchable by reason.

The prospect is challenging but also frightening. In particular, we
may feel tempted to approach the individuality of human nature,
human actions, and human creations in an attitude of defeatist awe. To
reject all generalization in this field looks good. Who would not like to
be the one who respects the ultimate mystery of all things? With the
smile of the sage one can, without effort, watch the sacrilegious and
clumsy manipulations of the professors. It is an attitude that triumphs in
conversation and noncommittal criticism. Unfortunately it gets us nowhere.

Psychology as a humanistic science is beginning to emerge from an
uneasy rapprochement between the philosophical and poetical interpretations of the mind on the one hand and the experimental investigations
of muscle, nerve, and gland on the other. And barely are we getting used

to what such a science of the mind might be like, when we are faced with attempts to deal scientifically with the most delicate, the most intangible, and the most human among the human manifestations. We attempt a psychology of art.

It is a recent example of the many cross-connections that are being established, during the construction of the great pyramid, between thus far unrelated disciplines of knowledge. "Psychology of Art"—there is a moment of silence during which a person confronted with this notion for the first time tries hastily to reconcile an approach and a subject matter, psychology and art, which do not seem to relate well. O yes, at second thought there appear some fleeting connotations: Leonardo's vulture, Beethoven's nephew, Van Gogh's ear. The prospect does not please the friends of the arts, and it may worry the psychologist.

The papers collected in this book are based on the assumption that art, as any other activity of the mind, is subject to psychology, accessible to understanding, and needed for any comprehensive survey of mental functioning. The author believes, furthermore, that the science of psychology is not limited to measurements under controlled laboratory conditions, but must comprise all attempts to obtain generalizations by means of facts as thoroughly established and concepts as well defined as the investigated situation permits. Therefore the psychological findings offered or referred to in these papers range all the way from experiments in the perception of shape or observations on the art work of children to broad deliberations on the nature of images or of inspiration and contemplation. It is also assumed that every area of general psychology calls for applications to art. The study of perception applies to the effects of shape, color, movement, and expression in the visual arts. Motivation raises the question of what needs are fulfilled by the production and reception of art. The psychology of the normal and the disturbed personality searches the work of art for manifestations of individual attitudes. And social psychology relates the artist and his contribution to his fellowmen.

A systematic book on the psychology of art would have to survey relevant work in all of these areas. My papers undertake nothing of the kind. They are due to one man's outlook and interest, and they report on whatever happened to occur to him. They are presented together because they turn out to be concerned with a limited number of common themes. Often, but unintentionally, a hint in one paper is expanded to full exposition in another, and different applications of one and the same concept are found in different papers. I can only hope that the many overlappings will act as unifying reinforcements rather than as repetitions.

These papers represent much of the output of the quarter of a century during which I have been privileged to live, study, and teach in the United States. To me, they are not so much the steps of a development as the gradual spelling-out of a position. For this reason, I have grouped them systematically, not chronologically. For the same reason, I did not hesitate to change the words I wrote years ago wherever I thought I could clarify their meaning. Removed from my original intimacy with the content, I approached the text as an unprepared reader, and when I stumbled, I tried to repair the road. In some instances, I recast whole sections, not in order to bring them up to date, but in the hope of saying better what I meant at the time.

Some of the earlier papers led to my book, *Art and Visual Perception*, which was written in 1951 and first published in 1954. Sections of the articles on perceptual abstraction, on the Gestalt theory of expression, and on Henry Moore are incorporated in that book. Others continued where the book left off, for instance, the attempts to describe more explicitly the symbolism conveyed by visual form. The short piece on inspiration provided the substance for the introductory chapter on creativity in my more recent book, *Picasso's Guernica*. Finally, in rereading the material, I was surprised to find how many passages point to what is shaping up as my next task, namely, a presentation of visual thinking as the common and necessary way of productive problem solving in any human activity.

Ten of the papers in this book were first published in the *Journal of Aesthetics and Art Criticism*. To mention this is to express my indebtedness to the only scholarly periodical in the United States devoted to the theory of art. In particular, Thomas Munro, its first editor, showed a great trust in the contribution of psychology. He made me feel at home among the philosophers, art historians, and literary critics whose lively propositions inhabit the hostel he founded and sustained. To him, as well as to my friends of the University of California Press, who are now publishing my fourth book, I wish to say that much of what I thought about in these years might not have been cast into final writing, had it not been for their sympathy, which encouraged the novice and keeps a critical eye on the more self-assured pro.

There are a few scientific papers here, originally written for psychological journals but free, I hope, of the terminological incrustation that would hide their meaning from sight. There are essays for the educated friend of the arts. And there are speeches, intended to suggest practical consequences for art education, for the concerns of the artist, and for the function of art in our time. These public lectures are hardly the products of a missionary temperament. In fact, I marveled why anybody would go to a theorist for counsel, illumination, and reassurance in practical matters. However, when I responded to such requests I noticed, bewildered and delighted, that some of my findings pointed to tangible applications, which were taken to be useful.

I. Keynotes

FORM AND THE CONSUMER

Art has become incomprehensible. Perhaps nothing so much as this fact distinguishes art today from what it has been at any other place or time. Art has always been used, and thought of, as a means of interpreting the nature of world and life to human eyes and ears; but now the objects of art are apparently among the most puzzling implements man has ever made. Now it is they that need interpretation.

Not only are the paintings, the sculpture, and the music of today incomprehensible to many, but even what, according to our experts, we are supposed to find in the art of the past no longer makes sense to the average person. Listen to what happens when one of the best known modern critics, Roger Fry, looks at a painting of the 17th century:

Let us note our impressions as nearly as possible in the order in which they arise. First the curious impression of the receding rectangular hollow of the hall seen in perspective and the lateral spread, in contrast to that, of the chamber in which the scene takes place. This we see to be almost continuously occupied by the volumes of the figures disposed around the circular table, and these volumes are all ample and clearly distinguished but bound together by contrasted movements of the whole body and also by the flowing rhythm set up by the arms, a rhythm which, as it were, plays over and across the main volumes. Next, I find, the four dark rectangular openings at the end of the hall

First published in the *College Art Journal*, Fall 1959, 19, 2–9.

impose themselves and are instantly and agreeably related to the two dark masses of the chamber wall to right and left, as well as to various darker masses in the dresses. We note, too, almost at once, that the excessive symmetry of these four openings is broken by the figure of one of the girls, and that this also somehow fits in with the slight asymmetry of the dark masses of the chamber walls (3, p. 23).

Now, this painting, attributed to Nicolas Poussin, tells the story of how Achilles was dressed as a girl by his mother Thetis and hid among the daughters of King Lycomedes because she did not want him to go to Troy and be killed in the war. In the picture, we plainly see Odysseus who in the costume of a peddler entertains the girls with his wares and traps the disguised Achilles by baiting him with a helmet and a shield.

No one could possibly miss seeing the six persons in the foreground of the picture. Roger Fry saw them too, but he hardly looked at them. He thought the story was boringly told and did not matter. Nor did he consider it relevant that the painter Poussin himself "would have been speechless with indignation" at the analysis of what the critic thought the picture was about.

Let me summarize what we have heard so far. A great artist has told a story. The story does not matter. The fact that he wanted to tell the story does not matter. The fact that he is supposed to have told it badly does not matter. His picture is great. It deals with rectangular hollows and volumes and contrasted movements and dark openings. At this point, if your and my senses still work, we feel a cold shiver as though touched by the wing of madness.

Yet Roger Fry was a very sane man. And equally sane are most of the men and women who speak and write and teach as he did. But Fry was fighting a battle. Art had fallen into the danger of losing form, mainly by trying to become a mechanically correct reproduction of nature. That art should make faithful reproductions had been maintained in theory for a long time. When Leonardo da Vinci and his colleagues talked about their craft, they discussed paints and tools and materials and hundreds of tricks as to how to represent animate and inanimate things in a strictly life-like manner. They had much less to say about what we now call the sense of form, namely, the capacity to furnish visible objects with such properties as clarity, unity, harmony, balance, fittingness, or relevance; because these virtues exert themselves naturally whenever any human being builds a boat, or makes a dress or a clay figure, or beats a rhythm, or sings a tune. But it was precisely in the age of

Leonardo that this natural gift of form began to suffer a rare disturbance, created by a civilization that was to replace perceiving with measuring, inventing with copying, images with intellectual concepts, and appearances with abstract forces. In the nineteenth century, to be a good artist had become much more difficult than it had been for two thousand years. And whereas normally one of the hardest tasks for a human being is to make an ugly object, an epidemic of ugliness now infected everything within the reach of the new civilization.

Therapy often requires radical measures, and it was the instinct of self-preservation that made sensitive critics insensitive to the perversity of such sentences as: "Art is the contemplation of formal relations." But that is what was said about painting and sculpture. In a neighboring field, the remarkable Eduard Hanslick, battling against the notion that music existed for the purpose of reproducing the feelings of the human mind, maintained instead that the content of music was "tönend bewegte Formen," that is, "sounding forms in motion" (5, ch. 2).

The consequences of such an approach are illustrated in Fry's analysis of the so-called Poussin. No doubt, it indicates a frightening estrangement of the sensory experiences from their meaning. At the same time, we must acknowledge the size of the threat to which such formalism was and is reacting. The danger shows not so much in the work of the few great artists who succeed in struggling to the heights, but—to speak only of painting and sculpture—in the middle-class of insipidly realistic portraits and landscapes, in the snapshots cast in bronze that celebrate the memory of famous men in our public squares, in the oppressive materialism of official Communist art, in the symbolic marble athletes on the façades of our own government buildings, in the shapelessness of old-fashioned ornaments and new-fangled "abstract" conglomerations of geometry and texture. Man's natural sense of form is indeed threatened, and a large-scale reclaiming action is in order.

But it is one thing to pay attention to the damage and quite another to restrict the concern of art to the elements of sensory phenomena. The assertion that "art is the contemplation of formal relations" must be confronted here with the fundamental and well-established principle that "good form does not show."

Let us remember that a well-mannered person is one whose manners we do not notice; that a good perfume is perceived as an aspect of the lady's own mood and character, not as an odor; that a good tailor or hairdresser fashions the person; that the art of the interior decorator or lighting designer has failed when it attracts attention to itself instead of making the room comfortable, elegant, dignified, cold, warm, or what have you; that the ingredients of a good salad dressing are hard to trace, and that the best musical accompaniment of a stage play or film intensifies the forces of the dramatic action without being heard by itself. The music at a funeral, in a church, or in a dance hall cannot serve its purpose if it is contemplated as a set of formal relations. And it is the funeral, the religious ceremony, and the carnival dance to which we must look for the prototypes of artistic experience, not the museum display of remote objects and the so-called "aesthetic distance" such display produces.

Is it not true that the great works of art are notoriously reluctant to yield their secret to analysis? Many useful and clever things are said about them, but what precisely creates the greatness in the face of an old man in a Rembrandt portrait, the desperate passion of a Beethoven quartet, the perfection of a Greek temple, or the intense freshness of a passage in Dante's *Commedia*? If we are admitted to the grace of such company, we surrender to the magic and barely remember the question: How is it done? The formal devices used are submerged in the statement, in the effect. Precisely this submergence is one of the prerequisites of the work's greatness.

Good form does not show. A statue representing a woman is a woman, not the shape of a woman—this holds true for a Roman Venus or a Gothic Madonna, and also for an African wood carving or the reclining figures of Henry Moore. And, in fact, even the woman is part of the form that disappears in order to leave only the pure visible embodiment of meaning or character. If, instead of meaning and character, you see a human body in the flesh, or if, instead of the human body, you see formal relations, something is wrong with the figure (1).

But where does this leave abstract art or music, which, after all, are nothing other than shapes, colors, sound, rhythm? Exactly the same principle holds true for them. In a successful piece of abstract art or music, a pattern of forces transmits its particular blend of calmness and tenseness, lightness and heaviness—a complete transubstantiation of form into meaningful expression. As soon, however, as the red circles or the blue bars, the crusts of metal or the carefully daubed areas of nothingness make themselves conspicuous; as soon as, in music, the harmonic progressions of the score or the tremolos of the instruments, the diatonic routine or the atonal irresponsibilities, the grating noises or the twelve-tone rows are heard as such, something is wrong with the painting, the sculpture, the music. Or, indeed, with the consumer.

For what has been said here requires reservations. Form is seen to dissolve into content only when the statement is made to conform to the beholder's way of perceiving things. Exotic manners, for instance, strike us with the strangeness of their formal devices. Foreign music may impress us as a display of odd sound-effects. In examining a piece of sculpture done in an unfamiliar style, we may be unable to get beyond the shape, which puzzles us or which we admire as original or as masterfully proportioned. Granted that educated Westerners have become capable of overcoming this obstacle to a remarkable extent for almost any style the history of art has brought forward anywhere. Flexibility, however, has its limits. Also we pay for it with an extremely unstable sense of form. Having trained ourselves to perceive in any idiom, there is no set of shapes, arbitrary and wilful as it may be, which we cannot welcome, but, on the other hand, there is no longer any one idiom into which we slip completely. Being strangers unto nobody and everybody, we find ourselves concerned with shapes.

It seems safe to say that the awareness of style, especially one's own style, is an unusual experience. The invariant attributes of one's own way of being and of doing things are hardly noticed. One cannot really see one's own face in the mirror, because what is always around tends to evade consciousness. Similarly, we cannot see the reflection of our personal manner in the objects we make. Robust cultures think of their own way as *the* correct way of making things, and distinguish it from the inferior efforts of the barbarians. In our midst, a genuine artist is likely to feel uneasy about what we call his style, since this aspect of his work is almost invisible to him. Cézanne looking at one of his landscapes is likely to have seen simply the mountain, which he had attempted to depict as accurately as he could. If somebody had suggested to him that surely he had changed nature in order to adapt it to his own style, it is likely he would have flown into one of his magnificent rages.

But Cézanne's style is only partly shared by the consumers. To them, his Mont Ste Victoire is one mountain among many others, which have been painted by Hiroshige or by Goya, by Brueghel or by Leonardo. If the consumers are fortunate, their minds will gain from this variety of views a rich, but unified conception of what a mountain can be. Otherwise, the mountain will vanish and a parade of styles will remain. The Cézanne landscape becomes an arrangement of post-Impressionist brushstrokes. Or, to use an example from opera: Mozart's young lovers no longer sing out their suffering and joy, but utter the melodies and rhythms of the late Baroque.

The eclecticism or, if you wish, the universality of our culture is not alone in being responsible for our worship of form. There are other, weighty causes, of which I can mention only one, namely, what I will call our "insignificant living." We neglect the human privilege of understanding individual events and objects as reflections of the meaning of life. When we break bread or wash our hands, we are only concerned with nutrition and hygiene. Our waking life is no longer symbolic. This philosophical and religious decline produces an opacity of the world of experience that is fatal to art because art relies on the world of experience as the carrier of ideas. When the world is no longer transparent, when objects are nothing but objects, then shapes, colors, and sounds are nothing but shapes, colors, and sounds, and art becomes a technique for entertaining the senses. Unconscious symbolism, to which we have been running for salvation, is much too primitive to shoulder the task by itself.

Art is the most powerful reminder that man cannot live by bread alone; but we manage to ignore the message by treating art as a set of pleasant stimuli. One of my students told me the other day that she found herself greatly disturbed when she attended a cheerful beer party in the living room of friends who had just acquired a very large reproduction of Picasso's *Guernica*. Undoubtedly the friends, being connoisseurs, thought of Picasso's outcry against the massacre of innocents as a decorative pattern of formal relations. And when I remember being shown through a very modern home in the hills of Los Angeles where a high-fidelity performance of Bach's *St. Matthew's Passion* was used to demonstrate that music could be piped through all the rooms of the house, including the laundry and the bathrooms, and also how often I have had to suffer from recordings of great music being used as background noise for conversation by otherwise well-bred and kindly people, I cannot but realize that music indeed may lose all depth of meaning and be reduced to sounding shapes.

The formalistic approach to art is a device for fending off the disquieting demands that are art's essence.[1] Listen to what the audience says after one of those concerts that are advertised by nothing but the name of the virtuoso, or in an art gallery, or at the theater during intermission. If they talk about what they just saw or heard, as they some-

---

[1] There are other ways of avoiding the issue. The tradition of discussing the subject matter instead of what it expresses survives in the search for clinical symbols.

times do, they will hold forth on what is good and what is bad, who imitates whom, and how the performance compares with the Budapest Quartet or with Jean-Louis Barrault, or that the second aria was too fast or that the last act betrays the latent homosexuality of the author. All these critical observations are presented with a chilly detachment that makes it perfectly clear that the speaker cannot have been in recent communion with Beethoven or Shakespeare, Verdi, or Matisse. The pose coveted by our young intellectuals is no longer that of the stirred lover of the beautiful but the poker face of the critic, who sniffs and judges. I cannot but think with gratitude of the Texas businessman whose wife showed me the precious Renoirs and Derains and Dufys they had on the walls, only to confess with a sigh of resignation: "But I have never been able to find a Picasso that does not upset my husband when he eats his dinner!" If a man has preserved the sense to know that Picasso is upsetting, the light may shine again some day in the darkness.

Everything seems to count except what the work of art is about. A friend of mine in the theater department talked with a colleague from out-of-town, who had just initiated a course in playwriting. Yes, he said, the students were doing well indeed. Some fine dialogue had been written, and there was increasing conciseness and logical sequence. "Of course," he added, "there is no content!" Such episodes make me wonder whether it is not high time for us to remember that where there is no content there can be no form.

The notion of composition for its own sake, which I illustrated with Fry's analysis of a painting, has its counterpart in the studio practice of some of our art departments, art schools, and professional artists. There is great refinement of technique, but little indication that unless the artist has something to say there can be no distinction between right and wrong, no preference for one technique as against another. By now, we start in kindergarten to overwhelm children with an endless variety of materials and tricks, which keep them distracted—distracted from the only task that counts, namely, the slow and patient and disciplined search for the one and only form that fits the underlying experience.

To be sure, artists have good reasons for being wary of discussing the ideas expressed in works of art. Any verbal shortcut threatens to replace the work in its particular concrete complexity and thereby threatens to paralyze the artist or blind the beholder. That is why artists prefer to deal with technique. But there is a decisive difference between the modesty of the artist who talks about paints and chisels while his every thought and move is in pursuit of his deepest vision, and the implied conviction that art is nothing but texture and space and formal relations.

Students are quick to pick up the teacher's attitude to art—indeed I have come to believe that what students learn from their teachers is mainly the attitude behind the teaching. Hence the widespread disorientation among young painters and sculptors, who have been trained to produce all the stunning effects, but have no criterion by which to choose among them. Hence also, among the more responsible and thoughtful, a profound cynicism—the inevitable consequence of playing a game of shapes that has no inner connection with the task of life. In an essay on Poussin, who seems to have become the paradigm of my argument, André Gide—speaking more convincingly than the critic across the Channel—asks us to recognize that thought (*la pensée*) motivates and animates all of Poussin's pictures. And, in this connection, he complains about some artists of our own time:

I should like to be understood. What displeases me is to have to listen to the dictatorial pronouncement: "This is a true painting precisely because it has no subject!" I dislike to see painting stripped of all spiritual value, and appreciation limited to matters of technique; to find our greatest painters address themselves carefully to nothing but our senses so that they are all eye, all brush. This deprivation, this voluntary insolvency, will, I believe, remain characteristic of our epoch, which has no hierarchy, and may expose it to severe judgment in the future—all the more severe, in fact, the more admirably these painters master their techniques. The pictures painted in our time will be recognized by their *insignificance* (4).

I am convinced that André Gide is not objecting here to abstract art but to what I earlier called "insignificant living."

Let us remember: even the great promoters of pure form were unwilling to assert that art is concerned with nothing but itself. Roger Fry admitted that art may express ideas, although he did so quite reluctantly and declared himself unable to explain what he meant. Hanslick observed on the subject of musical ideas: "Every concrete phenomenon suggests the class to which it belongs, that is, the idea which more directly pervades it, and continuing from there points to ever higher ideas, until the absolute is reached. This is true also for the musical ideas." And Clive Bell, hesitantly offering what he called his "metaphysical hypothesis" wrote, in 1913, the following remarkable sentences:

. . . we can only suppose that when we consider anything as an end in itself we become aware of that in it which is of greater moment than any qualities it may have acquired from keeping company with human beings. Instead of recognizing its accidental and conditioned importance, we become aware of its essential reality, of the God in everything, of the universal in the particular, of the all-pervading rhythm. Call it by what name you will, the thing that I am talking about is that which lies behind the appearance of all things—that which gives to all things their individual significance, the thing in itself, the ultimate reality. And if more or less unconscious apprehension of this latent reality of material things be, indeed, the cause of that strange emotion, a passion to express, which is the inspiration of many artists, it seems reasonable to suppose that those who, unaided by material objects, experience the same emotion have come by another road to the same country (2, p. 69).

Therefore, if we wanted to show that the painting attributed to Poussin [2] is a work of art, we could not content ourselves with a description of how its masses are "agreeably related" to each other. If nothing else restrained us from such decerebration, we should have to remember Poussin's own warning: "The first requirement, fundamental to all the others, is that the subject and the narrative be grandiose, such as battles, heroic actions, and religious themes . . . thus the painter not only must possess the art of selecting his subject, but judgment in comprehending it, and must choose that which is by nature capable of every adornment and perfection." Encouraged by the artist himself, we would attentively study the story of Achilles among the maidens, as presented in the picture. We would ask what the arrangement of the figures and the pattern of their gestures bring to the interpretation of the story, and we would try to discover meaning in the distribution of space and light. Perhaps we would find that all aspects of the picture, large and small, combine in presenting the story as a pattern of visual forces, which draws from the legendary episode the deeper theme of revealed masculinity, of power in the guise of grace. And, faced with a complete coincidence of eloquent shape and profound meaning, we might feel willing to say that we are in the presence of art.

But would not such an analysis involve us in an occupation which, as I suggested earlier, is not that of the consumer? The business of the consumer is to consume, that is, to enlighten and enrich his life through seeing and hearing, not to dissect the formal means by which such enlightenment and enrichment is accomplished. If it is true that what goes by the name of the aesthetic or critical attitude is often a device for escaping from the compelling call of art, then the television audience, in

---

[2] Is it a Poussin? Dr. Carla Gottlieb informs me that the painting, given to the Louvre by Paul Jamot in 1920, is not generally accepted as authentic.

the innocence of its full surrender to thrill, shudder, and suspense, is the only social group that functions as a genuine consumer of art.

This, indeed, is not far from being so. What better audience could a composer, performer, sculptor, or poet want than one as fully devoted to his visions as television viewers are to the horrors and sweetness of their own fare? But we remember immediately that the television spectacle and its public are geared to each other by a community of style, interest, and taste, which does not now exist in the arts. It did exist in the past. A Sicilian entering the Cathedral of Monreale around the year 1200 would be struck from the height of the apse by the fearful image of the blackbearded Pantocrator—he received the direct impact of a work of art. But nowadays the gaps separating artist from artist and artist from public can only be bridged by interpretation. I hope I have made it plausible that what we need is interpretation capable of opening the eyes and ears to the messages transmitted by form rather than distracting them with shapes.

Art controls the road that leads from the immediacy of our senses to what Clive Bell called "the ultimate reality." It is the road of man, and we cannot afford to block it.

REFERENCES

1. Arnheim, Rudolf. "The Robin and the Saint." This volume, pp. 320–334.
2. Bell, Clive. *Art*. London: Chatto & Windus, 1931.
3. Fry, Roger. *Transformations*. Garden City: Doubleday, 1956.
4. Gide, André. *Poussin*. Paris: Au Divan, 1945.
5. Hanslick, Eduard. *The Beautiful in Music*. London: Novello & Co., 1891.

AGENDA FOR THE PSYCHOLOGY
OF ART

The scientific psychology of art is no younger than scientific psychology in general. At the time of the early attempts to study phcnomcna of perception experimentally, Gustav Theodor Fechner obtained quantitative data on the psychology of visual proportions. Since then, general psychology has accumulated a large body of findings on perception and, more recently, has developed respectable methods for the investigation of the human personality, motivation, and social relations. Some work in the psychology of art has been done during this time. Every issue of the *Psychological Abstracts* mentions a few studies in the field. But one can hardly say that the psychology of art has kept pace with the accomplishments of general psychology. The lag is particularly evident if one is not satisfied with counting the number of contributions but asks the question: "To what extent have the essential features of the work of art, the artistic process, and the personality of the artist been subjected to valid psychological procedures?"

The relative scarcity of relevant studies is made all the more striking by the fact that an impressive amount of thinking, talking, and writing is devoted every year to the subject of art. What is more, the students of artistic practice and theory have become psychology-conscious,

First published in the *Journal of Aesthetics and Art Criticism*, 1952, 10, 310–314.

not just out of a fashion but because an increasing need for psychology has grown from their work. Art instruction has changed to art education, that is, art is being accepted as an essential instrument for the formation and expression of the human personality. Historians are accustomed by now to view the work of art as a manifestation of the mentality of a given culture, social group, or creative individual. And in psychopathology, concrete cases have shown dramatically that a disturbed person may grapple with his problems by means of artistic expression in painting, sculpture, music, literature, dramatics, or the dance.

Why has psychology failed, thus far, to respond more adequately to this challenge by providing aesthetic theory with a sounder basis of facts and concepts? There seem to be mainly two reasons. In the first place, there is too little contact between the two areas. A psychologist may feel the sting of curiosity when observing the strange skills that absorb some people for unknown reasons. Such curiosity is necessary but insufficient equipment. He cannot be expected to be an artist of merit himself, but unless he has learned to handle a brush or chisel or a musical instrument to a degree that will keep the feeling of genuine artistic experience alive in his eyes and ears and hands, no true advancement of our work is likely to come from him. The reason is, of course, that science requires not only the mastery of stringent method but an intuitive flair for the essentials and a keen anticipation of the truth to be verified. The careful application of the standard techniques of research will not in itself give a study in the psychology of art that indispensable flavor of authenticity which emanates from Delacroix's journals, Cézanne's conversations, or the writings of Van Gogh, Matisse, Henry Moore, or Paul Klee.

In the absence of such familiarity with the medium, one finds much effort spent on side issues, bad taste in the choice of examples, and the clinging to conventional notions about art, which are limited or outmoded or have never been true. I am referring, for instance, to the use of inferior works for the demonstration of artistic principles or to the idea that art is a kind of selective photography. There is need also for some knowledge of historical data. Otherwise it may happen, for instance, that a psychologist draws penetrating conclusions from the different look of two figures in a given picture without knowing that only one of them was done by the master himself and the other by a disciple or restorer.

In the opposite camp, we find many artists who are suspicious of psychologists. These artists combine remnants of the romantic prejudice that art excludes analytic reasoning with the notion that the psychology of art is entirely concerned with the uncovering of personal "complexes," that is, with information they believe to be irrelevant or even to produce harmful inhibitions. Artists and art educators need to be convinced that there is more to the psychology of art than that orgy on a bare mountain that psychoanalysts have been celebrating in recent years.

Then again, artists are attracted by the findings and language of the modern sciences. Their pronouncements are studded frequently with terms and quotations taken from nuclear physics, mathematics, psychoanalysis, and Gestalt psychology. More often than not one gets the impression that these scientific concepts fascinate them by the same evocative texture qualities that induce them to paste on their collages pieces of weather charts or technological blueprints.

Art historians and theorists have to refer constantly to principles of perception and motivation; but in many cases a lack of familiarity with the development of psychology makes them take for granted statements that were considered true in the days of Helmholtz and have since survived only in the so-called common sense thinking of the man in the street.

Thus, more intimate contact between art and psychology is the first prerequisite for progress. Once the wall between the two departments is pulled down, the student of art can expect to obtain from psychology a more solid foundation for the generalizations that play such an important role in all studio practice and particularly in the teaching of art. Similarly, the psychologist will find in works of art, as well as in informal observations recorded by artists, a wealth of information, which will serve not only this special field of study but will enhance the understanding of the human mind in general.

As a second obstacle to progress, the compulsive need for quantitative exactness should be mentioned. Discussions on the methods of general psychology have suggested that, while we strive for the eventual quantification of any scientific statement, we are likely to miss the vital core of our problems by limiting methods of procedure and the formulation of results to what can be measured and counted. Examples from the psychology of art are readily at hand. An artistic performance will be described by the numerical score it obtains in the judgment of a group of experts rather than by a qualitative analysis of its nature. The reaction to art will be determined by the number, rather than by the kind, of words it provokes or by the degree of skin perspiration in the beholder. The metronome speed of music can be subjected comfortably to statistics, but it is the rhythm rather than the beat that holds the secret, and we are guilty of neglect of duty if we fail to deal with rhythm because it requires qualitative description. The preference for quantitative investigations is also the reason why so much psychological work has been spent on attempts to derive a formula of beauty from mathematical proportions—a branch of study that in artistic practice has been little more than a quaint hobby, an attempt to canonize what had been achieved before in order to strangle the freedom and grace of what was to come afterwards. Compositional structure also has been treated as though it consisted of rigid geometrical patterns that were to coincide with salient points of the pictorial design—an activity in which the intellect can rejoice as long as it pays no attention to the fact that the eye fails to discover any such mechanical relation between the compositions of the masters and the superimposed geometry.

Some studies of this type can be considered useful as groundwork for a more adequate dealing with essential problems, but they are harmful when they take the place of true understanding. I do not see how one can hope to proceed in the field of art without trusting one's own intuitive judgment. For instance, if a psychological investigation requires distinction between good and less good artists, there is no point in pretending exactness by finding out who has had a one-man show or has been given more than ten lines in the encyclopedias, because this means nothing more than being objective about nonobjective decisions of art dealers, museum directors, or editors. One of the necessary qualifications is a sense of artistic value, and if a psychologist is convinced that Rubens is a better painter than Van Dyck, it is his duty to take the risk of going by that assumption. I am reminded of a passage in one of Chesterton's Father Brown stories. " 'There is another picture, Flambeau,' said Brown in his more mystical undertone. 'I can't prove it; but I can do more—I can see it.' "

The number of psychological studies that can and must be done in the field of art is overwhelming. Many of them are so simple that they can be carried out, at least in a preliminary way, by any clever and careful undergraduate, if his instructor does not compel him to repeat instead those workbook experiments that arouse no creative curiosity in either teacher or student. I will try to enumerate at random some of these problems in various psychological areas.

To start with motivation, some psychologists are still satisfied with the explanation that art is produced and consumed because it is "satisfying" or "pleasing"; but the hedonistic theory explains everything and nothing, so that until we ask *why* an activity is pleasing we have not even started our investigation. The only more specific theory of artistic motivation presented with consistency and vigor, is the psychoanalytic one. That theory is open to serious objections, but there is little point in complaining about the view analysts are giving us of the artistic process unless we remember that the absurdity of the theory springs from its one-sidedness, and that the one-sidedness exists because no sufficiently substantial alternate theory has kept the dialectic process of thrust and counterthrust going. Without that challenge movements grow unchecked until they become their own caricatures.

Another motivational theory that has become absurd through one-sidedness asserts that the work of art expresses and transmits emotions. It seems to me that it should be possible for psychologists to put their house in order to the extent that they come to distinguish the emotional component of mental activity from its motivational and cognitive aspects.[1] Once it is acknowledged that emotion is nothing but the tension that accompanies practically all psychical processes, the psychologist should be able to show that emotion cannot be the content of a work of art but only a secondary effect of the content, and that art is no more emotional than is any other reasonably interesting human occupation.

Research is also needed to determine the social aspects of artistic motivation. As matters stand now, nonartists keep repeating that the artist creates in order to communicate something to other people, whereas many artists either ignore this motive or explicitly reject it. A critical summary of the data that bear on this point is badly needed.

In recent years, a useful theory of human motivation based on the concept of equilibrium has been drawn from such varied sources as the principle of entropy in physics, homeostasis in physiology, and the law of simplicity in Gestalt psychology. In my opinion, application of this fruitful approach to the artistic process would not only provide the psychology of art with the foundation it lacks, but would also offer a dramatic illustration of motivational mechanisms in general.

Take now the problem of visual perception. No systematic attempt has been made to apply the principles of visual organization to the arts, and in this way to carry the theory of pattern structure beyond the point where Max Wertheimer left it almost thirty years ago. Art offers the best material for the analysis of more complex forms. Such investigation

---

[1] See "Emotion and Feeling in Psychology and Art." This volume, pp. 302–319.

should also include the problems of recognition and identification; that is, the concrete conditions that make a beholder accept a pattern as an image of something else, say, a human figure. What is the psychology of foreshortening and overlapping? And what are the perceptual criteria of distortion—that essential factor of most modern art?

Then there is depth perception. The study of painting seems ideally suited to get psychology over the stalemate of empiricism, because it is of no use to the painter to be told that the three-dimensional effect is based on past experience. What he needs to know is exactly what the psychologist is equipped to find out, namely, what particular configurations of lines, shapes, colors, etc., make for spatial dimensions. Nevertheless, James J. Gibson's recent work on texture gradients has been the only contribution since the basic studies of Kurt Koffka and Hertha Kopfermann. Also, there is no reason why the theory of figure and ground should still be in the state in which Edgar Rubin left it in 1915. Furthermore, what are the psychological effects of central as against isometric perspective? And what distinguishes the Egyptian principle of multiple aspects from the similar procedure of the Cubists?

Take color. Has anybody examined systematically the observations about the behavior of colors that artists like Kandinsky have recorded informally? What about the mood qualities of color described in Goethe's *Farbenlehre* and recently stressed by practical experiences in mental hospitals? What about the relations of color to sex and personality structure, which allegedly have been discovered in work with fingerpainting, children's art, and so forth? What about the valuable rules of thumb developed by fashion designers, stage designers, industrial designers, and interior decorators? In what way do painters of different periods take care of the phenomena of contrast and constancy and of the depth effect of hue and brightness? It is all terra incognita.

Has anybody studied the methods by which unified space is built through the succession of visual angles in the motion picture? How is the identity of visual units maintained or avoided in film cutting? In what way is the perception of movement on the screen related to the old studies by Karl Duncker and J. F. Brown? What about the tachistoscopic phenomena in the exposure of very brief film shots?

I will conclude with a reference to the psychology of expression. In music we have a number of studies on the adjectives people use to describe the content of various compositions. But, when it comes to the question *why* particular musical forms produce a particular musical experience, we are again paralyzed by the empiricist assertion that there is nothing to it but tradition and convention. Since James L. Mursell refuted this view in 1937, hardly any attempts have been made to demonstrate the structural kinship between specific expressive effects and specific patterns of rhythm, pitch, harmony, timbre, or volume. Until psychologists provide this foundation, the promising beginnings of musical therapy will not get beyond the intuitive hunches of practitioners.[2]

[2] Closely related ideas and bibliographic references can be found in Thomas Munro, "Methods in the Psychology of Art," *Journal of Aesthetics and Art Criticism*, 1948, 6, 225–235, and "Aesthetics as Science: Its Development in America," *ibid.*, 1951, 9, 161–207, as well as in Douglas N. Morgan, "Psychology and Art Today: A Summary and Critique," *ibid.*, 1950, 9, 181–196.

II. The Sense of Sight

PERCEPTUAL ABSTRACTION AND ART

INTRODUCTION

Art and abstraction seem to be incompatible if the two concepts are taken in the widely accepted sense. The artist is said to offer representations of concrete, individual cases. Abstraction is often defined as an operation that extracts elements or constituents common to a number of particular cases and presents them as a new sum or configuration. This extract, we are told, cannot be represented by a concrete, individual instance. Any particular object, for example, a table, allows visual representation, but such concreteness seems to be denied to the abstract concept "table." Again, abstraction is often described as an intellectual process, which elaborates mechanically recorded percepts, whereas the artistic process allegedly has nothing to do with thought; it is based on perception, intuition, feeling, etc.

On the other hand, "abstract art" has become a familiar term. And even apart from this extreme instance, it seems characteristic of many works of art, and particularly of many of the best, that they represent visual reality in a simplified fashion; they present types of objects, their general meaning rather than images of individual cases only—an achievement that sounds much like abstraction. The following attempt to ex-

First published in the *Psychological Review*, 1947, 54, 66–82.

amine some aspects of the relations between art and abstraction presupposes a revision of certain psychological concepts. This reinterpreta-
tion will eventually require a much more thorough justification than the
one offered here. Apologies are also in order for the apodictic manner in
which, again for the sake of briefness, these psychological propositions
are put forward.

PERCEPTUAL ABSTRACTION

A child draws a human head as a circle. This is not an attempt to reproduce the specific outline of a particular person's head but rather a general form quality of a head, of heads in general—namely, roundness.
Roundness is commonly thought of as an abstract concept. As such it
can be attributed to many or all heads, but—according to the traditional
definition of abstraction—no particular head ought to be able to represent it concretely to the eye. Yet, the child's circle is more than a mere
sign that stands for an intellectual concept, in the way in which ∞
stands for infinity. It is an image, a generally accepted image of that
roundness common to the shape of heads. The impossible seems
achieved—a perceptually concrete representation of the abstract.

The child's circle is no less concrete and individual than a photograph of any of the particular heads for which it stands. But it is a
representation that eliminates many of the perceptual characteristics of
heads and limits itself to a form that renders the structure of roundness
in a pure, clear-cut way. Thus the general quality of roundness drawn
from individual heads can not only be defined by an intellectual concept, but the particular structure it designates, which is realized less
clearly in the original shapes, can be presented to the eyes in a concrete,
individual form in which this structure is stripped of many accidental
complications. Such a purified, even though concrete, presentation of
structural qualities seems to fulfill the requirements of a true abstraction.

The contradictory use of "concrete" and "abstract" in the foregoing
is meant to illustrate the ambiguity of these terms. If we call "concrete"
everything that is perceivable, then the circle is just as concrete as a photograph of a head. But, within the realm of "concretely" perceivable
things, the circle may be described as an abstraction of the head. In the
following, the term "abstraction" serves to describe any simplified rendition of a (concrete) stimulus configuration.

Abstraction in primitive representation. Artistic abstraction involves a puzzling paradox as long as one considers abstraction as an intel-

lectual elaboration of perceptual raw-material and therefore as an operation that can be performed only at a relatively high level of mental development. In the field of art—and this is probably true also for the psychology of thinking—highly abstract forms appear at the most primitive stages, whereas highly realistic representations are found in culturally late periods such as Hellenistic or Renaissance art. The pictures made by a child or an American Indian, or a piece of early Egyptian sculpture show a high degree of abstractness, whereas Pompeian paintings or Michelangelo's *David* approximate "photographic" likeness so much more closely that less abstraction seems to have been needed to attain them (5).

The abstractness of children's drawings and other primitive pictorial representation is commonly explained by what may be termed the intellectualistic theory. The formula, "the child draws what he knows rather than what he sees" has become almost an article of faith. A typical exposition of this theory is given by Florence L. Goodenough (14), who clearly indicates that by "drawing from knowledge," she means drawing from intellectual concepts, as distinguished from memory images. Frequently, children's drawings are called "ideoplastic," meaning representations, according to the author of the term, Max Verworn (23), derived from what the draftsman thinks and knows of the subject rather than from a memory image.

The intellectualistic theory seems to have been suggested by the pictorial product, the child's drawings, rather than by what is known about the child's mind. In fact, a view according to which children create images of visible things by means of intellectual concepts is in striking contrast to the general observation that, at the early stages of development, mental life relies most directly on perceptual experiences. Is it probable that, for the purpose of producing visual images from visual objects, the child will choose the sophisticated detour via intellectual concepts? In particular, there is no evidence that young children possess the highly theoretical concepts of form, direction, proportion, etc., which they would need in order to solve the task at a nonvisual level. Probably the intellectualistic theory owes its origin and longevity to the fact that as long as perception is considered a purely passive "photographic" registration of the retinal image, striking deviations from that image can only be explained by the intervention of higher mental processes, such as intellectual conceptualization.

The attempt has also been made to account for the style of children's drawings by asserting that they are done from memory rather than from direct observation. The gradual transformation of memory images is indeed likely to play a role in the process. Experiments on the memory of form suggest that images change frequently in the direction of simplification, symmetry, etc. (17, pp. 493–506; 26, pp. 77–91). However, a discussion of this point seems unessential here because it is known that children's drawings that are done directly from the object do not differ in any important respect from memory drawings, and this not only when the child pays little attention to the model, but also when he concentrates on faithfully committing to paper what he is observing. Thus, the whole problem is already contained in the child's pictorial account of direct perception.[1]

Priority of global perceptual features. A less constrained explanation seems to suggest itself if one abandons the traditional conviction that structural whole-qualities like roundness are derived from individual percepts as a secondary, intellectual elaboration of the sense material. Gestalt research suggests that such over-all characteristics are not only directly perceivable but must even be considered the primary perceptual phenomena. They seem to strike the eye even before the more specific detail of a visual object is grasped. Louis W. Gellermann (11), for instance, has shown that young children and chimpanzees are able to transfer learning of one specific triangle to triangles of different form, size, position, etc.—an achievement that had been considered impossible for anybody who had not developed the intellectual concept "triangularity." In Koffka's experiments on memory images (26, pp. 43–44; 16), subjects often reported that they saw general characteristics of form, color, or movement, such as the shape of a coin or the fluttering of a flag, but not the further details necessary to determine the particular kind of coin or flag that appeared in the image.

If it is true that global, general features can be directly perceived and form the basic content of percepts rather than having to be distilled intellectually from a number of faithful "retinal" records, it cannot be maintained that "from the recognition of individual objects the child

---

[1] Another attempt to attribute to nonvisual processes the discrepancy between primitive representation and "photographic" faithfulness has been made by Löwenfeld (20, 21), who asserts that drawing in ground plan or side view springs from the essentially tactile experience of "haptical" persons, while visually minded persons draw "objective," i.e., perspective views. The theory ignores the fact that owing to what is known as the constancy of perceptual form, people do not see and therefore do not draw perspectively unless their cultural environment trains them to do so.

progresses by imperceptible stages to the recognition of classes of objects" (14, p. 67). Since the child grasps global class characteristics first and differentiates only secondarily between individual cases, no higher mental processes are needed to account for the abstract character of the drawings. Rather, this abstractness can be explained by processes that occur largely at the perceptual level, i.e., in a way more in keeping with the basic findings of child psychology.[2] This is also the first step toward a solution of the above mentioned genetic-historical paradox, which is due to still another ambiguity of the term "abstraction." Abstraction may simply indicate "a smaller quantity containing the virtue or power of a greater" (Samuel Johnson), regardless of how this "smaller quantity" has been obtained. Or it may mean the process indicated by the etymology of the word, that is, the act of reducing a configuration to a less complex one, as when a scientist succeeds in decreasing the number of concepts he previously needed for the description of certain phenomena or when an artist comes to prefer patterns simpler than the ones he employed before. The condition described in Johnson's definition may come about without the process indicated by the etymology. The highly abstract forms that characterize early stages of representation are not due to the simplification of previously more complex patterns. Rather, they spring, in perception as well as in pictorial representation, from a priority of simple, global forms. These may develop gradually into more complex ones, such as are required for more "realistic" representation. It follows that highly realistic images must not be interpreted as a direct registration of photographically faithful percepts but rather as the result of the gradual refinement of originally more abstract form patterns.

Perceptual concepts. A psychological difficulty arises if one tries concretely to realize what it means to see a general quality like roundness in a specific outline such as the contour of a human head. So far, Gestalt-psychology seems to state only that among the possible groupings of a given stimulus material, one will be chosen that yields the "best" structure, and that features which constitute the basic whole-structure of a configuration have a tendency to stand out and to be perceived first. That is to say, a selection or distinction of actual parts of the configuration on the basis of their structural function is said to occur. It would

----

[2] The occasional instances in which the representation is really determined by intellectual knowledge show convincingly how untypical it is. For instance, the child will come to draw a hand with the exact number of five fingers—as a rule after he has used star patterns that render the visual structure of the hand through an indefinite number of radial lines.

seem, however, that no mere grouping of or selecting from what is retinally given in the outline of a head could lead to the perception of "roundness." Also, experiments have shown that if the influence of the stimulus configuration is weakened through short exposure, dim illumination, distance in space or time, etc., figures are perceived that differ from the ones actually exhibited not by mere lack of completeness; rather, patterns result that represent the structure of the model in a simplified way, by means of regular, often symmetrical forms, which quite frequently are not contained in the model (17, pp. 141–144). It is as though the margin of freedom yielded by the lessened stimulus control enhanced a tendency of the receiving sense organ to produce simple, regular form spontaneously. This tendency may be basic for perceptual processes in general. Perhaps perception consists in the application, to the stimulus material, of "perceptual categories," such as roundness, redness, smallness, symmetry, verticality, etc., which are evoked by the structure of the given configuration. When we see a human face, is there, even as a first stage, a passive recording of all or some of the specific contours, sizes, shades of color, either in summation or in whole-configuration? Does not seeing a face mean producing a pattern of such general qualities as the slimness of the whole, the straightness of the eyebrows, the forward sweep of the nose, the blueness of the eyes? There is a fitting of perceptual characteristics to the structure suggested by the stimulus material rather than a reception of this material itself. Are not these whole-patterns of categories of shape, size, proportion, color, etc., together with the expression they carry, all we get and use when we see, recognize, remember? Are not these categories the indispensable prerequisites, which permit us to understand perceptually? [3] And does this not apply regardless of whether we content ourselves with the broad over-all impression of an object or examine its minutest detail? The number, kind, and subtlety of these categories will vary, but the more clear-cut and constant the structure of the stimulus configuration, the more definitely will it determine the pattern of categories that is the percept.

The perceptual categories can be described as general and abstract because they are not limited to any one object but are discovered in and applied to any object that fits them. They are not intellectual distillates gained through experience from a great number of cases, but are rather

---

[3] One is reminded of Dante's "Vostra apprensiva da esser verace tragge intenzione, e dentro a voi la spiega, sì che l'animo ad essa volger face" (*Purgatorio*, Canto XVIII, 22). Owing to the double meaning of the verb *spiegare*, the faculty of apprehension is described in this passage as "unfolding" the images of external reality at the same time as "explaining" them to the mind.

spontaneous "pure forms of sensory perception" (to borrow Kant's term), explainable possibly by a tendency to structural simplicity in the processes that take place in the visual cortex in response to stimulation. My assertion is that the individual stimulus configuration enters the perceptual process only in that it evokes a specific pattern of general sensory categories, which *stands for* the stimulus in a similar way that a scientific description of a network of general concepts is offered as the equivalent of a phenomenon of reality. Just as the very nature of scientific concepts prevents them from ever seizing the phenomenon "itself," percepts cannot contain the stimulus material "itself," either totally or partially. The nearest a scientific description can get to an apple is giving the measurements of its weight, size, shape, location, taste, etc. The nearest a percept can get to the stimulus "apple" is representing it through a specific pattern of such general sensory qualities as roundness, heaviness, fruity taste, greenness, etc.

If this theory is acceptable, the elementary processes of perception, far from being mere passive registration, are creative acts of grasping structure, even beyond the mere grouping and selecting of parts. What happens in perception is similar to what at a higher psychological level is described as understanding or insight. Perceiving is abstracting in that it represents individual cases through configurations of general categories. Abstraction, then, starts at the most elementary level of cognition, namely, with the acquisition of the sensory data.

This view requires us to speak of "perceptual concepts." For instance, we have to distinguish between the perceptual concept "weight," which refers to the kinesthetic experience of heaviness, and the intellectual concept "weight," defined as the force with which the earth attracts an object. Both equally fulfill the requirements of concepts by being general qualities applicable to specific cases.

The distinction between percept and concept also would seem to disappear. If the perception of an individual face is an abstractive process of the sort I have described, then the visual concept the observer obtains from that face is not different in principle from the visual concept of "the Chinese face" we may have obtained from a number of Chinese faces. Both are attempts to create perceptual patterns adequate to their referents, and it does not matter whether the referent consists of one case only or of several whose structure has something in common.[4]

---

[4] The term "general" is significantly ambiguous. Etymologically, it refers to something common to a number of cases, such as the German *allgemein*. However, when we speak of the "general outlines" of a particular face, we do not mean to

Representational concepts. The psychology of artistic abstraction involves not only problems of perception but also of representation. Perceiving a thing is not yet representing it. Still, considerable writing on the theory of art is based on the tacit assumption that a pictorial representation is simply a copy of a percept. Sometimes these theorists maintain that the percept of the referent or model object is, as it were, the raw material of representation from which the final shape of the work is derived by some kind of plastic surgery, namely, by the mere omitting or adding of elements, by changing or distorting, by dissociating and reassembling, etc.[5] I have asserted that what I called the perceptual concept is not derived from the stimulus configuration by mere selection, grouping, or rearrangement, but is rather its structural equivalent, a pattern of perceptual categories. In the same way, a pictorial representation is neither a copy nor a manipulation of a perceptual concept. Undoubtedly, the young child who draws the circle sees more than sheer roundness when he looks at a human head. Before he can draw at all, he is capable of distinguishing different people from each other. The perceptual pattern is refined beyond anything indicated by the child's drawings. Nor can the difference between what is perceived and what is produced on paper simply be explained as a lack of technical craftsmanship. By and large, the young child, and certainly the primitive artist, already possesses enough motor skill and visual control to produce the image he intends to. A child may not be able to draw a perfect circle, but as a rule he achieves enough of an approximation to make his intention quite clear to the spectator. The circle is not an unskillful rendition of a more complex or a more realistically intended form; it is a fairly exact representation of what the draftsman meant to produce.

The percept or memory trace of an object of reality does not gener-

refer to what it has in common with others but rather to its main, dominating, over-all features, which may remain untouched even when much detail is changed. Yet the two meanings of the term are closely interrelated. Sensible generalizations are drawn from individual cases that are similar with regard not merely to any element, but to essential structural features. That is to say, the "general" features of a particular specimen are likely to be those it shares with others of the same genus.

[5] Two examples quoted by Robert Goldwater (13) may illustrate this theory. John Constable: "Yet in reality what are the most sublime productions of the pencil but selections of some of the forms of nature, and copies of a few of her evanescent effects?" J. A. McN. Whistler: "Nature contains the elements, in color and form, of all pictures, as the keyboard contains the notes of all music. But the artist is born to pick, and choose, and group with science, these elements."

ally consist of lines or brush strokes and is for the most part not two-dimensional. It is the image of a three-dimensional body delimited from its environment by hue and brightness differences, etc. Some of its qualities can be reproduced in drawing and painting, others cannot. This means that wherever they cannot be reproduced directly, an equivalent must be developed from the means offered by the medium of representation. This is necessary also for an even more important reason. If perceiving consists in the creation of patterns of perceptual categories, adequate to the stimulus configuration, and if the artist's task includes the representation of such patterns, then he has actually to invent a pictorial form that more often than not cannot simply be "read off" from the percept. It is true that a lamppost easily suggests the straight lines by which it can be represented. But the roundness of a head is not present as a traceable outline, it is a whole-feature whose pictorial equivalent must be invented. A purely mechanical reproduction of an object through photography or plaster mold will generally allow identification of the object and render some of its characteristics, but its form will be, at least partially, chaotic, that is, incomprehensible if compared with a genuine representation of the model as a pattern of well-defined form. Representation consists in "seeing into" the stimulus configuration a pattern that fits its structure—often a laborious or even insoluble problem—and then inventing a pictorial counterpart for this pattern.[6] This can be done in innumerably different, all equally valid ways, as a visit to any art museum will tell. The sinuous lines van Gogh used for the representation of cypresses were not given in the stimulus configuration nor did the perceptual pattern that the artist produced in response to the stimulation consist of wavy strokes. These strokes were rather the pictorial equivalent of his perceptual concept, its materialization as tangible form, a translation into the pictorial medium rather than a reproduction.

Thus, representation consists in creating, with the means of a particular medium, an equivalent of a perceptual concept. The circle, for example, is directly derived from a graphic medium whose principal means are one-dimensional lines. The percept that gave rise to the circle

---

[6] This process should not be mistaken for "projection," that is, an imposition of essentially subjective meaning on a pattern of deliberately vague structures, such as a Rorschach inkblot. Representation always involves an interplay among the structure of the stimulus configuration, the formative process in the visual reception areas of the brain, and the attitude toward reality of the artist and his time.

would lead to a different representation if it were attempted with a brush, with cubic blocks, in clay, or in weaving. But whatever the medium, there will be structural similarity of the representation and the perceptual concept. Such a structural similarity of configurations in different media has been termed isomorphism in Gestalt theory.

The analysis shows that pictorial representation presupposes more than the formation of a perceptual concept. A way must be found to translate the percept into tangible form. Obviously this task is not performed by the pencil on paper, but by the mind that guides the pencil and judges the result. This requires what I propose to call "representational concepts." To return to our example: roundness is the *perceptual* concept that renders a structural particularity of the stimulus configuration "head"; the idea of a circular line by which roundness can be materialized as a tangible form is the *representational* concept needed to produce the circle on paper.[7] The translation of perceptual concepts into patterns that can be obtained from the stock of available forms in the particular medium will precede the actual drawing, continue during the drawing, and then again be influenced by what shows up on paper. Representational concepts are dependent on the medium for which they explore reality. When looking at a human figure, a sculptor forms a representational concept very different from the one of another artist who looks at the same figure with "woodcut-eyes."

Recent investigations, particularly the pioneer study of the art educator Gustaf Britsch (6) and the work of his disciple Henry Schaefer-Simmern (22), have evolved some of the rules according to which artistic form develops organically from the simplest shapes and directions (circle, straight line, horizontal-vertical framework) to more and more complex ones. Psychologically, this means that, for instance, the art of children and primitives cannot be understood as long as one describes them negatively by their mere falling short of what one chooses to call "correct" representation. Instead, we need a psychological reevaluation, similar to the successfully achieved aesthetical one. Primitive art must be considered positively as the manifestation of elementary representational concepts, which even at the earliest levels are capable of unified, consistent, and adequate representation to a degree often lacking in more "civilized," "advanced" artists. This new turn of the theory gives support to

[7] After what has been said before, the use of the term "concept" will not be misunderstood to mean an intellectualistic interpretation of perception and representation.

the claim of art educators that a human being's innate capacity for representation can be nipped in the bud if early in his training he is asked to reproduce "faithfully" a complex subject, for instance, a human model, with its intricate detail or if he is driven to imitate the advanced technique of the teacher. Such a procedure hinders the process of growth, which must carry the student through a gradual enrichment of his representational concepts to a level at which he can genuinely conceive and understand highly complex representations. Because of the innumerable disturbances that interfere in our time with the natural unfolding of such potentialities in the various aesthetic fields, many persons are needlessly deprived of the capacity of representing what they see in organized form or of enjoying sincerely what is offered in museums, concert halls, etc.

The new approach is likely also to reveal an intimate relation between the development of perceptual and representational concepts on the one hand and of mental growth in general, particularly in thinking, on the other. The interaction of the capacities to organize perceptual as well as thought-material of increasing complexity, the birth of thought, insight, understanding in the realm of perception and their development to more theoretical, intellectual processes deserve thorough psychological study. This will provide a more solid basis for "visual education," which at present relies on essentially empirical and practical principles. In particular, such investigations are likely to show that the merits of visual teaching-material are not limited to offering concrete, simple, near-to-life stuff to the young intellect; rather, the very perception and visual representation of such material, quite apart from intellectual elaboration, already contain processes of grasping and organizing of a kind needed in higher mental operations.

Representation requires abstract form. Artistic abstraction, then, is not a selective reproduction or a rearrangement of the model-percept but the representation of some of its structural characteristics in organized form. Meaning and expression of a pictorial object become manifest only to the extent that the representation consists of forms which are well defined with regard to their shape, proportion, direction, color, etc. This is particularly relevant in view of the traditional theory, which derived expression from what the observer knows, by past experience, about the psychological or physical state of the objects represented. The picture of a beast of prey was supposed to convey the expression of strength or ferocity because of what the observer knows about the nature of such animals or because, by empathy, he puts himself in the psychological and physical state suggested by the picture.

Actually, an image cannot convey artistic expression unless the form pattern by which the subject is represented contains structural characteristics that carry the desired expression. The drawing of a panther in a Persian illuminated manuscript (27) superbly renders the powerful but supple movements of the beast, which remind one of a steel spring. This is not attained by a careful reproduction of the outlines that might be found in the photograph of a panther but rather by the use of smooth but consistently bent curves standing for the animal's body as a whole as well as for every detail of its outline. The picture interprets the expressive qualities of the draftsman's perceptual concept "panther" through an adequate form pattern derived from the medium of representation, thus showing *the* panther through *a* panther and indeed creating an image of supple strength whose validity goes even beyond the presentation of a species of animal. An abstract, general content is conveyed by a specific individual image.

The organized pattern of shapes and colors, which in any work of art is the main carrier of the meaning and expression conveyed to the spectator, differs only in complexity from the circles, straight lines, and plain daubs of a young child's paintings. The form factor, which is so prominent in the highly abstract style of primitive representation, is equally present, though less striking, in even the most realistic work of art if it deserves the name of genuine representation. Thus, primitive pictures are particularly enlightening in showing the role that abstract form plays in any kind of representation. This insight is hampered by the intellectualistic theory (discussed before with regard to children's drawings), which has been used more generally to provide psychological explanations for two extreme kinds of artistic representation, the one formalized, stylized, often geometrical, the other naturalistic, approximating photographic faithfulness. Max Verworn explained the former as "ideoplastic" art, allegedly based on knowledge or thought, the latter as "physioplastic" art, a mechanical copy of the "retinal" projection (23). The theory is still alive in the minds of art theorists.[8] Apart from being based on an antiquated psychology of perception, such a theory creates an artificial dichotomy between what it considers two kinds of art, the one abstract and the other concrete, different both in their principles of representation and in the psychological processes from which they spring. As

---

[8] As a recent example, see Miriam Bunim's distinction of "conceptual" and "optical" representation (7). Also see "Art History and the Partial God," this volume, pp. 151–161.

I said before, this prevents the essential insight that the form element, which is so prominent in highly abstract art, is indispensable and exactly of the same kind in any naturalistic representation that deserves the name of art. On the other hand, the theory neglects the fact that perceptual observation contributes even to highly stylized work. When a South Sea islander paints the sea moved by the wind as a rectangle striped with oblique parallel lines, essentials of the model's visual structure are rendered in a simplified, but entirely un-"symbolic" manner. Albrecht Dürer's highly naturalistic studies of a hand, a face, a bird's wing are works of art only because the innumerable strokes and shapes form well-organized, even though complex, patterns, thus presenting an abstraction that interprets the subject. The two types of representation are nothing but the extreme ends of a scale that allows all possible styles of art to be arranged in a sequence leading from pure geometrical form through all degrees of abstractness to extreme realism.

Consequently, it seems insufficient to define the process of representation in relation to but one basis or point of departure, namely, the stimulus configuration of the objects portrayed. Representation is not simply a more or less faithful reproduction or simplification or variation of the perceptual material. Two opposite points of departure are needed: on the one side, the stimulus material of the object, and on the other, form, the indispensable precondition of visual understanding. Perceiving as well as representing a thing means finding form in its structure. The patterns of "nonobjective" art, if considered from the point of view of the world of natural things, are extremely abstract. They reduce the representation of reality to a visual equivalent of the universal physical and psychological forces that underlie nature and life and of their interplay. In this way they express harmony and disharmony, dominance and co-ordination, contrast and similarity, movement and rest, equilibrium and disequilibrium, and so forth. From the opposite point of view, however, that is, from the point of view of form, the basic, nonobjective patterns are not abstract. They are the very elements of visual comprehension, the building-stones of the composition the artist creates in order to represent the structure of the world in the way his temperament makes him see it.[9]

[9] Kurt Goldstein (12, p. 40) reports the case of a brain-injured patient who is unable to reproduce the V-shape with two sticks, but has no trouble when the model is turned upside down because now it means a roof to him whereas the V was "nothing." Goldstein explains that in the case of the "roof," the patient needs to deal simply with a known concrete object, while in the first case he would have

Form is sometimes considered a mere spice added by the artist to the representation of an object in order to make it pleasurable. Composition is often evaluated without any reference to the subject expressed by it. In opposition to this view, it must be asserted that, in art as well as in representation in general, form is an indispensable prerequisite for the perceptual characterization of the content. For instance, the invention of photography has not eliminated drawings for scientific illustrations, architectural and other technological drafting, etc. To be sure, a photograph gives in many ways a more faithful reproduction of a medical preparation, a building, or a machine. But what the picture is meant to show is not the object "itself" but rather some of its physical characteristics, such as shape, relative size of parts, etc. This information can be given only by means of lines, color and brightness values, shading, etc., and the more clearly the essential visual factors are brought out the better. The draftsman can reduce the representation to these essential factors. If it is important that two parts of an engine be shown as overlapping, he can employ contour lines that convey the effect of overlapping. If an indentation, a red speck, a curvature are what the physician or the biologist is to look for, the draftsman applies the rules of perceptual organization that govern these visual effects. That is to say, the draftsman interprets the object by bringing out relevant form characteristics. He produces an abstraction of the object's visual appearance by translating it into clear-cut form. Similarly, in a work of art, composition has the task of conveying, in the structurally most clear-cut way, such form characteristics as carry the desired expression. This, and only this, would seem to be representation.

to act on the basis of abstract ideas. This explanation is an example of what I mean by considering representation only from one basis, namely, the world of natural things. Simple figures are not primarily abstract derivates from concrete objects of the environment, they are rather the most immediately comprehensible stimulus configurations in their own right. They do not have to be related to objects in order to be understood visually. On the contrary, they are the closest structural equivalents of those perceptual categories that make it possible to identify objects. One does not need a roof to grasp a ∧ ; one needs the ∧ to be able to see a roof! Whatever the source of the patient's difficulty, it does not seem to be due to his being unable to produce or employ abstractions that are allegedly needed by the healthy person for dealing with basic visual patterns.

THE PSYCHOLOGICAL MEANING OF ARTISTIC
ABSTRACTION

So far, this study of artistic abstraction has dealt with the perception and representation of objects without considering the larger psychological context in which such processes occur. But some of their essential aspects can be explained only if one remembers that art is not the hobby of making reproductions, a game quite independent of other aims and needs, but is rather the expression of an attitude toward life and an indispensable tool in dealing with the tasks of life. Thus, if entire civilizations for hundreds and thousands of years did not go beyond a level of abstractness that Western children overcome within a few years, it would be superficial to account for this apparent limitation by saying that the artists of those civilizations were too primitive to develop their representational concepts beyond a certain level of complexity. Such an explanation may be valuable, for instance, when we analyze the artistic products of feeble-minded inmates in Western institutions. However, when it comes to the art of Egyptians or Africans, of the Pre-Columbians, the American Indian, or of the European Middle Ages, or, for that matter, if we wish to understand certain modern art of our own time, we must take into account the function of artistic representation in life and try to explain by means of our findings why under certain conditions representational concepts remain at, or return to, a level of high abstractness. This is a complex subject to which historians, anthropologists, and sociologists have devoted their attention. The following notes are meant to indicate directions an investigation could take with regard to our specific problem.

Form interprets environment. Highly abstract art can be disposed of as a primitive half-way achievement only as long as "photographic" realism is taken to be art's final aim. Actually, an unbiased look at the history of art shows that only very rarely, and under specific cultural conditions, has art pursued this aim. As a rule, rather abstract styles of representation have prevailed—not as preparatory steps on the road to something more perfect but as the fully materialized, adequate expression of certain conceptions of life and functions of art in life. Thus, it is necessary to account for the positive psychological values of artistic abstraction.

I have already pointed out that abstract representation differs from the corresponding stimulus configuration of the model by reproducing some essential features in a structurally purified way. Thus, it offers an interpretation of the model. This capacity is relevant for the explanation of the highly abstract style typical of primitive art. The origin of highly geometrical or "ornamental" forms as they are found in different periods all over the world has been frequently explained either as stimulated by the observation of simple shape in nature (the disk of the sun, the straightness of the horizon) or as a carry-over from certain handicrafts, particularly weaving, which, for purely technical reasons, produce simple patterns, such as triangles. These theories do not explain why simple shape, so rare in nature, should have been singled out and universally favored in the crafts of man, nor do they tell why geometrical patterns should have been invented or retained where no technical conditions suggested them. If, however, abstract representation accomplishes interpretation, then the style of primitive art may have to be related to the fact that man's orientation in his environment, so essential for his survival, takes place at first at an essentially perceptual level. In the child as well as in the primitive, theories about the forces that govern nature and life are derived from sensory observations. Now, according to the view presented here, perceptual understanding is possible only to the extent to which the stimulus material can be accounted for by patterns of perceptual categories. The simpler these patterns, the easier the understanding will be. This leads to the supposition that representations in simple form are attempts of the young mind to make the sensory environment understandable by presenting it as well-organized form. If this be so, it will be evident that art, far from being a luxury, is a biologically essential tool.

The functions of realism. Why did numerous cultural periods never pass beyond a stage of relatively high abstraction? The question is not likely to be answered adequately unless one realizes that it is just as necessary to wonder why in some instances artists strive toward more and more faithful reproduction of what corresponds to retinal projection. Order and comprehensibility, introduced into the visual environment by organized form, are not necessarily increased, and indeed are easily endangered, if the form patterns become more complex through increasing approximation to the "photographic" aspect of things. Perspective distortions of shape and size, overlappings, accidental aspects and positions, momentary reflections of color, and projections of light and shadow would, for the primitive, introduce a complication of visual reality that the elementary style of representation is able to avoid. The complex distortions of a nude painted by Tintoretto or Rubens do not directly convey the basic information about the structure of the human body that the child lays down laboriously through the creation of his "schematic" man. What then are the psychological conditions that in some periods make art develop toward a more faithful representation of the stimulus configuration?

Both the primitive and the man of the Western post-Renaissance world pay close attention to physical reality. But there are important differences. The modern scientist recognizes that the forces which determine physical events and can be read off or inferred from the appearance and behavior of material things are functions of the physical objects themselves. The primitive thinks of these forces as residing in invisible substances that merely dwell in bodies. In consequence, much of the detailed observation and representation of physical appearance and behavior that has become indispensable to modern science is less meaningful to the primitive. The illustrations contained in the handbooks of our natural scientists are faithful and detailed to a degree of concreteness that would have seemed superfluous and even confusing to their colleagues in the Middle Ages, in ancient Egypt, or in an African tribe. A corresponding attitude toward material reality distinguishes the post-Renaissance artists and their public from those of many other civilizations. The best European art of the past centuries, even where it still used conventional religious subjects, expressed a philosophy of the here and now. The physical concreteness of Michelangelo's figures, of Rembrandt's portraits, of Altdorfer's trees interprets and evaluates life in terms of material existence instead of presenting this existence as the mere object of immaterial powers.

The social function of art also changed in the post-Renaissance period. Art began to depict, for an ever-growing stratum of society, individual and transitory happenings of life. This called for a more realistic style.[10] Contrariwise, it is true for primitive as well as many of the higher and highest civilizations that the task of art consists in representing to the eye the meaning and the value of religion, government, etc.

[10] A cultural development that tended to separate religion, philosophy, art, and science from the pursuit of practical everyday tasks has enhanced this realism to a point where it has abandoned interpretative abstract form and degenerated into a mere indicator of the physical presence of desirable and otherwise emotionally "thrilling" things. The extreme example can be found in our commercial "art" and entertainment. Art becomes a substitute for the physical world, and an escape to a more pleasurable fictitious reality. According to Herbert Kühn (19) there is a relationship between artistic realism and civilizations based on exploitation and consumption.

The superindividual dignity of the divine ruler, which is untouched by the contingencies of time, requires the generality of highly abstract representation. This is particularly true for cultural periods in which the perceptual world is accepted only as a means of illustrating ideas to the senses. Early Christian art withdraws from the highly developed realism of the preceding era to a highly abstract style that rejects accidental and individual appearance and irrelevant detail, emphasizes what is constant and lasting, and resorts to symbolical representation.[11]

The preference for balanced form. As shown before, form must not be considered merely in relation to the reality of environmental objects, whose images it creates; it has a reality of its own, a world governed by its own laws, namely, the laws of perceptual organization. In pictorial representation, the organization of form is dominated by the task of creating a structural equivalent of the model-object. But, apart from its interpretative function, well-organized form has a value of its own for the organism. It is a characteristic reflection of analogous tendencies within the organism. This is another psychological aspect of the artistic creation, an extreme example of which is "ornament." Credit is due to Friedrich Kainz for having pointed out in 1927 that a more convincing explanation of ornamental form than the one mentioned above (p. 42) can be deduced from the Gestalt psychology of perception (15). I previously emphasized the priority of global perceptual features, which is suggested by these experimental studies. But equally relevant is the finding that there is a tendency in perception to create the most regular, symmetrical, stable form. This was the result of Max Wertheimer's investigation on the organization of visual stimuli (24, 25). Other studies (17, pp. 141–144) showed that when, through dim illumination, short exposure, distance in time, etc., the influence of the stimulus is

---

[11] The term "symbol" is frequently misused and has suffered from the devaluation to which many essential concepts have been subjected in our time. The Byzantine artist uses a symbol when he represents faithful Christians drawing strength from the spring of salvation through the image of two deer drinking from a fountain. But if the term is used to describe mere conventional patterns or signs, such as words standing for their referents, or the representations of physical objects in primitive art (the "symbolical" stage in children's drawings!), confusion is likely to result. In the psychology of dreams, the term would seem to be misused where it refers to substitution on the basis of mere perceptual or functional similarity (Freud's sex-"symbols"). On the other hand, dreams succeed in demonstrating psychological situations with an ingenuity and inventiveness that remind one of true artistic symbols. Cf., "Artistic Symbols—Freudian and Otherwise," this volume, pp. 215–221.

weakened, the receiving apparatus acquires the freedom of exercising a formative influence on the percept. Under such conditions, transformations result in the direction of more symmetrical and more regular structure. This suggests that in perception there is a tendency to the best possible equilibrium, related to what W. B. Cannon has described as physiological homeostasis for the organism as a whole (8). The implication is that well-organized visual form produces in the visual projection areas of the brain a correspondingly balanced organization. This adds a physiological explanation to the psychological and aesthetic fact that well-organized form produces pleasure.[12]

It is unsettled whether pure "design" is spontaneously produced by children and to what extent it exists in primitive art, but, if the preference for well-organized, "good" form is a basic characteristic of the perceptual process, it seems entirely likely that there is a strong motive for the creation of such designs, apart from or combined with the portrayal of objects. To be sure, a great amount of decorative ornament in our time is due historically to a decay of what was at some point representational meaning. And many patterns interpreted as mere decoration in primitive art are really representational (9). But, we must not overlook the fact that there is a genuine perceptual preference for well-organized form as such.

Dynamic complexity of form. The pleasurable effect of harmony, symmetry, etc., which is emphasized by classicistic art theory, can be derived from the above findings of Gestalt research. Even so, the organism does not tend simply to equilibrium. It strives to obtain a maximum of potential energy (18, pp. 319 ff.) and to apply the best possible equilibrium to it. Aesthetically, this may correspond to the old formula of unity in variety, that is, to the desire of organizing a maximum of dynamic richness in well-balanced form. Dynamic complexity can be obtained at any level of abstraction. A certain kind of modern art, for instance, some of Picasso's work, uses only a few highly simplified representational fea-

---

[12] Professor Erwin Panofsky has indicated to the author that medieval philosophy offers parallels to this view. Thus, Thomas Aquinas: Pulchra enim dicuntur, quae visa placent; unde pulchrum in debita proportione consistit, quia sensus delectatur in rebus debite proportionatis, sicut in sibi similibus, nam et sensus ratio quidem est, et omnis virtus cognoscitiva (*Summa Teologia*, pars I, qu. 5, art. 4). Ananda Coomaraswamy (10, p. 106) may have this passage in mind when he writes that, according to medieval aesthetics, "if the eye is satisfied, it is because a physical order in the organ of perception corresponds to the rational order present in whatever is intelligible."

tures as a base of departure for the construction of complex form patterns. The same is true, for instance, of the decorative designs on Peruvian pottery, the handicraft of the American Indian, or the Irish book illustrations of the early Middle Ages.

Realism, that is, increased concreteness, apart from creating new means of interpretation, serves also to obtain pleasurable complexity. L. Adam (1) has pointed out that the term "realism" has a double meaning. It may be understood as the faithfully detailed representation of objects "in themselves" and also as a method of picturing things "true to the optical impression of the model as observed at a given moment from a given angle." In both of these senses, realism enhances complexity. Young children's drawings do not use perspective, etc., that is, they are not realistic in the second sense. But, within this highly abstract style, the drawings often demonstrate the first sense of realism by their use of a great deal of detail. For instance, in the human figure, the child may elaborate on the design of dresses and such individual characteristics as earrings, missing teeth, mosquito bites, etc. Apart from its representational value, such realism leads to a complexity of formal relations, which can be expected to be pleasurable not only to the grown-up observer but to the young draftsman himself. At a higher level, the formal charms of intricate detail may be studied, for instance, in German and Dutch art.

In the second sense of realism, the transformations of shape and size through perspective, the amputations through overlapping, the emphasis on some parts and the elimination of others through light and shadow, and the modification of local color through reflections are important new means for the interpretation of objects (4, pp. 34–87). At the same time, however, such realism permits a sophisticated playing with form, color, light, and texture, which provides an epicurean pleasure in its own right.

Abstraction expressing mental detachment. My analysis has pointed out that form cannot be derived entirely from the objects represented in the work of art since it is at the same time a creative contribution of the organism. Three creative tendencies of this kind have been shown to be inherent in the form of a work of art: tendencies toward (*a*) simplification, (*b*) balanced, regular, symmetrical patterns, and (*c*) enriched structure. All three can be justified by genuine artistic purposes of representation and decoration. However, there also are conditions when any one of them seems to express a disturbance of the attitude to objective reality.

1) It is sound artistic principle (known in science as the principle of parsimony) that the form of any work should be as simple as its subject permits. In primitive pictorial representation, highly abstract form has been shown to be the adequate expression of the elementary approach to grasping and rendering global structural features. Far from expressing detachment from reality, the primitive, and to some extent the child, ignore "photographic" faithfulness in favor of the biologically important reality of "essentials." "Monumental" styles of representation emphasize the higher reality of ideas. Also, withdrawal from external reality may offer a chance for the expression of the subjective reality of the individual personality. Music or nonobjective art, even though they do not require such an attitude, are most favorable to its manifestation.

However, in some cases, a high degree of abstraction may express detachment from reality, an impoverishment that leaves representation with nothing but the perceptually determined play of empty forms. Such a detachment can be a consequence of the splitting-up of integrated culture into specialized activities, which tends to conceal the philosophical, religious, and social meaning of the individual's life, to destroy the artist's function in the community, and to reduce his task to a merely "aesthetic" one.

2) The tendency to simplification cannot be separated from the second tendency, to balanced, regular, symmetrical form. Just as experiments (17, pp. 141–144) have shown the perceptual mechanism to produce transformations in this direction to the extent to which stimulus control is reduced, so lack of contact with reality will lead to an overemphasis on form. Of course, predominance of form is justified when decoration is the primary purpose. However, one speaks of a "decorative" style negatively when a weighty subject fails to impress its meaning on the artist, who is consequently guided largely by formal values, such as in the case of Aubrey Beardsley representing the story of Salome and John the Baptist through ornamental lace patterns. In the doodles of persons whose attention is absorbed by other tasks, the predominance of the perceptual tendency to well-balanced, regular forms often leads to decorative, but otherwise empty patterns. Central control is reduced and therefore perceptual organization assumes peripheral control. Formalism caused by a detachment from the subject is characteristic of much modern art of minor quality.[13] Psychologically, this kind of abstractness can

[13] In scientific and philosophical theory, "decorative" systems are sometimes constructed, whose regular, symmetrical form patterns are not an adequate repre-

be described as a symptom of the emancipation of perceptual function from external and internal stimulus control.

3) Enrichment of the form pattern was described as providing new means of representational expression and an increase in genuine decorative values. Sometimes, however—and this happens particularly in highly abstract styles—the subject, or at least the task of representing the subject, seems to keep so insufficient a hold on the artist that, from a few remnants of representation, a complex pattern evolves, uncontrolled by the representational purpose and often overgrowing whatever representational elements exist in the work. It is a matter of aesthetic evaluation to decide whether some of the examples cited above (Picasso, Irish book illustrations) belong in this category or not. In this connection, it seems worthwhile to point out that sometimes the realism of perspective deformations, foreshortenings, overlapping, etc., may also have to be considered a neglect of essential contents in favor of explorations in purely formal complexity. Photographic faithfulness, which involves distortions and amputations of the "real" constitution of things, is so remote from the naïve conception of reality that even now a young artist has to undergo years of hard training and may have to rely on mechanical devices of measurement and projection if he wants to accomplish "correct" representation. This style of realism may come, paradoxically, from a kind of artist who is detached from the values and objectives of reality, who aspires to faithful reproduction of appearance for its own sake or is carried away by the stimulating charms of complex form. The aesthetic assertion that it did not matter whether a work of art represented a cabbage or a madonna came from a school of realists. Therefore, the rapid change from high Impressionism to highly abstract styles such as Cubism or Nonobjective Art is not necessarily what it appears to be on the surface, namely, a complete volte-face from the most careful service of reality to the boldest disregard of it. The extreme concreteness of realism and the extreme abstractness of some modern art may express an identical aloofness from reality, if by reality we intend the deeper meaning of life and nature.[14]

sentation of the facts at any level of approximation. (". . . *et comme dans notre esprit se forment symétriquement les hypothèses*," Paul Valery.)

[14] The interest in the perspectively deformed "retinal" projections as well as in the elementary building-stones of perceptual comprehension may be compared with our modern emphasis on psychology, that is, on the subjective reaction to external reality. One of the sources of this emphasis is a weakened interest in external reality itself. In this connection, one may also recall the tendency of post

As a final example, there are the pictorial creations of certain psychotics, particularly schizophrenics. Detachment from reality, which is characteristic of the psychological state of these patients, produces here again the symptom of form patterns abandoned to the play of perceptual organization. The drawings and paintings of these psychotics are described as highly abstract, stylized, geometrical, and ornamental (2, 3). One gets the impression that the receptor mechanism is organizing in a void. Frequently, however, the disease interferes even with the capacity for formal integration so that a chaotic agglomeration of representational remnants and other elementary forms results.

REFERENCES

1. Adam, L. *Primitive Art*. New York: Penguin, 1940.
2. Anastasi, Anne, and Foley, John P. A survey of the literature on artistic behavior in the abnormal: II. Approaches and interrelations. *Annals of the New York Academy of Sciences*, 1941, 42, 1–112.
3. ———. A survey of the literature on artistic behavior in the abnormal: III. Spontaneous productions. *Psychological Monographs*, 1940, 52, no. 6, 1–71.
4. Arnheim, Rudolf. *Film as Art*. Berkeley and Los Angeles: Univ. of Calif. Press, 1960.
5. ———. Gestalt and art. *Journal of Aesthetics & Art Criticism*, 1943, 2, 71–75.
6. Britsch, Gustaf. *Theorie der bildenden Kunst*. Munich: Bruckmann, 1926.
7. Bunim, Miriam S. *Space in Medieval Painting and the Forerunners of Perspective*. New York: Columbia Univ. Press, 1940.
8. Cannon, W. B. *The Wisdom of the Body*. New York: Norton, 1932.
9. Coomaraswamy, Ananda K. Ornament. *Art Bulletin*, 1939, 21, 375–382.
10. ———. *Why Exhibit Works of Art?* London: Luzac, 1943.
11. Gellermann, Louis W. Form discrimination in chimpanzees and two-year-old children. *Journal of Genetic Psychology*, 1933, 42, 3–27.
12. Goldstein, Kurt. *Human Nature*. Cambridge, Mass.: Harvard Univ. Press, 1940.
13. Goldwater, Robert. Art and nature in the 19th century. *Magazine of Art*, 1945, 38, 104–111.
14. Goodenough, Florence L. *Measurement of Intelligence by Drawings*. Yonkers, N.Y.: World Book, 1926.

Renaissance art to stress the process of creation, the strokes of the brush, the imprints of the modelling chisel or finger, the appreciation of sketchy drawings as works of art in their own right. See "Accident and the Necessity of Art," this volume, pp. 162–180.

15. Kainz, Friedrich. Gestaltgesetzlichkeit und Ornamententwicklung. *Zeitschrift für angewandte Psychologie*, 1927, 28, 267–327.
16. Koffka, Kurt. *Zur Analyse der Vorstellungen und ihrer Gesetze*. Leipzig: Quelle & Meyer, 1912.
17. ———. *Principles of Gestalt Psychology*. New York: Harcourt, Brace, 1935.
18. Köhler, Wolfgang. *The Place of Value in a World of Facts*. New York: Liveright, 1938.
19. Kühn, Herbert. *Die Kunst der Primitiven*. Munich: Delphin, 1923.
20. Löwenfeld, Viktor. *The Nature of Creative Activity*. New York: Harcourt, Brace, 1939.
21. ———. Tests for visual and haptical attitudes. *American Journal of Psychology*, 1945, 58, 100–111.
22. Schaefer-Simmern, Henry. *The Unfolding of Artistic Activity*. Berkeley and Los Angeles: Univ. of Calif. Press, 1948.
23. Verworn, Max. *Zur Psychologie der primitiven Kunst*. Jena: Fischer, 1917.
24. Wertheimer, Max. Untersuchungen zur Lehre von der Gestalt, II. *Psychologische Forschung*, 1923, 4, 301–350.
25. ———. Laws of organization in perceptual forms. In A *Sourcebook of Gestalt Psychology* (Willis D. Ellis, ed.). New York: Harcourt, Brace, 1939, 71–88.
26. Woodworth, Robert S. *Experimental Psychology*. New York: Holt, 1939.
27. *Manafi al-Hayawan* (*Description of animals*). Persian Manuscript, 13th century. New York: Pierpont Morgan Library, Ms. 500.

THE GESTALT THEORY OF EXPRESSION

What is the exact location and range of the territory covered by the term "expression"? Thus far, no generally accepted definition exists. In order to clarify what is meant by expression in the present paper, it is necessary to indicate (*a*) the kind of perceptual stimulus that involves the phenomenon in question, and (*b*) the kind of mental process to which its existence is due. This delimitation of our subject will show that the range of perceptual objects that carry expression according to Gestalt theory is unusually large and that expression is defined as the product of perceptual properties which various other schools of thought consider nonexistent or unimportant.

a) In present-day usage, the term expression refers primarily to external manifestations of the human personality. The appearance and activities of the human body may be said to be expressive. The shape and proportions of the face or the hands, the tensions and the rhythm of muscular action, gait, gestures, and other movements serve as objects of observation. In addition, expression is now commonly understood to reach beyond the observed person's body. The "projective techniques" exploit characteristic effects upon, and reactions to, the environment. The way a person dresses, keeps his room, handles the language, the pen, the brush, the colors, the flowers, the occupations he prefers; the mean-

First published in the *Psychological Review*, 1949, 56, 156–171.

ing he attributes to pictures, tunes, or inkblots; the story he imposes on puppets; his interpretation of a dramatic part—these and innumerable other manifestations can be called expressive in that they permit conclusions about the personality or the temporary state of mind of the individual. Gestalt psychologists extend the range of expressive phenomena beyond this limit. For reasons that will be discussed, they consider it indispensable to speak also of the expression conveyed by inanimate objects, such as mountains, clouds, sirens, machines.

b) Once the carrier of expression is determined, the kind of mental process that produces the phenomenon must be indicated. It is the contention of Gestalt psychology that the various experiences commonly classified under "perception of expression" are caused by a number of psychological processes, which ought to be distinguished from each other for the purpose of theoretical analysis. Some of these experiences are partly or wholly based upon empirically acquired knowledge. The mere inspection of many half-smoked cigarettes in an ashtray would suggest no connection with nervous tension to a visitor from a planet inhabited by nonsmokers. The letters EVVIVA GUERRA and EVVIVA DON PIO scribbled all over the walls of an Italian village will reveal something about the mentality of the natives only to someone who knows that these are words of homage to a champion cyclist and the village priest. In this essay, the use of past experience for the interpretation of perceptual observations will be excluded from the field of expression and referred to the psychology of learning. I shall be concerned only with instances in which, according to Gestalt psychology, sensory data carry perceptually self-evident expression. The way a person keeps his lips tightly closed or raises his voice or strokes a child's head or walks hesitatingly is said to contain factors whose meaning can be understood directly through mere inspection. Instances of such direct expression are not limited to the appearance and behavior of the subject's own body. They are also found in such" projective" material as the stirring red of a woman's favorite dress or the "emotional" character of the music she prefers. In addition, inanimate objects are said to convey direct expression. The aggressive stroke of lightning or the soothing rhythm of rain impress the observer by perceptual qualities that according to Gestalt psychology must be distinguished theoretically from the effect his knowledge exerts on the nature of these happenings. It is assumed, however, that practically every concrete experience combines factors of both kinds.

By pointing to expression not only in animate but also in inanimate things, we invite a terminological difficulty. The word "expression" implies an action; etymologically, that of "squeezing out." As long as expression is limited, in the traditional manner, to the outer manifestation of states of mind in man or animal, the meaning is clear. But what could possibly be expressed by the appearance of an object that has no mind? The theories of "empathy" or "pathetic fallacy," to which I shall come back later, helped temporarily. According to them, the mental state of the beholder was projected upon the object, making the object look as though it expressed a mind of its own. But, when projection was limited to its proper realm, there remained the genuine phenomenon of expression inherent in the perceptual appearance of the object itself. In that case, who expressed what? To settle this matter from the outset I would like to anticipate the main contention of this paper, according to which all percepts are dynamic, that is, possessed by directed tensions. These tensions are inherent components of the perceptual stimulus, just like the hue of a color or the size of a shape. But they have a unique property, not shared by the other components: being phenomenal forces, they illustrate and recall the behavior of forces elsewhere and in general. By endowing the object or event with a perceivable form of behavior, these tensions give it "character" and recall the similar character of other objects or events. This is what is meant by saying that these dynamic aspects of the percept "express" its character.

The perceived character may correspond to a similar physical state, for example, when the viscosity of tar is expressed in the visual character of its flow; or it may not, as in the passive limpness of the telephone receiver. Secondarily, expression may also refer, with or without justification, to a correlated state of mind. What counts first of all, however, is the character of the perceptual object itself, which is "expressed" through the directed tensions within it. The shape of the telephone receiver "expresses" the limpness that characterizes this particular perceptual object. But I am ahead of my conclusions.

Procedures and findings. What is expression, and what enables the observer to experience it? By means of which perceptual factors and in what way do stimulus configurations evoke such experiences in the onlooker? During the past twenty-five years or so, numerous experimental investigations have been devoted to the phenomena of expression, but hardly any of them have tried to answer our questions. Limited as they were to the connection between how a person behaves and what happens in him psychologically, they centered upon the certainly important problem: To what extent are observers, untrained or trained, gifted or

average, capable of obtaining valid information about a person's temporary state of mind or his more permanent psychical constitution from an
inspection of his face, voice, gait, handwriting, etc.?

This is true for the various matching-experiments, which are conveniently summarized by R. S. Woodworth and H. Schlosberg (24, pp.
113 ff.) and by G. W. Allport and P. E. Vernon (1, pp. 3–20). Similarly,
in the field of the projective techniques, psychologists have looked for
correlations between personality traits and reactions to environmental
stimuli. Almost invariably, these stimuli contain factors of the kind that
concern us here. But, so far, little explicit discussion has been devoted to
the question of why and how the given percepts provoke the observed
reactions. There is evidence that the whole structure of a face rather
than the sum of its parts determines expression (2). But which structural features make for what expression and why? In the Rorschach test,
the typical reactions to color are probably based on expression. But why
are "emotional" attitudes related to color rather than to shape? Ernest
G. Schachtel has done pioneer work in this field, pointing out, for instance, that responses to colors and to "affect-experiences" are both
characterized by passive receptivity (19). On the whole, however, questions of this kind have been answered by summary and scantily sup-
ported theoretical assertions.

A few remarks are in order on the investigations that have tested
the accomplishments of observers. A glance at the results reveals a curious contrast. One group of experimenters reports essentially negative
findings. Another, consisting mainly of Gestalt psychologists, asserts
that observers judge portraits, handwritings, and similar material with a
measure of success that clearly surpasses chance. Pessimistic generalizations have been drawn from the studies of the first type. The subject of
expression is sometimes treated with the buoyant unkindness that
distinguished the early behavioristic statements on introspection. This
attitude has not encouraged research.

The main reason for the conflicting results can be found in differences of approach. The investigators of the first type asked: How validly
can the bodily expression of the average person or of a random member
of a particular group of people be interpreted? They focussed on the important practical question of the extent to which expression can be re-
lied upon in everyday life. On the other hand, the Gestalt psychologists
preferred the common scientific procedure of purifying as carefully as
possible the phenomenon under investigation. They searched for the
most favorable condition of observation. A major part of their efforts

was spent in selecting and preparing sets of specimens that promised to demonstrate expression clearly and strongly (2, p. 8).

Some of the factors that may account for the often disappointing results obtained in experiments with random material are the following: (a) Everyday observation suggests that the structural patterns of character, temperament, mood, are not equally clear-cut in all people. While some individuals are pronouncedly depressed or lighthearted, strong or weak, harmonious or disharmonious, warm or cold, others strike us as indefinite, lukewarm, fluid. Whatever the exact nature of such indefiniteness, one might expect the corresponding faces, gestures, and handwritings to be equally vague in form and therefore in expression. When one examines material of this kind, one notices in some cases that the decisive structural features are not sharply defined. In other cases, factors that are clear-cut in themselves add up to something that shows neither harmony nor conflict but a lack of unity or relatedness, which renders the whole meaningless and inexpressive. Many telling examples can be found in the experiments with composite faces, made up of randomly assembled foreheads, noses, chins. If observers can cope with such material at all, they do so presumably by guessing what these artifacts are meant to mean rather than by directly perceiving the expressive impact of shapes. (b) The presence of a portrait photographer's camera tends to paralyze a person's expression, so that he becomes self-conscious, inhibited, and strikes an unnatural pose. (c) Candid shots are momentary phases isolated in time and space from the action and setting of which they are a part. Sometimes they are highly expressive and representative of the whole from which they are taken. Frequently, they are not. Furthermore, the angle from which a shot is made, the effect of lighting on shape, the rendering of brightness and color values, as well as modifications through retouching, are factors that make it impossible to accept a random photograph as a valid likeness. (d) If, for purposes of matching experiments, a number of samples are combined at random, accidental similarities of expression may occur, making distinction difficult, though every specimen may be clear-cut in itself. Further reasons for the lack of consistent results are discussed by Werner Wolff (23, p. 7).[1]

---

[1] Since there is no reason to expect that every photograph will reproduce essential features of expression, it would be interesting to know by which criterion the photographs for the Szondi test (18) have been selected. If an integral feature of the test consists in establishing the reactions of people to the person-

The conclusion seems to be that the recognition of expression has been proven reliable and valid only under optimal conditions. For the average face, voice, gesture, handwriting, etc., the results are likely to be less positive. However, in order to establish this fact reliably, the additional obstacles created by unsuitable experimental conditions will have to be reduced.

Associationist theories. What enables observers to judge expression? The traditional theory, handed down to our generation without much questioning, is based on associationism. In his essay on vision, Berkeley discusses the way in which one sees shame or anger in the looks of a man: "Those passions are themselves invisible: they are nevertheless let in by the eye along with colors and alterations of countenance, which are the immediate object of vision, and which signify them for no other reason than barely because they have been observed to accompany them: without which experience, we should no more have taken blushing for a sign of shame, than of gladness" (4, § 65).

Charles Darwin, in his book on the expression of emotions, devoted a few pages to the problem (7, pp. 356–359). He considered the recognition of expression to be either instinctive or learned.

Children, no doubt, would soon learn the movements of expression in their elders in the same manner as animals learn those of man [namely] through their associating harsh or kind treatment with our actions. Moreover, when a child cries or laughs, he knows in a general manner what he is doing and what he feels; so that a very small exertion of reason would tell him what crying or laughing meant in others. But the question is, do our children acquire their knowledge of expression solely by experience through the power of association and reason? As most of the movements of expression must have been gradually acquired, afterwards becoming instinctive, there seems to be some degree of *a priori* probability that their recognition would likewise have become instinctive.

In Darwin's view, the relationship between expressive bodily behavior and the corresponding psychical attitude was merely causal. Expressive gestures were either remnants of originally serviceable habits or due to "direct action of the nervous system." He saw no inner kinship between

alities of homosexuals, sadistic murderers, etc., two questions arise. (*a*) Is there a sufficient correlation between these pathological manifestations and certain clear-cut personality structures? (*b*) Are the latter suitably expressed in the photographs? These problems are avoided if the test is meant simply to investigate people's responses to a given set of portraits, whatever their origin.

a particular pattern of muscular behavior and the correlated state of mind.

A variation of the associationist theory contends that judgments of expression are based on stereotypes. In this view, interpretation does not rely on a person's spontaneous insight or repeated observation of what belongs together, but on conventions he has adopted ready-made from his social group. He has been told, for example, that aquiline noses indicate courage and that protruding lips betray sensuality. The promoters of this theory generally imply that such judgments are wrong, as though information not based on first-hand experience could never be trusted. Actually, the danger does not lie in the social origin of the information. What counts is that people have a tendency to acquire simply structured concepts on the basis of insufficient evidence, which may have been gathered first- or second-hand, and to preserve these concepts unchanged in the face of contrary facts. While this may make for many one-sided or entirely wrong evaluations of individuals and groups of people, the existence of stereotypes does not explain the origin of physiognomic judgments. If these judgments stem from tradition, what is the tradition's source? Are they right or wrong? Even though often misapplied, traditional interpretations of physique and behavior may still be based on sound observation. In fact, perhaps they are so hardy because they are so true.

Empathy. The theory of empathy holds an intermediate position between the traditional and a more modern approach. This theory is often formulated as a mere extension of the association theory, designed to take care of the expression of inanimate objects. When I look at the columns of a temple, I know from past experience the kind of mechanical pressure and counterpressure that occurs in the column. Equally from past experience, I know how I should feel if I were in the place of the column and if those physical forces acted upon and within my own body. I project my feelings into the column and by such animation endow it with expression. Theodor Lipps, who developed the theory, stated that empathy is based on association (16, p. 434). It is true, he also says, that the kind of association in question connects "two things belonging together, or being combined by necessity, the one being immediately given in and with the other." But he seems to have conceived of this inner necessity as a merely causal connection, because immediately after the statement just quoted he denies explicitly that the relationship between the bodily expression of anger and the angry person's psychical experience could be described as an "association of similarity, identity, correspondence" (p. 435). Like Darwin, Lipps saw no intrinsic kinship between perceptual appearance and the physical and psychological forces "behind" it. However, he did see a structural similarity between physical and psychological forces in other respects. After discussing the mechanical forces whose existence in an inanimate object is inferred by the observer through past experience, Lipps writes the following remarkable passage:

And to [the knowledge of these mechanical forces] is furthermore attached the representation of possible internal ways of behavior of my own, which do not lead to the same result but are of the same character. In other words, there is attached the representation of possible kinds of my own activity, which in an analogous fashion, involves forces, impulses, or tendencies, freely at work or inhibited, a yielding to external effect, overcoming of resistance, the arising and resolving of tensions among impulses, etc. Those forces and effects of forces appear in the light of my own ways of behavior, my own kinds of activity, impulses, and tendencies and their ways of realization. (16, p. 439)

Thus, Lipps anticipated the Gestalt principle of isomorphism for the relationship between the physical forces in the observed object and the psychical dynamics in the observer; and, in a subsequent section of the same paper, he applies the "association of similarity of character" even to the relationship between the perceived rhythm of musical tones and the rhythm of other psychical processes that occur in the listener. This means that with regard to at least one structural characteristic, namely rhythm, Lipps realized a possible inner similarity of perceptual patterns and the expressive meaning they convey to the observer.

The Gestalt approach. The Gestalt theory of expression admits that correspondences between physical and psychical behavior can be discovered on the basis of mere statistical correlation but maintains that repeated association is neither the only nor the common means of arriving at an understanding of expression. Gestalt psychologists hold that expressive behavior reveals its meaning directly in perception. The approach is based on the principle of isomorphism, according to which processes that take place in different media may be nevertheless similar in their structural organization. Applied to body and mind, this means that if the forces that determine bodily behavior are structurally similar to those that characterize the corresponding mental states, it may become understandable why psychical meaning can be read off directly from a person's appearance and conduct.

It is not my aim here to prove the validity of the Gestalt hypothesis.[2] I shall limit myself to pointing out some of its implications. Only brief presentations of the theory are available so far. However, Wolfgang Köhler's (12, pp. 216–247) and Kurt Koffka's (10, pp. 654–661) remarks about the subject are explicit enough to indicate that isomorphism on only two levels, namely, the psychical processes occurring in the observed person and the corresponding behavioral activity, would be insufficient to explain direct understanding of expression through perception. In the following, an attempt will be made to list a number of psychological and physical levels, in the observed person and in the observer, at which isomorphic structures must exist in order to make the Gestalt explanation possible.

Table 1: ISOMORPHIC LEVELS

A. *Observed Person*

I.	State of mind	psychological
II.	Neural correlate of I	electrochemical
III.	Muscular forces	mechanical
IV.	Kinesthetic correlate of III	psychological
V.	Shape and movement of body	geometrical

B. *Observer*

VI.	Retinal projection of V	geometrical
VII.	Cortical projection of VI	electrochemical
VIII.	Perceptual correlate of VII	psychological

Let us suppose that a person A performs a "gentle" gesture, which is experienced as such by an observer B. On the basis of psychophysical parallelism in its Gestalt version, it would be assumed that the tenderness of A's feeling (Table 1, level I) corresponds to a hypothetical process in A's nervous system (level II), and that the two processes, the psychical and the physiological, are isomorphic, i.e., similar in structure.

The neural process will direct the muscular forces that produce the gesture of A's arm and hand (level III). Again it must be assumed

---

[2] For that purpose, observations of infants are relevant. Even in his day, Darwin was puzzled by the fact that young children seemed directly to understand a smile or grief "at much too early an age to have learnt anything by experience" (7, p. 358). According to Charlotte Buhler (6, p. 377), "the baby of three or four months reacts positively to the angry as well as to the kind voice and look; the five-to-seven-months-old baby reflects the assumed expression and also begins to cry at the scolding voice and threatening gesture" on the basis of "direct sensory influence." Further evidence will have to come from detailed demonstrations of structural similarities.

that the particular dynamic pattern of mechanical action and inhibition in A's muscles corresponds structurally to the configuration of physiological and psychical forces at the levels of II and I. The muscular action will be accompanied with a kinesthetic experience (level IV), which again must be isomorphic with the other levels. The kinesthetic experience need not always take place and is not strictly indispensable. However, the perceived gentleness in the person's gesture will be experienced by him as a fitting manifestation of his state of mind.

Finally, the muscular forces of level III will cause A's arm and hand to move in a, say, parabolic curve (level V); and again the geometric formation of this curve would have to be isomorphic with the structure of the processes at the previous levels. An elementary geometrical example may illustrate the meaning of this statement. Geometrically, a circle is the result of just one structural condition. It is the locus of all points that are equally distant from one center. A parabola satisfies two such conditions. It is the locus of all points that are equally distant from one point and one straight line. The parabola may be called a compromise between two structural demands. Either structural condition yields to the other.[3] Is there any possible connection between these geometrical characteristics of the parabola and the particular configuration of physical forces to which we attribute gentleness? One may point to the kind of physical process that produces parabolic patterns. In ballistics, for instance, the parabolic curve of a trajectory is the result of a "compromise" between the direction of the original impulse and the gravitational attraction. The two forces "yield" to each other.[4]

---

[3] One can express this also in terms of projective geometry by saying that the parabola as a conic section is intermediate between the horizontal section, namely, the circle, and the vertical section, the straight-edged triangle.

[4] One of the principles on which the analysis of handwriting is based indicates that the script pattern reflects dynamic features of the writer's motor behavior, which in turn is produced by a characteristic configuration of muscular forces. The same isomorphism of muscular behavior and resulting visible trace has found applications in the technique of drawing. Herbert Langfeld (15, p. 129) quotes H. P. Bowie (5, pp. 35 and 77–79) concerning the principle of "living movement" (*Sei Do*) in Japanese painting: "A distinguishing feature in Japanese painting is the strength of the brush stroke, technically called *fude no chikara* or *fude no ikioi*. When representing an object suggesting strength, such, for instance, as rocky cliff, the beak or talons of a bird, the tiger's claws, or the limbs and branches of a tree, the moment the brush is applied the sentiment of strength must be invoked and felt throughout the artist's system and imparted through his arm and hand to the brush, and so transmitted into the object painted."

At this point, the description must shift from the observed person A to the observer B. B's eyes receive an image (level VI) of the gesture performed by A's arm and hand. Why should this image produce in B the impression that he is observing a gentle gesture? It may be true that the geometrical pattern of the gesture as well as the configuration of muscular forces that created this pattern can both be characterized structurally as containing compromise, flexibility, and yielding. But this fact in itself is not sufficient to explain the direct experience B is said to receive by his perceptual observation. It becomes clear at this point that the Gestalt theory of expression is faced not only with the problem of showing how psychical processes can be inferred from bodily behavior, but that its primary task consists in making plausible the fact that the perception of shape, movement, etc. may convey to the observer the direct experience of an expression which is structurally similar to the organization of the observed stimulus pattern.

A's gesture is projected on the retinae of B's eyes [5] and, by way of the retinal images, on the visual cortex of B's cerebrum (level VII). Correspondingly, B perceives A's gesture (level VIII). Is there a possible similarity of the geometrical structure of the stimulus configuration and the structure of the expression it conveys to the observer? We may go back to our mathematical analysis of the circle and the parabola. Simple experiments confirm what artists know from experience, namely that a circular curve looks "harder," less flexible than a parabolic one. In comparison with the circle, the parabola looks more gentle. One could try to explain this finding by assuming that the observer knows, through past experience, the geometrical characteristics of such patterns or the nature of the physical forces that frequently produce them. This would take us back to the associationist theory. Along Gestalt lines, another explanation suggests itself.

The projection of the perceptual stimulus on the brain, and particularly on the visual cortex, can be assumed to create a configuration of

[5] At this stage, a number of factors may interfere with the adequate projection of decisive characteristics of body A on B's receptor organ. In our specific example, it will depend, for instance, on the angle of projection, whether or not the perspective retinal image will preserve the essential structural features of the parabolic movement or transform it into a stimulus trace of unclear or clearly different structure. (In photographs and motion pictures, such factors influence the kind of expression obtained from the reproduction of physical objects and actions.) Similar factors will influence the veracity of other perceptual qualities which carry expression.

electrochemical forces in the cerebral field. The Gestalt experiments in perception suggest that retinal stimulations are subjected to organizational processes in the brain. As a result of these processes, the elements of visual patterns are perceived as being grouped according to Max Wertheimer's rules. Furthermore, any visual pattern appears as an organized whole, in which some predominant structural features determine the over-all shape and the directions of the main axes, while others have subordinate functions. For the same reasons, modifications of objective shape and size are perceived under certain conditions.

It will be observed that all these experimental findings focus upon the effects of the strains and stresses which organize the brain field. Is there any reason to assume that only the *effects* of these dynamic processes, namely, the groupings, the hierarchies of structural functions, and the modifications of shape and size, are reflected in perceptual experience? Why should not the strains and stresses of the cerebral forces themselves also have their psychological counterpart? It seems plausible that they represent the physiological equivalent of what is experienced as expression.

Such a theory would make expression an integral part of the elementary processes of perception. *Expression, then, could be defined as the psychological counterpart of the dynamic processes that result in the organization of perceptual stimuli.* While concrete verification is obviously far away, the basic assumption has gained in concreteness since Köhler and Hans Wallach explained phenomena of perceptual size, shape, and location through the action of electrochemical forces (14). The future will show whether the theory can be extended to covering the phenomena of expression.

It is possible now to return to the question of how the perception of shape, movement, etc. may convey to an observer the direct experience of an expression that is structurally similar to the organization of the observed stimulus pattern. I referred previously to the constellations of physical forces that will induce an object to pursue a parabolic path. The physicist may be able to tell us whether the example from ballistics is invertible. Will a parabolic pattern, such as the one projected on the brain field, set off, under certain conditions, a configuration of forces that contain the structural factors of "compromise" or "yielding"? If so, isomorphism of the cerebral forces in the observer and those described as levels I-V could be established.

This brings the description of isomorphic levels to an end. If the presentation is correct, the Gestalt-theoretical thesis would imply that an observer will adequately gauge another person's state of mind by inspection of that person's bodily appearance, if the psychical situation of the observed person and the perceptual experience of the observer establish structural similarity by means of a number of intermediate isomorphic levels.

Expression as a perceptual quality. The definition given above suggests that expression is an integral part of the elementary perceptual process. This should not come as a surprise. Perception is a mere instrument for the registration of color, shape, sound, etc. only as long as it is considered in isolation from the organism, of which it is a part. In its proper biological context, perception appears as the means by which the organism obtains information about the friendly, hostile, or otherwise relevant environmental forces to which it must react. These forces reveal themselves most directly by what is described here as expression.

There is psychological evidence to bear out this contention. In fact, the observations of primitives and children cited by H. Werner (21, pp. 67–82) and Köhler (13) indicate that "physiognomic qualities," as Werner calls them, are even more directly perceived than the "geometric-technical" qualities of size, shape, or movement. Expression seems to be the primary content of perception. To be aware of a fire as merely a set of hues and shapes in motion instead of experiencing the exciting violence of the flames presupposes a very specific, rare, and artificial attitude. Even though the practical importance of, and hence the alertness to, expression has decreased in our culture, it cannot be maintained that a basic change has taken place in this respect. Darwin noted that people sometimes observe and describe facial expression without being able to indicate the features of form, size, direction, etc. which carry it (7, pp. 359–360). In experimental work, one notices that even with the object directly in front of their eyes, subjects find it a hard and uncomfortable task to be aware of the formal pattern. They constantly fall back upon the expressive characteristics, which they describe freely and naturally. Everyday experience shows that observers may clearly recall the expression of persons or objects without being able to indicate color or shape. Solomon Asch notes: "Long before one has realized that the color of the scene has changed, one may feel that the character of the scene has undergone change" (3, p. 85). Finally, there is the fact that the artist's, writer's, and musician's approach to his subject is principally guided by expression.[6]

Generalized theory. Thus far, the phenomenon of expression has

[6] This has led to the erroneous notion that all perception of expression is aesthetic.

been discussed essentially in its best known aspect, namely, as a physical manifestation of psychical processes. However, some of the foregoing considerations implied that expression is a more universal phenomenon. Expression does not only exist when there is a mind "behind" it, a puppeteer that pulls the strings. Expression is not limited to living organisms that possess consciousness. A flame, a tumbling leaf, the wailing of a siren, a willow tree, a steep rock, a Louis XV chair, the cracks in a wall, the warmth of a glazed teapot, a hedgehog's thorny back, the colors of a sunset, a flowing fountain, lightning and thunder, the jerky movements of a bent piece of wire—all convey expression through the various senses. The importance of this fact has been concealed by the popular hypothesis that in such cases human expression is merely transferred to objects. If, however, expression is an inherent characteristic of perceptual factors, it becomes unlikely that nonhuman expression should be nothing but an anthropomorphism, a "pathetic fallacy." Instead, human expression will have to be considered a special case of a more general phenomenon. The comparison of an object's expression with a human state of mind is a secondary process. A weeping willow does not look sad because it looks like a sad person. It is more adequate to state that since the shape, direction, and flexibility of willow branches convey the expression of passive hanging, a comparison with the structurally similar psychophysical pattern of sadness in humans may impose itself secondarily.

Expression is sometimes described as "perceiving with imagination." In doing so, D. W. Gotshalk explains that "something is perceived as if it were actually present in the object of perception, although literally it is only suggested and not actually there. Music is not literally sad or gay or gentle; only sentient creatures or creatures with feeling, such as human beings, could be that" (9). If our language possessed more words that could refer to kinds of expression as such, instead of naming them after emotional states in which they find an important application, it would become apparent that the phenomenon in question is "actually present in the object of perception" and not merely associated with it by imagination.

Even with regard to human behavior, the connection of expression with a corresponding state of mind is not as compelling and indispensable as is sometimes taken for granted. Köhler has pointed out that observers normally deal with and react to the expressive physical behavior in itself rather than being conscious of the psychical experiences reflected by such behavior (12, pp. 260–264). We perceive the slow, listless, "droopy" movements of one person as against the brisk, straight, vigorous movements of another, but do not necessarily go beyond the meaning of such appearance by thinking explicitly of the psychical weariness or alertness behind it. Weariness and alertness are already contained in the physical behavior itself. They are not distinguished in any essential way from the weariness of slowly floating tar or the energetic ringing of the telephone bell.

This broader approach has practical consequences. It suggests, for instance, that the phenomenon of expression does not belong primarily under the heading of the emotions or personality, where it is commonly treated. Granted that the study of expression has great contributions in store for these fields of psychology and that thus far they are almost untapped. However, the experience of the past decades shows that little progress will be made unless the nature of expression itself is clarified first.[7]

Secondary effects. Strictly speaking, the phenomenon of expression is limited to the levels V to VIII in Table 1. That is, the term expression, as used here, refers to an experience that takes place when a sensory stimulus affects the visual projection areas of an observer's brain. The processes that may have given rise to the stimulus, as well as those the cortical stimulation provokes in other brain centers of the observer, are supplementary.

Once perceptual stimulation has taken place, a number of secondary happenings may follow. (1) The observer B may deduce from the expression of A's bodily behavior that particular psychical processes are going on in A's mind; that is, through the perception of level V, the observer gains knowledge about level I. The observation of a gentle gesture leads to the conclusion: A is in a gentle mood. This conclusion may be based on an isomorphic similarity between the observed behavior and a state of mind known or imaginable to the observer. In other cases, the conclusion may rely on past experience. Yawning, for instance, conveys the direct expression of sudden expansion; but the connection between yawning and fatigue or boredom must be discovered by learning. The same seems to be true for the spasmodic outbursts of sound we call laughter, which in themselves are so far from suggesting mirth that they

---

[7] Once this is done, it will be possible and necessary to approach the further problem of the influences that the total personality exerts upon the observation of expression. To Vincent van Gogh, cypress trees conveyed an expression they do not have for many other people. Cf., Koffka (10, p. 600).

remain permanently incomprehensible to the chimpanzee, who other-wise "at once correctly interprets the slightest change of human expres-sion, whether menacing or friendly" (11, p. 307). It is important to realize that an expression may be correctly perceived and described, yet the inferences derived from it may be wrong. If, in an experiment, 80 per cent of the observers agree on an "erroneous" attribution, it is not sufficient to dismiss the result as an instance of failure. The high amount of agreement represents a psychological fact in its own right. The relia-bility of the observers' responses to a perceptual stimulus is a problem quite different from the validity of such responses, that is, the question whether the observers' diagnosis is "correct."

(2) The observed expression may bring about the corresponding state of mind in B. In perceiving A's gentle behavior, the observer him-self may experience a feeling of tenderness. (Lipps speaks of "sympa-thetic empathy" as distinguished from "simple empathy" [16, p. 417].) (3) The observed expression may provoke the corresponding kinesthetic experience, for example, a feeling of relaxed softness. The effects de-scribed under (2) and (3) may be instances of a kind of "resonance" based on isomorphism. Just as a sound calls forth a vibration of similar frequency in a string, various levels of psychological experience, such as the visual, the kinesthetic, and the emotional seem to elicit in each other sensations of similar structure. (4) The perceived expression may remind B of other observations, in which a similar expression played a role. Thus past experience is considered here not as the basis for the apperception of expression; instead, the direct observation of expression becomes the basis for comparison with similar observations in the past.

The role of past experience. While there is no evidence to support the hypothesis that the central phenomenon of expression is based on learning, it is worth noting that in most cases the interpretation of the perceived expression is influenced by what is known about the person or object in question and about the context in which it appears. Mere in-spection will produce little more than over-all impressions of the forces at work, even though the experience may be strong and clear-cut. In-creasing knowledge will lead to more differentiated interpretations, which will take the particular context into account. (As an example, think of the expression conveyed by the behavior of an animal whose habits you do not know and the changes that occur with closer acquaint-ance.) Knowledge does not interfere with expression itself, it merely modifies its interpretation, except for instances where knowledge changes the appearance of the carrier of expression, that is, the percep-tual pattern itself. For instance, a line-figure may change its perceptual structure and therefore its expression if it is suddenly seen as a human figure. A lifted eyebrow is seen as tense because it is perceived as a deviation from a known normal position. The expression of Mongolian eyes or Negro lips is influenced, for a white observer, by the fact that he conceives them as deviations from the normal face of his own race.

In Gestalt terms, past experience, knowledge, learning, and memory are considered as factors of the temporal context in which a given phenomenon appears. Like the spatial context, on which Gestaltists have concentrated their attention during the early development of the theory, the temporal context influences the way a phenomenon is perceived. An object looks big or small depending on whether it is seen, spatially, in the company of smaller or larger objects. The same is true for the temporal context. The buildings of a middle-sized town look tall to a farmer, small to a New Yorker, and correspondingly their expression differs for the two observers. Mozart's music may appear serene and cheerful to a modern listener, who perceives it in the temporal context of twentieth-century music, whereas it conveyed the expression of violent passion and desperate suffering to his contemporaries in relation to the music they knew. Such examples do not demonstrate that there is no intrinsic connection between perceptual patterns and the expression they convey, but simply that experiences must not be evaluated in isolation from their spatial and temporal whole-context.

Knowledge often merges with directly perceived expression into a more complex experience. When we observe the gentle curve of a coachman's whip while being aware at the same time of the aggressive use of the object, the resulting experience clearly contains an element of contradiction. Such contradictions are exploited by artists; compare, in motion pictures, the uncanny effect of the murderer who moves softly and speaks with a velvety voice.

Finally, the perceptual experience of expression can be influenced by the kind of training known in artistic and musical instruction as making students "see" and "hear." By opening the observers' eyes and ears to what is directly perceivable, they can be made to scan the given sensory pattern more adequately and thus to receive a fuller experience of its expression. A neglected or misled capacity for responding perceptually can be revived or corrected.

The role of kinesthesia. Frequently, people feel that another person, whom they are observing, behaves physically the way they themselves have behaved before. They get this impression even though at that time they probably did not watch themselves in a mirror. It may be that they compare their own state of mind as they remember it from the former occasion with the expression conveyed by the bodily behavior of the other person and/or with the state of mind reflected in that behavior. Probably the kinesthetic perception of one's own muscular behavior plays an important part in such situations. If muscular behavior and kinesthetic experience are isomorphic, it becomes explainable why at times one is so keenly aware of one's own facial expression, posture, gestures. One may feel, for instance: Right now, I look just like my father! The most convincing example is furnished by actors and dancers, whose bodily performance is created essentially through kinesthetic control. And yet their gestures are visually understandable to the audience. This suggests that there is a valid correspondence between bodily behavior and the related kinesthetic perception. The problem of what enables an infant to imitate an observer who smiles or shows the tip of his tongue belongs in the same category. Of particular interest is the fact that the blind express their feelings—even though imperfectly—in spite of their inability to observe expression in others visually. The blind also understand their own gestures on the basis of their kinesthetic experiences. As Pierre Villey says: "The blind man, like the person who sees, is aware of the gestures he makes when under the influence of various emotions. He shrugs his shoulders and raises his arms to express his disdain and amazement. The same gestures recognized by him in a statue will evoke within him the same sentiments" (20, p. 320).

Isomorphism would seem to account also for the fact that it often suffices to assume a particular posture (levels III and IV) in order to enter into a corresponding state of mind (level I). Bending the head and folding the hands is more than an accidentally chosen posture of praying, which derives its meaning merely from tradition. The kinesthetic sensation accompanying this posture is structurally akin to the psychical attitude called devotion. "Bowing" to a superior power's will is a mental condition so directly related to the corresponding bodily gesture that its common linguistic description uses the physical to describe the psychological. Rituals not only express what people feel but also help them to feel the way the situation requires. By straightening our backbones, we produce a muscular sensation akin to the attitude of pride, and thus introduce into our state of mind a noticeable element of bold self-sufficiency.[8]

[8] William James's theory of emotion is based on a sound psychological observation. It fails when it identifies the kinesthetic sensation with the total emotional experience instead of describing it as a component that reinforces and sometimes provokes emotion because of the structural similarity of the two.

The "practical" motor activities are also accompanied more or less strongly by structurally corresponding states of mind. For instance, hitting or breaking things generally seems to evoke the emotional overtone of attack. To assert merely that this is so because people are aggressive would be an evasion of the problem. But, if the dynamic character of the kinesthetic sensation that accompanies hitting and breaking resembles the emotional dynamics of attack, then the one may be expected to evoke the other—by "resonance." (This kinship makes it possible for aggressiveness, wherever it exists, to express itself through such motor acts.) Probably this parallelism holds true for all motor activity. Muscular behavior such as grasping, yielding, lifting, straightening, smoothing, loosening, bending, running, stopping seems to produce mental resonance effects constantly. (In consequence, language uses all of them metaphorically to describe states of mind.) The psychosomatic phenomena of pathological "organ-speech" ("I cannot stomach this!") may be considered the most dramatic examples of a universal interdependence. The range and the importance of the phenomenon are not acknowledged as long as one studies expression only in motor activities that are not, or not any more, serviceable. It seems safe to assert that all motor acts are expressive, even though in different degrees, and that they all carry the experience of corresponding higher mental processes, if ever so faintly. Therefore, it is inadequate to describe expressive movements as mere atavisms, as Darwin did. Many of them are physical acts that take place because of their inner correspondence with the state of mind of the person who performs them. To use one of Darwin's examples: a person who coughs in embarrassment is not simply the victim of a meaningless association between a state of mind and a physical reaction, which was or can be serviceable under similar circumstances. Rather he produces a reaction that he experiences to be meaningfully related to his state of mind. The bodily accompaniment completes the mental reaction. Together they form an act of total psychophysical behavior. The human organism always functions as a whole, physically and psychically.

This view permits an application to the theory of art. It highlights the intimate connection of artistic and "practical" behavior. The dancer, for instance, does not have to endow movements with a symbolic meaning for artistic purposes, but uses, in an artistically organized way, the unity of psychical and physical reaction that is characteristic for human functioning in general.

In a broader sense, it is the direct expressiveness of all perceptual qualities that allows the artist to convey the effects of the most universal and abstract psycho-physical forces through the presentation of individual, concrete objects and happenings. While painting a pine tree, he can rely on the expression of towering and spreading this tree conveys to the human eye, and thus can span in his work the whole range of existence, from its most general principles to the tangible manifestations of these principles in individual objects.

Illustrations. Earlier I pointed out that experimenters have been concerned mostly with the question whether and to what extent observers can judge a person's state of mind from his physical appearance. In consequence, the psychological literature contains few analyses of perceptual patterns with regard to the expression they convey. An example of the kind of material that is badly needed in this field is David Efron's study on the gestures of two ethnical groups (8). He describes the behavior in New York City of Eastern European Jews and Italians from south Italy by analyzing the range, speed, plane, coordination, and shape of their movements. A comparison of these findings with the mental attitudes of the two groups would probably produce excellent illustrations of what is meant by the structural similarity of psychical and physical behavior. Among the experimental investigations, H. Lundholm's 1921 study (17) should be mentioned. He asked eight laymen in art to draw lines, each of which was to express the affective tone of an adjective given verbally. It was found, for instance, that only straight lines, broken by angles, were used to represent such adjectives as exciting, furious, hard, powerful, while only curves were used for sad, quiet, lazy, merry. Upward direction of lines expressed strength, energy, force; downward direction, weakness, lack of energy, relaxation, depression, etc. Recently, R. R. Willmann had thirty-two musicians compose short themes, meant to illustrate four abstract designs (22). Some agreement among the composers was found concerning the tempo, meter, melodic line, and amount of consonance, chosen to render the characteristics of the drawings. Subsequently, the designs and compositions were used for matching experiments.

Because of the scarcity of pertinent material, it may be permissible to mention here an experiment that is too limited in the number of cases and too subjective in its method of recording and evaluating the data to afford a proof of the thesis. It is presented merely as an example of the kind of research that promises fruitful results.[9] Five members of

---

[9] The data were collected and tabulated by Miss Jane Binney, a student at Sarah Lawrence College.

the student dance group of Sarah Lawrence College were asked individually to give improvisations of the following three subjects: sadness, strength, night. Rough descriptions of the dance patterns that resulted were jotted down by the experimenter and were later classified according to a number of categories. Table 2 presents the findings in an abbreviated form. The numerical agreement is high but obviously carries little weight. As a point of method, it may only be mentioned that instances of disagreement cannot be taken simply to indicate that there was no reliable correspondence between task and performance. Sometimes, the task allows more than one valid interpretation. For instance, "strength" expresses itself equally well in fast and in slow movement. "Night" is less directly related to one particular dynamic pattern than sadness or strength.

Table 2: ANALYSIS OF DANCE MOVEMENTS IMPROVISED BY FIVE SUBJECTS

	Sadness:	Strength:	Night:
Speed:	5: slow	2: slow 1: very fast 1: medium 1: decrescendo	5: slow
Range:	5: small, enclosed	5: large, sweeping	3: small 2: large
Shape:	3: round 2: angular	5: very straight	5: round
Tension:	4: little tension 1: inconsistent	5: much tension	4: little tension 1: decrescendo
Direction:	5: indefinite, changing wavering	5: precise, sharp, mostly forward	3: indefinite, changing 2: mostly downward
Center:	5: passive, pulled downward	5: active, centered in body	3: passive 2: from active to passive

Most tempting is the comparison between the movement patterns and the corresponding psychical processes. Such comparison cannot be carried through with exactness at this time mainly because psychology has not yet provided a method of describing the dynamics of states of mind more exactly and scientifically than do the descriptions found in novels or everyday language. Nevertheless, it can be seen from our example that the dynamic patterns of expressive behavior permit relatively concrete and exact descriptions in terms of speed, range, shape, etc. Even the crudely simplified characterizations given in the table seem to suggest that the motor traits through which the dancers interpreted sadness reflect the slow, languishing pace of the psychological processes, the indefiniteness of aim, the withdrawal from the environment, the passivity—all of which distinguish sadness psychologically.

The fact that expressive behavior is so much more readily accessible to scientific description than are the corresponding psychical processes deserves attention. It suggests that in the future, psychologists who undertake the task of reducing complex mental processes to configurations of basic forces may choose the study of behavior as the most suitable method. Already, the analysis of handwriting has led to a number of categories (pressure, size, direction, proportion, etc.) that invite a search for the corresponding psychological concepts.

The foregoing experiment also shows why it is fruitless to dismiss the phenomena of expression as "mere stereotypes." If it can be demonstrated that the dynamics of psychical and physical processes are structurally interrelated, and that this interrelation is perceptually evident, the question of whether and to what extent the performance and its interpretations are based on social conventions loses importance.

REFERENCES

1. Allport, Gordon, and Vernon, Philip E. *Studies in Expressive Movement.* New York: Macmillan, 1933.
2. Arnheim, Rudolf. Experimentell-psychologische Untersuchungen zum Ausdrucksproblem. *Psychologische Forschung*, 1928, 11, 2–132.
3. Asch, Solomon E. Max Wertheimer's contribution to modern psychology. *Social Research*, 1946, 13, 81–102.
4. Berkeley, George. *A New Theory of Vision.* New York: Dutton, 1934.
5. Bowie, Henry P. *On the laws of Japanese painting.* San Francisco: P. Elder & Co., 1911.
6. Buhler, Charlotte. The social behavior of children. In Carl Murchison (ed.), *A handbook of child psychology.* Worcester, Mass.: Clark Univ. Press, 1933, 374–416.
7. Darwin, Charles. *The expression of the emotions in man and animals.* New York: Appleton & Co., 1896.
8. Efron, David. *Gesture and Environment.* New York: King's Crown Press, 1941.
9. Gotshalk, Dilman W. *Art and the Social Order.* Chicago: Univ. of Chicago Press, 1947.
10. Koffka, Kurt. *Principles of Gestalt Psychology.* New York: Harcourt, Brace, 1935.

11. Köhler, Wolfgang. *The Mentality of Apes.* New York: Harcourt, Brace, 1925.

12. ———. *Gestalt Psychology.* New York: Liveright, 1929.

13. ———. Psychological remarks on some questions of anthropology. *American Journal of Psychology*, 1937, 50, 271–288.

14. Köhler, Wolfgang, & Wallach, Hans. Figural after-effects. *Proceedings of the American Philosophical Society*, 1944, 88, 269–357.

15. Langfeld, Herbert S. *The aesthetic attitude.* New York: Harcourt, Brace, 1920.

16. Lipps, Theodor. Aesthetische Einfühlung. *Zeitschrift für Psychologie*, 1900, 22, 415–450.

17. Lundholm, H. The affective tone of lines. *Psychological Review*, 1921, 28, 43–60.

18. Rapaport, David. The Szondi Test. *Bulletin of the Menninger Clinic*, 1941, 5, 33–39.

19. Schachtel, Ernest G. On color and affect. *Psychiatry*, 1943, 6, 393–409.

20. Villey, Pierre. *The World of the Blind.* London: Duckworth, 1930.

21. Werner, Heinz. *Comparative Psychology of Mental Development.* New York: Harpers, 1940.

22. Willmann, R. R. An experimental investigation of the creative process in music. *Psychological Monographs*, 1944, 57, no. 261.

23. Wolff, Werner. *The Expression of Personality.* New York: Harpers, 1943.

24. Woodworth, Robert S., and Schlosberg, Harold. *Experimental Psychology.* New York: Holt, 1964.

PERCEPTUAL AND AESTHETIC ASPECTS OF THE MOVEMENT RESPONSE

Psychologists speak of movement responses to the Rorschach inkblot cards. Artists assert that in pictures or sculpture the forms and colors "move." Such statements contain a paradox since they attribute movement to visual patterns in which no physical locomotion occurs. What is the nature and origin of these psychological reactions?

In most instances, the movement response does not seem to involve the illusion of actual locomotion. Probably, very few people see the "pink bears" in Rorschach Card VIII as actually climbing upward. Nor do the angels in Tintoretto's paintings look as though they were really propelled through the pictorial space. The movement response is a different perceptual phenomenon, which is hard to describe, even though it is clear and strong enough as a common experience. Visual forms are striving in certain directions. They contain directed tensions. They represent a happening rather than a being. All this occurs without the sensation of displacement in space.

Empiristic explanation. Illusions of locomotion do occur, but, except for such specific phenomena as the so-called autokinetic effect, which requires an unstructured field, they are rare and weak. The traditional psychological approach does not distinguish between illusions of

First published in the *Journal of Personality*, 1951, 19, 265–281. I am indebted to Dr. Kurt Badt for some of the bibliographic references.

locomotion and what I shall call "visual dynamics." [1] The explanation is empiristic and has essentially two versions. The movement response is said to presuppose that the observer recognizes, in the pictorial forms, objects he has previously seen in motion, such as a galloping horse or running water. By means of association, he endows the percept with motion.

However, common observation shows that some pictures of moving bodies give the dynamic effect while others do not. Some snapshots of football players show intense action, while in others the figures look awkwardly arrested in midair. In a good work of sculpture or painting, bodies swing freely. In a bad one, they may be stiff and rigid. [2] These differences are observed although the good and the bad pictures have equal chances of being associated with past experience.

This objection can be met by another, more refined version of the empiristic theory, according to which the associations are not based on the objects as such (horses, water) but on the shapes, directions, brightness values, etc., by which objects are represented in the picture. From everyday experience, certain perceptual phenomena are known to be connected with movement and objects that move. For instance, movement through water leaves a wedge-shaped trace. Boats, arrows, birds, airplanes, motor cars show, wholly or in parts, pointed, converging shapes. Similarly, any oblique position of an object indicates potential physical motion since it deviates from the zero-positions of hanging perpendicularly or lying on the ground. An oblique object is often in the process of actually moving toward or away from the vertical or horizontal positions of rest. Again, shaded brightness values are observed in fast moving objects, such as wheels, cars, flags, arms, legs. Therefore, according to this version of the empiristic theory, it can be assumed that any picture that presents objects by means of such perceptual qualities as wedge shapes, oblique directions, shaded surfaces will give the impression of movement, while the same objects will look stiff in pictures that do not fulfil the perceptual conditions.

Essentially, this assertion is borne out by the facts. The theory also has the advantage of suggesting an explanation of the strong dynamic

[1] Throughout this paper, the term "movement" denotes visual dynamics, not the illusion of locomotion. The autokinetic effect consists in the illusion of erratic movements performed by a stationary dot of light in a totally dark room.

[2] Leonardo da Vinci called such a figure "doubly dead, since it is dead because it is a figment and dead again when it shows neither movement of the mind nor of the body." (Quoted by Justi [5, p. 480].)

effect often produced by abstract pictorial forms, which are not directly related to objects of daily life experience. A wedge-shaped form is dynamic regardless of whether or not it reminds the observer of an arrow or a boat or any object at all.

Visual dynamics and locomotion. However, both versions of this theory would make us expect the appropriate visual patterns to convey the illusion of locomotion or, at least, that the contradiction between the familiar motion and the perceived lack of it would make the pictorial object look paralyzed, as though it had been suddenly stopped in its course, like a motion picture in which still shots have been inserted. Instead, the illusion is rare and the paralysis effect occurs only when the proper perceptual conditions are not fulfilled.

In fact, it can be shown that tendencies to actual locomotion within visual forms are apt to block the dynamic effect in question. This occurs when a pictorial or sculptural composition is incompletely balanced or when elements do not fit the pattern of which they are a part. Why is balance an indispensable factor of aesthetic composition? One of the reasons, which is often overlooked in discussions of the subject, is that visually, just as physically, balance represents the state of distribution in which all elements have come to rest. In a balanced composition, all factors of shape, direction, location, etc. are mutually determined by each other in such a way that no change seems possible and the whole assumes the character of "necessity" in all its parts. An unbalanced composition looks accidental, transitory, and therefore invalid. Its elements show a tendency to change place or shape in order to better fit the total structure. Under such conditions, visual dynamics appears inhibited in the unbalanced elements. They look paralyzed, abruptly stopped in their tracks and retained in their places by force. Paradoxical as it may sound, the quality painters and sculptors call the movement of static form does not unfold freely, unless any notion that the object should actually change or move is rigorously checked by balanced composition.

The difference between the dynamics of still forms and actual locomotion can be illustrated also in another way. It is sometimes asserted that the still picture of a moving body represents a momentary phase picked from the actual movement and is perceived as such by the observer. According to this view, if one sees the picture of a blacksmith swinging a hammer, one imagines the total motion, of which it is a small fragment—one thus completes the incomplete. Actually, the picture of the blacksmith has its own independent dynamics, which can be shown by the fact that the intensity of the perceived movement depends exclusively on the positions of body, arm, and hammer in the picture itself. If one examines the series of photographs taken of blacksmiths at work by Eadweard Muybridge, one realizes that the full impact of the blow appears only in those pictures which show the hammer lifted high (8). Intermediate phases are not seen as transition stages of the smashing blow but as a more or less quiet lifting of the hammer; intensity depends on the angle represented. Assumptions of what is actually going on have a remarkably slight influence on the perception of the picture. Similarly, in snapshots of a man walking, the step will look small or large depending on the given angle between the legs—regardless of the size of the actual step from which the picture is taken or believed to be taken. If one of the legs appears in a vertical position, the observer does not see a man walking but one standing on one leg and lifting the other. The skirt of a dancer will appear as moving or as a rigid, motionless object, depending on its shape caught by the camera (8, series 62). The windmills in Dutch landscapes stand still if their arms are painted in a vertical-horizontal position. They move when the arms are tilted asymmetrically, even though both kinds of position are known to be phases of actual motion.

For this reason, painters in the nineteenth century were quite right in asserting that the traditional posture of the galloping horse with its four out-stretched legs—seen, for instance, in Géricault's *Derby at Epsom*—is correct, while the actual positions revealed by photography are pictorially wrong. Only the maximum spread of the legs translates the intensity of the physical motion into visual dynamics, even though no running horse ever assumes that position (10, 14). More often than not, paintings of "snapshot horses," influenced by photography, can only be understood, but not seen, as moving.

For the same reason, Carl Justi (5, p. 479) and others objected to the theory of the "pregnant moment" in the visual arts expounded by Gotthold Ephraim Lessing in his *Laocoön*. Lessing maintained that action should be represented in sculpture or painting not at its climax but at a point a few moments before the maximum, because only in that way would the imagination of the spectator be given free play to conceive a dynamic increase beyond the given phase (7, III). Justi knew that Lessing's notion of imagination was alien to the nature of art. The artist "will not leave free play to phantasy but fasten it to the spell of his creation." The spectator "must not add this and that in his mind but grasp the thought of the artist, if he is capable of it. The highest achievement to which he can aspire is not the belief of seeing *more* but the recognition of what the artist has seen." [3]

Visual dynamics in art. Thus, visual dynamics is not illusion or imagination of locomotion, but the perceptual equivalent of locomotion in a static medium. It is not the projection of one kind of perceptual experience (locomotion) upon another, but a perceptual phenomenon in its own right. In fact, it is one of the basic features of perception, not limited to occasional examples but pertaining to all visual percepts unless specific obstacles block the effect. One of the most elementary statements that can be made about any work of art is that it represents a dynamic pattern. Sometimes the whole work is organized around one dominant center, from which movement radiates throughout the entire area. In other cases, two or more centers of movement create a contrapuntal pattern. From the main arteries of the composition, the movement flows into the capillaries of the smallest detail. Any description of a work of art in terms of static geometric shapes ignores its main animating feature, namely, the fact that all form is primarily visual action.

The static analysis of pictorial composition is akin in spirit to the traditional psychological approach that considers geometric shape as the primary content of percepts, to which such qualities as movement may be added subjectively and secondarily. Actually, the dynamic effect of a perceptual object is probably more elementary than its outlines or proportions. The soaring of a mountain peak, the spreading of a treetop, the protruding of a nose or chin strike the eye of the observer more directly and are better remembered than the geometric properties of the shapes that create these dynamic effects. The phenomenon is perhaps more universally and more strongly apparent in art than it is in nature, because the artist fashions his pattern in such a way that the movement of form flows clearly throughout the work. In nature, the shapes of objects are often so irregular that the corresponding dynamic factors block each other rather than combining in an over-all flow. Also, natural objects are seen in accidental combinations and overlappings, which further interfere with the dynamics of form.

Every work of art is built on a scale of dynamic values. Usually, some elements establish what may be called the zero-level of movement

---

[3] Recently, a well-known poet, after being told by a psychologist that his Rorschach test revealed "lack of imagination," commented: "They don't seem to realize that years of hard training as an artist have enabled me to see an inkblot when I am shown one rather than to indulge in loose associations."

by means of vertical or horizontal orientation, symmetrical shape, or central position. Even these elements are not without dynamics, since their quietness is nothing but the limiting case of movement. The extent and "pitch" of the dynamic scale varies from work to work, from artist to artist, from period to period. The dynamic value of any one perceptual element depends on the scale of its context. A gesture of a hand in a medieval miniature, which looks free and strong in its own surrounding, might appear stiff in a work of larger or higher dynamic scale, for instance, in a painting by Veronese. Hence the frequent misinterpretations of dynamic qualities, by which a critic calls a Byzantine mosaic lifeless or a Baroque ceiling overexcited, because he applies his own scale of movement to works conceived in another.

Perceptual conditions. Some references have already been made to the particular perceptual factors that go with visual dynamics. Since no systematic investigation of these factors seems to exist, I can only refer to the findings of keen individual observers, as they are available in the field of the arts. For example, Heinrich Wölfflin has analyzed the architecture, sculpture, and paintings of the Italian Baroque style. One of the basic characteristics of this style, according to him, is movement (15). Among the formal traits of the Baroque style, Wölfflin notices a "tension in the proportions," expressed, for instance, in the change from circular to elongated shape, from the square to the rectangle. He finds a "sense of direction." Also, there is ample use of convergent and divergent shapes as well as of curved contours and surfaces. Instead of the right angle, softly fluent transitions lead from one direction to another. Juxtaposition of elements is replaced by overlapping. In the representation of the human figure, the limbs do not act independently and freely, but draw the rest of the body into the movement.

The development from Renaissance to Baroque style is characterized by an increase of movement. A similar development can be traced, for example, in Greek sculpture. Here the composition of the early works is based on the vertical and horizontal. The frontal orientation of the figures makes for symmetry. The limbs are at rest or only slightly active. Later, the movement factor is enhanced by an increasing use of oblique directions. The posture of the figure becomes asymmetrical, the body is twisted, the spatial orientation of the planes changes throughout. Curved lines and volumes become more frequent, and forms overlap. There are constant turns of direction. The limbs are bent and active.

No detailed analysis of these and other movement factors can be given here. However, it may be pointed out that gradients of perceptual qualities seem to make for movement. Every wedge-shaped form involves a gradual increase or decrease of size. If the contours of such a form are curved rather than straight, the gradual change of size accelerates, and the movement effect is enhanced. More generally, oblique direction can be defined dynamically as a gradual withdrawal from, or approach to, the zero-positions of the vertical or horizontal. Shading, which also makes for movement, represents a gradient of brightness values.

When form units overlap, movement results from the tension created by the incompleteness of the covered units. The tendency to reestablish completeness by pulling the overlapping units apart is experienced as a dynamic effect.[4]

Eye movements. I pointed out before that illusory locomotion of perceptual shapes is not identical with the dynamic effect but rather tends to block it. Under certain conditions, however, the time sequence inherent in the act of perception will produce an animation effect. If one looks rapidly through a series of Muybridge's snapshots, the scanning movement of the eye produces a motion-picture-like succession of phases. As the eye shifts along the series of twelve pictures, one sees a man leap or catch a ball. This animation effect can also be found in works of art. In Peter Bruegel's painting of the blindmen guiding each other to disaster, the row of six figures represents progressive phases of the same action. The eye of the observer, by scanning the picture from left to right, transforms coexistence into sequence—it records successively the acts of walking, stumbling, and falling into the brook. Auguste Rodin, in his conversations with Paul Gsell, mentions similar examples, for instance, that of Watteau's *Embarkment for Cythera* (11). He also maintains that such progressions are frequently supplied by the artist within the body of one figure. As the observer's eye moves along the figure, he sees one posture turning into another. Thereby inactivity changes into action. If one arm of a statue hangs downward while the other is lifted, the observer integrates the two positions into successive phases of the motion of lifting. One can go further and show that the scanning of a wedge-shaped form will produce a time sequence of decreasing or in-

---

[4] The conditions of the dynamic effect are closely related to those of depth perception. In certain configurations, tensions in two-dimensional patterns can be relieved by the three-dimensional perception of the same stimuli. See my *Art and Visual Perception*, Chapter V.

creasing size and thus convey the locomotor effect of contraction or expansion.

However, it is important to realize that this animation effect is identical neither with what we have called visual dynamics nor with the illusion of locomotion. Attempts to explain visual dynamics by actual or potential eye movements will only confuse the issue. When the moving glance connects a spatial sequence of phases into a temporal sequence, the resulting motion-like experience is quite different from the perception of directed tension within a pattern, or the illusion of its actual displacement in space. As the glance moves along the dynamic axis of a pattern, it may reinforce the movement inherent in the pattern itself. But, photographic recordings of eye movements have shown that the trace of the scanning glance is quite erratic; it follows the compositional lines of the picture only occasionally, for instance, when the whole is dominated by one or two striking features (4). Also, most pictorial patterns consist of so many divergent movements that an attempt to scan them separately, even if successful, would never lead to a unified grasp of the whole. Eye movements serve essentially to change the fixation point, that is, to bring the various areas of the perceptual object successively into the focus of sharp vision.

Subject matter. I have dealt with the form factors that determine visual dynamics regardless of what the observer knows about the nature of the objects represented. This seems justified in that no difference in principle exists, in a painted landscape, between the movement perceived in the sinuous contour of a coastline or in the shape of the waves. The swinging outline of a beret in a Rembrandt portrait can be just as dynamic as the skirt of a dancer drawn by Toulouse-Lautrec, even though the beret is known to be motionless while the skirt is known to be moving. Also, it has been pointed out that no knowledge will produce the movement effect unless the proper perceptual features are present. However, knowledge can play a role in stressing the basis, or zero-position, from which the given pictorial form represents a deviation. The raised arms of a man convey stronger visual dynamics than the branches of a tree or an abstract pattern rising at the same angle because the man's arms are understood as being lifted from their normal hanging position. The elongated faces in El Greco's or Modigliani's paintings have stronger dynamics than an abstract oval of the same shape because they are seen as distortions of the normal face. In these cases, the interaction between memory traces and the given percept strengthens the dynamic tension.

Gestalt explanation. In "The Gestalt Theory of Expression" I raised the question whether there is any reason to assume that only the *effects* of the physiological processes that lead to perceptual organization are reflected in perceptual experience. Why should not the strains and stresses of the physiological forces themselves also have their psychological counterpart? Accordingly, expression was defined as the "psychological counterpart of the dynamic processes that result in the organization of perceptual stimuli." Expression is closely related to visual dynamics. The theory that the movement effect psychologically reflects the stresses of electrochemical forces in the brain field of vision is a purely hypothetical suggestion for the construction of the kind of "pseudobrain model" that Edward C. Tolman has called inevitable and desirable (3, p. 48).[5] But the following discussion of Rorschach's M-response will show that the adoption of such a theory, which would make movement an integral feature of the percept itself, may have practical consequences.

Rorschach's theory. Hermann Rorschach (12) defines the M-response as the "feeling of movement" (*Erfühlung der Bewegung*) an observer derives from a pictorial form when his interpretation is not only determined by the shape of the object but also accompanied by kinesthetic reactions (*Zuflüsse*). Whether or not, in his view, the experience involves the illusion of actual locomotion is not clear, but he stresses the difference between the "feeling of movement" and the mere apperception of form, which only secondarily is interpreted as being in motion.

Rorschach's implicit psychological assumptions, which are based on traditional theories of perception, can be formulated as follows. The perception of a pictorial pattern cannot furnish anything but static form. Therefore, the element of movement must be a contribution of the observer's past experience. The observer may interpret the perceived form as an object that, by its nature and posture, is known to be in a state of movement (a flying bird, a bowing waiter). He therefore draws the conclusion that the perceived thing is in motion. Such a reaction is not scored as an M-response by Rorschach since, in this instance, the move-

[5] Why do the perceptual features produced by physical motion—such as wedge shapes—give rise to the psychological movement response? Gestalt theory can attempt to explain this correspondence by pointing out that the brain processes on which vision is based, being physical, are subject to the laws of the physical world. If a boat moving through water produces a wedge-shaped wake, might not a wedge-shaped stimulus in that brain field produce, inversely, the kind of dynamics experienced as "movement"?

ment factor derives simply from an intellectual inference. In other cases, however, the identification of the perceived form with an object in movement provokes empathy in the observer. He feels in his own body the kind of muscular sensation that, by analogy to his past experience, he assumes to be felt by the flying bird or the bowing waiter. This is the M-response. As a rule, it will be provoked only by human figures or animals with "human-like" movements (bears, monkeys, etc.). However, Rorschach says, occasionally there are subjects who are capable also of kinesthetic empathy with animals of any kind, with plants, and even with geometrical figures and single lines.

Rorschach's clinical evaluation of the M-response is directly related to his assumptions about the perceptual process. If the M-response is due to an endowment of the percept with subjective sensations, then a person who offers many M-responses can be expected to be one who is rich in associations, meets observations with productive ideas, and has a fertile imagination. In other words, an abundance of M-responses will be characteristic of people who concentrate on their thoughts and, often, their fantasies. Such persons will tend to be absorbed by their inner mental life rather than adapted to the outside world. According to Rorschach, this expectation is essentially borne out by his clinical findings.[6]

There is, then, a decisive difference between Rorschach's theory and the one presented in this paper. Rorschach holds that the feeling of movement is nothing but kinesthetic empathy. I maintain that it is an inherent feature of visual perception itself.

Kinesthesis. The widespread notion that the dynamic components of perception can be explained only as contributions of the muscle sense is probably due to the tacit assumption that the impact of physical forces cannot be experienced except when these forces act within the observer's body. Thus, when someone watches a bird in flight, the energies producing the flight are in the body of the bird and are therefore inaccessible to the observer. But, when muscles contract or expand within his own body, he can become aware of them. A moment's reflection shows that this view derives from a confusion of physical and psychological facts. The immediate basis of any percept, whether visual or

---

[6] Later developments of Rorschach theory and practice have not altered these basic assumptions (6, 13). However, D. Rapaport has questioned the kinesthetic basis of the M-response and related it, instead, to the Gestalt concept of balance (9, p. 212).

kinesthetic, is the stimulation of the pertinent brain centers. As far as stimulation is concerned, it makes no difference whether the physical processes that activate the sensory nerves are located within the body of the observer or outside it. In neither case are these physical forces directly "accessible" to perception. If we assume that the visual stimulus obtained by the observation of a bird in flight offers nothing but a configuration of such formal properties as shape, color, and locomotion, then there is no reason to assume that a kinesthetic stimulus transmits anything but similar formal properties, namely, those corresponding to the displacement of muscular tissue, joints, and tendons (extension, contraction). If, however, we believe that, in addition to these purely formal qualities, the kinesthetic stimulation involves dynamic factors, which show up psychologically as experiences of tension or distension, we cannot think of these dynamic factors naïvely as a direct grasp of muscular energies but must assume that the dynamic properties of the situation created by the stimulation of the projection areas in the brain find their counterpart in the kinesthetic percept. If so, however, there is no reason to deny the existence of similar dynamic factors in the stimulated field of the visual projection center and, correspondingly, in visual perception. In other words, there is no difference in this respect between the physiological bases of visual and kinesthetic perception. Recourse to kinesthesis is of no help in explaining the dynamic properties of visual perception, since this requires assumptions about the nature of kinesthetic stimulation which can be made with equal justification, or lack of it, for visual stimulation itself.

This observation is not meant to deny the fact that visual perception can be accompanied by kinesthetic components. While looking at a picture of a man who is turning his head, one may feel a tension of the neck. But how often and how strongly such sensations occur is extremely hard to determine. Rorschach admits that the establishment of the kinesthetic factor is the most delicate point of the whole test. It may be suspected that Rorschach used this factor as the only criterion for the presence of the M-response not because empirical observation told him so but because no other principle of explanation was in sight.

Undoubtedly, there is an important difference between the mere perceptual acknowledgment of dynamic factors and the full experience of their impact. In particular, it is characteristic of artistic vision that, for instance, the gesture of an arm is not noticed simply as a displacement in space but is felt as being soft or abrupt, graceful or jerky. But such experiences are not limited to artists. The dynamic component is a part of the everyday experience of movement. Strictly speaking, there is probably no such thing as a perception of movement devoid of dynamics, even though there may be great individual differences in the strength and awareness of it.

There is no evidence that the sensation of visual dynamics is due always, or mainly, to kinesthetic empathy. From what I said before, it follows theoretically that dynamics are just as likely to be perceived visually as kinesthetically. Since we are dealing with visual objects, and therefore the primary stimulus is visual, it seems reasonable to assume that the movement response arises from the dynamic components of the visual percept. Secondarily, in some cases this response may be accompanied and reinforced by kinesthetic sensations, which occur in "resonance" with the isomorphic visual process (pp. 66, 69). It is improbable that kinesthetic responses arise unless the figural properties of the stimulus have provoked a strong visual movement response first.

Clinical inferences. These assertions, if justified, can be expected to have a bearing on the clinical interpretation of the Rorschach test. In the view of Rorschach and most of his followers, the kinesthetic response is the only kind that goes beyond a mere acknowledgment, or assumption, of the presence of movement. The dynamic aspects of vision itself are ignored. There is, however, a difference between the two kinds of response, which may well prove to be significant clinically. The dynamic components of vision are as much a part of the percept as are form or color. They are localized by the observer in the perceived object itself. They are no more "subjective" than are shape or size. On the other hand, the kinesthetic response to a visual object is indeed a subjective contribution of the observer. As he experiences the visual dynamics of the percept, a corresponding muscular sensation is aroused in his own body. In the first case, the observer is concentrated on the perceptual impact of the object "outside." In the second, the focus of the experience shifts to personal feelings inside.

In discussing the "feeling of movement," Rorschach does not distinguish between these two sources of the response, and in many cases there is no telling which of the two prevails. Is there really any reason to anticipate that in every case a strong sensation of visual dynamics will go with an abundance of "inner life," that is, with "introversion"? Would one not expect to find it, on the contrary, in the devoted observer, who concentrates on absorbing all the qualities of what he sees in his environment?

The question arises whether the personality syndrome that Rorschach relates to an abundance of M-responses does not actually contain two quite different attitudes and their combinations. At the one extreme, there might be the kind of person who strongly feels the visual dynamics of percepts because he is passionately interested in the outside world and experiences its properties sharply and fully. The richness of his experiences would account for the variety of associations available to his thinking and the lack of rigid stereotypes. He has "imagination" in the literal sense, that is, the capacity to turn thoughts into images and hence to think concretely and colorfully in terms of perceptual symbols. His feelings are not determined essentially by what is like himself or appealing to his own past experiences but by what comes to him from outside. The range of his apperception corresponds to the range of the phenomena he meets during his constant explorations. He is open-minded, curious, and adaptable. His movement responses will not be limited to human or "human-like" figures but will be aroused by any stimulus possessing the pertinent perceptual properties. He may even respond more strongly to nonrepresentational patterns, which exhibit the perceptual properties more purely.[7]

At the other extreme, there would be the kind of person for whom external stimulation essentially fulfills the function of pulling the trigger that sets inner activities into motion. He responds to the outside world to the extent to which he rediscovers himself in it. To him, perceptual stimulation is the point of departure for speculation and the play of internally motivated associations. His imagination is in the nature of fantasies, that is, rich subjective productions, only slightly connected with the environmental experiences that gave rise to them. This personality attitude would correspond to the kinesthetic variety of the movement response.[8]

Both descriptions might fit the characteristics that Rorschach enumerates for the people who give many M-responses. But, obviously, they refer to basically different "experience types." It seems possible

[7] Some Rorschach workers seem to presuppose that pure forms and colors are "abstract" and, therefore, that the perception of such patterns without primary reference to subject matter is due to a sophisticated aesthetic attitude or to remoteness from reality. According to Rapaport, restriction to the "vague" (!) movement-impressions derived from the formal "abstract" characteristics of the inkblots "bespeaks inhibition of the associative processes" (9, pp. 217–218).

[8] Compare Herman A. Witkin's recent findings, according to which "a tendency to rely mainly on the visual framework or mainly on bodily experiences represents a fairly general characteristic of the individual's orientation" (3, p. 157).

that this hidden dichotomy might explain some of the inconsistencies that have hitherto complicated the clinical interpretation of M-responses.

Perceptual structure of inkblots. The instruction of the Rorschach test ("What might this be?") limits the testee to responses connected with, and derived from, the subject matter he recognizes in the cards. Consequently, the theoretical discussions of the test in psychological literature show the same limitation. But, since the attributions of meaning are induced by the figural patterns, it would seem useful to analyze their objective perceptual properties in terms of the Gestalt rules of grouping, figure and ground, etc. Rorschach selected the ten figures intuitively according to criteria of simplicity and rhythm. They had to be ambiguous enough to allow for a multiplicity of interpretations, but, on the other hand, structured enough to elicit some kind of reaction. They could not be "unstructured" since observers do not offer much comment on formlessness.

In the few attempts that have been made to discuss the structure of the Rorschach patterns, the tools of the modern psychology of perception have not been used (1, 2). It would not be difficult to show in detail that perceptual qualities in the ten blots counterbalance each other in such a way that mutually exclusive groupings would have an equal chance to occur if neither memory traces nor personality factors influenced the act of vision.[9] For instance, in Card II, a similarity of color suggests grouping the reds against the blacks, while consistency of form ("good continuation") unites each red spot with an adjacent black area because of continuous contour lines. In all the cards, contours are organized in such a way that they may either lop off smaller units or swing across the vertical axis and thus connect areas in both halves of the blot. The symmetry of the whole blot causes horizontal connection between corresponding form and color units, and thus counteracts groupings within each half of the blot. In Card II, a white central area readily assumes figure character because of its symmetrical shape, convexity, and enclosedness; but, when the glance encompasses the whole card, this white area combines equally well with the outer white surface of the card and thereby creates a background for the black figure. There is also an ambiguous hierarchy of perceptual units within each card; that is, different units compete for the role of dominant structural features,

---

[9] Since the inkblot cards cannot be reproduced here, I must refer the reader to Rorschach's original publication (12).

which then determine the organization of the rest. In consequence, the over-all structure of each blot can be seen in several mutually exclusive ways.

Strongly dynamic forms prevail throughout the cards. This is because the blots were produced by mechanical pressure exerted on liquid paint. Card I is full of obliquely oriented wedges. In Cards IV and V, a large inverted V-shape tends to dominate the whole. On the other hand, the strength of both the vertical and horizontal directions makes the pattern of Card VI relatively stiff; however, a shading of brightness values produces strong movement, which is further enhanced by its three-dimensional quality. The locomotion associated with the subject matter is sometimes enhanced by perceptual qualities, for instance, in the swinging curve of the bowing waiters of Card III; whereas the climbing bears of Card VIII are pathetically short of visible pep.

The symmetry of the patterns has two important effects on movement. It reinforces each dynamic form by duplication and at the same time it provides balance. Each unit is "pinned down" by its opposite number, which thereby, according to the preceding discussion of balance (p. 76) fulfills one condition for the free unfolding of dynamic properties.

Clinical value of percepts. Rorschach clinicians use the "popularity" of responses as an objective basis for the evaluation of individual behavior. A perceptual analysis of the cards would allow a comparison of individual interpretations with the objective properties of the stimuli. For instance, the degree of visual dynamics inherent in each pattern as a whole, as well as in parts, could be determined with some accuracy by application of the perceptual criteria that make for movement. This would provide a yardstick for measuring the extent to which a response conforms to, or deviates from, the stimulus.

If perceptual organization is the counterpart of personality organization, as George S. Klein and Herbert Schlesinger have recently suggested (3, p. 32), the most direct and striking reflection of the testee's personality might be the visual structure he finds in the inkblots. Rorschach clinicians pay some attention to perceptual properties with regard to color and shading, but they obtain information on whole-vs.-detail responses and on movement only indirectly—and therefore quite incompletely—through the content interpretations offered by the observers.

The question would be: What kind of pattern does the observer see when he looks at the card? Just as some artists interpret their environment by strongly dynamic forms while others prefer relatively static ones, testees could be expected to find significantly different degrees of visual dynamics in each inkblot as a whole and in its parts. For instance, is Card I seen essentially as a combination of three vertical blocks or as a system of soaring diagonals? Is Card VII essentially a quiet U-shape or a conglomeration of mobile units, which fly in all directions? The modifying influence of the search for subject matter hides this basic response.

Finally, it would be desirable to separate testees with strong movement responses into those who react mainly to the visual dynamic properties inherent in the percept and those who rely mainly on subjective tensions aroused by empathy.

REFERENCES

1. Beck, Samuel J. Configurational tendencies in Rorschach responses. *American Journal of Psychology*, 1933, 45, 433–443.
2. Brosin, Henry, and Fromm, E. Some principles of Gestalt psychology in the Rorschach experiment. *Rorschach Research Exchange*, 1942, 6, 1–15.
3. Bruner, Jerome S., and Krech, David. *Perception and Personality*. Durham, N.C.: Duke Univ. Press, 1949.
4. Buswell, Guy Thomas. *How People Look at Pictures*. Chicago: Univ. Chicago Press, 1935.
5. Justi, Carl. *Winckelmann und seine Zeitgenossen*. Vol. III. Leipzig: Vogel, 1923.
6. Klopfer, Bruno, and Kelly, D. M. *The Rorschach Technique*. Yonkers, N.Y.: World Book Co., 1942.
7. Lessing, Gotthold Ephraim. *Laokoon*. London: Bell, 1890.
8. Muybridge, Eadweard. *The Human Figure in Motion*. London: Chapman & Hall, 1901.
9. Rapaport, David. *Diagnostic Psychological Testing*. Vol. II. Chicago: Year Book. Pub., 1946.
10. Reinach, Salomon. La représentation du galop dans l'art ancien et moderne. *Revue archéologique*, 1900, 36, 217–251, 441–450, 37, 244–259; 1901, 38, 27–45, 224–244, 39, 1–11.
11. Rodin, Auguste. *Art*. Boston: Small, Maynard, 1912.
12. Rorschach, Hermann. *Psychodiagnostik*. Berne and Berlin: Huber, 1921. (In English, *Psychodiagnostics*. Berne: Huber, 1942.)
13. Schachtel, Ernest G. Projection and its relation to character attitudes and creativity in the kinesthetic responses. *Psychiatry*, 1950, 13, 69–100.
14. Sizeranne, R. De La. Géricault et la decouverte du cheval. In *Géricault raconté par lui-même et par ses amis*. Geneva: Callier, 1947.
15. Wölfflin, Heinrich. *Renaissance und Barock*. Munich: Ackermann, 1888.

PERCEPTUAL ANALYSIS OF
A RORSCHACH CARD

In present-day Rorschach work, the inkblots are described essentially on the basis of the subject matter observers see in them. While this approach corresponds most closely to established Rorschach practice, I suggested in my paper on the "Movement Response" (p. 74) that the objective perceptual characteristics of the blots as visual stimuli could and should be explored in their own right.

Such an analysis may be useful for at least three reasons: (1) The structure of the spontaneously perceived visual pattern may reveal a direct and elementary kinship with the dynamics of the observer's personality. For instance, one person may perceive Card I as a relatively stable and static configuration of vertical and horizontal units, while another may see triangular shapes flying away obliquely from a central axis. The isomorphism of percept and personality may conceivably offer a more immediate access to the root pattern of psychical forces than does the detour via subject matter. (2) The objective nature of a Rorschach stimulus is commonly determined statistically by the frequency of "popular" attributions of subject matter. A perceptual analysis could show

This study was done in collaboration with Abraham Klein and was first published under the names of both authors in the *Journal of Personality*, 1953, 22, 60–70.

that some of the perceived formal configurations follow more naturally from the given structure of the pattern while others do violence to it, thus objectively distinguishing the relatively more stimulus-determined from the more observer-determined responses, regardless of how often they occur. (3) As far as general psychology is concerned, the rules of perceptual organization that have been formulated thus far (7, 8) are derived from simple geometrical figures. The analysis of more complex patterns requires the use of more elaborate categories and, therefore, must lead to a restatement of the methods of perceptual analysis in general.[1]

Why has no such systematic analysis been undertaken? Perhaps because the Rorschach blots were considered "unstructured" and their interpretations "purely subjective." But these terms betray a one-sided conception (6). A visual stimulus should be called unstructured or amorphous only when it is impossible to find an organized perceptual pattern in it. This may happen when the given forms are so vague that the eye cannot take hold of definite shape and color characteristics (as, for instance, in certain cloud or ground formations) or when a random distribution of items does not add up to any over-all structure (as, for instance, a heap of old tools in a junk shop). It is true that, in some of their details, the inkblots can be called unstructured. "Shaded" areas are vague in texture, and some portions of the blot contours are successions of unrelatable small shapes. But an outstanding perceptual feature of the ten standardized cards is that—mainly, because of their symmetry —they offer to the first glance a striking total picture, which is far from being unstructured.

The inkblots are suitable for projective work because they are ambiguous. Ambiguous patterns are not unstructured. They are combinations of different structures that are mutually exclusive. Ambiguity also should not be confused with complexity (3). A sad smile is complex but not ambiguous; a portrait that looks sometimes happy and sometimes sad is ambiguous. The Rorschach blots, then, allow attribution to different, relatively clear-cut and mutually exclusive perceptual patterns.

What is meant by "subjective"? A reaction is subjective to the extent that it is not demanded by the stimulus. Subjectivity may be involved in either or both of the two kinds of attribution that occur in perception: (1) an organized pattern is attributed to the given stimulus,

---

[1] These methods can be applied fruitfully to the pictorial arts. Cf., Abraham Klein's detailed perceptual analysis of a painting by Picasso (5).

as when four lines are seen as a rectangle; (2) the perceived pattern is seen as an image of another object, e. g., the rectangle as a familiar geometric figure or as a window or a brick.[2] Subjective responses are possible when more than one visual pattern can be attributed to the stimulus or when the perceived pattern (or patterns) can be seen as an image of more than one other object. But the possibility of subjective responses does not alter the fact that the stimulus in itself is a perceptual entity that can be defined objectively by measurable shape, size, proportion, orientation, color, etc. The rules of visual organization derive from such objective properties, and their application can produce an objectively valid result, which is not just the investigator's personal "Rorschach."

In the following, a sample analysis of Rorschach Card I will be undertaken. It does not claim to be complete. It is meant to outline a method and to show how certain perceptual configurations follow from the objective structure of the blot. In particular, concrete conditions for perceptual ambiguity will be described.

Grouping and subdivision. These are reciprocal terms. Grouping combines elements or parts in a whole; subdivision breaks a whole down into elements or parts. Gestalt theory describes this difference by saying that grouping proceeds "from below" whereas subdivision proceeds "from above." Both grouping and subdivision are guided by the Gestalt rule of simplicity, which asserts that a visual pattern is organized by the mind in such a way that the simplest, most regular, most symmetrical structure results. Grouping by similar shape, color, etc. is enhanced when the combination of parts helps to simplify the over-all structure; otherwise it is resisted. Subdivision is favored when the parts in themselves and their mutual relations are simpler than the undivided whole. A circle is always seen as one undivided whole because any subdivision would make for a less simple pattern. In a square, a subdivision into four edges is compelling.

However, oneness and distinctness do not necessarily exclude each other. In most cases, a structural hierarchy is created by the relative strength of the whole and the parts. A hierarchy is not ambiguous. But, when the unity of the whole is approximately as strong as the independence of the parts, subordination gives way to an ambiguous coordination of two different conceptions which are mutually exclusive.

[2] The two processes influence each other. The perceived pattern will determine what object is seen. But familiarity with, need for, or expectation of a given object may also help to determine—within the range of freedom offered by ambiguous stimulus structure—the kind of pattern that is perceived.

In Card I, the almost homogeneous blackness of the blot against the white ground, and its symmetry about a central vertical axis, establishes a strongly unified pattern. Symmetry makes for correspondence of parts. These parts may be seen as similar in shape and location, but still self-contained entities, or they may merge in one integrated whole. The latter condition will occur when the corresponding parts (1) lie sufficiently close together, (2) add up to a sufficiently simple pattern, and (3) are not separated by obstacles that are relatively too strong. For instance, the white areas D (Figure 1) correspond compellingly to each other, but they are not easily seen as forming one pattern because a relatively large area of different color separates them. On the other hand, the symmetrical lines *a* are easily seen as pieces of a unified bowl-shaped form, which tends to prevail in spite of the four relatively small and clearly segregated protrusions M, N.

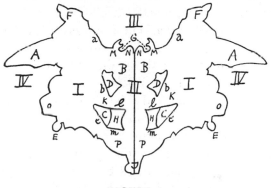

FIGURE 1

Although the symmetry of the whole blot enhances its unity, the internal white areas C and D produce an effective subdivision by establishing a central black column II. This column is itself symmetrical and therefore tends to be a relatively self-contained unit. In consequence, the lateral areas I seem also self-contained although they are not symmetrical in themselves. Thus, the blot is easily subdivided vertically into three columns. But this subdivision is delicately balanced against the conception of the whole blot as one unit. If the four white spots were larger, the blot might break up irreparably into three entities; if they were smaller, they might be too weak to counteract the over-all coherence. Rorschach chose his cards, with admirable sensitivity, in such a way that perceptual ambiguities are created throughout by the balance of different, mutually exclusive conceptions.

In addition to the splitting-up of the total pattern into three vertical units, many other subdivisions are possible, all the way down to the smallest detail. A portion of a whole will tend to appear as a segregated part when (1) it can be seen as having a relatively simple shape in itself and (2) there is enough structural discrepancy between it and its context. For instance, the promontories A are easily seen as segregated parts because their shape approaches the simplicity of a triangle and the directly adjoining areas are sufficiently different in direction and shape.

A part is perceived as a separate unit, but at the same time it plays its role in the larger contexts of its environment. In the Rorschach blots, the position of parts is often ambiguous in that they fit equally well into more than one context. As indicated in Figure 2, the triangular wings A[3] can appear as parts of the lateral columns I, but they can just as easily combine with B in the large crossbar A, B, B, A, which may be seen as connected with, or disconnected from, the vertical column II. The stimulus pattern suggests these and other subdivisions, although none of them predominates.

FIGURE 2

Shape. A stimulus can be said to have shape only to the extent that an organized pattern can be attributed to it. Most of the lines and masses that constitute the Rorschach blots are only rough approximations of such patterns. In these cases, attribution occurs by one of two methods. Either the small and irregular detail is "not counted" perceptually, by being overlooked in favor of the larger dimensions of the stimulus. (For instance, the white areas IV may be seen as triangular, in spite of the many minor deviations from triangular shape [Figure 3, A]). Or, some of the small detail is reinforced in its characteristics. Protrusions are made more protruding, curvatures more curved, contrasting directions more contrasting, etc. Thus, the same white areas IV may be seen to look like Figure 3, B. These procedures may be called instances

[3] Throughout this paper, parts of Card I are identified by the letters given them in Figure 1, unless specific reference to another figure is made. The reader is urged to consult a copy of the actual Rorschach card while reading this analysis.

of "leveling" or "sharpening"—terms coined by Friedrich Wulf (9) to describe changes that occur in the recall and pictorial representation of visual figures. In the blots, the shape of many contours and masses is ambiguous so that it equally favors either procedure.

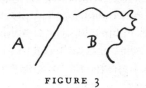

FIGURE 3

The decisive feature of visual shape is not the outer contour but what may be called the "structural skeleton." The skeleton is established by the main axes. Although often not explicitly given, the axes are still effective, and their arrangement determines the identity of the pattern to such an extent that a given outline may produce completely

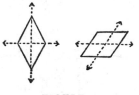

FIGURE 4

different patterns depending on what structural skeleton is perceived in the figure. Compare, for instance, the diamond and the parallelogram of Figure 4, in which a change of orientation changes the framework of axes. Ambiguity results when several structural skeletons fit the same stimulus pattern equally well. This happens very frequently in the

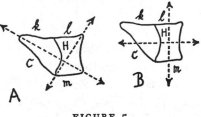

FIGURE 5

Rorschach cards. For example, areas C and H assume a quite different character depending on the position of the axes (Figure 5). In A, there is a strongly dynamic, obliquely oriented structure, which culminates in the white peak, whereas in B, an approximately vertical and horizontal framework, based on the grey area H, produces a more static impression. In the same way, Card I as a whole conforms to a variety of skeletons, three of which are indicated in Figure 6.

Each structural skeleton produces a system of corresponding parts. For instance, in Figure 5A, *c* and *k*-plus-*l* are corresponding edges in a kitelike pattern, while in Figure 5B, a grey rectangle makes *l* and *m* corresponding parts. Framework of axes, correspondence of parts, and subdivision are the three main features of shape that determine the perceptual character or identity of a visual pattern.[4]

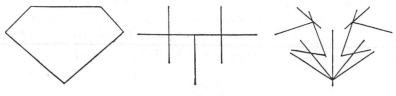

FIGURE 6

Similarity. Wertheimer's various rules of grouping (8) can be considered applications of the one rule of similarity, according to which elements resembling each other in any perceptual aspect tend to be grouped together.[5] Thus, "proximity" is similarity of location, "good continuation" is a consistency that derives from similarity of shape, orientation, and location, and so forth. As previously mentioned, all relations among parts are dependent on the structure of the whole pattern, but piecemeal similarities nevertheless represent some of the ingredients that contribute to the total structure. Similarity may apply to any perceptual factor, such as location, shape, size, orientation, direction, color, texture, etc. The relative degree of similarity among parts helps to determine the degree of their perceptual connectedness. Thus, the strong similarities created by the symmetry of the Rorschach blots make for horizontal ties between pairs of corresponding parts.

[4] In Kurt Gottschaldt's experiments (4), the identity of figures is destroyed largely by changes of these three features.

[5] It is too rarely remembered that Max Wertheimer himself called his rules of grouping "a poor abstraction" in the very paper in which he presented them for the first time. He called the rule of similarity "a special case of the law of good Gestalt" and asserted that visual patterns should not be treated in terms of "distances and relations between pieces" but as wholes, divided into subwholes, which had to be explored "from above to below."

The edges *b* and *c* in Figure 1 may be seen as belonging together because of their similar oblique orientation. If, in addition to similarity of orientation, the units are located in such a way that they roughly continue each other, they can be seen as one unified, consistent form. (The example of the contour lines *a, a* has been cited earlier.) The protrusions E and M can be seen as related because they are of similar size and have similar functions as small outer appendages of a large mass, even though the large distance between them (low similarity of location) weakens the relationship.

The homologies created by the symmetry of the whole blot are so strong that they easily overcome large distances and differences of orientation of the parts. Thus, the triangular wedges F are readily seen as corresponding parts even though they are far apart and point in opposite directions. Similarity of shape, size, and orientation may outweigh dis-

FIGURE 7

similarity of color or brightness. For instance, the white areas C may be seen as resembling, and therefore belonging to, the dark areas F. Vice versa, the common factor of whiteness may connect the outer background with the inner spots C and D in spite of great differences in size, location, shape, etc. It is evident that the large number of perceptual factors that may create similarity constitutes a source of ambiguity. One of these factors may tie together two or more parts by similarity while another segregates them by dissimilarity.[6] Or, similarity may put a given part into mutually exclusive contexts. For instance, contour *a* may be seen as continued across the outer contour, but it also connects with *b* on the basis of the same rule of consistent shape, orientation, and location. The grey area H fits into the triangular pattern C, but also participates in the bell-shaped section of the central column III (Figure 7).

[6] The distinction between similarity and dissimilarity is used for the sake of convenience only. Actually, there is no such dichotomy but rather a continuum from high to low degrees of similarity.

The continuity of any contour line, whatever its shape, represents a strong factor of similarity. The eye willingly follows the "coastline" of the blot in its erratic course. However, when a contour has marked breaks, other connections may overrule its continuity. In Figure 8, continuity of contour would make for the connection of the edges *a, b, c, b, a*, etc. But, given the rectangular break between *a* and *b* on the one hand, and the strong similarity between *a* and *a* on the other, the ob-

FIGURE 8

server's eye may interrupt the contour and connect *a* and *a* by crossing the vertical bar. This makes for segregation of areas. Card I abounds in examples (F, A, E, J, M, N). When the strength of such a cross-connection is balanced by the strength of the continuity of contour, perceptual ambiguity results.

Direction and movement. All visual patterns possess inherent movement, essentially following the direction of their axes. This movement is particularly evident when the pattern displays a gradient. Gradients of size, leading from a broad base to a narrow peak (Figure 9), are frequent in the Rorschach cards (A, F, C) and produce outward-

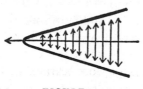

FIGURE 9

bound movement. An obliquely oriented visual object is seen in Figure 10 as deviating from the basic positions of the vertical or horizontal, and consequently there is a gradient of distance from these spatial coordinates. Thus, while the protrusions A roughly coincide with the horizontal, the obliqueness of F increases the dynamic effect of the wedge-shaped form.

In the case of protrusions planted on a broad base, movement tends to take the direction from the base toward the free end. In principle, however, the direction of all movement is ambiguous. The blot as a whole, or its median vertical axis in particular, may be seen as moving either upward or downward. Gradients of shading stimulate movement from the darker to the brighter color or vice versa. The protrusions F may be related to the horizontal or to the vertical, and in either case, may be seen as moving away from or toward the coordinate. The obliquely oriented pair of claws M may be seen as closing or opening. The difference between flexor and tensor movement described by Rorschach often has an objective perceptual basis in this ambiguity of visual movement.

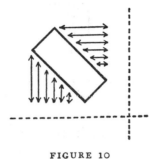

FIGURE 10

Third dimension. All contours separate two adjoining areas. In most cases, one of the areas seizes the contour while the other, contourless area is seen as extending underneath the first. This splits the whole pattern into two spatial planes, the first area occupying the nearer plane and becoming "figure," the second occupying the farther plane and becoming "ground." (Some of the factors that make for seizure of the contour have been described by Edgar Rubin [7].) In Card I, the total black blot tends to be figure because it is enclosed by its white surroundings and because it possesses more texture. In the detail, however, the figure-ground relationship is more ambiguous. Since convexity makes for figure, all black protrusions may be seen as extending over white ground. But, for the same reason, the white bowl III may be seen as lying on black ground. Narrowness also makes for figure, so that the black areas F, A, E, etc. tend to lie on top. But the white areas IV are also sufficiently narrow to be able to snatch the contour and to become white figure on black ground. The small white areas G may protrude over black, just as the claws M may protrude over white.

The white spots C and D tend to be seen as part of the white ground when the card is perceived as a whole. But, when it is not, they easily appear as figure because they are surrounded by relatively large areas of black and because they are of fairly simple shape. (According to P. Bahnsen [2], the more simply shaped pattern becomes figure.) In the card as a whole, this latter conception would make for a three-plane structure (Figure 11A), the white spots assuming the front plane, the black pattern the middle, and the white environment the back plane. If spots C and D are seen as a part of the ground, the whole structure remains limited to two planes (Figure 11B). A principle of economy seems to operate in figure-ground relations, simplifying the three-dimensional structure by reducing it to a minimum number of planes.

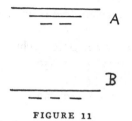

FIGURE 11

It follows that there is a perceptual connection between range of view and figure-ground formation. A restricted view is needed in order to make the inner white areas appear as figure.

Expression. Once the main perceptual traits of a pattern have been analyzed, it becomes possible to describe the expressive qualities that derive from them. For instance, there is the stability of horizontal-vertical axes or the excitement and tension of oblique ones. There is the metallic smoothness of some contour lines or the tattered look of others; the sturdy compactness of a large, uninterrupted mass or the frailer, more sensitive quality of a strongly subdivided, honeycombed pattern. The expression conveyed by a visual pattern will be as ambiguous as the perceptual structure that creates it. But it is possible to distinguish between expressive traits that follow naturally from the stimulus and others that do it violence. The objective expressive properties of the stimulus can be compared with what individual observers report seeing. This requires and deserves an investigation of its own.

REFERENCES

1. Arnheim, Rudolf. Gestalt psychology and artistic form. In L. L. Whyte (ed.), *Aspects of Form.* Bloomington: Indiana Univ. Press, 1951.
2. Bahnsen, Paul. Eine Untersuchung über Symmetrie und Asymmetrie bei

visuellen Wahrnehmungen. *Zeitschrift für Psychologie,* 1928, 108, 129–154.

3. Frenkel-Brunswik, Else. Intolerance of ambiguity as an emotional and perceptual personality variable. In J. S. Bruner and D. Krech (eds.), *Perception and Personality.* Durham, N.C.: Duke Univ. Press, 1949, pp. 108–144.

4. Gottschaldt, Kurt. Ueber den Einfluss der Erfahrung auf die Wahrnehmung von Figuren. *Psychologische Forschung,* 1926, 8, 261–317.

5. Klein, Abraham. *Visual Organization in a Painting by Picasso.* Unpublished Master's thesis. New York: New School for Social Research, 1950.

6. Luchins, Abraham S. The stimulus field in social psychology. *Psychological Review,* 1950, 57, 27–30.

7. Rubin, Edgar. *Visuell wahrgenommene Figuren.* Copenhagen: Glydendal, 1921.

8. Wertheimer, Max. Untersuchungen zur Lehre von der Gestalt, II. *Psychologische Forschung,* 1923, 4, 301–350.

9. Wulf, Friedrich. Ueber die Veränderung von Vorstellungen (Gedächtnis und Gestalt). *Psychologische Forschung,* 1922, 1, 333–373.

A REVIEW OF PROPORTION

One of the basic visual experiences is that of right and wrong. In particular, the partitions of lines or other linear distances, and the shape of rectangular surfaces or bodies impress us not only as what they are but also by telling us whether or not they are what they ought to be. The shape of a house, a shelf, or a picture frame may repose contentedly or show a need to improve by stretching or shrinking. The sense of proportion is inherent in the experience of perception, and—like all other perceptual properties—is dynamic. Rightness is seen not as dead immobility but as the active equipoise of concerted forces while wrongness is seen as a struggle to get away from an unsatisfactory state of affairs. Well-balanced shape is a main source both of the harmony found in many products of nature and man and of the pleasure given by that harmony.

How are we to account for our capacity of judging spatial relations? It may be contended that, like other ethical judgments, these also are imposed upon the individual by authorities, and that the sense of proportion is therefore a gift of the Freudian superego: Good shape is simply what we have been taught is good. But this theory nips our curiosity in the bud. It passes the problem on to the science of social interaction and declines to ask why some patterns, rather than others, are selected by the authorities. And it does not explain the universal validity of such

First published in *Journal of Aesthetics and Art Criticism*, 1955, 14, 44–57.

judgments, which enables us to understand and appreciate the art work of other individuals and civilizations, whether or not they agree with our own preferences.

It seems more fruitful to assume that properties inherent in the perceptual patterns themselves impinge upon us and largely account for our reactions. Such a theory must take two different forms. First, we acknowledge that every person, and indeed every organism, has certain general biological needs. A person or animal requires clarity and simplicity for the purpose of orientation; balance and unity for tranquillity and good functioning; variety and tension for stimulation. These needs are better satisfied by some patterns than by others. The square and the circle are simple and balanced. A slight deviation from a simple shape is ambiguous, hard to identify. A rectangle of the ratio 2 : 1 may disturb us by implying unity and rectangularity while threatening to break up into two squares. The proportion of the golden section—in which the smaller part is related to the larger as the larger to the sum of both, and which yields a ratio of roughly 8 : 5—may successfully combine unbreakable unity with lively tension.

It may be objected that such desirable or undesirable properties in geometric shapes provoke a strong reaction even when they are of no conceivable biological value. To be sure, the balance of a house or the dynamic tension in a well-proportioned human body indicate stability and vitality, which are profitable to life, but why bother with a rectangle on paper? Recent psychological experiments on the interrelation of perception and personality suggest, however, that certain general needs of the mind will manifest themselves, by analogy, even in reactions to perceptual situations that have no practical import. For instance, Else Frenkel-Brunswik (2) found that people whose social insecurity made them demand clear group distinctions were disturbed by a set of line-drawings in which a cat gradually changed into a dog. This means that a central tendency of the mind, such as the need for clear distinctions, may reverberate in purely peripheral reactions—a theory likely to be correct in cases like the one just cited. The reaction of the observers to the pictures is hardly explainable by the perceptual conditions of the experiment, but it makes sense as a reflection of deeper personal needs.

In other instances, however, the perceptual reaction does not seem to be due to an imposition of deep-seated needs on peripheral behavior but to a pervasive tendency, which governs organic functioning at various physical and mental levels. Balance is such an over-all principle. The psychology of motivation interprets human striving as a need for balance;

but balance is also assumed to govern the physiological forces organizing the processes of vision in the brain. Therefore, when we assert that the need for balance is at the root of the sense of proportion, we concede a rather broad organic base to that sense.

In the following, I shall assume that an optical stimulus pattern—produced, for example, by a drawing of a rectangle, at which the observer is looking—when projected on the pertinent brain field, will arouse in that field a corresponding pattern of physiological forces. Thus, the static stimulus pattern will be translated into a dynamic process governed by the principle of balance, and the resulting tensions in the physiological field will have their counterpart in visual experience. This theory explains how we can judge spatial relations without measuring the lines or planes involved. Intuitive judgment, based simply on the inspection of a pattern as a whole, is assumed to rely on the strength and directions of the tensions experienced in the perceived object. Such intuitive judgment can be most sensitive even to compositions of geometrically or numerically complicated structure because, instead of figuring out the single elements and their connections piecemeal, the mind can rely on the tensions resulting from the integrated action of all the forces concerned. More generally, this means that whereas the calculating mind can only approximate the Gestalt by establishing a network of relations, the perceiving mind can fully realize it by relying on the field of interacting forces itself.

However, the intuitive procedure has serious drawbacks. It is delicate, easily disturbed by external influences, and its findings do not offer proof to the intellect. An observer's assertion that the shape of an object is "good" or "right" can be confirmed only by exposing other observers to the same object and obtaining a similar result. Fortunately, the simpler the pattern, the surer becomes the judgment, and the greater is the agreement among observers. The surest result is obtained when we compare the lengths of lines or objects placed side by side. The simplicity of such a pattern of parallels is so strong that subjective inferences are almost powerless and disagreement is negligibly small. Therefore, it is tempting to reduce complex visual judgments to combinations of this simple one. Here, then, we have the beginning of measurement by yardstick.

There is no difference between the basic art of measuring and any other intuitive judgment. Measuring is purely visual, only simpler and safer. But its application makes for grave differences indeed. Measurement dismembers any pattern, and therefore must be handled with caution when it is used to analyze the spatial structure of a whole. Also, measurement introduces numbers into spatial relations, and numbers can be manipulated abstractly without any reference to the object to which they were applied. Hence two risks, amply documented by examples from the study of visual proportions. First, the roving compass, blind to the Gestalt qualities of the object, uncovers identical distances here and there, whether or not such correspondences are based upon true structural kinship. A scaffold of units does not produce an organized whole. Secondly, numbers, obtained by measurements, are juggled about independently, with arithmetical relations replacing the forgotten visual ones. These are Pyrrhic victories of calculation over vision.

Yet, abuses do not disqualify procedures, and the persistent attempt to find the measure of beauty has not remained without encouragement. Some simple measures are obviously related to visual goodness, notably the ratio 1 : 1, basis of all symmetry. Most spectacular was, of course, the Pythagorean discovery that the perceived harmony of musical intervals is paralleled by simple numerical ratios of spatial distance on the string and the flute. This discovery—made more substantial by our present-day knowledge of the simple relations between the wave frequencies of musical sounds—permanently established the conviction that harmony depends on spatial measure. When Le Corbusier takes pains to show his studies in proportion are valid by pointing out that he comes from a family of musicians, he speaks in the same Pythagorean mood that made it imperative for Renaissance architects to study the theory of musical harmony. "More than these thirty years past, the sap of mathematics has flown through the veins of my work, both as an architect and painter; for music is always present within me" (3, p. 129).

According to the Pythagorean doctrine, simple numbers and their mutual relations, as well as the simple geometrical figures that obey such measures, represent the innermost secret of nature. All existing things, complex as they may be, are made up of geometric building-stones. The human body, masterwork of nature, soon came to be considered the revelation of perfect measure. "For without symmetry and proportion," says Vitruvius, "no temple can have a measured composition; that is, it must have the exact measure of the members of a well-shaped human body" (8, book III, ch. 1). Once an ideal human figure, which obeyed the demanded simple numerical measurements, had been constructed, it served in turn to prove the sanctity of the canon: the law of the cosmos could be read off from that of the microcosm. This piece of circular reasoning has maintained its power to our day.

The rationalization of proportion, designed to overcome the uncertainty of intuitive perceptual judgment, suited the demand for scientific exactness that arose in the Renaissance. It satisfied the yearning for objective description, and yielded a rule that governed the bewildering complexity of things. It helped to make art respectable by demonstrating that the shape of its products was not arbitrary. And, wherever the scientific ideal and procedure weakened the intuitive powers of the artist or the connoisseur, the crutch of measurement was offered to support the untrustworthy eye.

At the same time, the reduction of shape to measurement recommended itself for the practical purpose of identifying and reproducing a given product. Mass production demands standardization, and standard shapes are impractical as long as they are not defined by measurement. The ancient Egyptians used a network of vertical and horizontal lines to manufacture statues of specific shape, and, in the treatise of Vitruvius, the Pythagorean metaphysics of number is transformed into a set of recipes, designed to meet the demand of the imitative Roman style of architecture.

It seems natural that a modern architect, endeavoring to revive the art of proportion, should insist on the aspect of standardization. Le Corbusier is aware of the responsibility involved in selecting standards that suit the functions of the object. His aim is: "To standardize, which is to run the risk of arbitrary choice, and the reverse of that risk: a wonderful freeing of the methods of economic production" (3, p. 107). He believes that a suitable set of standardized units is offered by his "modulor," which he obtains in the following manner. He starts, in the Vitruvian tradition, from the human body (Figure 12). He divides the total height, from the feet to the hand of the vertically raised arm, into two equal parts, at the level of the navel, and assumes that this total height is divided according to the golden section at the wrist level of the downward hanging arm (86 : 140). Similarly, the distance from the feet to the top of the head is also divided by the golden section, in this case at the level of the navel (70 : 113). These two ratios are used as the bases for two independent sequences of numbers, both meeting the condition of what is known to the mathematician as the Fibonacci series. Each element is equal to the sum of the two preceding ones, and throughout the sequence the relation between neighboring values roughly approaches the proportion of the golden section. (Thus the ratio 86 : 140

gives rise to the sequence: . . . 33, 53, 86, 140, 226, 366 . . . , continued ad infinitum in both directions.)

How well does this set of sizes suit the purposes of standardization? Standardization demands that the number of units employed be as small as possible and that the units combine readily with each other. The first condition seems to be met by the modulor since the number of the proposed values is small within any range of size. Thus, for the opening of a normal door, the modulor, if I am not mistaken, practically re-

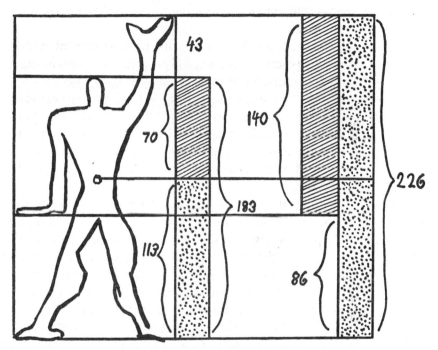

FIGURE 12. (Adapted from Le Corbusier, *The Modulor*, by permission of the Harvard University Press)

stricts the choice to a breadth of 70 cm. and a height of 226 cm., and thus limits production to only one size. The combination of units is not as well taken care of because only a very few are multiples of each other. Within each of the two series, units can be combined only by means of their neighbors. For example, the three contiguous values 33, 53, 86 fit nicely together (33 + 53 = 86), but no multiples of either 33 or 53 match 86. This weakness, which follows from the nature of the Fibonacci series, has also aesthetic consequences, to be discussed shortly.

Standardization aims at facilitating the functional relations between things. Since most manufactured objects are "either containers of man or extensions of man" (3, p. 60), they must be related functionally to their user. Of course, in an informal way, houses, furniture, and tools have always been adapted to the human body, but Le Corbusier hopes to standardize these relations by deriving his scales from the main proportions and dimensions of the body. Unfortunately, however, the human figure cannot be standardized, and since the stature of any population is distributed statistically in a bell-shaped curve, it seems ludicrous to specify the relation between man and his objects to the fraction of an inch. In fact, Le Corbusier worked originally with a scale custom-tailored for an average 175 cm. Frenchman, until he remembered "that in English detective novels, the good-looking men, such as the policemen, are always six feet tall." Since the modulor is meant to apply to world-wide production, the inventor settled for 6 feet (182.88 cm.), explaining that it would be better for a measure to be too large rather than too small, "so that the article made on the basis of that measure should be suitable for use by all"—an argument unlikely to be appreciated by short people.

Le Corbusier's insistence on his particular scale becomes understandable if one ignores its pretended functionalism and interprets it instead as a Romantic variation of the Pythagorean philosophy. The traditional doctrine of proportion related architectural shape to man because his body was an example of perfection, not because he was to live in the building. The architect was expected to create in the image of man, and therefore the relative proportions of the model, not its absolute dimensions, were considered. Whereas, in this view, man, the child of Nature or of God, revealed the secret of cosmic harmony to the builder, the more recent theory of empathy viewed the humanization of architecture as the means by which man "compels inhuman nature to his need" (5, p. 179). Man is a stranger in a chaotic setting of plants, streams, and mountains, so he creates in his buildings something of his own kind, orderly shapes he can understand; he "transcribes in stone the body's favorable states" (5, p. 177). Both theories imply a division between man and his work: the first sees man as a mere model to be contemplated and copied from a distance, the second sees the building as the remote object of sympathetic appreciation.

To Le Corbusier, man and the world he builds are an indivisible unity. Just as man is an outgrowth of nature, so the building, the furniture, the machine, the painting or statue, are outgrowths of man. The builder and his work are interdependent like the snail and its shell. Man enlarges his scope by his works, and the works receive their meaning from man's use of them. It follows from this Romantic view that man and his creation must be conceived as one integrated organism. Hence Le Corbusier's preference for the golden section, which to his forebears was the essence of cosmic mathematics, whereas to him it is the formula of life, discovered by scientists in the body structure of plant and animal. Hence also his two proportional series, which embed the human body in a continuous scale from the infinitely small to the infinitely large, presenting man as *natura naturans* and *natura naturata*.

This is an eminently modern philosophy, well suited to provide our biological outlook with an aesthetic superstructure. But it is a philosophy—applicable to the arts only if it assumes visible form. The reasoning mind may find coherence and consistency satisfactorily symbolized in the arithmetical properties of the modulor series. Are they equally evident to the eye? Obviously, the virtues of the system must be tested in practice and can hardly be evaluated in the abstract. Only a few general considerations can be tentatively advanced here.

If one particular ratio of spatial distances is to be preferred, the golden section is certainly a good candidate. Art historians and psychologists can testify that the eye distinguishes this particular relation—in the twofold sense of recognizing and liking it. Similarly, the ratio 2 : 1, introduced into the modulor by the fact that the values of the one series are twice as large as those of the other, is easily recognized by the eye and can be put to good use. Continuity, by which a series of steps leads the observer from the smaller to the larger units and thus helps to knit the whole structure together, is a basic prerequisite of all artistic composition. To reaffirm and codify it, with explicit inclusion of the human dimensions, seems particularly welcome in view of a modern preference for "monumental" buildings that make the visitor feel lost like a beetle in a cigar box. However, Le Corbusier's arithmetical progression of values does not guarantee continuity; it merely suggests it. Since it remains for the artist to pick from the scales the values he wishes to combine, he must still rely on his intuitive judgment for obtaining those unbroken chains of relationships that produce the unified hierarchy of any good composition. Within each of the two series, only the contiguous values have a simple relationship to each other. The more distant ones do not. And, as far as the relations between the two series are concerned, each value of the one has the ratio 2 : 1 to its opposite number in the other, but, otherwise, the relations between members of the two series

are far from simple. For example, for a cornerstone, designed to symbolize the principle of good proportion, Le Corbusier picked the ratio
183 : 86, one value from each series. No simple relation between the two
is apparent, and, if the resulting shape "possessed dignity and elegance,"
these qualities are not explained by the fact that both values lie somewhere on the two series.

It looks as though in Le Corbusier's system the harmony of the
compositional whole is pieced together by a creeping sequence of con-
cords between neighbor and neighbor, thus neglecting the cross-
connections of distant elements. A comparison, which may or may not
be appropriate, will at least illustrate the point. The musical diatonic
scale provides for the unity and density of the compositional fabric not
by simply equalizing the intervals between neighboring steps. One does
not have to walk the scale in order to connect one tone with another.
Any two tones are directly connected by more or less simple auditive
and arithmetic relations, and the varying degrees of concordance make
for a rich palette of expressive values. Also, transposition of pitch—
which may be compared to the transposition of visual size—produces
patterns related to each other not only by homology, that is, by similarity of proportion, but also by a comprehensible harmony between each
tone of one and any other pattern. Every tone of the C-scale directly relates to every tone of the D-scale. Not so the values of Le Corbusier's
two series.

The publication of *The Modulor* again raises the more general
questions: Is there any justification for applying measurement to visual
proportion? And, if so, when and in what way should it be applied? This
subject has not been controversial for very long. In all advanced civilizations, artists and other craftsmen seem to have felt little hesitation
about using all the faculties of their minds—perception, intuition,
thinking, calculation—wherever they served a purpose. The fear that
formulae might curtail the eye's freedom did not arise as long as visual
judgment preserved its natural power. The Romantic admonition that
intellect and intuition are antagonists began to exert its influence when
there were reasons to suspect that calculation, instead of the eye,
was being used for the tasks that require constant and final visual control.
Needless to say, no fully developed artist has been prevented by such
controversy from using conceptual thinking to sharpen his intuitive generalizations, to cast them into less perishable shape, and to make them
communicable. If there is no objection to making a mental note of the
fact that, say, "blue recedes and red advances," there should be none to
the rule that the golden section creates a good proportion since the first

statement is no less intellectual than the second. The problem is not whether abstract operations are applicable to the arts but whether those that involve number and calculation are.

The objection can take two forms. Either, the adversary may say: "It is possible and perhaps likely that simple arithmetical or geometrical relations are at the bottom of all visual harmony. But, the search for such formulae should remain a hobby for the theorist; they are harmful to creative work because artists can attain harmony only by intuition." I shall consider this form of the objection a prejudice, based on false dichotomizing and refuted by centuries of artistic practice, particularly in architecture, which by its very nature involves constant measuring and figuring. The other objection does not question the procedure as such, but protests against some ways of its application. It raises the basic question of what in the nature of things subjected to measurement justifies it and what kinds of measurement can be shown to be more appropriate than others.

It is useful to reformulate that question as follows: To what extent are the objects of rationalization rational? The term "rational" as used here does not mean what it means to the mathematician. By "rationality," I mean the extent to which the visual structure of a pattern and the parts that compose it are simple, clear-cut, identifiable. If, for instance, the lengths of all the parts in a given pattern are multiples of a given unit, the pattern is fully rational in terms of such measurement. This is one kind of rationality, based on measurement. There is another kind, based on geometric simplicity. A pattern becomes more rational, as the geometrical relations by which it can be defined become simpler. In this sense, the relation of a circle to its diameter, or of a square to its diagonal, is highly rational, even though in both cases the algebraic ratios lead to infinite fractions. The question is, then, to what extent and in what way visual objects can be reduced to rationality.

In the history of art, both criteria of rationality have been used. One of them is based on measurement by yardstick. In its most elementary version, it relies on the single module, that is, it defines all parts and relations as multiples of one unit. This procedure, as we shall see, affords only a minimum of structural understanding. The opposite method of measurement starts from the whole, rather than from an element. It defines the parts as fractions of the whole and thereby makes the whole, as it were, the module.[1] For instance, in Vitruvius' analysis of the human

[1] On the history of proportion, consult Erwin Panofsky's classic investigation (7, pp. 55–107).

body, the head is ⅛ of the total height; the face and hand are ⅒ each; the foot is ⅙; the cubit ¼, and so on (8, book III, ch. 1). Here, then, are several different units of subdivision, pointing perhaps to a number of different structural levels, and thus representing a subtler analysis than the crudely equalizing technique of the single unit. On the other hand, the method of building the whole from multiples of one element creates, at its own primitive level, a simple unity that the more complex method lacks; for this latter procedure relates the various subdivisions of the body only indirectly to each other, namely by their reference to a common whole, while the relations between them are neglected. It is as though several incongruous networks had been superimposed upon the same pattern.

In the same analysis in which Vitruvius uses modular measurement, he also applies a fundamentally different method by pointing out that a body with out-spread limbs can be inscribed in a circle. Here the procedure is geometric. Rationality is obtained, not by applying a linear yardstick, but by fitting the object to some other, simple shape. Geometric planning with compass and ruler was practiced by the medieval masons. While not excluding the yardstick, they freely profited from such incommensurable relations as that between the circle and its diameter or that of the golden section.

Le Corbusier's modulor represents an uncomfortable compromise between the two methods. Being based on the golden section, it is by nature geometric. But all of his ratios are translated into numbers, which requires a rounding off of the infinite fractions. By this artifice, a geometric principle of structure is forced into arithmetical shape. An even more serious ambiguity is introduced by the fact that, in order to obtain a continuous sequence, Le Corbusier uses the Fibonacci progression, in which the relations between neighboring units meander toward the golden section but are not identical with it. Thus, in the twilight of arithmetic approximation, two different structural principles—one based on addition, the other on ratio—are made to fit each other.

As a system of measurement, Le Corbusier's scale is a sophisticated variation of the module principle. Instead of keeping the size of the unit constant, the scale increases it gradually according to an arithmetical progression. This procedure (as was pointed out before) limits rationality to contiguous units and makes distant ones incommensurable. It shares with most of the other systems the weakness of not doing justice to the integrated structure of a whole pattern, in which parts are directly interrelated even when they belong to very different size levels. Instead, one might say, it merely traces linear paths of rationality through such patterns.

Whatever the virtues and flaws of particular methods, the conviction that the search for rational shape is justified has been greatly encouraged by the scientific discoveries about the nature of matter. The Pythagorean trust in number arose from the yearning for order and was based on little evidence. The confidence of modern science is better founded because its rational models are confirmed experimentally. To the modern scientist, simple number and geometric shape as such are not the ultimate principle, they are only the formal manifestation of physical forces holding each other in balance. The atomic model is, of course, the prize discovery of the rationalist. If at the foundation of all matter there is so regular, simple, and symmetrical a pattern as any order-loving mind could dream up, then it may seem sensible to expect that the shape of the things around us is based on rationality.

Such reasoning, however, has to be met with caution. It is modular thinking, an oversimplified assumption that the macroscopic world is a mere multiplication of a smallest unit. Crystals come closest to confirming this view because their regular shapes do indeed reflect an extension of the atomic order. Commonly, though, we find even at the molecular level a structure more nearly chaotic than orderly; if a drop of water and a large body of water exhibit regular shape, this regularity comes about, despite molecular disorder, through the action of macroscopic forces, which, by the way, are not the same for both. According to D'Arcy Thompson, "the spherical surface of the raindrop and the spherical surface of the ocean (though both happen to be alike in mathematical form) are two totally different phenomena, the one due to surface-energy, and the other to that form of mass energy which we ascribe to gravity" (6, p. 57). When it comes to organisms, according to C. H. Waddington, "the forces which hold the elementary parts in a certain orderly relation to each other are not derived from the affinities of just a few kinds of units, but arise from the interactions of very numerous active entities" (9, p. 45). In other words, what I have called "modular thinking" is defeated by the fact that, as we ascend the scale from the atomically small to the astronomically large, we encounter levels of near-chaos and also "integrative levels," as A. B. Novikoff has called them, at which the whole is not the sum of its parts: "Knowledge of the laws of the lower level is necessary for a full understanding of the higher level; yet the unique properties of phenomena at the higher level cannot be predicted a priori from the laws of the lower level" (4). A landscape is essentially chaotic, but it lies in the scale of sizes between the orderly shapes of, say, a flower and the terrestrial globe.

Thus, while the order of things cannot be derived from the atomic module, the striving of physical systems toward equilibrium produces orderly shape at various integrative levels. This confirms the soundness of our search for rationality. It also indicates, however, that more often than not the order of structure is not of the purely additive, "modular" kind but involves an integrated organization of the whole pattern. The structural models we invent and apply must take this fact into account.

What has been said holds not only for the physical shape of the things around us but also for perceptual patterns, which are produced by the sense of sight and are reflected in the work of artists. Here again we have a gap between integrative levels: The patterns that are seen are not mere extensions of the perceived physical objects. But the gap can be bridged by a reference to the projection area in the brain, which, as I said in the beginning, translates retinal patterns into configurations of field forces. If the physiological brain field is indeed controlled by a tendency toward balance, then the structure of patterns will assume the simplest possible shape, that is, strive toward the greatest possible rationality. And, since here again we are dealing with an integrative level, patterns perceived, created, and understood by the eye—in either nature or art—are again more likely to be analyzed adequately by a system that envisages features of a total structure rather than an accumulation of units. This means, for instance, that patching pictorial compositions together by means of rectangles considered perfect for one reason or another is unlikely to produce a visual whole; nor does such piecemeal analysis do justice to a good work of art—even if the mosaic of modules fits the structural seams and corners of the work fairly well. For it is one thing to construct a rational model that serves to make a reproduction of a pattern, and another to hit upon the particular model that reveals the pattern's essential structure. Vitruvius' measurements make it possible to copy a given Greek temple quite faithfully, but they tell us very little about the underlying principles that render the over-all appearance of such buildings so harmonious.

Although we must demand adequacy from the geometric or arithmetic model, constructed for the purpose of rationalization, we should not expect it to fit with mechanical precision, unless, of course, the model itself served for the construction, as is often the case in architecture. But sculptured or painted human figures constructed in strict obedience to compass and yardstick—just as, for instance, the mechanical applications of central perspective in pictures—exhale a deadly chill. Architecture can afford a simple order because, instead of portraying reality, it has the more limited task of representing lawfulness in a natural setting. But no portrayal of reality—be it representational or "abstract"—can present law itself instead of its embodiment in things, for it is in the nature of reality that the manifestations of each lawful process should be interfered with by those of other such processes. Without such interaction, an object becomes complete and therefore isolated, and nothing can be complete except the universe, or the total work of art (which is an image of the whole), or the rational model (which isolates some features of the whole so that we may understand).

The rational model, then, is related to its referent the way any law is related to the things in which it is manifest. Just as the norm of the oak leaf is not perfectly realized in any one specimen, so no rule of proportion can be expected to appear perfectly in any thing. This makes the task of finding such a rule harder rather than easier, for, instead of being satisfied when a model roughly applies, we must find out, through judicious examination of many specimens, toward which principle the species converges. To a given human body, any number of structural principles can be applied approximately, and "the" human body patiently stretches and squeezes itself to accommodate this or that theory. The paintings of the masters have been interpreted with many and often contradictory schemas. This does not mean that they possess no intrinsic order but that to define it takes more than mechanical measuring and fitting. It requires the kind of scientific method that permits distinction between the essential and the accidental.

The simpler the configuration of forces to which an object is subjected, the simpler its shape will be. The smallest organisms are less controlled by gravity and are therefore more regularly shaped. It is easier to be symmetrical in water than on land—but the more rational the shape, the less "real" does the creature look. At primitive or early stages of organic development, there is little differentiation of function and, therefore, simple shape. As the configuration of the forces that control the organism becomes more complex, so does shape. When the human mind is young, the simplicity of its functioning is reflected in the simple shape of its controlled manifestations, for instance, in the drawings of children. These drawings are made up of near-geometric patterns, and it is for this reason—not because they are not faithful likenesses—that they tend to look unrealistic. As the mind grows, so does the complexity of its creations. The typical product of the mature artist is so intricate that only intuitive perception is capable of organizing and unifying the multiplicity of forces that make up the whole. If we try explicitly to identify—geometrically or arithmetically—all of its parts and relations, we are, at best, left with a collection of pieces.

What we can do, however, is to fit rational patterns at various levels of approximation to the work. If we describe a picture as a triangular composition, we let escape almost everything except one feature of the work's skeleton, which may still be the basis of the whole. And, from this most generic level, we can descend to more subtle ones and obtain differentiations of the primary pattern. But at a certain point of the approach to rationality we are stopped. It is the point up to which the scientist can find lawfulness in the intricacy of the individual specimen. The compositional schemata with which the artist starts his work on the empty paper or which the art theorist draws on the photographs of paintings or buildings are such approximations. They are possible because all organized wholes are hierarchic. Such wholes do not grow like unplanned cities, in which each new unit is determined mainly by its direct neighbors—making the whole chaotic. Organized wholes grow by differentiation of a germ structure, and each detail is determined by the law of the whole. This means they have layers of order, which descend from the highest and simplest to more and more complex ones. The order found at each level is true. The edge of a knife is straight even though under the microscope it reveals its irregularities. And when the statistician "smooths" a curve, he is not cheating but trying to clean the intrusions of lower orders off the higher one. How deeply our rational understanding can penetrate into the hierarchy of layers depends on the acuity of our tools, the foremost of which is the mind.

It is necessary here to distinguish between lawfulness and rationality. Every product of nature or man can be assumed to be entirely lawful in the sense that it is composed by the interaction of simple forces. Therefore, even the most complex shape is, in the last analysis, a composite of simple shapes. Things are lawful even though the degree of their organization may be low. The chaos of dancing gas molecules is but the lowest degree of order. Some modern painters limit the organization of their pictures to spot-to-spot relations plus an over-all uniformity: the statement is meager, the hierarchy is narrow, and coherence is weak, but these works are as completely lawful as any other existing thing. The basic lawfulness of all things justifies the search for rationality. But whereas lawfulness is an objective property, rationality describes the extent to which an observer can fit an object to a definable pattern; it is, therefore, always a matter of degree.

I said earlier that the shape of any object must show the effect of interaction in order not to appear isolated and dead. Therefore, perfect geometric shape and very simple proportion are likely to be rare. A potentially simple shape is often modified under the influence of the context in which it appears. Gustav Th. Fechner, studying proportion, spoke of *"kombinatorische Mitbestimmung."* [2] For instance, space value in architecture is affected, as Geoffrey Scott has pointed out, "by lighting and the position of shadows: the source of light attracts the eye and sets up an independent suggested movement of its own. It is affected by color: a dark floor and a light roof give a totally different space sensation to that created by a dark roof and a light floor. It is affected by our own expectancy: by the space we have immediately left. It is affected by the character of the predominating lines: an emphasis on verticals, as is well known, gives an illusion of greater height; an emphasis on horizontals gives a sense of greater breadth" (5, p. 170). This means that, in their search for rational shape, investigators may have to concentrate more on potential simplicity than, as they have done so far, on actual simplicity. The tendency to simple shape is inherent in any one unit but is often modified by the context, in the same way in which, say, an egg is a potential sphere modified by pressure while the shell hardens. A telling example is given in Fechner's studies. When he asked observers to choose between rectangles of different shapes, he found a preference for proportions approaching that of the golden section. But when he measured the proportions of hundreds of museum paintings, he discovered that, on the average, a considerably shorter rectangle was preferred: about 5 : 4 for upright pictures and about 4 : 3 for horizontally extended ones (1, section 44). A moment's reflection shows why this should be so. In an empty rectangle, the ratio between the two linear distances—roughly that of our postal card—is pleasant enough. But when it comes to a pictorial composition that is to be read not only in the directions of

[2] Fechner writes: "Some shapes or ratios, taken by themselves, may surpass others in being more pleasurable. Yet they are never used in isolation, but combined with neighboring shapes or relations, either of the same object or of the environment, or with shapes inscribed in the object itself or crossing it. Each shape, each ratio is codetermined, in the impression it produces, by a direct or associative relation to other forms and ratios, which are apprehended together with it . . . This I have called codetermination by combination" (1, p. 187; my translation).

the two main dimensions but as a more closely knit whole, in which every point of the area is to be related to every other, the distances in the longer dimension would be relatively so large as to be unbridgeable for most purposes. Innumerable examples in which proportions are influenced by practical usage also come to mind.

From what was said in the beginning, it follows that shape preferences will not only be determined by the degree of balance attained through the interplay of physiological forces in the visual apparatus. Often these purely perceptual aspects will be overlaid and modified by motivational needs at higher psychical levels. Examples can be drawn from what is generally treated under the headings of "taste" or "style." The rectangle of the golden section and the square may be equally balanced, but they carry different expression or meaning, the one showing directed tension, the other compact symmetry. The expressive differences between slimness and thickness, straightness and curvedness; the relatively relaxed proportions deriving from the module and the tenser incommensurable ones—all these properties are well suited to reflect basic human attitudes. They have specific biological and cultural connotations, for instance, in the proportions of the human figure. When the title of "Miss Universe 1955" was given to a girl who measured 36 inches at the bust and hips and 24 at the waist, it is not enough to point out that her body satisfied the Pythagorean ratio 2 : 3 and perhaps looked harmonious for that reason and that her torso could be inscribed, possibly, in the rectangle of the *Divina Proportione*. We must also see that these particular measurements helped to make her the visual symbol of what a woman is today in this culture, and that the perhaps equally harmonious women of Rubens or the Pre-Raphaelites project a different style of life.

Preference for the particular degree of rationality to which a given pattern aspires is in itself the expression of a deep-seated attitude. The range from Mondrian, Nicholson, Albers to, say, Rodin, reaches from an extreme need for safety, order, and reason to an equally radical enjoyment of lively complexity; and the demands of the Pythagorean adepts of the yardstick and the compass do not lead to absolute beauty but are only the manifestation of a particular style. So long as the analysis of rational shape remains a tool of the fully developed mind, it can help to make perceived order explicit. When it replaces vision and stifles expression, it becomes a game *in vacuo*.

REFERENCES

1. Fechner, Gustav Theodor. *Vorschule der Aesthetik*. Leipzig: Breitkopf & Härtel, 1876.
2. Frenkel-Brunswik, Else. Intolerance of ambiguity as an emotional and perceptual personality variable. In Bruner, Jerome S., and Krech, David (eds.) *Perception and Personality*. Durham, N.C.: Duke Univ. Press, 1949.
3. Le Corbusier. *The Modulor—A Harmonious Measure to the Human Scale Universally Applicable to Architecture and Mechanics*. Cambridge, Mass.: Harvard Univ. Press, 1954.
4. Novikoff, A. B. The concept of integrative levels and biology. *Science*, 1945, 209–215.
5. Scott, Geoffrey. *The Architecture of Humanism*. Garden City: Doubleday, 1954.
6. Thompson, D'Arcy W. *On Growth and Form*. London: Cambridge Univ. Press, 1942.
7. Panofsky, Erwin. *Meaning in the Visual Arts*. Garden City: Doubleday, 1955.
8. Vitruvius Pollo. *The Ten Books on Architecture*. New York: Dover, 1960.
9. Waddington, C. H. The character of biological form. In Whyte, Lancelot L. (ed.) *Aspects of Form*. Bloomington: Indiana Univ. Press, 1951.

III. The Visible World

ORDER AND COMPLEXITY
IN LANDSCAPE DESIGN

Order may be defined as the degree and kind of lawfulness governing the relations among the parts of an entity. Such lawfulness, or obedience to controlling principles, derives from the over-all theme or structure, to which the behavior of all parts must conform; it also applies to the make-up of each part within itself. Without order, the organs of the human body would work at loggerheads with each other, and the various functions and strivings of the mind would fight each other chaotically. Without order, our senses could not function: the visible shape of an object must be clearly organized if we are to recognize, remember, and compare it with others. Furthermore, if there were no order in nature, we could not profit from experience since what we have learned serves us only so long as like things look alike and similar consequences follow from similar causes. If the world were not orderly, and the mind unable to perceive and create order, man could not survive. Therefore, man strives for order.

Complexity is the multiplicity of the relationships among the parts of an entity. By multiplicity I do not mean quantity. A pattern may consist of many parts connected by many relations and yet be quite simple, as in, for example, a formal rose-garden. And the relations be-

Unpublished paper, written in 1960 for a handbook of landscape architecture.

tween a few parts may add up to a most complex whole, as for instance, in an artfully trained and trimmed Japanese pine.

Order and complexity are antagonistic, in that order tends to reduce complexity while complexity tends to reduce order. To create order requires not only rearrangement but in most cases also the elimination of what does not fit the principles determining the order. On the other hand, when one increases the complexity of an object, order will be harder to achieve.

Order and complexity, however, cannot exist without each other. Complexity without order produces confusion; order without complexity produces boredom. Although order is needed to cope with both the inner and outer world, man cannot reduce his experience to a network of neatly predictable connections without losing the stimulating riches and surprises of life. Being complexly designed, man must function complexly if he is to be fully himself; and to this end the setting in which he operates must be complex also. It has long been recognized that the great works of man combine high order with high complexity.

Different states of mind call for different degrees of order and complexity and, in consequence, produce different interpretations of nature. If the mind is in need of measure and limpid harmony, it will either conceive of nature as an orderly cosmos (the way the Pythagoreans and the neo-Platonists did), or abhor it as the savage foe of reason and safety (as shown by Western man's attitude toward mountainous wildernesses from the Middle Ages until fairly recently). If, on the contrary, the mind longs for inexhaustible and unpredictable abundance, and rejects order as artificial, it will either seek refuge in the unfathomable variety of nature or condemn its lawfulness as mechanical. The historian is accustomed to distinguishing these attitudes as the Classic and the Romantic.

It is because of nature's own inherent ambiguity that such contradictory views can be held concerning its order. Science suggests that, in the last analysis, everything in nature is regulated by a few basic laws. In this sense, nature has high order, which manifests itself visibly in the planetary system or in the star-shape of the daisy's petals. In the solar system as well as in the daisy, a simple constellation of forces determines the entire structure, practically without disturbance; hence their orderly look. However, when we scrutinize an uncultivated setting of trees and shrubbery, we notice no such undisturbed order. The potentially regular shape of each tree is diverted from its symmetry by the influence of wind and sun and is further crippled by the presence of other trees. In the natural landscape, we tend to observe order in the large and in the small but less so in the intermediate range. Looking from a distance, we see perhaps a forest or a town fitting itself smoothly to the simply shaped slope of a mountain; the mountain, together with other mountains, forms a fairly orderly massif because the forces that shape forests and mountainscapes have something of the same simplicity that creates the flower's symmetry. But, when we consider the natural objects of more nearly our own size, we find a different situation. Here also, it is true, we discover approximations of harmony, due to such over-all conditions as the lay of the land and the proportionate distribution of space result-ing from the struggle for light and water; but at the same time there is equally evident a lack of coordination. Branches move in complicated paths, and there is little visible relationship between this bush and that fallen stump, this rock and that patch of wild flowers. The forester and the botanist discern an orderly interplay of supply and demand, but the form-seeking eye finds an often most welcome disorder.

What is *disorder?* It is not the absence of all order but rather the clash of uncoordinated orders. An accumulation of pieces assumes the quality of disorder only when within each piece, or group of pieces, there appears a clearly discernible order, which, however, is neither con-tinued nor contradicted by the neighboring order but is rather ignored, denied, distorted, made incomprehensible. The relationship between partners is disorderly when there is no clear-cut way of telling whether they conform or contrast, whether they are coordinated or subordinated. The term "disorder," as I use it here, describes a structu-ral condition. It also implies a condemnation in the sense that disorder interferes with optimal human functioning. Nevertheless, given certain needs, disorder may be attractive and desirable. For example, it provides a crude, anarchic form of freedom and as such it offers relief to the vic-tims of regimentation.

Man's attitude toward nature is, in part, his reaction to the order or disorder he observes in it. This reaction, we may safely say, reflects his feelings about the kind of order he experiences in his own mind as well as in the community of his family, social group, or nation. For ex-ample, the heated controversy during the eighteenth century between de-fenders of the formalized French garden and the partisans of the looser English style must surely be considered one aspect of the fight for liber-alism against the rigid autocracies of the past.

When it comes to landscaping and gardening, that is, to man's shaping of nature, we must refer to another basic attitude, namely the varying notions about the origin of order, as far as the relations between man and nature are concerned. It has been asserted that in Christianity the evaluation of nature depends largely on whether nature is viewed as the creation of God or as the product of the defection from God. In the first case, nature appears as the incarnation of the divine order, and man, a child of nature, creates order when he acts as an executor of natural order. In accordance with this view, desirable order is what looks natural, and geometrical forms introduced by man appear as a dangerous impoverishment of the true order. Thus, the battle for the "English" garden was fought in the name of nature, and care was taken to keep the formal order of the man-made landscape immanent rather than explicit. Man enters the garden gate not as the master of nature but as its prodigal son, humbly returning and graciously readmitted to the benefits of the order from which he strayed. This attitude appears most clearly in the pantheistic conceptions of our Western culture and, with due allowance for basic differences, in Chinese Taoism and its later modifications of the fifteenth century Japanese Zen gardens. The design of the ancient Japanese gardens is, of course, most carefully controlled —with the intention, however, of hiding the formative contribution of man.

When, on the other hand, man alone is privileged to be eligible for salvation; when he is believed to be endowed with the spirit, and is thereby distinguished in principle from beast and plant; when, to put it in secular language, he alone has reason, measure, and proportion, then he is considered the master of nature and assumes the right and the mission of imposing order—human order—upon the disorderly raw material of the physical world. The consequence is a style of gardening in which man is not enveloped and absorbed by nature but is canopied and framed by subservient natural objects, which, like guards of honor, line the paths he treads, and adopt the patently man-made shapes of rectangles and cubes, spheres and cones, walls and arches. The garden becomes a vegetable extension of architecture; in the words of Bartolomeo Ammanati, one of the designers of the Boboli gardens in Florence: "What is built must serve as guide and be superior to what is planted" (Le cose che si murano debbono essere guida e superiori a quelle che si piantano).

Even the most radical topiary art, however, cannot—and indeed does not wish to—suppress the natural properties of plants to the extent to which, for instance, a stone will assume the shape imposed upon it by a mason. Even the accommodating boxwood reveals a natural structure totally incongruous with the geometrical envelope applied by the "fantastic admirers of symmetry" (4, p. 14). Therefore, complaints about the violation of nature are easily aroused. Nowadays, we are inclined to consider landscaping as one of the many arts whose products are half artifact, half nature, and which should display rather than hide their twofold character. Foremost among these arts are the dance and the theater, which have experimented occasionally with the extreme formalization of the live human figure (classical ballet, expressionistic robots). Photography and the motion picture also have tried to stylize natural objects and movement by various means. Experience seems to indicate, however, that such hybrid media achieve their happiest results when they frankly admit the contribution of the natural raw material by keeping the imposed order loose, open, and partial.

Another way of making this point is to say that the order of man-made landscapes varies as to the degree of their *definition*. By definition, I mean the extent to which intended order is carried through in a setting or an individual object. In André Le Nôtre's Versailles gardens, definition is at a maximum. In the English style, which developed during the late eighteenth century, order is sometimes reduced to a loose spacing and grouping of plants, rocks, and water, which are otherwise left to their own devices. Note here, however, that the defining is done not only by man but by nature as well. In some trees and shrubs, such as the perfect Christmas tree, the willow, or the fern, all shapes seem to fit neatly into an over-all pattern; and a piece of granite offers more definition to the eye than does volcanic rock. A gardener who wishes to interfere with nature as little as possible may introduce a modicum of order by selecting plants of high natural definition. It is obvious that, on the other hand, nature actively interferes with definition. Plants grow and die; the seasons produce and remove foliage, change colors, play with moisture and snow; the movement of the sun, the moon, and the clouds constantly modifies the distribution of light. The visual definitions worked out by man are subject to endless incursions, and the shapes created by nature itself are always being destroyed.

Definition should not be confused with another dimension of order, which I shall call *rationality*. The classical French garden and the classical Japanese garden are both of particularly high definition. In the Zen gardens, the shape of each tree, each rock, the outline of each pond is as completely controlled as are the symmetries and geometric contours of Versailles. And yet there is a profound difference, which we may describe by saying that the French preferred rational patterns whereas the

Japanese were committed to irrational ones.[1] I call a shape or relation visually rational when the eye can understand it as being formed according to some simple principle, such as straightness, symmetry, constant curvature, etc., and thus can use it as one of the models by which the mind codifies nature. The square is a rational shape to every person with an undamaged brain, whereas the rectangle of the golden section cannot be visually recognized or reproduced with certainty by most persons. The most rational patterns are those the eye can reduce to the relation of equality; and it is possible, though open to verification, that only ratios reducible to equality can be identified by the eye.

Irrational shapes need not be disorderly. On the contrary, the rectangle of the golden section conveys to most observers the satisfying impression of being "just right," balanced, and harmonious—as was demonstrated by Gustav Th. Fechner's experiments in the nineteenth century. However, they cannot tell with precision why this is so, whereas they can be made to see that the distances between any corresponding points on parallel lines meet the condition of equality. In architecture, many shapes and relations are rational while in painting rationality is an exception. The designers of the Japanese gardens avoid straight lines and parallels. The units of size and distance they employ in shaping and arranging natural objects are not multiples of each other. Shapes are not geometrically regular. And yet we receive the impression of complete control, complete lawfulness. Nothing, we feel, could be changed without disturbing the balance of the whole. Everything is committed to its shape and rooted to its place by the necessity of the total order.

We noted that the low-definition landscape offers an escape from all-encompassing order. It diminishes subservience and presents instead the anarchic freedom of the spontaneous, the unrequired, the independent. The highly defined irrationality of the Japanese garden, on the other hand, presents a supreme universal order, into which man can fit himself by sensing it and letting it emanate from himself. But this experience of order is not based on the intuitive recognition of measurable relations. Rules and classifications are applicable, but they deal only with balance, structural similarities, etc., not with exact measurement. It is

[1] Throughout this article, I shall refer to three basic types of man-made landscape, namely, the "geometrical," the "natural," and the "calculatedly irrational." These types are, of course, abstractions. Their properties are embodied only approximately in the French, the English, and the Japanese gardens, which I make play the three parts for the sake of a more concrete presentation.

important to remember, nevertheless, that this irrational order builds up to occasional highspots of frank rationality, such as the stone lantern, the bridge, and the building. These clearly man-made objects do not express the mastery of man over nature. They do not appear to be opposing nature or imposing their character upon it. Rather, rationality is presented as the ultimate outgrowth of the intangible order, a manifest confirmation of what the eye senses everywhere without being able to prove it. These tokens of rationality reassure man but do not tell him that he is in charge as does the French garden. The highly rational garden pattern in the French tradition proclaims man's triumph over nature, upon which he has imposed his own kind of order, subjecting nature to quantitative rules and classifications. We can sum up the character of these three archetypes of garden by comparing their different attitudes toward human dwellings: the low-definition garden hides the house; the highly defined, irrational garden leads up to the house, and the rational garden is dominated by it.

Having surveyed some over-all qualities of order we shall now analyze four particular types, namely, (*a*) homogeneity, (*b*) coordination, (*c*) hierarchy, and (*d*) accident. At the level of minimum complexity, we find *homogeneity*. This simplest kind of order is obtained by applying some common quality to the entire pattern. A lawn, for example, derives order merely from its over-all plane shape, green color, and leafy texture. An expanse of water or a gravel road also has order by homogeneity. However, texture does not require straight evenness. A meadow sprinkled with wild flowers or a border of randomly mixed colors can be said to have the character of texture, because we speak of *texture* when we do not perceive the particular relations among individual parts but only the over-all similarity of the whole surface. With increasing distance from the observer, almost any landscape, as for example, a mountainscape or a stretch of cultivated fields viewed from an airplane, tends to become texture. Texture results when the elements of the pattern appear quite similar or when their shapes and interrelations vary so irregularly that they cancel each other out instead of adding up to a distinct design. Uncultivated natural growth tends to assume this quality, and indeed almost any landscape or garden in its over-all aspect possesses the texture of vegetation, which distinguishes it from the different texture of man-made architecture. Depending on the taste of the times, the architect and designer will emphasize this difference of textures by giving the buildings shapes and colors contrasting with those of nature; or play down the difference, either by adapting the buildings to the texture of nature (ivy-covered walls, artificial ruins) or, vice versa, by applying architectural geometry to the garden.

Texture is not disorderly since disorder, according to my earlier definition, is the observed clash of uncoordinated orders. Rather, texture is orderless, as far as the internal relations of the pattern are concerned. So low is the level of this sort of homogeneous structure that it assigns no individual differences to its constituent parts. Since one place is like another, the visitor is not invited to identify or discern any part, nor is his own location or motion defined by the pattern. Therefore, a homogeneous order induces an unspecified mood rather than an articulate response, a drifting rather than an oriented aiming. Its boundlessness affords the elation of a primitive sense of freedom, the sense of "open spaces."

Such undefined roaming does not fit the spirit of the Japanese gardens and therefore we find homogeneous expanses used as "ground" rather than as "figure." Lakes are cut into by jagging tongues of land and are further punctured by islands and isolated rocks, and the raked gravel areas of the Zen gardens are either beset with distinctly patterned groups of stones or serve as the base for agglomerations of shrubs and trees. Thus, the inarticulate surfaces assume the function of "negative" space.

At a somewhat higher level of complexity, we find a type of order I call *coordination*. In a coordinated pattern, all the parts constituting the whole are of similar importance and carry similar weight. The most elementary form of coordination is rather like what I just described as homogeneity. In an orchard, for example, the trees are so much alike as to add up to a homogeneous assembly. Often, however, the units of a coordinated pattern are quite different from each other. On a small scale, this sort of order may provide for the pleasant combination of a piece of lawn, a group of shrubs, a pond, a few trees, etc., each holding its bit of ground and displaying its difference from the neighbors. On a larger scale, we find the subdivision of a piece of property into orchard, herb garden, pleasure garden, etc., or—to use a gigantic example—the collection of Greek and Egyptian landscapes and buildings reproduced in Hadrian's Villa in Tivoli. The demand that, in an orderly whole, everything should be in its proper place is fulfilled to the extent that a place is assigned to each kind and function. However, such a plan may show no order in the relations between the parts. To avoid such disorderly coordination, the gardener will see to it that the various units are sufficiently distinguished from one another by contrast, yet made to harmonize.

But, even the judicious observance of contrast, variety, and harmony keeps the pattern at a relatively low level, at which order is defined only by the piecemeal relations between neighbors. Thus, Christian C. Hirschfeld, the German historian of horticulture, illustrating the need of variety, demands that: "The open shall alternate with the closed, the light with the dark, the charming with the melancholy, the wild and romantic with the graceful . . ." (2). Neighbors can be distinguished from each other clearly enough, but no over-all organization of the pattern defines the particular place to which a given element is assigned, or the particular function it is to fulfill.

In calling this sort of order low, I am merely describing its place on the scale of complexity. In no way am I implying that it should be considered inferior for the purpose of landscape design. On the contrary, this level of coordinated structure suits a broad range of needs by striking a balance between too little order and too much. It replaces the diffuse mood and aimless roaming induced by homogeneous expanses with stimulating alternations and oppositions, and it defines the visitor's position and progression locally, thereby supplying him with partial orientation in space. At the same time, it leaves him with some of the freedom of being nowhere, instead of pinning him down at a spot completely determined by the garden's total design. The virtues of such a structure are especially evident when it provides a succession of surprises, as it does in the Japanese stroll-gardens of the 16th century by "stringing miniature scenic gems with garden paths leading to ceremonial tea-houses" (3).

The organization of a coordinated structure need not be limited to piecemeal local relations among neighbors. It can attain a very tight order, in which each unit is determined in its individual place and appearance by a completely defined over-all network. An example is the famous stone garden of the Ryoanji temple in Kyoto. There, five small groups of rocks are placed on a rectangular court of raked, white gravel in such a manner that nothing could be changed without destroying the delicate balance of the whole.

The high degree of definition in such a pattern naturally raises the level of complexity since more traits are called into play. Even so, the fact that the five units are coordinated, that is, have the same importance in the whole, limits the pattern to statements about homologues. There is no way of presenting the differences between what is dominant and what is dependent, what is central and what is peripheral. Given this structural limitation of the arrangement as a whole, it is significant that, within each of the five groups at Ryoanji, the stones tend to form a kind of pyramid, thus introducing, secondarily, the higher structural order of hierarchy.

A *hierarchy* is an order of some complexity, in which the elements are distributed along a gradient of importance. The dominant structural element may be a central point, as in a circular arrangement, or an axis, as in axial symmetry. The traditional European garden often combined both of these forms. It was laid out in relation to a "head" and a "spine," that is, to the central spot of the castle or mansion and the axis of the central avenue. In a pyramid or cone, two hierarchical dimensions, namely height and size, act as "co-variants": With increasing height, the horizontal sections get smaller, so that the greatest height is also distinguished by being limited to one point, which adds the qualities of rarity, uniqueness, and centrality to that of top position. The dominant structural element is the "theme," either simple or complex, to which the rest of the pattern is subordinated.

In a highly defined hierarchical pattern, each part is determined by its relation to the central theme. Whereas in a coordinated structure all parts are homologous with each other, a hierarchy generally contains many different groups of homologues, each with its own particular relation to the dominant center. In a symmetrical set-up, for example, "each alley has a brother, and half the garden just reflects the other" (Alexander Pope). Since the function of any one part can be understood only in its relation to the whole, an organized pattern such as a hierarchy must be surveyable in order to make sense; that is, the view must be sufficiently unobstructed and the pattern must be either so small that it can be encompassed with a glance or so simple that a guiding image of the whole can be acquired and retained.

In the most radical version of hierarchy, the whole pattern depends directly on one center. Mostly, however, the over-all structure consists of a group of subordinate hierarchies, from which in turn further and still smaller hierarchies may derive. Such a set-up loosens the coercive centralization by giving the subordinate structures a modicum of autonomy. At the same time, every local hierarchy, in repeating the structure of the whole on a smaller scale, strengthens the consistency of the total pattern.

Since hierarchies are made up mainly of groups of homologues, we may say that they tend to be graded arrangements of coordinated structures, with the coordination serving as a stabilizing and simplifying counterbalance of the effect created by the whole. Inversely, coordinated structures become more complex, more dynamic when each of their constituents in itself represents a small hierarchy—as in the Ryoanji garden.

Evidently, hierarchical order is keyed to a state of mind that welcomes a centralized organization or upon which the power and glory of such centralization is to be impressed. Coordination, on the other hand, stands for a sort of federal set-up, in which each subject is at the same time an associate member of the government, that is, in which the governed are also the governors—a most dignified blend of freedom and constraint.

In addition to the types of order mentioned up to now, there exists another one, particularly congenial to the spirit of our own times, namely the order of *accident*. Accident would seem to be the opposite of order, and it is indeed so when events actually take place without reference to each other. Such clashes are identical with what I defined as disorder. For the purpose of the present paper, I am referring to accident not as a method of producing a landscape but as an effect to be obtained through planning. Disorder, although created by means of accident, is not a valid representation of accident. Disorder defines no relationships whatever, whereas accident is a well-defined structural condition, namely, the relationship of independence, which can be brought about only by disciplined organization. The order of accident can be highly defined and is, of course, always irrational. Among the styles of landscaping in the past, it is most nearly represented by that of the Zen gardens, which probably arouse so much attention nowadays for this very reason. In these patterns, order is not achieved by an explicit principle—such as the principle of similarity or equality in the simpler kinds of coordinated pattern or that of gradation in the hierarchies. Instead, the order is implicit. It is due only to the individual configuration of the individual parts constituting it. This structural pattern, demonstrating the kind of order attainable in, and appropriate to, a decentralized community, has been prevalent in much modern art and music and can be expected to exert its influence on modern landscaping as well.

Up to this point, order has been described as a matter of various kinds of grouping—a rather static affair. If the order of a landscape offered nothing but spatial distributions, it could hardly contribute to conveying that sense of life we cherish so greatly. But, fortunately, all perception is dynamic, and therefore order, as an aspect of perception, is dynamic also. Each of the aspects or elements of which visual patterns are composed is perceived as a pattern of forces, and these forces radiate in various directions and create a gradient of decreasing intensities around each center. This means that, quite apart from its actual shape, every visual object—be it a tree, a stone lantern, or a spot of bright color —is perceived as the center of a hierarchy, with "directed tensions" issuing from the center or pointing toward it. Depending on the structure of the whole plan, these elementary hierarchies will fit into a more comprehensive pattern of a similar dynamic character or they will compensate each other in the framework of what I have called a coordinated structure. Thus, a hierarchy has an inherent direction or sequence whereas in a coordination system the various tensions balance out to an animated standstill. In a state of disorder, the over-all effect tends to be static because the various irregularly directed forces add up to nothing better than a sort of visual "noise."

The perceptual dynamics of a tree can be described as centering in the roots and the stem, from which forces issue through the network of the branches, expanding from the center toward the periphery. This is an example of directed tensions being perceived as one-way tracks. Mostly, however, they point both ways, ambiguously. For example, the conic envelope of a fir tree leads upward to the top as well as downward from the top. Similarly, terraces and sloping steps are visually directed upward and downward.

The directions of the forces created by such visual dynamics contribute greatly to the physiognomy of the setting. There is an almost complacent stability in patterns spreading within the horizontal plane, whereas upward and downward movement implies a dramatic interaction with the force of gravity. In the abbot's garden of the Nanzenji temple in Kyoto, there is a most impressive accumulation, raising the visitor's glance from rocks and spherical shrubs near the ground to treetops, rooftops, and finally the slope of a wooded hill beyond the precinct.

In addition to dynamic shape, actual movement also helps to enliven the order. There are informal variations introduced by the motions of plants in the wind. There is the movement of water. Again, the Japanese gardens supply us with clear-cut examples. The picture gardens, composed to be viewed from one definite vantage point inside the house, derive their dynamics from asymmetrical placement and the kind of accumulation just described, thereby justifying Basho's haiku: "The mountain and the garden move entering the summer parlor." In addition, a stream of water often travels through the picture garden, issuing generally from a waterfall on the left, eastern corner and traversing the pond, which occupies the center of the sight. Thereby an order of sequence is superimposed upon the timeless order of the picture landscape, and the onlooker is induced to view the elements of the composition not only in their togetherness but also in succession.

In the stroll-garden, on the other hand, the changing viewpoint of the walking visitor provides a succession of settings and a perspective shifting of relative positions within each setting. Given the infinite variety of arrangements deriving from the moving viewpoint, there is naturally no valid order to many of these aspects in itself. The sequences tend rather to be made up—like much music or film action—of rigorously composed highspots connected by transitional passages, which are ordered in time rather than in the simultaneity of space.

The time character of sequences is compelling only when the structure of the total pattern is not completely surveyable but, instead, reveals itself in a succession of small or large surprises. When we walk around a tree to view it from all sides, we experience not so much a succession of views as the gradual exploration of a given immobile spatial order. But a drive around a lake or mountain of complex shape may assume the character of an orderly or disorderly sequence. Thus, gardens meant to convey a sense of permanent solidity tend to be surveyable; whereas a conception of life as constant change expresses itself in gardens that shun vistas and lead us along the crooked path of wonder.

REFERENCES

1. Arnheim, Rudolf. *Art and Visual Perception*. Berkeley and Los Angeles: Univ. of Calif. Press, 1963.
2. Hirschfeld, Christian C. L. *Theorie der Gartenkunst*. Leipzig: Weidmann, 1779–1785.
3. Tatsui, M. *Japanese Gardens*. Tokyo, 1959.
4. Walpole, Horace. *On Modern Gardening*. New York: Young, 1931.

THE MYTH OF THE BLEATING LAMB

Not long ago, the American Council of Learned Societies invited its representatives at various colleges and universities to report on the state of the creative arts in their institutions. In his reply, one of the representatives, a member of the art department of a large university, gave a melancholy description of a prevailing administrative view of the subject, which contained the following sentence: ". . . art by itself seems useless and is too often classed as an ornament to the curriculum, a frivolity suited to students too stupid for engineering, a dumping ground for athletes, and a training ground for paraplegic therapy" (1, p. 16).

These harsh words characterize an attitude against which art teachers have been fighting at all levels of education, from the elementary grades through college. It is the attitude of those who consider art a pleasant distraction from duty, a leisure-time activity to be indulged in during the few hours left over after the "necessary" fields of study have been taken care of. The situation looks discouraging; but even a sympathetic observer of this struggle for recognition cannot help realizing that, more often than not, the arguments brought forward by the advocates of art education in defense of their subject are hardly suited to change the minds of their opponents. These advocates when called upon to justify

An unpublished essay developed from "What Do the Eyes Contribute?," *Audio-Visual Communication Review*, September–October 1962, 10, 10–21.

their claims, tend to speak of art as nothing better than an enjoyable skill or an emotional release. They insist that art will round out the student's knowledge and experience without explaining what particular values will accrue to him from such additions to an already overloaded curriculum.

No responsible educator or student should be expected to spend time and money on art so long as beauty is spoken of as something that "pleases without interest." It will be necessary to revive in our minds the awareness of the vital functions the arts fulfill. In the last analysis, this requires a general evaluation of sensory activity, of which art is the finest flower. The underestimation of art is only a particular consequence of the underestimation of the senses.

Percepts as Raw Material. We are the victims of a tradition according to which the senses furnish nothing better or worse than the raw material of experience. The physical world, although magnificently organized by the laws of nature, is supposed to present no such lawfulness to the eyes. The appearance of the world—we are told—is shapeless, and shapeless is the image caught and transmitted by visual perception. It takes the so-called higher processes of the mind to elaborate the raw material, that is, to do what we thought had been done for us during the six days described in the Book of Genesis: namely, to separate heaven from earth, the waters from the land, and light from darkness, to distinguish from each other the sun and the moon, the moving, flying and creeping things, and to tell a man from a woman. All this, we are assured, is not directly perceived by us. It is laboriously brought about by mental operations remote from the primary experience of perception: by memory, by association, by learning, and perhaps by thinking.

Where such beliefs began to be held—and partly because of them —education became limited almost exclusively to the indirect manipulation of experience by means of words and numbers; and the senses came to be associated with sex, which had been separated from love as fatefully as seeing had been separated from understanding. Sensation became sensuality—at best a pleasant pastime, at worst a sinful distraction from the higher pursuits of the mind and the spirit.

The view that the artist is limited to a primitive, animal-like recording of sensory data while the more advanced type of Homo sapiens is capable of thought was expressed with amusing straightforwardness by one of the founders of modern psychology, Ivan P. Pavlov, in a speech he entitled "Concerning the Artistic and Thinking Human Types."

Addressing his Wednesday morning seminar at the physiological laboratory of the Russian Academy of Sciences, the 85-year-old father of conditioning said in 1935:

Now, gentlemen, let us turn to the following question. When we analyzed nervous patients in the neurological clinic, I came to the conclusion that there are two specifically human neuroses—hysteria and psychasthenia; I related this conclusion to the fact that man offers two types of higher nervous activity, namely, the artistic type, consequently analogous and close to that of animals, which also perceive the external world in the form of impressions exclusively and directly by means of receptors, and the other, intellectual type, which functions with the help of the second signaling system. Thus, the human brain is composed of the animal brain and of the purely human part relating to speech. It is this second signaling system which is beginning to prevail in man. It can be assumed that under certain unfavorable conditions, when the nervous system is weakened, this phylogenetic division of the brain takes place anew; then probably one individual will use predominantly the first signaling system while the other will use predominantly the second signaling system. And it is this that divides men into artistic natures and purely intellectual abstract natures (18, pp. 589 ff.).

Images through knowledge. In dealing with the relation of the senses to understanding, knowledge, and thought, the psychologist cannot help involving himself in an age-old controversy, which ultimately rests on a basic difference between an extroverted and an introverted attitude. The extrovert contends that man functions under the impact of the outer world and that his ways of thinking about it and his image of it are dictated by the nature of that outer reality. The introvert considers the outer world amorphous; order, character, and lawfulness are imposed upon it by a mind stocked with ideas that are inborn, inbuilt, or adopted from other minds. The problem concerns, first of all, the relation between outer and inner world and, secondly, that between image and abstract concept. We ask: How much of the visual organization we experience in the world as we see it is determined by the nature of the images impinging upon the eyes? How much of the operations of thought is performed within the medium of images?

In the psychology of perception, the empiricist theory, according to which the very image we receive from the outer world must be credited to nonperceptual capacities of the mind, has been given new luster by the recent demonstrations and formulations of the so-called transactional school. The concept of transaction should exclude onesidedness, and in fact the founder of the school, Adelbert Ames, Jr., has described perception as the "ongoing interaction of three components of your total situation," namely, the expectations of the perceiver, the physical object perceived, and the physiological process of perception. He was careful to point out: ". . . the demonstrations also disclosed that the content of perception was at least in part a consequence of the 'object' of the perception; that is, was dynamically related to unperceived light-ray-bundles impinging on your eyes and to your physiological structure patterns. The three: content, object, physiology make a dynamic triad —a triangle" (2). Nevertheless, the introverted slant has dominated the formulations of the school. Thus, in a booklet on the transactional approach to perception, W. H. Ittelson and H. Cantril start out by establishing the central problem of perception as the study of "the degree of correspondence between the significances which we externalize and those which we encounter"; but the encounters drop out of sight when perception is defined later as "the process by which a particular person, from his particular behavioral center, attributes significances to his immediate environmental situation" (13).

The emphasis on past experience as the shaping agent in perception has given aid and comfort to similarly oriented theorists of art. Art historians, accustomed to stressing the importance of tradition and convention, were easily persuaded to accept a corresponding view of visual processes. In particular, E. H. Gombrich's book *Art and Illusion* is a monumental attempt to devalue the contribution of perceptual observation (8; 3). Gombrich suggests that the world of the senses is an impenetrable puzzle and that images are understandable only when maker and beholder share a set of conventions, by which statements about visual reality can be coded and decoded. At the beginning of his eleventh chapter, he describes the history of art as "the forging of master keys for opening the mysterious locks of our senses to which only nature herself originally held the key" (8, p. 359). Since, according to him, what we see as reality depends on what we expect to see, the effect of illusion is obtained when an image matches the preconceptions of the observer.

Do words shape the visible world? The most spectacular example of the introverted view of perception has come from the so-called linguistic determinists. Since the visual world in itself is taken to be shapeless, some nonperceptual power must be doing the job of separating one object from the next, discovering similarities and differences, inferring generalities from individual instances, and establishing the character of any particular thing or species. This power is said to be language—language, the entirely man-made medium, which names things by arbitrary signs rather than embody them; language, the supreme demonstration of man's capacity to detach himself from direct intercourse with reality! It is to language that we are supposed to owe the world as we see it.

This extraordinary perversion starts in the eighteenth century with Johann Gottfried von Herder and Wilhelm von Humboldt and finds its modern advocates in philosophers such as Ernst Cassirer and more particularly in the linguists Edward Sapir and Benjamin Lee Whorf. All of them eloquently describe the visual world as shapeless. The experience of sight, says Herder in his essay on the origin of language "is so bright and over-resplendent, it supplies such a quantity of attributes, that the soul succumbs to the manifoldness" (11). The visual world is "dispersed in infinite complexity." He calls the sense of vision "too subtle" because what it tells us is "confusing and empties our heads." Vision, according to Herder, "presents us with everything at once and frightens the novice by the infinite expanse of its simultaneity." Some hundred and fifty years later, Cassirer echoes this view by speaking of the "rhapsody of perception" (4, p. 27). Whorf, in turn, tells us that "the world is presented in a kaleidoscopic flux of impressions which has to be organized by our minds—and this means largely by the linguistic system in our minds" (21, p. 213). The world of sight appears as a colorful nightmare, truly the invention of men of words.

Language is assumed to be the mold into which the amorphous raw material of vision is cast. Humboldt remarks in one of his anthropological investigations: "Man lives with his objects chiefly—in fact, since his feeling and acting depends on his perceptions, one may say exclusively—as language presents them to him. By the same process whereby he spins language out of his own being, he ensnares himself in it; and each language draws a magic circle round the people to which it belongs, a circle from which there is no escape save by stepping out of it into another" (4, p. 9). To Herder, human beings are distinguished from the instinct-driven animals by what he calls *Besonnenheit*, reflection. "Man gives proof of reflection when the power of his soul acts so freely that he can segregate, if I may say so, one wave in the entire ocean of sensations which rushes through all of his senses—segregate it, stop it, direct his attention to it, and be conscious of his attention. He gives proof of reflection when out of the whole drifting dream of images that passes by his senses he can collect himself in one moment of wakefulness, dwell voluntarily upon one image, observe it lucidly and more calmly and pick out for himself characteristics which show that this is the object and no other." And reflection, he asserts, is made possible by speech (11).

Our own contemporaries put the matter more bluntly. "It is not only in the organization and articulation of the conceptual world," writes Cassirer, "but also in the phenomenal structure of perception itself—and here perhaps most strikingly—that the power of linguistic formation is revealed" (5, vol. 3, p. 15). And Whorf: "Segmentation of nature is an aspect of grammar. We cut up and organize the spread and flow of events as we do, largely because, through our mother tongue, we are parties to an agreement to do so, not because nature is segmented in exactly that way for all to see" (21, p. 240).

As an illustration of the theory, Herder describes how primitive man, confronted with a lamb—"white, gentle, woolly"—exercises his capacity for reflection by seeking a characteristic of the animal. Suddenly the lamb bleats, and lo! man has found the distinguishing trait. "This bleating, which has made the liveliest impression on his mind and which freed itself from all other properties of sight and touch, stood forth and entered most deeply into his experience—'Ah! You are the bleating one!' —and it remains with him" (11). The notion that the visual characteristics of an object are incapable of being distinguished and remembered unless they are associated with sound and thus related to language, I propose to call the myth of the bleating lamb.

Needless to say, Herder's account of the origin of perceptual organization is purely fictional, and anybody is at liberty to replace it with another. Thus, the Italian architect, Leonardo Ricci, untouched by linguistic determinism, wrote recently in a curious treatise called *Anonymous (20th Century)*:

Sight is the most sensitive, or rather, the most evident, of the human senses. Thus when men tried consciously to express themselves to one another, they must have tried, before any other, that language which today is called painting. And so it came about that one man looking at the moon and trying to refashion its form on the wet sand, or dipping his own hand in color and pressing it on a stone, or trying to imitate the form of a running animal, began to talk with the others. It was true that they could all see the moon and hands and running animals. But how could any one of them know whether the others saw exactly what he saw? And then—someone comes upon the place where another man has drawn the moon. He looks at the drawing and he sees the moon the way the other saw it! He feels like shouting with joy. Now, things are different: for one man has smashed the door between himself and another, opened the way to pass to the other! And since that time, nothing has changed (19, p. 130).

Words and thought. Ricci is just as convinced as Herder was and, to me, more convincing. But the word-struck theorists proceed from their first assertion—that the visual world is, in itself, invisible—to a second, which is not easily reconciled with the first. While assuring us that the senses are incapable of producing articulate form, they also maintain that these same senses perceive only individual objects and that in order to generalize, that is, to form concepts, one must go beyond, and away from, perception. Cassirer adopts this familiar philosophical assumption. He explains that for animals there are no stable "things" with constant attributes; animals are unable to detach, from the complex totality of perceptual experience, particular attributes by which a certain content can be recognized and identified. The sameness of things "is not at all a factor that is contained in the immediate experience—on the plane of sensory experience itself there is no 'recurrence of the same.' Every sense impression, taken purely as such, possesses a peculiar, never recurring timbre, or tinge. Where the purely expressive character of this timbre or tinge predominates, the world is not yet homogeneous and constant in our sense" (5, vol. 3, p. 120). Elsewhere, Cassirer speaks of the need "to deliver the contents of sensory or intuitive experience from the isolation in which they originally occur" (4, p. 32). Practically, this means that, as Sapir has argued," even comparatively simple acts of perception are very much more at the mercy of the social patterns called words than we might suppose. If one draws some dozen lines, for instance, of different shape, one perceives them as divisible into such categories as 'straight,' 'crooked,' 'zigzag,' because of the classificatory suggestiveness of the linguistic terms themselves. We see and hear and otherwise experience very largely as we do because the language habits of our community predispose certain choices of interpretation" (15, p. 162). This means that you call a line a zigzag not because you see that it has a zigzag shape; on the contrary, you see the line as a zigzag because you are used to calling it that way!

The theory culminates logically in the contention that there can be no thinking except in words. Sapir is of the opinion that "the feeling entertained by so many that they can think, or even reason, without language is an illusion. Thought may be a natural domain apart from the artificial one of language, but speech would seem to be the only road we know of that leads to it." And there is an almost pathological tinge to his rhetorical question: "Would we be so ready to die for 'liberty,' to struggle for 'ideals,' if the words themselves were not ringing within us?" (20, pp. 15–17). We are reminded here of the kind of semanticist who sounds as though he would like to convince us that if we could only eliminate the ambiguity of words there would be no further disagreements among the inhabitants of this earth.

Form inherent in vision. Occasionally, the adherents of this introverted approach to the psychology of cognition acknowledge that there are facts not easily reconciled with their view. Thus Whorf commends Gestalt psychology for "the discovery that visual perception is basically the same for all normal persons past infancy and conforms to definite laws, a large number of which are fairly well known" (21, p. 163). In fact, the main antidote to the prevalent introverted slant has come from Gestalt psychology. As soon as perceptual experiments were directed toward the behavior of the stimulus pattern as a whole rather than toward isolated elements, it became clear that a visual stimulus has a character of its own that strongly influences what is seen. To be sure, on its arrival at the retinae of the eyes, the stimulus is amorphous in the sense that there is no interaction among its elements likely to influence perception substantially. But it contains objective properties of shape and color—such as similarity, geometric form, symmetry, complementarity—which steer the organizational process in the brain field. To cite just two experimental studies, one older, one more recent: K. Gottschaldt showed that the parts that appear as discernible entities within a total pattern are determined for the average observer by the relation between the structure of the part and the structure of the whole (9). In the research of A. Michotte, the experience of causality—that is, the observed effect of the forces inherent in one object upon the movements of another—turned out to be an integral part of the percept itself, strictly dependent on stimulus conditions such as the relative direction and speed of the moving objects (16). This dependence of the percept upon the stimulus, however, is not a point-to-point relation between items of the retinal and the perceptual fields, as J. J. Gibson (otherwise a strong proponent of this approach) has asserted, but follows the rules of structural organization (6).

The compelling effect of visual structure operates not only in spatial patterns but also in time sequences, as in the perception of movement or in the interaction between memory images and direct perception. Thus, the spatial and the temporal contexts act with and against each other. The outcome of this interaction is determined by the relative strengths of the two contexts; but the immediate presence of a strongly organized percept is very hard to overrule or even to modify by memory factors. Significantly enough, in practically all experiments demonstrating the effect of past experience, an ambiguity or some other structural looseness in the perceived pattern is seized upon by the memory trace or set.

As far as the relation of perception to the acquisition of general concepts goes, the Gestalt psychologist has to point out, first of all, that vision is not an isolated mechanism intent on recording stimuli for the recording's sake. The senses developed rather in the course of evolution as a means of coping with the physical world. Such coping, whether based on instinct or on learning, consists in dealing with individual things on the basis of what kind of thing they are. The individual case can be foreseen neither by instinct nor by learning. One copes with a staircase, a can-opener, a threat, or an offer by means of the properties they have as species. Hence perception, too, must be geared to generic properties from the outset. The level of generality will depend on how much differentiation the purpose demands. Early concepts will be very broad, to be broken down later.

The experimental evidence for what psychologists call "stimulus equivalence" refers mostly to motor reactions rather than to perception, but to reactions based on perception nevertheless. The experiments strongly suggest that perception starts with broad generalities. It is true, however, that in certain cases the theory clings to traditional assumptions. Thus, when Pavlov found that his dogs reacted to a whole range of sound pitches after having been trained with a particular one, he inferred from the reaction that the originally specific stimulus had spread along an extended range of such stimuli, thus causing a corresponding generalization of the response (17, pp. 113 ff.). Related to this notion of generalization by oozing, as one might call it, is a tendency among theorists to explain stimulus equivalence by the alleged fuzziness of percepts at early stages of development. According to this view, animals or young children are able to react to, say, triangular shape regardless of variation of size, proportion, or orientation for the same reason that may make a near-sighted man find all women equally beautiful. Gestalt psychologists have had to face this approach on early occasions, as, for example, in 1913, when G. E. Müller explained the gradual transformation of memory traces by the *Konvergenzprinzip*, according to which the mental images of different objects "converge with increasing imprecision toward an extremely imprecise image" (23; 24). Gestalt psychology suggests, instead, that perception does not consist in the mechanical recording of stimulus material, either detailed or blurred, but in the grasping of structural features, which gives the character of generality to any percept and eliminates the difference in principle between seeing an individual thing and seeing a kind of thing—the difference between percept and concept.

This Copernican turnabout of the theory—according to which the early knowledge of the world does not develop from perceived particulars to abstract generalizations but is based on primary generalities within perception itself—explains many manifestations of the young or primitive mind. It enables us, for example, to recognize in the pictorial representations of children or archaic art the reflection of early stages of perceptual concept formation rather than to misinterpret them as the manifestation of an intellectualistic or "haptic" approach.

This new view, however, should not make us forget that after differentiated patterns have been acquired, generalization will often take place along the lines of traditional logic. In a paper on perceptual learning, the Gibsons forcefully make the point that learning is not a matter of "enriching previously meager sensations" with the help of past experience but of "differentiating previously vague [!] impressions" (7). They assert that learning does not consist in moving away from and beyond the percept but in differentiating the percept itself: in the response to "variables of physical stimulation not previously responded to." In their paper, the Gibsons report an experiment in which subjects learned gradually to distinguish between very similar scribbles presented to them. While this demonstration is of great value, we must keep in mind that by presenting almost identical items and asking for discrimination, the Gibsons stacked the cards in favor of discrimination between items. If, on the contrary, subjects are faced with a set of very different figures and asked to find some similarity among them (as, for example, in C. L. Hull's experiment of 1920 with Chinese characters containing a common radical [12]), the differentiation of the percept will lead to the discovery of similarities rather than differences; that is, to generalization. But, here again, it is a thorough scrutiny of the percept that leads to progress in learning.

Visual thinking. Perceptual abstraction lays the foundation for perceptual thinking. Reasoning is in no way limited to the manipulation of words and numbers. Wolfgang Köhler has shown that the speechless apes with which he experimented were capable of genuine problem solving (14). In fact, we have evidence from much more highly esteemed primates that the most creative kind of scientific reasoning in fields such as mathematics and physics is based on perceptual experiences rather than words or formulae. There is a chapter, "Discovery as a Synthesis," in the French mathematician Jacques Hadamard's book on the psychology of invention in the mathematical field, where he relates how surprised he was when he ran into the belief that no thought is possible without words (10). He had his first hint of it when he read in a newspaper article in 1911: "The idea cannot be conceived otherwise than through the word and only exists by the word." "My feeling was," adds Hadamard, "that the ideas of the man who wrote that were of poor quality." In an enquiry about the matter, he received a letter from Albert Einstein, which says: "The words or the language, as they are written or spoken, do not seem to play any role in my mechanism of thought. The psychical entities which seem to serve as elements in thought are certain signs and more or less clear images which can be 'voluntarily' reproduced and combined. . . . These elements are, in my case, of visual and some of muscular type. Conventional words or other signs have to be sought for laboriously only in a secondary stage, when the mentioned associative play is sufficiently established and can be reproduced at will" (10, appendix II).

If it is true that genuine creative thinking, which makes for progress in the sciences and other exercises of the intellect, consists in the handling of perceptually conceived objects and forces, much of our education, from grade school to graduate school, may be doing an efficient job of interfering with the development of this most precious capacity of the human mind. By reducing the work of the growing brain as much as possible to words and numbers, we may be reducing the thinking of our pupils and students to the accumulation and reshuffling of formalized chips or "bits," as the communication engineers call them. Those engineers also tell us that computing machines cannot think.

If it is true, as the philosopher Wittgenstein once wrote beautifully in his notebooks, that "die Worte sind wie die Haut auf einem tiefen Wasser" (22, p. 52), that is: words are like the skin on a deep water, then we must penetrate beneath the skin. We must see to it that in every field of study, whether natural or social science, geography or history, or literature, the student proceeds from the mere husks of communication to the play of the real forces to which communication points; and these forces are most efficiently conceived and handled by our highest sense—the sense of vision. To put it more practically: We must preserve for secondary and higher education the approach so successfully applied at the level at which, I believe, education in the United States does its finest job, namely, in kindergarten and the first grade.

Visual aids. This brings up the question of the so-called visual aids. To be sure, the value of direct visual experience is admitted by everybody in the field of education. Particularly, the contribution of photography in all its forms has revolutionized teaching and learning in most

areas of study. However, even the use of visual aids may be hampered by
the blinders of the introverted approach. This approach does not deny
that visual material is indispensable; but it thinks of it as raw material
only. If the image of the world, outside of the schoolroom or indoors on
the projection screen, is believed to be amorphous in itself, a film or lantern slide will be considered satisfactory if it is an authentic recording of
the pertinent subject matter. Suppose, for example, the processes of cell
division or the child-rearing practices on a Pacific island are to be studied: it will suffice that the pictures be genuine and complete since all the
selecting, comparing, generalizing, and interpreting are assumed to be
accomplished by the "higher" mental operations of the beholder
anyway.

If, however, the educator has come to understand that all these
components of learning are inherent in the very act of perception and
that truly productive thinking—during, after, and before direct perception—is done by means of images, he will realize that the visual material will have to fulfill certain requirements in order to do its job.

What are some of these requirements? First of all, we need to keep
in mind that perceiving consists in the grasping of structural features.
Consequently, all subject matter must be presented in a way that makes
such grasping possible. At the most elementary level: How many separate objects are seen in the picture? Does this number correspond to the
intended meaning? Or are objects being separated that should be perceived as one, or vice versa? We have no right here to rely on the
student's expectation or knowledge. The picture itself must steer perception. How it accomplishes this feat has been demonstrated in great detail by Gestalt psychologists. The shape of contours, the contrast of
brightness, the structure of the over-all pattern will determine what is
seen. Whether an object fades into the background or stands out as a
segregated entity depends again upon perceptual factors; and the meaning of what is seen is influenced by this visible relationship of figure and
ground.

More subtly, we notice that objects are not simply either separate
or united but relate to each other in different degrees, thus creating a
complex hierarchy that leads from the over-all pattern to the smallest
detail. This varying closeness of connection between elements is not
automatically transmitted by just any authentic photograph. Contrasts
may be blurred or misleading breaks may be created if angle, distance,
and lighting are not judiciously chosen. Often a photograph, in spite of
all its authenticity, is not the best visual interpreter; rarely will it do the

job without the help of other means such as schematic drawings, graphs, etc. A good drawing identifies and interprets the subject by means of clearly defined visual properties. A photograph, which is a mechanical impingement of light stimuli, must be carefully controlled in order to explain the subject rather than merely expose the student to it. It is a pious superstition to believe that the student sees, say, a printing machine or a sperm fertilizing an egg, just because the pictures he looks at have been taken of these objects.

To see a printing machine means to understand certain things about it—things that appear within the picture as shapes, directions, and movements. In order to truly perceive what the sperm is doing, the beholder must see "penetration" translated into a clear-cut sequence of moving or yielding elements of form. I have watched groups of schoolchildren stare at the small television screen on which vague smudges of black and grey purported to represent the dikes of Holland or the heartbeats of a frog. Whatever effect these phantoms may have had upon the children, it was not visual education.

Visual education must be based on the premise that every picture is a statement. The picture does not present the object itself but a set of propositions about the object; or, if you prefer, it presents the object as a set of propositions. These propositions are stated in visual language. For instance, a "comparison" is made by means of visible similarity and parallelism. A "sequence" is shown by visible continuity. "Cause and effect" are shown by an observable proximity in time or space or both. "Change" is shown by something changing—it must be seen, not just talked about.

True visual education presupposes that the world can present its inherent order to the eye and that seeing consists in understanding this order. The human mind must bring into play all of its capacities at the very first contact with the object; there is no preparatory phase of pure reception. The thinking on which all true learning is based takes place at the source and continues to draw on it.

Art makes the world visible. Only in an educational setting that is dedicated as a whole and in all of its activities to the purpose of making the world visible can the cultivation of the arts in theory and in practice make true sense. Art is never quite itself when it floats as an island of visibility in an ocean of blindness. It begins to make sense when it is conceived as the most radical attempt to understand the meaning of our existence through the shapes and colors and movements that the sense of sight grasps and interprets. Taken seriously in this fashion, art is not light entertainment for the after-work hours. It is wonderfully exhaust-ing. "I never thought so hard," a student of painting will say after wrestling for a few hours with a compositional problem. And if, at a visit to the museum or in a class on the history of art, a student immerses himself truly in the work of a master, he will feel that he has been subjected to a rare discipline of all of his mental powers.

A visual problem is hard to escape from. It takes hold of the mind directly, without the mediation of alphabets and digits. The questions it asks, the demands it makes, and the imperfections of your own response stare you in the face, embodied, tangible, haunting. If you try a perfunc-tory solution, your shallowness will show. If you apply somebody else's answer to your problem, it will look at you like a stranger. Nobody's thinking will do but your own, and every incompleteness will hurt like a wound.

Art is so wonderfully exhausting also because it raises the question of our entire existence every time. No artist can be a specialist. The more truly he concentrates on the work of his brushes or chisels, the more im-mediately the shapes and colors will confront him with the question: Who are we? And: Where are we? The work of art makes the world visible. No human quest for wisdom can go farther.

REFERENCES

1. American Council of Learned Societies. *Newsletter*, March 1962, 13, 16.
2. Ames, A., Jr. *Interpretative Manual for the Demonstrations in the Psychology Research Center*. Princeton, N.J.: Princeton Univ. Press, 1955.
3. Arnheim, R. "Art history and the partial God." This volume, pp. 151–161.
4. Cassirer, E. *Language and Myth*. New York: Dover, 1946.
5. ———. *The Philosophy of Symbolic Forms*. New Haven, Conn.: Yale Univ. Press, 1957.
6. Gibson, J. J. *The Perception of the Visual World*. Boston: Houghton Mifflin, 1950.
7. Gibson, J. J., and Gibson, E. J. Perceptual learning. *Psychological Review*, 1955, 62, 32–41.
8. Gombrich, E. H. *Art and Illusion*. New York: Pantheon, 1960.
9. Gottschaldt, K. Ueber den Einfluss der Erfahrung auf die Wahrnehmung von Figuren. *Psychologische Forschung*, 1926, 8, 261–317. (English summary in Willis D. Ellis. *A Sourcebook of Gestalt Psychology*. London: Kegan Paul, 1938.)
10. Hadamard, J. *The Psychology of Invention in the Mathematical Field*. Princeton, N.J.: Princeton Univ. Press, 1945.
11. Herder, J. G. von. *Ueber den Ursprung der Sprache*. Berlin, 1770.

12. Hull, C. L. Quantitative aspects of the evolution of concepts. *Psychological Monographs,* 1920, no. 123.
13. Ittelson, W. H., and Cantril, H. *Perception, A Transactional Approach.* Garden City: Doubleday, 1954.
14. Köhler, W. *The Mentality of Apes.* New York: Harcourt, 1925.
15. Mandelbaum, D. G. (ed.) *Selected Writings of Edward Sapir.* Berkeley and Los Angeles: Univ. of Calif. Press, 1949.
16. Michotte, A. *La perception de la causalité.* Paris: Vrin, 1946.
17. Pavlov, I. P. *Conditioned Reflexes.* N.Y.: Dover, 1960.
18. ———. *Experimental Psychology and Other Essays.* N.Y., 1957.
19. Ricci, L. *Anonymous (20th century).* N.Y., 1962.
20. Sapir, E. *Language.* N.Y.: Harcourt, 1949.
21. Whorf, B. L. *Language, Thought, and Reality.* N.Y.: Wiley, 1956.
22. Wittgenstein, L. *Notebooks 1914–1916.* Oxford, 1961.
23. Woodworth, Robert S. *Experimental Psychology.* N.Y.: Holt, 1938.
24. Wulf, F. Ueber die Veränderung von Vorstellungen. *Psychologische Forschung,* 1922, 1, 333–373. (English summary in Willis D. Ellis, *op. cit.*)

ART HISTORY AND THE PARTIAL GOD

They say, namely, that what the mind can sense and in many ways perceive is not the mind itself nor existing things but only things that are neither in themselves nor in any place; which means that the mind solely by its own power can create sensations and ideas which are not of real things. This amounts to regarding the mind partially as God. They say further that we, or our minds, have a freedom of such a kind that we constrain ourselves, that is, our minds, and indeed our very freedom. For after having contrived some fiction and given it its assent, the mind can no longer conceive or fashion it in any other way, and it is also forced by its fiction to conceive of other things in the same manner in order not to oppose the initial fiction; thus, because of that initial fiction, they are also forced to admit the absurdities which I have mentioned and which we shall not fatigue ourselves to refute by any demonstrations.

—SPINOZA. *On the Correction of the Understanding.*

The interpretation of pictorial representation has gradually shifted from the object to the subject. Nature in its absolute and independent existence used to be considered the stable target the artist endeavored to reach. But, with the turn toward psychology, the theory of art began to take cognizance of the difference between the physical world and its appearance, and, subsequently, of the further difference between what is seen in nature and what is recorded in an artistic medium. The importance of formative factors inherent in the person, or acquired by experi-

A review written for the *Art Bulletin*, March 1962, 44, 75–79.

ence and historical tradition, was increasingly stressed: What is seen depends on who is looking and who taught him too look. The introverted approach (as the psychologist might classify it) to the problem of representation has found its most significant expression in a book unlikely to be surpassed in the extremeness of its theoretical position, the eloquence of its pleading, or the thoroughness of its documentation— E. H. Gombrich's *Art and Illusion* (2).

Given the complexity of Gombrich's presentation, it seems useful to enumerate some of the basic assertions contained in his eleven chapters:

Introduction. From antiquity to Ruskin, the history of art has been viewed as the striving toward an ever more successful imitation of nature. The development from early schematic forms toward the lifelikeness of recent Western art was interpreted as reflecting the change from the representation of what is known to that of what is seen. A growing interest in the traditional shapes into which all imagery is cast found support in the recent psychological discovery that perception does not start from particular sensations but from global generalities.

Chapter I. Even the lifelikeness of a painting by Constable is not due to a mere transcription, but to a translation into the terms of the medium. Although a simple code of shapes and colors can suffice to produce readable images, such codes can attain any level of subtlety.

Chapter II. Mental sets created by an epoch make the works of a particular style understandable to its public. The tendency to use the familiar in order to represent the unfamiliar leads to curious aberrations even in documentary pictorial reporting. Schemata are needed to describe the world.

Chapter III. A work of art will "come to life," not by its actual faithfulness, but by meeting the needs and expectations of the period.

Chapter IV. Early art defines pictorial objects only to the extent needed to inventory the content of the depicted scene. An interest in narration accounts for the exceptional event of naturalism in Greece. By detaching pictures from their social context, the Greeks invented "art" as we know it.

Chapter V. Even the Greeks had canons of proportion; and instructional books on how to draw various objects served as a basis for the art of the West and China. Such devices influenced the technique of the masters. To the postmedieval artist, traditional schemata are the starting point for corrections, which may revise these schemata beyond recognition.

Chapter VI. The beholder's share in the reading of images is evident in the interpretation of inkblots, stimulating scribbles, and Leonardo's damp walls. Effects of perspective and texture rely on what the beholder perceives. Painters entertain the public with the evocative magic of their brush strokes.

Chapter VII. Expectation creates illusion, and knowledge fills gaps. Incomplete shapes are supplemented by the beholder's "projections," which presuppose a mental set and a sufficiently empty "screen." Ambiguity is the key to the problem of image reading.

Chapter VIII. The illusion of spatial depth illustrates the power of suggestion. The clues for distance are interpreted by what is known from past experience. So are the contributions of light and shade to the rendering of volume. Cubism attempts to destroy the illusion of space.

Chapter IX. In order to create illusionistic art, it is not enough to forget what one knows about nature. One must work out "patches" that can be mistaken for an object in the distance. Illusionism must take into account the perceptual modifications caused by the mutual influence of shapes and by colors. Illusionistic art grew out of a long tradition. Changes come about when inherited schemata are tested against the actual appearance of nature.

Chapter X. When the proper mental set exists, details can be dispensed with. Caricatures are accepted because their simplicity excludes contradictory clues. They do not derive primarily from the observation of nature but from arbitrary scribbles and the reshuffling of elementary features. In general, artists present equivalences rather than likenesses.

Chapter XI. The expression of shapes and colors is not absolute. It can only be understood when the range of alternatives is known. Expression is cast into historically determined categories and modified further by the artist's background and personality.

While Gombrich offers his book as a study in the psychology of pictorial representation, he links art with illusion in his main title. His insistence on illusion is, at first, puzzling. One cannot assert that all representation aims at illusion without expanding the meaning of the term to an extent unlikely to be acceptable to the author. If, however, illusion is but one variety of pictorial effect, then one cannot treat representation in a book on illusion without severely mutilating one's subject. How precisely the two concepts are related in the author's mind is not easily discovered since his book offers many pertinent observations on how illusions might come about, but does not define the term. That it has only one meaning can hardly be maintained by anybody who studies Gombrich's numerous and varied examples.

In its authentic sense, "illusion" in art refers to instances in which an image is taken by an observer to be the physical object it represents. It causes the sort of mistake Zeuxis made when he tried to lift the painted curtain from Parrhasios' picture. Such effects, obviously rare, are of theoretical interest only as the limiting case of a particular species of pictorial effect. They are to be distinguished from what happens when an image is taken to be physically "real" in some respects although, and because, it is known to be only an image. This is what must have happened, I believe, when the trees and trains in Lumière's movies were seen to be in live motion, although the audience realized it was watching black-and-white photographs, or when Giotto's figures were seen truly weeping and gesturing, although they were smaller than life size and flat on the wall (2, p. 60). If the term illusion is still needed here to describe the fact that images were reacted to as though they presented physical reality, it is nevertheless distinctly awkward to have to speak of "partial illusions." The concept illusion derives from the dichotomy of seeing physical reality vs. seeing images of that reality, and this dichotomy is much too crude to describe even the most elementary visual effects.

The artist is rarely concerned with making things look real. He wants them to come alive. Is this a quest for illusion? What was it Donatello was struggling for when he cursed his *Zuccone* for not speaking to him (2, p. 94)? He was not asking for the magic power of Pygmalion. He wanted to shape and combine his sculptural volumes in such a way that their constellation would display "visual dynamics" appropriate to a human figure. Nowhere in the arts, except for the few episodes of extreme illusionism, can "to be alive" have meant to be like living beings —the difference between nature and simulacrum must have always been obvious. Works of art not only *are* equivalences—to use Gombrich's term—they also must have always been seen as such. "To be alive" meant to display the *perceptual* quality of liveliness. Since this quality can be found in both animate and inanimate objects, in physical objects as well as in their images, the artistic distinction between lifeless and alive is strictly perceptual, not ontological. For this reason, an investigation based on the ontological concept of "illusion" cannot but miss the fundamental problem of pictorial representation. In terms of the dichotomy of image vs. physical reality, the aliveness of the image must appear as a paradox to be attributed to "the peaceful coexistence in man of incompatible attitudes" (2, p. 113).

Gombrich implies that illusion is created by mimetic art and that mimesis started and ended somewhere in history. He is well aware of the arguments that make the old distinction of conceptual and perceptual art untenable (2, pp. 87, 293), but he clings to it, although with a new twist: All art is conceptual in that it relies on traditional schemata rather than on mere perception; but the Egyptian or the child uses his concepts to draw what he knows, whereas the "Greek revolution" initiates a way of using such concepts for the purpose of drawing what is seen. Gombrich continues to refer to "the conceptual style of Egypt" (2, p. 126), which enumerates rather than describes and "is concerned with the what, not the how" (2, p. 134). In an admirable paragraph, he points out that the chessboard and chessmen are particularized in their appearance only to the extent to which the game requires discrimination (2, p. 119). But, instead of demonstrating that this sort of functionalism is characteristic of all art, he reserves it for the "conceptual" procedure of the Egyptians, as distinguished from what happens in Greek art, which produces "the possibility of a real trompe l'oeil" (2, p. 127). A difference in principle is also said to exist between the medieval artist, for whom "the schema is the image" and the postmedieval artist, for whom the schema "is the starting point for corrections, adjustments, adaptations, the means to probe reality and to wrestle with the particular" (2, p. 173). But, is it fair to medieval art to confront a Leonardo sketch of a rearing horse with Villard de Honnecourt's pedagogical paradigms?

A similar artificial distinction is maintained for the other end of the historical development. Cubism is "the last desperate revolt against illusion" (2, p. 281), which had been brought to a climax by the Impressionists. Here again a difference in principle between mimetic and nonmimetic art is implied. Gombrich pokes fun at my suggestion that since again and again in the course of the past centuries, and particularly in the nineteenth, paintings that had been rejected as mere splashes of paint have come to be accepted as lifelike, the process of adaptation might continue to make works of Picasso, Braque, or Klee "look exactly like the things they represent" (2, p. 27; 1, p. 93). If Gombrich does not share this assumption, where exactly does illusion end? With Cézanne? With Léger? With *Guernica*? We are not told, and obviously we cannot be told. When I wrote the sentence in question, it did not occur to me that the admittedly incautious formulation could be misunderstood to mean that I was referring to illusion. What I meant was that in Van Gogh, Renoir, Cézanne, we no longer see patches of paint but sunflowers, nudes, mountains. It is a perceptual phenomenon, best described by saying that the form is consumed by the object. This prerequisite for art of any style is met when shapes and colors fit into a unitary pattern, which makes the beholder see a constellation of perceptual forces; that is, when the work "comes alive." One way of recognizing this experience is by thinking of the difference between a good and a not-so-good Kandinsky. An unsuccessful work is an agglomeration of shapes and colors. In one we call successful, we see thrusting, twisting, expanding visual agents interact in a concerted play of forces. Similarly, in a Cézanne, the pigments disappear in the appearance of the colorful object; whereas a mediocre painting may look *bunt* (an untranslatable German word describing a potpourri of unintegrated colors). Whether or not a work "comes alive" in this way does not depend on the degree of its naturalism. It fails to do so when its visual organization lacks unity or does not fit its subject, or when the perceiver is attuned to a different style of form. "Aliveness" rather than "illusion" must be acknowledged as the goal of pictorial representation if one wishes to avoid artificial distinctions and to do justice to the continuity of the aesthetic experience across styles. Gombrich explicitly states that he is not pleading "for the exercise of illusionist tricks in painting today" (2, p. 7); but the fact remains that the ill-defined objective of "illusion" is the only one he supplies.

One finds this further confirmed when one discovers that, in Gombrich's view, the nonmimetic image is accepted by the beholder only because and when he shares with the artist certain conventions as to what an image should look like. These conventions make the beholder fill in what is missing in the non-naturalistic painting or statue! Thus, illusion becomes possible even here because, by a trick of the mind, the work is made to look like the real thing. In other words, the nonmimetic image is no exception to the rule that representation requires illusion; but the beholder's knowledge of what he is supposed to supply and his imagination are needed to remedy its incompleteness. Imagination is the capacity to "project what is not there" (2, p. 208). Thus, the empty spaces, "waiting to be filled in by our imagination" (2, p. 208), in Hellenistic or Chinese paintings are attractive because they turn purely passive reception into a do-it-yourself job, enabling the beholder to do part of the work. This notion of imagination, a crude leftover from the illusionistic aesthetics of the past, surely precludes any appreciation of the representational and expressive values of visual form. Did Rembrandt refrain from rendering "every stitch," as Van Eyck had done, and instead paint a gold braid with one stroke of the brush because completeness was no longer needed, convention having become able to replace detail (2, p. 332)? Or was it not rather that the omission was demanded by a new content to be expressed?

Gombrich is not mainly interested in the end product of pictorial representation but rather in the ways it is accomplished. In his opinion, representation becomes acceptable when it fits the schemata of realization to which the perceiver is accustomed. The artist paints what the reservoirs of his memory offer him as the proper form for his subject. These reservoirs contain the schemata supplied by the artist's teachers and by other models of the past. Beyond that, they equip him with the expectations necessary to see anything at all: We see what we assume is "out there." Here Gombrich avails himself of the traditional doctrine of empiricist psychology, which commands a large following even today, especially among American psychologists. Since neither the shapes, sizes, colors, and brightness values, nor the space we see, correspond to the data supplied by the retinal image, a theory is needed to account for the discrepancy. The traditional answer is that man and animal see the world the way they know it to be. Recently, this claim has been accompanied dramatically with the exhibition of a set of clever optical illusions, thought up and constructed by Adelbert Ames, Jr. They are referred to by Gombrich (2, p. 248) and have aroused much attention beyond the pale of psychology. It is therefore necessary to repeat here that these demonstrations do not prove the theories that come with them. The past experiences to whose effect the demonstrations are credited are hypothetical; they are neither created nor controlled in the experimental situation.

The results also conform equally well to the predictions of Gestalt psychology, which relates the perceptual organization and corresponding physiological brain processes reflected in these experiences to the general tendency toward states of minimum tension in the physical world. The student of art is entitled to know that a stringent decision on the validity of the two theories has been all but impossible for two reasons: (a) normal perception without previous experience occurs only in newborn creatures, whose experiences are hard to explore (when the inception of vision is delayed, as in animals reared in darkness or in blind persons acquiring sight in adult life, normal functioning is impeded); (b) since there is nothing new under the sun, no experimental situation can be devised of which the empiricist could not claim—although he could not prove his contention—that the results were caused by past experience. However, what counts for the student of art is that, to the best of this reviewer's knowledge, the empiricist approach to perception has been all but sterile, whereas Gestalt psychologists have supplied us with an enormous amount of experimental information on the particular conditions of form and color that produce visual patterns in nature and in art. Gombrich is aware of this material (2, p. 262); but his attempt to disprove the principle of simplicity (2, p. 264) shows that he has not made himself familiar with it. (Gestalt psychology predicts that contradictory structural features lead to ambiguous percepts.) In accordance with his own views of human behavior, Gombrich has taken from psychology what he was ready to find in it.

He neglects the body of concrete Gestalt research, which is indispensable for any psychology of pictorial representation, because it illustrates the vital contribution to visual perception made by the "stimulus object." He concentrates on the particular situations in which the steering power of the object is weakened by ambiguous and chaotic structure, that is, on the inkblots, the scribbles, the reversible figures, the optical tricks. Therefore, historians might consider his theoretical enterprise as a parallel to the practice of the Surrealists and their diabolic delight in showing that the world of our experience is unreliable (see especially, 2, p. 395). Gombrich's approach leads to a preference for marginal material, since, in most styles of art, ambiguity is excluded or of minor importance. When he refers to the ambiguity of the pictorial image, he has in mind that, theoretically, any image stands for an infinity of projections and also permits an infinity of groupings. But he fails to stress the fact that, perceptually, the choice of interpretation is severely limited by the structure of the work of art.

In its broadest formulation, Gombrich's basic thesis cannot be said to be controversial: Neither perception nor representation are mere passive recordings of the outer world as it impinges upon the mind. His impressive documentation certainly gives the coup de grâce to the opposite view in aesthetics. As far as perception is concerned, our best guess is nowadays that stimulus material, although not organized within itself, tends to fit certain patterns of organization better than others, and thereby strongly controls perception. On the other hand, the shapes to which such material is fitted are determined by the tendency to simple structure in the nervous system. This immediate perceptual response to the given situation is overlaid by the influence of memory patterns created by past experiences. Nobody denies the importance of these learned responses. It is not surprising, for example, that a Japanese, accustomed to isometric perspective, which obtains three-dimensionality through the strong and elementary perceptual effect of slanted parallels, sees the

more complex pattern of central perspective as distorted (2, p. 267).
But such examples do not prove that the capacity of perspective to create space is due to convention in the first place.

Gombrich's contention that all art is conceptual reflects his view,
which *is* highly controversial, that images are made before the world of
sensory experience has had its effect on the image maker. In reading his
book one encounters again and again the curious notion that "always
. . . making will come before matching, creation before reference"
(2, p. 99). The image maker gropes in the dark like a monad and somehow wrests correspondences with nature from his medium. This belief
appears clearly in Gombrich's treatment of caricature. He cites without
protest Rodolphe Toepffer's view, according to which caricature is based
on the fact that "physiognomics . . . could be learned by a recluse who
never sets eyes on any human being" (2, p. 339). By varying a scrawl
systematically, and by simply reshuffling primitive traits, the variety of
possible faces is obtained (2, p. 340). The implication that creativity
originates in a state of blindness explains why Gombrich, when faced
with the crucial question of how the first image could ever have been
made if nature can only be seen in terms of already existing pictures,
offers the startling answer: "But after all, we have seen that the first picture was not intended as a likeness. There are few civilizations that even
made the change from making to matching . . ." (2, p. 314).

Gombrich would assume that the recognition of the human face is
based on "some kind of inborn disposition" (2, p. 103) rather than admit that the impingement of the outer world upon the mind induces the
making of images. The observation that simple geometric shapes do indeed underlie the structure of organic bodies is dismissed as some sort
of Platonic superstition (2, p. 162). One is reminded of Schiller's reaction, which, at the first encounter of the two poets, made Goethe so
desperate that it delayed the beginning of the famous friendship: "Das
ist keine Erfahrung, das ist eine Idee!" (This is not an experience, it is
an idea!)

The impression emerges that the world of our senses is an all but
undecipherable puzzle, which can be solved only by long and special
training. "The history of art may be described as the forging of master
keys for opening the mysterious locks of our senses to which only nature
herself originally held the key. They are complex locks which respond
only when various screws are first set in readiness" (2, p. 358). All such
a statement reflects is the pathological disturbance in the relationship
between man and perceptual reality that has recently beclouded West-

ern civilization. Although Gombrich is no friend of modern art, he strikingly shares its basic attitude.

Why, in a discussion of expression, focus upon the undeniably valuable observation that expression is understood correctly only when the range of possible choices is known (2, p. 368)? One can talk sensibly about this limiting condition only after one has duly acknowledged and explained the surely remarkable phenomenon that shapes and colors carry expression in the first place. And when evidence is found that a pictorial device may not work, although the beholder knows perfectly well what the painter is trying to show (2, p. 212), why not conclude that knowledge will not help when the perceptual conditions are unsuitable and that, therefore, the analysis of perceptual conditions is imperative for the study of representation?

Gombrich asserts repeatedly that the purpose of his book is to answer the question why art has a history (2, pp. 291, 388). This is indeed a test question, since his emphasis on the influence of tradition would make us expect art to subsist in a state of inert uniformity. Apparently, for Gombrich, the question is identical with the much more limited one: Why did it take "mankind so long to arrive at a plausible rendering of visual effects that create the illusion of lifelikeness" (2, p. 291)? But, even this more limited query raises the basic problem. If I understand the author correctly, he believes that historical changes occur when the artist checks the traditional schemata against nature (2, pp. 173, 322), thereby breaking out of "the prison of style toward a greater truth" (2, p. 320). The inherited formulae supply a target for correction and modification. But surely a theorist cannot invoke appeals to the standards of nature if he asserts at the same time that the view of nature itself is always the product of traditional schemata! Similarly, one cannot assert that perception is "primarily the modification of an anticipation" (2, p. 172) without telling on what data the modification is based. One cannot "code" (2, p. 181) what one has not got. If "there is no reality without interpretation" (2, p. 363), the theory would seem to be caught in its own trap. Only by admitting that the experience of nature has a great deal of autonomy after all, can one get out of the dilemma.

Even if this admission were made, however, the answer would seem much too narrow. Is the history of art nothing better than the story of how a faulty likeness of nature was gradually improved? Do not changes in the artistic conception of nature derive from changed attitudes toward life and world? And is not the history of art the history of these changing conceptions? Gombrich states explicitly that the history of art consists in telling us from whom artists got their vocabulary (2, p. 317). But surely, to object to this view and to insist that the history of borrow-. ings must be considered subsidiary to that of creative discoveries is more than a Romantic idiosyncrasy (2, p. 381). When both Manet and a minor Victorian painter use the same Impressionistic device for representing crowds (2, p. 216), is there no answer to the question of what is more important, the common inheritance or the difference between a great innovator and an undistinguished craftsman? Furthermore, if conventional devices make a picture readable, they are also known to deaden it. And the psychology of representation is presumably the story of how things "come alive."

Here it is well to remember also that, according to psychological findings, tradition or "habit" in itself is never an explanation of behavior. We must indicate the continued needs that make a practice survive. In the human realm, inertia is not an admissible motive. Thus, even the history of traditional schemata is a part of the history of attitudes.

At this point I realize why Gombrich's book, with all its wisdom and charm, its abundance of striking source material and impressive erudition, leaves me nevertheless with the sort of letdown one experiences after having been shown around the backstage areas of an opera house. His is a book of exposure rather than of revelation. Nowhere does it deal with the core of artistic representation, namely, with what takes place when an artist, or period of art, possessed by a vital conception of human existence, rallies all available tools and resources to invent a profoundly significant visual form. To look at some of the inherited tools is certainly useful, but only as long as we realize that this is what we are doing.

In offering the foregoing critique, I am fully aware that progress in any field of knowledge tends to come from one-sided theses. Gombrich has made the strongest possible case for his position. He has also revealed with admirable clarity its weaknesses, at which the counterthrust must aim. In his Preface, Gombrich assures his readers that he will not play safe. He has kept his promise.

REFERENCES

1. Arnheim, R. *Art and Visual Perception*. Berkeley and Los Angeles: Univ. of Calif. Press, 1963.
2. Gombrich, E. H. *Art and Illusion*. New York: Pantheon, 1960.

ACCIDENT AND THE NECESSITY OF ART

The immediate impulse for this inquiry came from the practices of certain modern artists, writers, and composers who deliberately rely on accident for the production of their work. One of our more experimental composers is said to be fond of drawing a large staff of five lines on a piece of paper, putting it on the floor, dropping a handful of pennies on it at random, and then using this accidental assortment of notes as a musical composition. The Surrealists took over a parlor game in which a group of people write a poem or draw a figure collectively without seeing each other's contributions (*cadavres exquis*). They also cultivated automatic writing—the technique of jotting down as fast as possible and without reflection or choice any phrases that come to mind. These are extreme examples of a rather widespread tendency, which includes the scrap-heap as a supplier of inspiration for sculptors, the adoption of nature's shapes and textures in collages and assemblages, the exploitation of the chance effects of running paint, molten metal, etc.

Lawfulness in science and art. Offhand, the use of accident would seem to be the very opposite of what the artist is expected to do, since

First published in the *Journal of Aesthetics and Art Criticism*, 1957, 16, 18–31.

one of the functions of art is that of discovering order, law, and necessity in the seemingly irrational world of our experience. Art is a basic instrument in man's struggle for survival, which requires him to understand something of the nature of things by observing them, and to predict their behavior by what he has understood of their nature. Schiller, in the preface to *Die Verschwörung des Fiesco zu Genua,* points out that in reality the hero of his play perished by accident, but that this course of events had to be changed because the nature of the drama does not tolerate casual motivation or the limitation of fate to a narrow range of events (den Finger des Ohngefährs oder der unmittelbaren Vorsehung). "Higher beings are capable of seeing the tenuous cobweb threads of a deed run through the entire expanse of the universe and perhaps attach themselves to the remotest boundaries of the future and the past— where the human eye sees nothing but the mere fact suspended in free air. The artist, however, makes his selection for the narrow view of humanity, which he wants to instruct, not for keensighted omnipotence, by which he is instructed."

In order to go beyond the puzzling surface of the apparently accidental, man has developed two techniques, which in their perfected and professionalized form are science and art. By science, I mean the interpretation of events through conceptual generalizations. Art serves a similar purpose by making images, through which the nature and functioning of things can be experienced. In its early stages, scientific thinking imposes a simple order by a few sweeping generalities, such as that all heavenly bodies move in circles or that the sexual instinct is the root of all human motivation. Under the impact of reality, science gradually refines its descriptions to take care of complexities and variations—so that at times the intricate tissue threatens to hide the underlying structure. And since enlightenment through order remains its aim, science must constantly try to organize the increasingly unwieldy material under simple over-all forms.

Art goes about its job in a rather similar way. It also starts with simple generalities. We find them in the elementary symmetries of children's drawings or the sculpture of early civilizations; we find them in the black-and-white characters of fairy tales and legends. Under the impact of reality, art, too, develops toward more and more complex patterns in order to take care of the variety of appearances and the peculiarities of the individual mind. In Western art, growing complexity takes the form of increasing realism. The simple, schematic figures found in the archaic styles and later in Byzantine art give way to the highly individualized likenesses of human beings shown in a wide variety of attitudes and settings.

Accident as subject matter. Now, realism enhances the element of chance in the relationship between the work of art and its ultimate purpose. For, when we proceed from a Byzantine saint to a Rembrandt portrait, we move farther away from the prototypical image of man, which is the final aim of the representation of man in art. Rembrandt envisages man in the likeness of a particular individual that happened to capture his attention. The gesture and posture of Michelangelo's "David" are more specific than those of a Romanesque knight, and the costumes, perspectives, lights, and groupings of Renaissance art are rich in accidental features. Accident always refers to relations, and, when we call a relationship accidental, we express our belief that it did not come about through a direct cause-and-effect connection between the parties concerned. The stylized Byzantine features are more closely controlled by the primary concept of man than is the Rembrandt figure, which shows the intrusion of extraneous individual encounters. The difference may be expressed also in the language of the statistician by saying that with increasing realism, the solution offered by the artist becomes a less probable one.

We must add hastily that while in science the more schematic image may be considered nearer the truth, art is not satisfied with the bare quintessence extracted from the variety of appearances. To a larger or smaller extent, it always uses the chance inventory of the artist's world and the chance perspective of his personal outlook in order to present the prototypical essence under ever new aspects. And while from the point of view of the ultimate prototype, the particular individualization produced at a particular time is an accidental rendering, there is nothing accidental about it as far as the maker of the image is concerned. As art proceeds toward increasing individualization, each new step may seem to add arbitrary or accidental particulars to what was determined by necessity at the earlier level. But, once the new approach is understood, its specification of the image will turn out to be required by the new, more individualized conception of the theme. For instance, by the standards of medieval art, an individual portrait face would be considered inappropriately particularized for the purpose of representing sanctity, royalty, or the sufferings of the passion. It took a new interest in the specific manifestations of human nature before such features could be considered acceptable, pertinent, and indeed necessary.

Fra Angelico's "Annunciation" in San Marco (Figure 13) might have looked disorderly, like our snapshots, to an observer accustomed to the formally arranged religious paintings of, say, the thirteenth century. The architectural setting is losing its symmetrical relationship to the figures and is perceived from an oblique angle. The two figures would seem to our observer to have been caught or placed somewhere at random, and the vanishing point toward which the perspective converges would appear similarly accidental. Actually, Fra Angelico's composition springs from a new, more complex order, which determines the position

FIGURE 13. After Fra Angelico's "Annunciation," San Marco, Florence

of each object with necessity. The balanced serenity of the Virgin is conveyed by her central position in relation to the right-hand frontal arch, and is contrasted with the forward push of the eccentrically placed messenger. But the larger frontal arch overlaps smaller ones, and, with regard to this subordinate framework, the Virgin, too, is placed eccentrically—an expression of her timid withdrawal, that counterbalances the advance of the angel and is properly made secondary to her more "official" attitude of poise. We also notice that the seemingly accidental angles of the perspective produce a wedge of oblique shapes, which underscore the forceful intrusion. Here, then, the concern of a new age with the human aspects of arrival, announcement, bewilderment, and modesty modulates the traditional static symmetry of the religious scene. The deviation from the prototype turns out to be not accidental but an essential pictorial device for interpreting the interaction of two sets of forces: the dogmatic and the psychological.

The phenomenon repeats itself at more advanced levels, for instance, when Tintoretto's "Last Supper" in San Giorgio Maggiore looks like a rush-hour turmoil to an observer brought up on Leonardo. It is only after we have understood that the oblique position of the main scene, the violent variations of figure sizes and postures, the crowding, the overlapping, and the splashes of light create a new, intensified version of the old drama, that the apparently accidental use of the accidental is revealed as a necessity.

In the course of the centuries, the ever bolder presentation of accident serves various purposes. A humorous application of the kind of pattern that creates emotional frenzy in Tintoretto produces the merry confusion of the Dutch tavern scenes in the work of Jan Steen or Ostade, and a similar teeming disorder depicts the casual abundance of material wealth in the still-life arrangements of choice food stuffs and other luxuries. Later, accident is used by the Romantic artists to defy the rigid order of rationalism; and the same device points up the imperfection of everyday life in the harsh statements of social critics and naturalists, from Hogarth to George Grosz.

As illustrated by these examples, increasing individualization not only makes the relationship of the image to the ultimate prototype more and more unpredictable, but also weakens the bond of necessity among the elements of the represented scene. A seventeenth century portrait of a married couple is a highly particularized rendering of the subject of man and woman, and, as such, it also depicts a highly "improbable" combination of two citizens, one among millions of equally possible ones. While in the example of the double portrait, the combination depicts the necessity of a particular union, the grouping of highly individual elements can also serve to represent the instability and fleetingness of relations. It can depict constant change and also isolation and disorder. Some painters of the nineteenth century insist on gathering, within the frame of the picture, figures that seem to have little or nothing to do with each other. The milling crowd in any of the great Baroque scenes was at least united by a common center of action so that even though a great deal of turnover was suggested in the secondary episodes, the over-all constellation appeared stable. In Degas' "Cotton Market in New Orleans" (Figure 14) there is no such focus. The participants are all in the same business, but they hardly trade with each other. As though they were unaware of each other's presence, they read their papers, test their samples, and work on their ledgers. In other pictures of the period, people walk past each other in the street, dancers hurry crisscross without any evidence of choreography, holiday-makers are spread irregularly over a lawn and look at the river instead of each other. Viewed with the eyes of the pictorial tradition, these figures may appear scattered over the canvas at random, but again it is only by the standards of an older order that the relations presented in the composition seem to be devoid of necessity. The composition ceases to appear

FIGURE 14. After Edgar Degas' "Cotton Market in New Orleans," Musée de Pau

accidental and instead becomes compelling and unchangeable as soon as we recognize that the lack of a common purpose, the atomization of society in an age of individualism, is precisely the theme of these pictures. They suggest a communal pattern in which all joints are loose. No over-all constellation holds the crowd together, and hence there is no limit to the changes that may occur in the relationships between the participants.

Accident interpreted by necessity. Our sketchy survey reveals in Western painting an increasing use of accident, that is, of showing objects in relations that have not come about by direct cause-and-effect connections between them, and of presenting subject matter less and less directly related to the fundamental prototypes that art is expected to interpret. It also becomes evident, however, that, while accidental relationships crept into the subject matter, the artistic representation of their effects was not based at all on chance selection or grouping. These works depict particularized necessity with the utmost compositional precision, and, when they wish to present the accidental character of relations, they do so not by elements thrown together at random but by a calculated pictorial interpretation of accident. In Fra Angelico's "Annunciation," among all the possible relationships by which accident could connect the figures with the architecture, the painter has chosen those that precisely express the attitudes of the angel and the Virgin. Similarly, among the innumerable groupings in which accident could combine the figures of the cotton market, Degas presents one that shows with great visual precision that these people are not concerned with each other. For instance, he collects all the heads of the background figures in one horizontal row, and another, oblique line leads from the man with the top hat in the foreground via the newspaper reader to the head of the bookkeeper. Degas thus makes us see his men in relation and discover the paradoxical isolation of people whom life has thrown together.

Degas and some other painters of his generation used the theme of accidental encounter as a subject matter to portray indifference, isolation, unawareness. The Cubists carry the principle further and make it express the conflict of everything with everything. In the best works of this school, great skill is applied to defining with visual precision the oblique relationships among the single cubic units. These units constantly interfere with each other, breaking into each other's contours. They tend to destroy the remnants of over-all compositional groupings and instead evenly fill the entire surface within the picture frame. This is a logical development because when structure is reduced to a one-to-one interaction between individual elements, no larger shape can build up. The pattern can extend forever. In its pure and extreme form, this style represents a level of order that, although intricate, is quite low— because it lacks hierarchy and diversity. But a definite form of order it still is: it is classically described in Plato's *Timaeus* as *ananke*, which is put in opposition to the lawful cosmos (4, pp. 159 ff.). In the realm of *ananke*, necessity is reduced to the causal action of any one object upon any other, and all of these actions add up to nothing more organized than an over-all balance. To use a modern and practical example: a completely free economy would function according to this structural pattern.

Accident as a compositional principle. The most recent and radical phase of the trend we are examining is the use of accident not merely as subject matter but as the formal principle of the pictorial composition itself. There is, of course, a difference between portraying chance artistically and producing a chance assortment of shapes. All the examples discussed here so far showed that in painting certain effects of accident were interpreted compellingly through such means as the controlled deviation from symmetry or from the basic framework of the horizontal and vertical, also through the irregular distribution of objects in space, through overlappings that cut across the structure of things at oblique angles, etc. Now, the accidental throwing together of elements does not always produce disorder, deviation, lack of connection, or interference. It will not depict obliqueness of relation only but rather any kind of relation: some will have order or even symmetry, others will be quite irrational; some will be harmonious, others discordant. But, since they are all thrown together by chance, none of them can make its particular point.

This can be demonstrated by the increasing number of dismal examples that have accumulated in the Western art of the past centuries when the compositional patterns of realism became so complex that the average painter's and sculptor's eyes could no longer organize them. Here accidental patterns were produced not by intent but by the degeneration of the sense of form. The desire for the faithful imitation of nature finally conquered man's natural and traditional need of visual order and meaning to such an extent that the occasional great master was increasingly hard put to impose organization and significance upon the multiplicity of appearances. In looking, for example, through the American *trompe l'oeil* still lifes, one finds that in the work of a relatively better painter, such as William M. Harnett, the assorted household goods are organized in such a way that the place and function of each object are defined by an over-all pattern. This pattern makes it possible for pictorial devices such as the irregular distribution of objects or the overlapping at oblique angles to attain visual necessity and thereby to interpret the charms of chance. In the lesser members of the same school, the passion for mechanical reproduction and a very modern fascination with disorder produce random displays, which the beholder's eye can identify but not understand. The phenomenal chaos of accident, from which man seeks refuge in art, has invaded art itself.

Photography should be mentioned here since, by mechanically reproducing the visual surface pattern of the physical world, it introduces accident into every one of its products. The artifices of selection and transformation draw an approximate order from this raw material, but a photograph is never more than partially comprehensible to the human eye. In fact, the uniqueness and cultural worth of photography—just as, incidentally, the charm of mobiles—lies precisely in the encounter of natural accident and the human sense of form. As a medium of art, however, photography will always suffer from the inherent compromise.

What objection is there aesthetically to random patterns? Not that they are not interesting, suggestive, stimulating. They are—as anybody can testify who has looked at a pebbled beach, the New York City skyline, or certain modern painting and sculpture. There is also great recreation in an occasional escape from sense. It cannot be said either that such patterns are unbalanced. Even the most outlandish conglomeration of elements can be made to balance perfectly about one central point. But stimulation, pleasure, and balance are not enough. A work of art must do more than be itself: it must fulfill a semantic function, and no statement can be understood unless the relations between its elements form an organized whole.

The "statistical" use of accidental patterns. There is one means by which accidental agglomerations can acquire organization and meaning, namely, quantity. The larger a random collection of elements is, the more the individual characteristics of the elements and their interrelations will recede while their common properties will come to the fore. The more diverse the material, the larger the quantity of elements, needed to produce some order, will have to be, and the more generic will be the qualities they share. If the pattern is given a semantic function, these common properties will represent the statement the pattern makes. Such statistical induction works not only by intellectual extraction but also by simple perceptual inspection. If we observe two persons who happen to sit next to each other, say, on the long bench of a waiting room, meaning may emerge accidentally from their combination (for instance, "young and old"). As the row of people on the bench gets longer, the individual connections we have made between the first two, and those between any other members of the group begin to neutralize each other, and instead certain common properties, perhaps that of "metropolitan man" or "resignation," or what have you, present themselves.

What is noteworthy about this inductive procedure is that it neglects all relationships between the items concerned except their resemblances. This is why it alone can extract order from chance patterns, but this is also why its yield is so poor. When examined piecemeal, the random collection seems to possess the wealth of universality since it contains an enormous variety of being, behaving, and relating. But the riches turn out to be useless when we attempt to draw the essence from the whole.

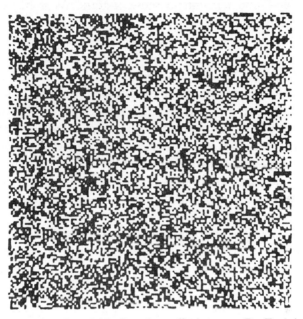

FIGURE 15. A random field of 19,600 cells (courtesy Dr. Fred Attneave, San Antonio, Texas)

This letdown is nicely illustrated by a recent experiment of Dr. Fred Attneave, a psychologist, who is interested in the theory of visual information (2). He divided a square-shaped surface into 19,600 little squares, each of which he had either left white or painted black in the order suggested by a table of random numbers (Figure 15). Since only chance predicted the color of any one square, a maximum of piecemeal information was furnished by every unit of the pattern. Yet, looking at the total result, the psychologist was impressed with its monotony, which struck him as remarkable because he had previously associated homogeneity with redundancy, and the random field had been constructed to be completely nonredundant. Which goes to show that piles of accidents add up to very little.

Attneave observes that the sequence of point-by-point communications, when viewed as a whole, changes into "texture." We may define texture as the result of what happens when the level of perceptual comprehension shifts from the scrutiny of individual structural relationships within their total context to that of over-all structural constants.

The random field of Figure 15 bears a striking resemblance to a well-known type of modern painting. (If reference is made here to certain works by the late Jackson Pollock [Figure 16] or Mark Tobey, it should be understood that this paper is not concerned with individual artists but rather with a general principle, which may be embodied more or less perfectly in a given painting.) Such a picture can be perceived only as texture—not because the number or size of the units of which it is made up go beyond the range of the human eye's capacity but because the units do not fit into more comprehensive shapes. The number of elements is large enough so that their variations as to color, shape, size, direction, relative position, etc. compensate each other, and a common denominator of textural qualities such as prickliness, softness, excitation, viscosity, mechanical hardness, or organic flexibility emerges from an inspection of the whole. All movements, also, are compensated so that nothing "happens," except for a kind of molecular milling everywhere.

A similar effect can be observed, by the way, in modern music. The Italian music critic, Fedele D'Amico, remarks that in Dallapiccola's *Canti de liberazione*

. . . all the lively flashes remain a private experience of the composer. At best, the devotees of Dallapiccola (those, like myself, for whom a page of his represents under any condition a fascinating invitation to scrutiny) can partly reconstruct them, the way one reconstructs a document; but in the performance they are covered by an opaque shroud, they do not come through. The energies that make up the single elements of the piece exist, but they are visible only under the microscope. In practice, they neutralize each other to the point of forming an immobile, homogeneous, and dull substance. The law of entropy is fulfilled, in front of our eyes, billions of years in advance (5, p. 141).

What was said before about the compositional principle in Cubist painting holds true even more strongly for the texture painters. The pattern in itself is endless so that its limits are dictated only by the rule of parsimony, which prescribes in this case that the number of units employed should not be larger than that needed to attain the effect of global uniformity. Furthermore, the level of the structure is low because

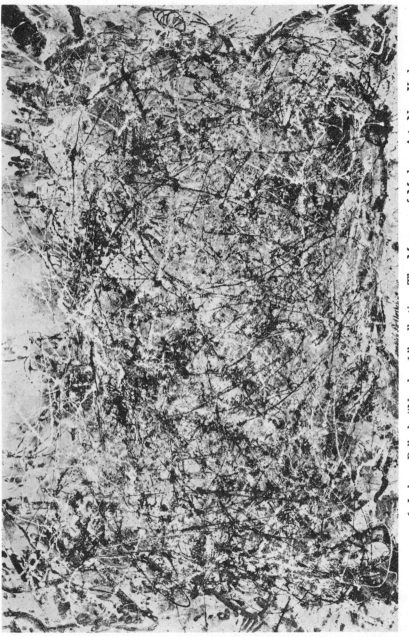

FIGURE 16. Jackson Pollock, "Number I," collection, The Museum of Modern Art, New York

it lacks diversity and hierarchy. As far as diversity goes, such pictures typically look more like Figure 15, which derives its variations from nothing but a standard-size square in one of two colors, than they do like the junk-shop type of still life—their spiritual ancestor—whose texture is made up of many different objects. Lack of diversity, that is, the fact that the same kind of thing happens all through the picture, seriously limits the importance of the content that can be conveyed. An artistic statement, be it representational or "abstract," hardly begins to be interesting until it deals with segregated, different entities, whose interrelations are worked through. All such distinctions are here submerged in the texture pattern.

Another minimum demand on a work of art is hierarchy. In order to hold our attention, the dominant masses, which determine the basic "plot" of the work at the top level of structure, are made up of secondary units, whose interrelations represent an enriching refinement of, or counterpoint to, the top structure. Additional, lower structural levels often develop the main theme down to the capillaries (1, p. 51). The complexity of human existence demands some such corresponding complexity from even the simplest work of art if we are to recognize ourselves in it. The statements produced even by the most artful filigree texture, however, are as disconcertingly elementary as a train whistle or a flash of light.[1] In no way can such texture work be compared with the over-all uniformity of pattern found in the mature style of the masters, as for instance, in Cézanne's late watercolors. For, in the masterwork, the multiform manifestations of life are brought into an over-all unity that still preserves all the richness, whereas texture pattern by itself reduces the content to the poor extract of perceptual induction.

The spontaneous stroke. An extreme of accident, that is, minimum lawfulness of relation, is embodied in the texture patterns. To produce them by human rather than by mechanical means is quite difficult because in all organic behavior—be it perceptual, motor, or intellectual, conscious or unconscious—there is a measure of spontaneous order. On the other hand, an admixture of accident is also one of the trademarks

---

[1] In biology, the higher organisms are distinguished from the lower by an increasing differentiation of functions. In still another field, namely, architecture, Kevin Lynch (11) has described a similar morphological distinction between primitive and advanced human settlements. In his examples, the aerial photograph that most resembles the pictorial texture patterns here discussed is that of the city village of Kano in Nigeria.

of human behavior, owing to the multiplicity of impulses that complicates all organic functioning. We have learned to value the charm of such imperfection since we met the immaculate products of machines.

This modern taste for the human "touch" derives historically from the new appreciation of creative man that developed during the Renaissance. As long as the artist's task was defined as the making of objects that met specifications of correctness, faithfulness, and proportion, the marks of the maker were carefully wiped off.[2] The change took place slowly, however. In a recent monograph on "the handwriting of painters," Vojtěch Volavka (13) notes that even Leonardo objects to "penellate terminate e tratteggionati aspri e crudi," and that Vasari takes a dim view of Titian's late paintings, "condotte di colpi, tirate via grosso, e con macchie . . ." Vasari admits that while these paintings cannot be looked at from close by, they appear perfect from a distance, and that the effect is beautiful and stupendous "perchè fa parere vive le pitture," but he concludes that it would have been better for Titian's reputation if in his last years he had used painting only as a pastime. The artistic virtues and vices of the "divided" stroke, as Volavka calls it, play a part in the controversy of the classicist school of Poussin against the colorists around Rubens; and to Diderot, the paintings of Chardin were crude and only tolerable when viewed from a distance. Apparently, there is no true appreciation of the "touch" before the late eighteenth century. For a long time, the bold innovation must have been taken as an arbitrary intrusion of the maker into the world of the making.

In the meantime, however, an admiration developed for the virtuoso, who with a few rapid but controlled strokes outpaints the slow average craftsman. By the conspicuous traces of the *bravura*, masters such as Titian, Velasquez, or Rubens authenticated the products of their workshops. What was boasted and admired here was not so much a pictorial quality of the work as the facility of the making. It was the capacity, acquired through decades of practice, to attain a perfectly controlled objective by a motor process that in itself was not controlled but spontaneous, and whose traces on the canvas showed the freshness, elegance, and ease of the freedom from conscious guidance. The artist must have experienced a partial surrender to an organic power—often interpreted as divine inspiration—quite different from the capacity to

[2] The effects of Hellenistic impressionism on medieval painting can be neglected in this discussion.

calculate, plan, and carefully accompany the stroke: he may have felt awe, pride, and the relief of confidently delegating responsibility to an ingenious agent.

Accident as a creative device. The free brush stroke of the Baroque, then, was a first step toward the surrender of artistic initiative. It was not before the time of the Romantic movement, however, that the contribution of spontaneous forces was explicitly acknowledged and sanctioned. Herbert Read says: "What was achieved in this first phase of Romanticism was a dissociation of the will, as the active aspect of the intellect, and the imagination. The will was seen as always inhibiting or distorting the free play of the imagination, and this 'free play' was identified with the 'real self.' The unconscious, the dream world, became a refuge from an impersonal and harsh materialistic world" (12, p. 117). We notice that by then the helpful power had been identified as the unconscious, and also that the surrender was no longer limited to a technical detail of execution but tended to apply to the very conception of the work of art.³ When, finally, in the twentieth century, the Surrealists entered the scene, the necessity behind the seemingly accidental images of dreams had been confirmed by Freud, so that we are not surprised to find André Breton say in the first of his manifestos of Surrealism: "I should like to sleep, to be able to deliver myself to the sleepers the way I deliver myself to those who read me with open eyes" (3, p. 25). And he tells of a fellow writer who when he went to bed put a sign on his door: *Le poète travaille.* Breton did not hesitate to assert that "psychical automatism" was a technique for expressing "the real functioning of thought" (3, p. 45). How valid is this claim?

Passivity and the unconscious. The psychological discussion has been made difficult by the fact that the term "unconscious" has become a catch-all for whatever activities lie beyond conscious control. In conse-

---

³ Not everybody was pleased with the new trend, however. In a letter dated July 26, 1800, Schiller wrote to Goethe: "I am enclosing a new magazine, which was sent to me and which will surprise you by showing you the influence of Schlegel's ideas on the latest art criticism. There is no telling what this bustle will come to; but neither production itself nor artistic sensibility can profit from such hollow and empty buffoonery. You will be astonished to read that true production in the arts must be entirely unconscious, and that your genius in particular is credited with the great merit of acting entirely without consciousness. You are quite mistaken, therefore, if you continue your untiring effort to work with the utmost thoughtfulness and to become aware of the process within yourself. Naturalism is the sign of mastery, and Sophocles is supposed to have worked that way."

quence, all of them tend to be indentified with the very specific kind of unconscious process that is treated in analytical depth psychology. It is assumed, for example, that any surrender of awareness at all will open automatically the resources of wisdom that, according to the Romantic version of psychoanalysis, hide in the treasure house of the unconscious. In order to point up the confusion, it may suffice roughly to distinguish (*a*) the basic motivational strivings investigated by psychoanalysis, (*b*) the creative cognitive processes that also operate below the level of consciousness and are responsible for intuitive insights and for the flash solutions of stubborn scientific or artistic problems, (*c*) the automatic practicing of skills or aimless doodling, made possible by a detachment of partial psychical functions from central control; and, finally, (*d*) such purely physical chance operations as the throwing of dice or pennies, which are not controlled by any agency of the mind at all, unless the dice are subject to telekinesis.

Since the nonconscious is a house of many mansions, there is no reason to believe that whenever conscious control lapses, the deepest layers of the mind will respond automatically. More normally, what comes to the fore in relaxation will be the fairly disorganized result of the interaction among the various layers. When the process is close to the surface—as in daydreams, doodles, or free associations—automatisms will go into action, daylight thoughts and the afterimages of recent experiences will float by, modified through erratic intrusions from deeper levels. In dreams, the proportion will be reversed; but the stream of unconsciousness is no more orderly than that of consciousness. According to Jung, "dreams that satisfy logically, ethically, and aesthetically are, of course, exceptions. As a rule, the dream is a peculiar and strange contraption, distinguished by lack of logic, dubious morals, unattractive form, and obvious contradiction or nonsense" (10, p. 11). Such mental products can be interpreted analytically, but they are nothing better than raw material artistically.

Furthermore, we must not be caught by the prejudice that the mental layers most remote from consciousness are the "deepest" ones, and that, therefore, they are the most valuable for artistic creation. (They may be "deepest" in a purely topological sense only.) Presumably, little of genuine value will arise either in the extreme depth, namely, from the crude primitivism of mainly "archetypal" vision, or at the extreme surface, that is, from the flatness of mainly perceptual or intellectual productions. Any true work of art requires the cooperation of all the essential layers of the mind—not, however, in the form of the erratic interpenetration I just described as the state of relaxation. Art is no occupation for relaxed people. The resources of the mind must be forged into organized shape by conscious and unconscious discipline, which requires the effort of concentration.

Accident is a shrewd helper, and the unconscious is a powerful one. Art has always profited from both—but only as assistants. The sudden inspirations of creative men seem to take place after insistent wrestling with the problem, and the Zen Buddhists, who preach against conscious control and wilful effort, do not recommend sleep, distraction, or parlor games: "A painter seats himself before his pupils. He examines his brush and slowly makes it ready for use, carefully rubs ink, straightens the long strip of paper that lies before him on the mat, and finally, after lapsing for a while into profound concentration, in which he sits like one inviolable, he produces with rapid, absolutely sure strokes a picture which, capable of no further correction and needing none, serves the class as a model" (9, p. 64).

Withdrawal and surrender. The texture paintings to which I referred are probably somewhere in between accidental production and the guided interpretation of accident. On the one hand, they are due to what I described as the detachment of partial psychical functions from central control. Some relatively self-contained mechanisms, such as motor behavior or perception, can operate practically on their own. When released from control, they will rely on routine reactions and automatic skills—as when one drives a car without being aware of what one is doing or when the brush of Frans Hals plays over the canvas—or they will betray their detachment from the central concerns of the mind by the monotony and lack of organization of their performance. We can thus account for the weave of strokes, which surely is not constructed but is rather the largely spontaneous product of what a pair of hands and a pair of eyes felt like doing at a given time in a given material.

However, the evenness of the pattern throughout the pictures discussed here suggests that something more than laissez-faire accounts for the result. We know from doodles that, when the hand is left alone, the monotonous rhythms of the detached process will be disrupted by impulses, reminiscences, and associations from other areas of mental functioning. In the texture patterns, we look in vain for the projections from the unconscious that attract the psychologist's attention in doodles.[4]

[4] Compare, however, the views of Anton Ehrenzweig (6; 7).

Only by careful supervision throughout the work will the artist obtain such perfect homogeneity of texture, and the control he exerts must be guided by a definite image of what he is trying to accomplish.

This image is clearly the visual display of a maximum of accident, spread with mechanical universality, and not even alleviated by the islands of sense that would intrude if the mind were left to its spontaneous impulses. We recognize the portrait of a life situation in which social, economical, political, and psychological forces have become so complex that, at superficial inspection, nothing predictable seems to remain but the meaningless routine of daily activities, the undirected milling of anonymous crowds. The well-defined mutual independence of the individual units, observed in Degas and even in the Cubists, has given way to a lack of any definable relation at all.

Fascination, fear, contempt, withdrawal, but also the strong temptation to take part—we can only guess at what the artist feels about the subject matter of such paintings. In any case, the very depicting of standardized chaos makes him share the attitude he illustrates. The machine-like monotony of production has been brought to further perfection since Seurat and the Pointillists tapped out their paintings through thousands of frighteningly uniform color dots. Such performance reflects a willingness to accept the façade of shapelessness as the intrinsic substance and nature of our world. It expresses that surrender of initiative to transcendent powers that makes people entrust themselves to gods, ghosts, instincts, archetypes, accident, or the mathematics of probability, "when there is distress of nations and perplexity." [5]

REFERENCES

1. Arnheim, Rudolf. *Art and Visual Perception*. Berkeley and Los Angeles: Univ. of Calif. Press, 1954.
2. Attneave, Fred. Some informational aspects of visual perception. *Psychological Review*, 1954, 61, 183–193.
3. Breton, André. *Les manifestes du Surréalisme*. Paris, 1946.
4. Cornford, Francis M. *Plato's Cosmology*. London: Kegan Paul, 1937.
5. D'Amico, Fedele. *I casi della musica*. Milan: Saggiatore, 1962.
6. Ehrenzweig, Anton. The modern artist and the creative accident. *The Listener*, January 12, 1956, 53–55.
7. ———. The mastering of creative anxiety. In *Art and Artist*. Berkeley and Los Angeles: Univ. of Calif. Press, 1956.
8. Eliot, T. S. *Four Quartets*. New York: Harcourt, 1943.

[5] Compare here section V of T. S. Eliot's "The Dry Salvages" (8).

9. Herrigel, Eugen. *Zen in the Art of Archery*. New York: Pantheon, 1953.

10. Jung, Carl G. *Die Welt der Psyche*. Zurich: Rascher, 1954.

11. Lynch, Kevin. The form of cities. *Scientific American*, April 1954, *190*, 54–63.

12. Read, Herbert. *Icon and Idea*. London: Faber and Faber, 1955.

13. Volavka, Vojtěch. *Die Handschrift des Malers*. Prague, 1953.

MELANCHOLY UNSHAPED

When you have to attend to things of that sort, to the mere incidents of the surface, the reality—the reality, I tell you—fades.

—JOSEPH CONRAD. *Heart of Darkness.*

When a specialized subject is treated intelligently, its particular essence is described by means of general categories. Caught, as it were, in the focus of a battery of floodlights, the illuminated theme points back, in turn, by reflection to the remote sources that make it visible. In this sense, Siegfried Kracauer's book, *Theory of Film* (4) is probably the most intelligent book ever written on the subject of the film. While the author, a veteran film critic and sociologist, exercises restraint by limiting himself to his specific task, the breadth of his thinking constantly tempts the less disciplined reader to apply the findings of the book to the other arts and to enlarge on the diagnosis the author suggests by his lucid description of the symptoms. The book centers about two main issues, one aesthetic, the other philosophical. By examining the nature of the photographic medium, it suggests what the proper domain of film is and ought to be. After this is done, it raises the question of what particular function the film can fulfill in our cultural situation. Both con-

First published in the *Journal of Aesthetics and Art Criticism*, 1963, 21, 291–297.

siderations are based on the assertion that the film, in the words of the subtitle, brings about a "redemption of physical reality."

The aesthetic discussion takes off from the fact that photography, more than any other medium of visual art, limits the artist's freedom of shaping the forms he invents. The optical image of the physical world imprints itself mechanically upon the sensitized surface, and the artist influences rather than molds a given material by means of selection, the control of the light, and the angle of approach, etc. On the strength of the assertion that a medium serves the artist best when it is used in accordance with its most characteristic properties, Kracauer believes that the cinema should make a virtue of the encounter of unshaped outer reality and human formative power; it should display rather than subdue the nature of untreated physical existence. "Works of art consume the raw material from which they are drawn, whereas films as an outgrowth of camera work are bound to exhibit it. . . . Along with photography, film is the only art which leaves its raw material more or less intact. In consequence, such art as goes into films results from their creators' capacity to read the book of nature. The film artist has traits of an imaginative reader, or an explorer prompted by insatiable curiosity" (4, p. x). Many filmgoers would be willing to agree that the cinema is at its most cinematic, and therefore most likely to succeed, when it draws expression from the spontaneous appearance and behavior of real life; but they might hesitate to share the author's radical conviction that this condition must be fulfilled if film is to be film. "In an aesthetic interest," says Kracauer, "[the photographer] must follow the realistic tendency under all circumstances" (4, p. 13). "It is evident that the cinematic approach materializes in all films which follow the realistic tendency" (4, p. 38). And, of the newsreel: "It meets the minimum requirements of the cinematic approach as a matter of course, with the realistic tendency prevailing over the tendency towards form construction" (4, p. 194).

What distinguishes the photographic image? The objects it shows, we may be tempted to say, tend to be so complex in their shape and coloring and in their relations to each other that the eye experiences them as irrational, that is, as unrelatable to defined visual forms. In fact, the visual world presents itself as a continuum, devoid of clear-cut breaks, and expanding beyond any frame. It is, furthermore, a world of individuality. It shows the particular specimen or instance in the uniqueness of its details—its difference from other things of its kind. The consequence is a display of bewildering variety.

As we look this description over, we realize that it is true, but in a one-sided way. It is true only by contrast with the highly controlled images that the visual arts commonly produce. Whether it describes the world as we typically see it is quite another matter, which will be discussed later. Undoubtedly, photography is best equipped to show the visual world in all its bewildering complexity. But can it be maintained that "of all the existing media the cinema alone holds up a mirror to nature" (4, p. 305)? To the best of our understanding, we live in a physical universe in which the constellations of basic forces run the gamut from the simplest order to unfathomable complexity. Man's senses are geared to a particular range of magnitude, located between the atomic and the astronomic realm, and in this realm we observe conglomerations of shapes that lack most of the simplicity found at other cosmic levels. This intricate landscape is our reality in the most immediate sense. But it is not the only reality to which the human mind can refer. Whether, in trying to answer the question: What is reality?, we look at what is close at hand or what is remote, apparent to the eye or hidden, superficial or essential, shaped or unshaped, is a matter of philosophical outlook or, aesthetically, of style.

What the cinema is so well equipped to redeem is not "physical reality" but a particular version of it, namely, the view of a boundless, indeterminate, unfathomable world. We recognize this outlook as Romantic —a Romantic image obtained by photographic realism!

Kracauer's aesthetic claim comes under the heading of *Materialgerechtheit*, that is, the demand that the medium should guide the artist's approach. This demand—in itself characteristic for some, but not for all styles of art—enjoins the sculptor to derive his shapes from the wood, the metal, the stone, or the painter to invent in terms of oil, watercolor, etc. However, in the case of the film, the character trait emphasized by Kracauer does not belong to the materials employed but to the subject matter, which in photography is a part of the medium itself. Change the subject matter from a street crowd to a drawing for an animated cartoon—and you have changed the medium! For this reason, Kracauer states that his book must be "a material aesthetics, not a formal one. It is concerned with content" (4, p. *ix*). Now the aesthetic analysis of subject matter is indispensable, but necessarily partial since no medium of expression can be understood through its subject matter alone; also it must evaluate the subject matter as to what it contributes to the artistic purpose, not according to some alien criterion, such as whether or not it is "authentic." This, Kracauer, a seasoned filmgoer of sure taste, does in practice almost by instinct; but his insistence in theory on limiting film to realism leads to ambiguity. Thus, he declares certain kinds of highly stylized films—*Caligari, Gate of Hell, Hamlet, Metropolis*—eligible because they employ movement; but movement, which is indeed "cinematic" by definition, is not a category of content. It is a formal or perceptual element of expression, which draws authentic cinema from the most unrealistic shapes. Again, in discussing spoken dialogue, Kracauer rightly warns of the danger of opening up the region of discursive reasoning, which does not depend on images. The spoken word "is most cinematic if the messages it conveys elude our grasp" and if, instead, we are presented with "a sort of word carpet which, woven from scraps of dialogue or other kinds of communications, impresses the audience mainly as a coherent sound pattern" (4, pp. 107, 110). Quite so, but discursive reasoning is surely not unrealistic; nor does the film resist it because it is not physical. Rather, it is unvisual and antivisual. We conclude that the criteria of the "cinematic" and the "realistic" overlap but do not coincide. In fact, there is a passage in Kracauer's book in which he admits that "what accounts for the cinematic quality of films . . . is not so much their truth to our experience of reality or even to reality in a general sense as their absorption in camera-reality— visible physical existence" (4, p. 116). Precisely.

Kracauer is at his best when he illustrates in detail "the medium's affinity with the flow of life" (4, p. 72). The film gravitates toward "an open-ended, limitless world which bears little resemblance to the finite and ordered cosmos set by tragedy" (4, p. x). The predilection for endless streets, shapeless crowds, accidental detail, for loosely knit episodes, and open-ended plots is simply an extension of the characteristics of the photographic image itself. Since the camera preserves the physical world in its "virgin indeterminacy" (4, p. 69), that world, in turn, must put forward its indeterminate aspects. Kracauer is certainly correct in pointing out how easily the more stylized variety of film—historical chronicles or fantasies—reveals its lowly derivation from the mechanically photographed material world by slips that only the alertness of an ingenious filmmaker can avoid. But, when we look at these flaws dispassionately, we are likely to conclude that they occur not because those films are not realistic but because they have failed to eliminate realism sufficiently. It is true that the ocean waves that intrude upon Hamlet's soliloquy are more directly congenial to the film medium than the "dream orbit" of Sir Laurence Olivier's labyrinthine castle of Elsinore. But the slip does not make the entire undertaking artificial.

Here the argument runs into two general aesthetic problems. One, which I cannot take up on this occasion, concerns the value of attempts to stretch a medium from its natural center toward its periphery.[1] The other refers to the rather delicate criteria of the stylistic consistency or "reality level" (3, p. 15) of a work of art. In a film, consistency is guaranteed most simply and safely when all elements of the camera technique, performance, setting, and action conform to the same reality level. A glance at the actual practice suggests, however, that combinations of discordant elements are acceptable or indeed enrich the meaning by significant contrast if one condition is observed: There must be no contradiction within one and the same dimension of the medium. Thus, the ludicrous aspects of *Caligari* are not due to the artificiality of the setting as such. The solidly Euclidean continuity of space, revealed by the movements of the actors, appears as an embarrassing giveaway only because the scenery attempts to break up that unity of space in the manner of Expressionist and Cubist painting. There is a contradiction within the dimension of space. On the other hand, the thoroughly "stagy" acting in the early comedies of Chaplin and Keaton—the most formidable demonstration against the universal validity of Kracauer's thesis—is reasonably compatible with the realistic streets and rooms because the stylization is limited to human behavior. In *West Side Story*, to use a more recent example, the dances of the street gangs do not jar unduly with the realistic acting or the authenticity of the Manhattan slums in which they take place. They are inserted as self-contained units of action—like the ballets in Molière's plays or the arias in classical opera —and the steps and leaps of the dancers, although highly stylized, fit the realistic pavement of the setting; the trite prettiness and sentimentality of the young lovers in the same film do disturb, not only because of their artistic inferiority, but because they do not match the realism of the rest of the acting. In Alain Resnais' *Last Year at Marienbad*, actors of realistic appearance freeze into tableaux vivants—the logical climax of their remote, stylized gestures. The contrast between behavior and appearance creates the familiar Surrealist effect of revealing the unreal in the real. It is worth noticing that this film, just as others of its kind, meets Kracauer's criterion not by realism but by the flagrant violation of it—by the broken chains of time, space, and causality; the fragmentation of episodes; the elusive settings; the openness and emptiness obtained by omission. To exclude such possibilities from the cinema would mean to impoverish it without justification. As to consistency: the rule of intact

[1] On the definition of artistic media, consult Th. Munro (6, chapter X).

but separate dimensions has been shown to apply also to the combinations of media, such as film image and speech, music and dance, etc.[2]

Kracauer's presentation may call for correction and clarification, but the core of his thesis is surely valid and important: The photographic medium has made its most significant contribution by depicting the world, more extremely than has ever been done before, as an unbound, loosely knit continuum. This interpretation was made possible by the invention of photography; but the extent to which the space and time of our daily lives have become occupied by photographs cannot be explained simply by the fact that they are technically available. Photography was allowed to imbue Western civilization so thoroughly because it made possible the most radical manifestation of a tendency that began with the turn toward lifelikeness in the arts and sciences of the Renaissance and culminated in the Impressionist conception of the transient, teaming "flow of life."

There is a curious ambiguity in the striving toward lifelikeness. While it leads away from convention, from simplified, petrified generalities to the freshness, complexity, and concreteness of direct experience, it also induces the mind to lose itself in the intricacies of the particular and thereby distracts it from active understanding and participation, which must be based on the grasp of generalities. Plato first warned us of this danger, and thinkers and artists have been aware of it ever since, as witness a recent example in the arts, the writings of Piet Mondrian.

In the light of this situation, we examine Kracauer's answer to the question: What is the mission of the cinema in our time? Modern man, he points out, has become ideologically shelterless; in fact, he has lost all guiding ideas. At the same time, he has been deprived of true contact with reality. "This then is modern man's situation: he lacks the guidance of binding norms. He touches reality only with his fingertips. Now, these two determinants of contemporary life do not simply exist side by side. Rather, our abstractness deeply affects our relations to the body of ideology. To be precise, it impedes practically all direct efforts to revamp religion and establish a consensus of beliefs" (4, p. 294). How can we get out of this predicament? Perhaps the film is the gateway. Perhaps the way to "the evasive contents of the inner life . . . , if way there is, leads through the experience of surface reality" (4, p. 287).

"The moviegoer watches the images on the screen in a dream-like

----

[2] See my essay, "A New Laocoön: Artistic Composites and the Talking Film" in (2).

state. So he can be supposed to apprehend physical reality in its concreteness" (4, p. 303). This is a bold non sequitur, in view of what Kracauer recognizes immediately before: he defines the film artist as "a man who sets out to tell a story but, in shooting it, is so overwhelmed by his innate desire to cover all of physical reality—and also by a feeling that he must cover it in order to tell the story, any story, in cinematic terms—that he ventures ever deeper into the jungle of material phenomena in which he risks becoming irretrievably lost if he does not, by virtue of great efforts, get back to the highways he left" (pp. 303–304). Here exactly lies the problem. After all, it is the surface of reality we explore when we touch it only with our fingertips. Do we find that modern man, surfeited with photographs that crowd out the words in his reading matter and are the staple of his leisure time edification, is being led back to the highways? He is immensely better informed about the epidermis of the world at large, the appearance of what goes on; but we have good reasons to call him less wise than his counterpart of the prephotographic era. The addicts of photography seem highly distracted. They think less well. Their ever stimulated curiosity makes them lose themselves in the capillaries of the particular rather than move on the mainstream of life. Photographic information, potentially a magnificent source of knowledge, seems to serve as a powerful distraction from insight. The mere exposure to the visible surface of the world will not arouse ideas unless the spectacle is approached with ideas ready to be stirred up.

Earlier, I described the lifelike image as complex, irrational, continuous, and particularized, but left the question open as to whether this was a typical view of reality. In fact, it is not. Psychologists have come to see that perception cannot be understood as a mechanical recording of stimuli. Perception develops in the service of needs. Animals and humans look in order to survive, which means they have to orient themselves by distinction and generalization. True, the perception of early man is richer—as demonstrated by the complexity of primitive languages. But that complexity is organized by the stark simplicity of conception we find reflected in primitive and folk art and in the drawings of children. That "stylized" simplicity is the prototype of genuine concreteness, of elementary closeness to reality!

It takes the later refinement of fatigued cultures to become aware of, and interested in, the irrationality of minutely scanned surfaces; it takes the passive sensitivity of the unengaged spectator. Here we are greatly helped by a remark of Kracauer's on the possible role of melancholy in photographic vision: "Now melancholy as an inner disposition not only makes elegiac objects seem attractive but carries still another, more important implication: it favors self-estrangement, which on its part entails identification with all kinds of objects. The dejected individual is likely to lose himself in the incidental configurations of his environment, absorbing them with a disinterested intensity no longer determined by his previous preferences" (4, p. 17). This observation, valid for individuals, also applies to phases of civilization.

If melancholy is a prevalent disposition of our time, we might expect artists to be concerned with its portrayal and perhaps with the mobilization of forces able to counterbalance or even overcome it. In fact, melancholy does pervade our visual art and literature. However, it is necessary here to distinguish carefully between the artistic representation of a state of mind and the manifestation of its symptoms. Artistic representation, as we find it, for instance, in the opening lines of T. S. Eliot's "Prufrock," shapes the experience of melancholy with the forms of a given medium. When the poet speaks of "half-deserted streets . . . that follow like a tedious argument of insidious intent," he describes endlessness, identified by Kracauer as a typically modern, "photographic" experience, but he does so not by means of endlessness itself but by a sharply defined sequence of words. The poem may be the expression of a melancholy man; but, as is every work of art, it is the product of a most unmelancholy occupation. The same is true for good films. In De Sica's *Umberto D.*, the im-pertinence of the lonely man's environment is characterized with all the precision of aesthetic economy. Such Neorealism is profoundly different from the amorphousness of a photographic reality recorded mechanically and at random. The "open form"—to use H. Wölfflin's (8) term—is characterized in the arts by a less direct dependence of the composition on the central theme. It works with an abundance of material rather than with scarcity, with coordination rather than subordination. However, the difference between open form and closed form—or between the epic and the dramatic style (1)—must not be misinterpreted as a difference between one kind of composition controlled by the criteria of unity and necessity and another using "free" material, undetermined by function.

The recent tendency toward the dissolution of form has begun to manifest itself also in the cinema. As an example, one may cite Antonioni's *L'Avventura*, a film of some merit, which meanders, however, perfunctorily through quantities of half-digested material, for instance, in the aimless and endless roaming of the characters on the island in the central sequence. I may be doing injustice to this particular work; but, assuming that it is what it appeared to me to be: is this a new, legitimate way of interpreting dissolution by unorganized form or is it a clinical symptom of the mental dejection it purports to portray—melancholy unshaped?

Kracauer has given a valuable clue to the theory of modern art by spelling out, for the first time, the consequences of a strong admixture of raw material, as it distinguishes the photographic medium. The primary question to be raised here is not whether such a medium is an art (4, p. 39). This question is unanswerable because "art" is not a filing cabinet for certain objects and activities that "belong." Art is an attribute found in all objects and activities to a larger or lesser degree, namely, the capacity of making reality visible. Now visibility is brought about by form, and—as we know, for example, from the comparison of plaster casts of human faces and sculptured portraits—untreated raw material tends to make the object invisible. Therefore, in the photographic medium, the ratio between raw material and the formative (artistic) element is such as to strengthen the share of the former and to reduce visibility. This loss may be compensated by gains of another kind, but the loss needs to be recorded.

The realistic tendency in Western art has produced a gradual decrease in visibility, complementary to an increasing surrender of the formative capacity of the human mind to the raw material of experience. This development, as I mentioned before, comes to a climax in Impressionist painting, in which the world of objects approaches total invisibility in favor of faithfully rendered surface appearance. It seems significant that nonrepresentational painting repeats and continues the same development by a gradual lessening of the formative factor. Some leading recent varieties of abstract art, an acknowledged parallel to the late Impressionism of Monet, have shifted from pattern to texture (see preceding essay), which is tantamount to saying that they no longer permit the eye to organize the material presented. It is becoming increasingly clear that this abandonment of pictorial organization, with the concomitant loss of visibility, is nothing else but the yearning for the unshaped, a return to the raw material of reality.[3] For, to illustrate the trend by the work of its most significant recent representative, what else is the consummate

---

[3] The same attitude prevails in the more recent insipid imitations of advertising and other popular imagery as well as the mechanical copying of foodstuff, excrements, or human limbs. Although externally so different from abstract texture art, these "realistic" products of painters and sculptors manifest a similar surrender of formative power to the shapelessness of the environment.

craftsman Jean Dubuffet trying to accomplish with his artful use of viscous varnishes that create "enigmatic branchings" by repelling the oil, with his enamels that "become decomposed, causing a fine network of fissures and crackles," his wrinkles and curlicues, child-scribbles and impulsive gestures of the brush, with his bark and leaves of trees, tar, asphalt, putty, clinkers, old sponges, butterfly wings, and fragments of burned automobiles—what else but an ever more faithful reproduction of nature, nature at its most amorphous, remote from the formative impact of man and equally remote from its own formative powers? "These pictures provide me with peace . . . great peace of rugs and naked and empty plains, silently interrupted distances whose homogeneity and continuity cannot be altered. I love homogeneous worlds with neither landmarks nor boundaries, which are like the sea, snowy mountains, deserts and steppes" (6, p. 139). There is little doubt about the attitude that inspires this preference for what Dubuffet himself calls a kind of continuous universal soup with the savor of life itself: "The kingdom of formal ideas always appears to me of very little virtue beside the seignioral kingdom of stones" (6, p. 72).

Here the realistic tendency reveals itself as the relinquishment of the active grasp of meaning that characterizes man's relationship to reality when he is in full possession of his mental powers. The development is brought to its logical completion when the materials of the painter are no longer considered as means of representation but as objects for their own sake, additions to the material world itself: "I see no great difference (metaphysically, that is) between the pastes I spread and a cat, a trout or a bull. My paste is a being as these are. Less circumscribed, to be sure and more emulsified; its ordinance is stranger, much stranger certainly; I mean, foreign to us, humans, who are so very circumscribed, so far from being formless (or, at least, think ourselves to be)" (6, p. 63). The painter cultivates his pastes and fluids as a gardener cultivates the soil; he becomes a breeder and trainer. He no longer produces images but matter. And the matter he is creating with the refined chemicals of a late civilization is the world before the Creation, the attractive infinity and variety of the chaos. It is the escape from the duty of man—the final refuge and the final refreshment.

This essay has critically discussed a contention which in its most radical formulation holds that a shift from man-made form to the unshaped raw material of experience constitutes a return to concrete reality, from which alone new thought can arise. It has become necessary to point out that genuine realism consists in the interpretation of the raw material of experience by means of significant form and that therefore a concern with unshaped matter is a melancholy surrender rather than the recovery of man's grip on reality. Perhaps, then, we are witnessing the last twitches of an exhausted civilization, whose rarefied concepts no longer reach the world of the senses. But it is also possible that by cleansing the mind of all shapes we are approaching the nadir we must touch in order to rise again. Perhaps in this confrontation with primordial matter we resemble the underworld shadows of the Odyssey, eager to drink from the sacrificial blood so that the scenes of life might come back once more.

REFERENCES

1. Arnheim, Rudolf. Epic and dramatic film. *Film Culture*, 1957, 3, 9–10.
2. ———. *Film as Art*. Berkeley and Los Angeles: Univ. of Calif. Press, 1960.
3. ———. *Picasso's Guernica: the Genesis of a Painting*. Berkeley and Los Angeles: Univ. of Calif. Press, 1962.
4. Kracauer, Siegfried. *Theory of Film*. New York: Oxford Univ. Press, 1960.
5. Munro, Thomas. *The Arts and Their Interrelations*. New York, 1951.
6. Selz, Peter. *The Work of Jean Dubuffet*. New York: Museum of Modern Art, 1962.
7. Wölfflin, Heinrich. *Kunstgeschichtliche Grundbegriffe*. Munich: Bruckmann, 1920.

FROM FUNCTION TO EXPRESSION

The aesthetic status of function and functionality in architecture and the other applied arts has been uncertain and uneasy. If an object is designed for a practical purpose, will this intention of the designer and the utility of the object advance or hamper the artistic value of the product? Or is function aesthetically indifferent? In the present essay, I shall undertake to show that functionality, that is, the fitness of an object for a nonaesthetic purpose, enters the realm of art by way of visual expression. To this end it will be necessary, first of all, to rehearse some of the views on the relations among the three concepts: fitness, beauty, expression.

Fitness and beauty. At the level of innocence, questions of art are solved without being explicitly propounded. Adolf Loos, a Viennese architectural reformer of the early twentieth century, speaks of the peace of a mountain lake: The mountains and the clouds are reflected in the water, and so are the farmhouses and the village churches—"they look as though they had not been built by human hand." But a discord shatters the peace "like an unnecessary clamor. In the midst of the houses of the farmers, built not by them but by God, there stands a villa. The product of a good or a bad architect? I do not know. All I know is that peace, calmness, and beauty are gone." And Loos asks: "Why is

First published in the *Journal of Aesthetics and Art Criticism*, Fall 1964, 23, 29–41.

it that any architect, good or bad, will desecrate the lake? The farmer will not. Nor will the engineer," who builds the boats and the railways (11).

Loos suggests that the farmer's consciousness is entirely concerned with the purposive aspects of his house: the roof, the door. His sense of beauty is guided instinctually. His house is "as beautiful as the rose or the thistle, the horse or the cow." The capacities of creating good proportions, harmony of color, fitting shape, and striking expression operate intuitively as they do in the painting of a child or in primitive handicrafts. There is "instinct"; there may be also some convention of how to make things. But any aesthetic evaluation is limited here to: this is right, this is wrong! This looks good, this looks bad! There is no conscious recourse to individual standards. The question of how to combine fitness and beauty does not arise either in the making or in the judging of the object. Nor does the aesthetic status of fitness come up for discussion. This, however, does not absolve the aesthetician from facing these questions when the work of the farmer, the engineer, the child, or the primitive is to be considered.

Once the issue does come up, there are first of all two radical solutions. One can either maintain that functionality has nothing to do with art, or that art excludes functionality. Thus, the Bauhaus architect Hannes Meyer is reported to have said that "it is an absurdity to talk about the modern style in terms of aesthetics at all. If a building provides adequately, completely, and without compromise for its purpose it is a good building, regardless of its appearance" (16, p. 393). And Loos asserted that architecture should be counted among the arts only to the minor extent to which it is concerned with tombs and monuments, since the contamination of art and material purpose "profanes the highest." He was preceded by Schopenhauer, who remarked that architecture, to the extent to which it fulfills practical purposes, cannot be called an art since, when it serves utility, it serves the Will, that is, material needs, rather than pure cognition (22, book 3, § 43).

Such formulations ignore the issue. The functionalists did acknowledge the existence of the problem but maintained that, in practice, there need not be any difficulty since strict adherence to practical requirements would automatically meet the demands of beauty. They pointed to nature, which, they said, attains perfect beauty unintentionally through sheer practicality. Thus, Frank Lloyd Wright, speaking of a flower, concluded: "Law and order are the basis of its finished grace and beauty; its beauty is the expression of fundamental conditions in line, form, and color, true to them, and existing to fulfill them according to design" (8, p. 60).

Clearly, Wright and Louis H. Sullivan in their theorizing were not advocating the intuitive pursuit of aesthetical requirements. They believed that by some happy correspondence beauty was produced when utility was intended. What they admired in nature was not the mere attractiveness of biological abundance, vitality, or colorfulness. Nor were they impressed only by the visible evidence of fitness in plants and animals. By beauty, they meant order and harmony, balance, proportion, unity, parsimony, etc.

These properties, wherever they are found in nature, seem to derive mainly from two conditions. First, natural objects are created by the very forces that constitute them. The shape of the ocean wave results directly from the action of propelled water. The flower is grown rather than made, and therefore its external appearance consists of the perceivable effects of the processes of growth. The muscles that move an animal's body also shape its contours. The simpler and more unified the constellation of these physical forces—and this is the second condition—the simpler and more unified the result of their manifestation will look. Symmetrically grouped forces will make for symmetry in the blossom, the starfish, the atomic model. When shape and motion are produced by the forces that constitute the natural object or body, they will look parsimonious and graceful. The optimum solution of the functional problem is worked out physically under the pressure of the tendency toward a state of minimum tension and, in the organism, as the streamlining effect of Darwinian evolution. To some extent, these physical virtues will be reflected in appearance.

Man-made objects, on the other hand, are produced by external forces, whose relations to the shapes of these objects are far from simple. Compare the forces that make a clay pot or wooden table-leg on a potter's wheel or lathe with those that grow an apple or a human leg; or compare the operations of building a steeple or casting a rocket with the sprouting of an asparagus! Because of this fundamental difference, the human craftsman must envisage the intended shape and judge the obtained shape in the light of desired properties and then direct his hands and tools accordingly. In doing so, he discovers that function alone does not determine shape, and it is at this crucial point that the analogy with nature also lets him down.

Natural shape is not accounted for wholly or even essentially by function. There are hundreds of ways of being a tree, a fish, or a bird, and while, of course, each organism was formed by a set of determining conditions, there is no way of explaining the difference between an oak and a maple by reference to their present needs or function. In spite of Horatio Greenough's admonition, we view this diversity as "the result of Omnipotence at play for mere variety's sake" (5, p. 117). The random factors that, according to Darwinism, offer the freedom necessary for the gradual perfection of each species also make one species different from the next. It may be true that once one is cut out to be a turtle, a turtle's shape and color reflects the most convenient way of leading a turtle's life, but the character or style of the turtle is not essentially accounted for by function. Similarly in man and in the human product. Apart from its function, which is taken care of by the skill and imagination of its maker more or less successfully, the object is shaped by the character of producer and consumer. This character is a complex and, in our particular civilization, quite unstable set of determinants, traditional preferences, indoctrinations, personal needs, an unsure sense of perceptual propriety, and conflicting social pressures and influences. The resulting steering force is capricious and unreliable.

Evidently, this disorientation of the maker cannot be avoided by suppressing the influence of human character altogether. Physical function alone will not determine the object. What is more, the reduction of function to physical fitness is quite arbitrary in an object made for human use. The term "function" in its broadest sense would include all purposes a building or implement is meant to fulfill. It would refer not only to the comfort of the body but also to that of the mind. In this broader sense, fitness would comprise the very properties that functionalism was meant to combat. Even the worst excrescences of the nineteenth century would be functional. To use Richard Neutra's example: the picture of Abraham Lincoln painted on the billiard ball certainly helped to satisfy the needs of the man who believed that without that picture he would not win (18, p. 108). Functional also would be the bed wrought in sterling silver by a New York firm for a Maharajah and manned (if that is the word) on its corners with four life-sized silver nudes, who smiled at the sleeper realistically and cooled him with silver fans.

In this true generality, "function" would be no distinguishing characteristic at all. Every object fit to serve the wishes of its owner would be functional. On the other hand, to reduce function to physical fitness is not a functional decision but an act of character, that is, of personal or period style. Granted that in an age of disturbed taste it may be more

sensible to try to reduce the decisions of the architect or designer to objectively determinable requirements than to mislead him by unsuitable
aesthetic standards. If his individual sense of form happens to be in
good order, he will intuitively meet the aesthetic demands he believes
he is ignoring. But, although the approach may work in practice, the
problem remains unsolved theoretically.

A few examples may help to demonstrate that pure functionalism
does not eliminate the need of stylistic choice. To conceal the mechanism of a sewing machine in a shell of straight-line L-shape may make
the object safe, clean, storable, etc.; but it is also the expression of a
mind that is not curious about how an implement operates "inside" as
long as it works. Nor does a reduction to simplest shape produce pure
functionality. In the furniture and implements designed at the Bauhaus,
we discover by now a preference for elementary geometry, not derived
from function but dictated by the character of its makers and more directly expressed perhaps in Feininger's and Klee's Cubism or in Schlemmer's "Mechanical Ballet" of human robots (2). The same kind of
stylistic idiosyncrasy will soon be discovered in the alleged functionality
of what Lewis Mumford calls "the vast repetitive inanity of the high-rise
slab" (15, p. 160). Functionality can be claimed convincingly for the very
opposite style; thus, W. C. Behrendt discussing Wright: "For it is not
the aim in forming the structure to represent the geometric idea of
space, but to create for the individual life, which unfolds itself within
that space, an accurately adjusted shell. This explains the strange irregularity of these plans, which exhibit irregular contours with numerous projections, and also single rooms of various shapes with manifold juttings
and recessions" (16, p. 397).

Functionalism calls for still another comment. Admittedly, nature
under the pressure of the physical striving for balance and the Darwinian principle of selection can produce shapes that satisfy standards of
proportion, harmony, order, unity, etc. These criteria define "beauty" in
the traditional sense of the term, but they do not meet the requirements
of art. In fact, flowers, animals, or human beings may be called beautiful
but they are not in themselves acceptable as art. The kind of shaping
and arranging they undergo by the hands of the painter or sculptor who
uses them does not serve primarily to improve on the often exquisite
beauty of the model objects. The principal task of the artist is to introduce appropriate meaning. Not that the objects of nature are aesthetically meaningless. They may convey peace or ferocity, power, striving, or
laziness. But, in doing so, they use only the vocabulary of visual meaning. The natural object as a whole rarely constitutes a complete state-

ment of meaningful expression because its external appearance was not devised for that purpose. External expression comes about in the natural object as an unintentional by-product of physical organization, and therefore is not likely to meet the particular conditions of visual unity, consistency, and composition that must be fulfilled in an artistic statement.

There are, of course, theorists who fully acknowledge the aesthetic aspect of the architect's or designer's task. However, they tend to think of beauty as an additional virtue of the useful object. Fitness is one thing, beauty another. Thus, Leone Battista Alberti maintains that the architect should deserve praise "both for the wonderful and ravishing beauty of his works and for the necessity, serviceableness, and strength of the things which he has invented." Beauty is defined by Alberti as the harmony of all the parts: "the just composition and relation of the lines among themselves" (1, pp. 119 ff.). In our own century, the architect Walter Gropius tells us that "the slogan 'fitness for purpose equals beauty' is only half true. When do we call a human face beautiful? Every face is fit for purpose in its parts, but only perfect proportions and colors in a well-balanced harmony deserve that title of honor: beautiful" (7, p. 4). Finally, a quotation from a modern furniture designer may serve as an example of how the average craftsman talks about these matters nowadays. Jens Risom asserts that furniture must be both functional and decorative: "It is important for a chair to be comfortable and for a cabinet to fully satisfy the storage requirements. At the same time it is, of course, important for us to like its looks, for it to have a well-proportioned and pleasant appearance, to be made of good materials in a good, craftsmanlike manner. In other words, we must like its 'design'" (21, p. 43). In this sort of statement, no relation between function and beauty is envisaged theoretically.

Beauty and expression. Beauty is treated traditionally as an entity totally separate not only from function but also from expression.[1] As far as the relation of beauty to expression is concerned, Vitruvius asserts

---

[1] I should like to make it quite clear that what I am objecting to is not the mere separation, for the purpose of theoretical analysis, of factors that interact organically in the phenomenon under investigation. Such separation is inevitably required by scientific procedure. What I do object to is the notion that a work of applied art comes about by the combination of three factors that are independent in principle from each other. Beauty, I believe, is that property of form that makes expression pure and strong. Fitness, as will be shown, provides the theme for what a building or implement expresses. And no beauty of form can be conceived without reference to that theme of fitness.

that architecture must meet six criteria. Four of these refer to the requirements of beauty, namely, order, arrangement, eurythmy, and symmetry. The fifth, economy, comes closest to what we call utility. Finally,
propriety demands that "the temples of Minerva, Mars, and Hercules,
will be Doric since the virile strength of these gods makes daintiness entirely inappropriate to their houses. In temples to Venus, Flora, Proser-
pine, Spring-Water, and the Nymphs, the Corinthian order will be found
to have peculiar significance, because these are delicate divinities and
so its rather slender outlines, its flowers, leaves, and ornamental volutes
will lend propriety where it is due" (28, book 1, chapter 1). Here
Vitruvius is dealing with expression. He thinks of physiognomic properties of form, reflecting the personality of the gods to whom the buildings
belong; but these properties are quite unrelated to his criteria of beauty
on the one hand and utility on the other.

There is no need to belabor the point by further quotations from
writings on the theory of art. But it may be worth mentioning that even
psychologists tend to neglect expression when they deal with problems
of aesthetics. For example, if we consult the recent survey of *The Experimental Psychology of Beauty* by C. W. Valentine, we find that the
book is limited to the traditional notion of beauty (26, p. 6). On the
implicit assumption that beauty is a generic harmony, not amenable to
more specific description or response, the author asserts that for most
practical purposes the question: "Do you think this is beautiful, and
why?" can be replaced with: "Do you find this pleasing?" In fact, the
bulk of the studies available in English, as summarized by Valentine, are
concerned with preferences for anything from a single patch of color to a
poem by Dylan Thomas. These studies are singularly unrewarding aesthetically because they report only as a by-product what people perceive when they face a work of art. In contrast, the space given in the
book to expression, i.e., to the very foundation of art, is startlingly small;
and in the studies of expression which are mentioned, the phenomenon is
often sidetracked by a concern with subject matter in painting and, in
music, by the comparison with the so-called emotions.

Expression and fitness. The tendency in psychology to neglect expression or to separate it from other mental functions is not limited to
aesthetics. Expression has remained a stranger in psychology. In the
English-speaking countries, one branch of psychology, exemplified by
behaviorism, has been mainly concerned with the practical aspects of
activities, such as how animals go about getting something to eat. In dealing with such "functional" activities, behaviorism has limited its en-

quiries to what can be described quantitatively; it has ignored the rest or filed it away under the heading "general behavior." Clinical psychology, on the other hand, is concerned with the interplay between states of mind and goal-directed striving; but clinicians cannot be said to have paid enough attention to the corresponding external unity of perceptually expressive and purposive behavior. They tend to study the outward manifestations of character and mood apart from goal-directed activity, as for example, in the so-called projective tests, that is, in acts of contemplation and context-free performance. Thus, we notice a split between the investigation of purposeful behavior and that of expressive behavior. Expression is either entirely neglected or treated as the detached externalization of the mind, a luxury of behavior, useful for diagnosis, but quite separate from a person's or an animal's effort at getting things done. In line with this attitude, experimental psychologists have generally limited their studies of expression to artificially produced material: stereotyped facial grimaces and gestures staged by actors, schematic line-drawings, etc. Here again, expression is isolated from its context.

In one of the very few significant papers on the subject published during the past two decades in this country, the split shows up clearly. Writing on "the expressive component of behavior," A. H. Maslow mentions that "most acts of behavior have both an expressive and a coping component," but distinguishes acts of coping from acts of expression throughout his paper (12; 13, chapter 11). While this separation is in itself significant for what I am trying to show, it is less important than the tendency to treat expression as something outside the mainstream of behavior. Expressive behavior is described by Maslow as unmotivated and useless. It is an epiphenomenon, an end-in-itself. It has no effect on the environment, it is not functional. Ripping away a merely expressive neurotic symptom, says Maslow, will do no harm because it plays no vital role. Expression refers to what a person is, rather than what he does. It is "the stupidity of the moron, the smile and the springy walk of the healthy person, the benevolent mien of the kind and affectionate, the beauty of the beautiful woman," etc. (12; 13, chapter 11).[2]

[2] Compare the following remark by Wolfgang Köhler: "In discussing our problem, philosophers and psychologists may have concentrated too much on the expressive movements which accompany *emotions*. At any rate, equally relevant facts have virtually been ignored: behavior in the most *practical* sense of the word tends to be seen as organized in forms which copy the organization of corresponding inner developments" (10, p. 231).

Such views and practices of psychologists set the stage for the consideration of a similar state of affairs in the arts. In training students for the applied arts, expression is all too often either ignored or separated from function. To cite a famous example: Instruction at the Bauhaus consisted of technical training and the development of the sense of form—*Werklehre* and *Formlehre*. *Formlehre* consisted of Perception, Representation, and Formation; and formation (*Gestaltung*), in turn, dealt with color, space, and composition: it was thought of as the teaching of visual grammar (6, p. 44; 24). Expression was not mentioned in the official curriculum. When the Bauhaus teachers did refer to it, they spoke of expression as a property of color, shape, or space as such (in the manner of Kandinsky), unrelated to function.

This neglect of the vital connection between function and expression is traditional. I mentioned that Vitruvius thought of propriety as a requirement entirely separate from the demands of beauty and economy in a building. When Adolf Loos refers to the subject he, too, treats expression as an isolated property: "Architecture arouses moods in us. Therefore it is the task of the architect to make this mood precise. The room must look *gemütlich*, the house 'livable.' The courthouse must appear like a threatening gesture to secret vice. The bank building must say: Here your money is stably and safely deposited with honest people" (11).

The separation of expression from physical function is most evident in discussions of symbolism in architecture. Certain shapes that carry meaning, mostly a conventional meaning, are applied to a building. A medieval basilica may be laid out in the form of the cross; the Presbyterian church in Stamford, Connecticut, has the shape of a fish; Andrea Palladio recommended that our temples be made round because the circle is "the most proper figure to show the unity, infinite essence, the uniformity and justice of God" (19, p. 240). In this circumscribed sense, symbolism is a property possessed by some buildings, but not all. It is an explicit element applied to the building for the sake of communication. John E. Burchard, in an enlightening paper on symbolism in architecture, speaks of the "steady devaluation of the symbolic purposes of architecture" and the "sterility of the symbolic aspirations of the best modern architects." And he raises the question whether symbolism is necessary in the architecture of our time (3; 30).

Earlier, and with a broader prospect, Hegel thought of architecture as the lowest among the arts because its medium is matter, subject only to the laws of gravity, and therefore unsuitable for the representation of the spirit (9). When Hegel calls architecture symbolic, he means to describe its mode of representation as inferior. More particularly, he also defines as "symbolic" the earliest of three phases of architecture, which he describes as the symbolic, the classic, and the romantic. The ideas expressed in early architecture are nothing better than "shapeless, general representations, elemental, variously segregated and confused abstractions of nature, mixed with thoughts of spiritual reality." Being abstract and indefinite, these ideas are suitably represented by matter itself, which is just as abstract and generic. In towers, obelisks, or mazes this early and mostly Oriental architecture gives expression to broad social and religious ideas. In the second, the classic phase, Greek architecture incorporates the function or utility of the building and becomes a shell, a surrounding for men and gods. It thereby relinquishes expression and, instead, develops beauty, that is, harmony of proportion: "Through the music of its proportions it raises mere utility towards beauty." In the third or romantic phase, represented by the Christian Gothic, expression is combined with utility; but here the demands of beauty remain unheeded. In the Gothic cathedral, utility, although it is present physically, vanishes nevertheless from sight, giving the whole building the appearance of an independent existence. Practical utility is transformed into what serves the subjective devotion of the mind. As distinguished from the objective ideas expressed in early, symbolic architecture, the buildings of the romantic phase receive their meaning and value from what the feeling mind (*das Gemüt*) puts into it. The external medium as such is indifferent and inferior. "The spirit," says Hegel, "puts no final trust in it and cannot dwell in it."

What strikes me as symptomatic in these and similar utterances is that expression is considered a supplementary component, which may or may not be present. The obelisk, the cathedral have expression; the farmhouse, the Greek temple, the modern skyscraper have not. Characteristic, also, is Hegel's tendency to make expression a privilege of man. In itself, architecture, being nonrepresentational, is considered by him as purely material, inferior, limited to the play of physical forces. The expression of the spirit can be attained only when the human figure is represented, as in sculpture, or when the human element is brought in by the observer, who can project his subjective feelings even on the unfeeling stones of the builder.

In order to remedy this state of the theory, it is necessary, first of all, to point out that expression is an objective property of all organized patterns of shape and color. It is an inherent aspect of every perceptual quality whatever, of size, space, movement, illumination, etc. It is found in the percept of every object or activity, human or nonhuman, animate or inanimate, useless or useful, man-made or natural, in fine art or applied art. Expression can be weakened and disturbed by inarticulate, disorganized patterns, but it can never be absent. As an aspect of perception, expression is cerebral rather than retinal, that is, it arises in the brain rather than in the eye, but it is lawfully dependent on the stimuli recorded by the eyes. Every change of shape, for example, makes for a corresponding change of expression. Given the expressive character of all functional shape, we must now elucidate the particular relationship of function and expression.

The visibility of fitness. Fitness as a criterion for the making of useful objects has rarely been limited to the demand that the objects should suit their practical purpose physically. Almost invariably there is the further request that the function of the object and its fitness to fulfill that function should be visible.

This is, first of all, a requirement of utility. Man must rely on his eyes to make use of a building, a teapot, or a machine. Therefore the object should show what it is for, how it goes about serving its function, and how it is to be handled. It is useful to be able to see where the door is and how it opens; the shape of the teapot should distinguish the spout from the handle; and the handles of a machine are quickly found if they are painted yellow while the machine itself is green and its electric switches and plugs are red for safety's sake (4).

From the practical point of view, however, visibility can be undesirable as well as desirable. Concealment may be more useful than display, for example, in camouflage, in trap-doors and safes, in the hiding of the doors of streamlined automobiles, or the covering up of buttons and zippers.

Beyond practicality, the request that an object should show its purpose is sometimes raised in the name of honesty and truth. An object must not tell a lie; therefore it must display its function, and also the material of which it is made, the physical forces that sustain and press it, its strength and weight. Thus, Palladio complains about Baroque architecture: ". . . instead of columns or pilasters, which are contrived to bear great weight, one ought not to place those modern ornaments called cartouches, which are certain scrolls that are but an eye-sore to the artists and give others only a confused idea of architecture . . . such nonsensical things as cartouches are altogether superfluous because it is impossible that the joists or any other timber whatsoever could really perform what these represent; and since they are feigned to be soft and weak I know not by what rule they can be put under anything heavy and hard" (19, p. 232). This architect is not speaking in the interest of public safety. No danger of physical collapse is involved. He defends an ethical principle that has been asserted sometimes but not at all times and not always with regard to the same aspects of the object.

In the broadest sense, this principle derives from man's desire to be aware of his condition, that is, to understand his existence. In the perceptual realm, it makes for the wish that things look the way they are. We are reminded here of the traditional belief in the symbolic significance of appearance in nature. The Renaissance notion of the human body as a microcosmic image of the macrocosm may serve as an illustration; or, a more specific example, Schopenhauer's view that the anatomical relationship of head to torso in man and animal expresses the varying dependence of cognition (Erkenntnis) upon physical need. In the lower animals, head and torso are still closely fused; whereas in man, as exemplified by the Apollo of Belvedere, the freely turning head shows a mind no longer subservient to the care of the body (22, book 3, § 33).

The visibility of nature is one of the cherished tenets of the functionalists. It served them as a model and also gave status to their architectural claim. "It stands to reason," wrote Louis H. Sullivan, "that a thing looks like what it is, and, vice versa, it is what it looks like. . . . The form, oak tree, resembles and expresses the purpose or function, oak; . . . so the form, wave, looks like the function, wave; . . . and so does the form, man, stand for the function, man; the form, John Doe, means the function, John Doe; the form, smile, makes us aware of the function, smile; so, when I say: a man named John Doe smiles—we have a little series of functions and forms which are inseparably related, and yet they seem very casual to us" (25, p. 43). I have already pointed to the main cause of this transparency. Natural objects are created by the very forces that constitute them. Their visible shape is largely an externalization of the state of affairs inside. Therefore the correspondence of what is outside with what is inside does not have to be provided for explicitly. On the other hand, this correspondence is far from complete. For one thing, mechanical processes and states tend to manifest themselves but chemical ones often do not. Also, as mechanisms grow more complex, the formal independence of their components becomes increasingly impractical, as shown by the human body, which conceals most of its functions in a streamlined envelope of relatively simple shape. Such streamlining, known as "styling" to designers, is surely functional in the sense of physical practicality and survival; but it is just as surely not functional in the sense of the visual display of function. Significantly, Frank Lloyd Wright, speaking of the "geometry that is the idea of every form" admonished his disciples to study "a quail, a snail, a shell, a fish. They yield their secret readily, and are easier to grasp than dogs and horses and humans because they are a little nearer origins, a little more primitive" (8, p. 129).

Works of visual art, of course, will display their physical nature only to the extent that a piece of sculpture may visibly derive its shapes from the nature of the wood, stone, or metal of which it is made; but to the mobility of limbs in the Apollo of Belvedere there corresponds the total rigidity of the marble of which it is made, and the textures of silk or flesh in a painting have no physical counterpart. Even in buildings, which are physical objects for physical use, the correspondence between physical structure and perceptual appearance is severely limited. The untruthful statics about which Palladio complained is not limited to Baroque buildings. Geoffrey Scott reminds us that "in point of structural fact" every upward movement in the Gothic edifices, much applauded for their soaring spires and pinnacles, "is a downward one, seeking the earth" (23, p. 85). If the Gothic building makes a valid statement, as it surely does, it cannot be about its own physical nature.

Translation into expression. At this point it is necessary to ask more precisely in what particular manner the appearance of an object can reflect its physical functioning. After all, we have a problem here. It is not obvious, for example, how the goings-on within the three-dimensional volume of a building can project themselves upon its two-dimensional outer surface. Furthermore, since physical function comes down, in the last analysis, to the behavior of forces, how are such physical forces to be portrayed in the visual appearance of an object?

What we call the functional look of an object cannot be described as the externalization of internal physical forces (although it may be brought about by such externalization). Instead, functional appearance is due to a translation of physical forces into visual language. A simple example will make this clear. Compare two glasses, one the shape of a truncated egg (Figure 17a), the other diverging at the rim, tulip-fashion (Figure 17b). The first may be as ready to deliver its liquid content as the second, but, visually, the expression of containing prevails uncontested in the contour of the first until the convergence toward closure is suddenly cut by the opening. In the second, the gesture of containing turns gradually into that of opening and giving. What we see, in other words, is the expressive behavior of a pattern of visual forces. This pattern is related to the pattern of physical forces that constitutes the function of the object. But the relation is not necessarily close or simple. The correspondence is never complete. The external shape selects for visual presentation and interpretation only a few among the actual physical features of the object. These features may not be faithfully portrayed. They may be intensified or weakened. The translation into visibility can take advantage of all the freedom translators possess. In fact, the appearance may present features not physically contained in the object. In such instances, the beholder attributes the externally visible dynamics to the volume of the perceptual object as a whole rather than limiting it to

FIGURE 17a   FIGURE 17b

the outer skin. The object is perceived as a solid not only spatially but also dynamically. The Gothic building does indeed soar, and the body of the racing car is seen as animated throughout by the forces that constitute its appearance. In other words, what happens in the perception of the functional object is not that internal forces manifest themselves outside but, on the contrary, that perceived external forces are projected upon the inside. (It is the task of the maker to see to it that the appearance reflects physical functioning to the proper extent and in the proper manner.)

An impressive example in point is the simple post-and-lintel construction in architecture. While it represents visually the interaction of load and support with insuperable clarity, it is in no way a faithful image of the static forces actually involved. If the physical forces had the opportunity to create their own congenial form, they would produce a continuous object of complex curvature. Pier Luigi Nervi refers in this connection to the shape of flower-cups, leaves, eggs, shells; and he states that only re-enforced concrete has enabled us to apply these functional shapes to architecture (27, p. 104). However, in spite of the discrepancy and the concomitant overweight of the structure, we call the rectangularity of the gate or temple functional because it portrays the underlying physical situation with the simplicity of a child's drawing. Nervi's design may render the static forces more closely, the way a more mature painting may be more realistic. But it seems correct to say that even the Nervi construction remains an image of the physical forces rather than their direct manifestation.

Even in the shaping of implements that are strictly limited to practical use, the "functional" appearance of the object is a visual interpretation of its nature. What is the job of the industrial designer? According to one of them, P. Muller-Munk, laymen tend to think of industrial design only in relation to consumer goods: "They are ready to recognize that design is a necessary part of implements, ballpoint pens, chinaware, and all other paraphernalia in our department stores and specialty shops" (14, p. 97). But they seem to have a hard time recognizing that, in addition, design must be regarded as a significant quality factor in machines, technical instruments, and other equipment. This is to be expected as long as form is thought of exclusively as a matter of pleasant proportions and harmonious relations. There would seem to be little need for such luxury in the workshop and factory. But here as anywhere else, form is no luxury. Given the nature of their products, industrial designers are bound to realize that it is their task to explain the nature of the object by its appearance, that is, to create a pattern of visual forces correspondent to the physical pattern that is characteristic for the functioning of the object. Thus, Ralph Caplan demands that the designer "interpret technology to the layman by fashioning products that are intelligible," (29, p. 39) and Muller-Munk observes that "the working process of an automatic mail-sorting machine must be clearly comprehensible and manifest to the average buyer and even more so to the personnel that will use it. The arrangement of the connecting parts, the sequence of movements, the physical attitude of the operators, not to mention the choice of colors and the placement and shape of control instruments, all these elements concern the designer just as much as they do the engineer" (14). Perceptual equivalents must be invented by the designer for all significant physical characteristics and relations; and beauty turns out to be an essential attribute of good industrial design because the order and clarity brought about by harmony of shape and good proportion are necessary to make the pattern readable. Beauty is a means of clarifying expression.[3]

Function as subject matter. Function, it will now be seen, plays the same part in the aesthetics of the useful object as subject matter does in painting and sculpture. The physical function is no more and no less foreign to the building or the vase as an aesthetic object than is the physical body of a person portrayed in a painting or statue. Function, far from being outside the aesthetic realm, is the very theme, the central subject matter of all applied art. And just as our knowledge of the physical and mental nature of human beings amplifies and modifies the human image presented by the painting or statue, so our knowledge of the physical functioning of a useful object amplifies and modifies the pattern of perceptual forces offered by its appearance.

FIGURE 18

The parallel between representational and applied art may be illustrated by the following simple example. Figure 18 shows the outline of a wooden clothespin. As little girls have long discovered, it can also be seen as a human figure. Therefore it can illustrate the similarity and differences of the two kinds of representation. The shapes constituting the visual object have an intrinsic expression of their own. The symmetry, the narrow vertical, the round head, the swelling of the "trunk," the outward swing of the "legs" characterize a definite dynamics of behavior, regardless of any reference to what they may represent. This expression

[3] It stands to reason that a perceptually meaningful surface cannot simply be applied to a finished construction. A significant order of appearance tends to presuppose a corresponding order of the actual mechanism. Hence the demand of designers to be called to collaborate with the technicians from the very beginning.

is differently modified by the two referents. When the object is seen as a pin, the head is a firm knob, to be gripped; it is a subordinate base for the central function of clasping, located in the legs. When the object is seen as a human figure, the head becomes dominant and the legs act as a base. The spatial orientation is upright. Instead of the passive virtue of being graspable, the head now expresses the compactness of a generator radiating energy. The legs, no longer tense with the contradiction between their outward swing and their potential task of compressing a piece of laundry, serve as a leisurely pedestal to the elevated head and trunk: the interstice is now empty and neutral space rather than the very focus of the squeeze. Evidently, to maintain that the awareness of the object's function is irrelevant to the perception of its shape would be as erroneous for the clothespin as it would be to state for the human figure that "the subject matter does not count." It is also worth mentioning that, when architecture, pottery, etc. are recognized as representational arts, they can no longer be described as "abstract art" as they often are or cited for the purpose of demonstrating that pure abstraction is feasible and indeed familiar to all civilizations.[4]

It is time to return to the notion of "expression." Function, we now formulate, enters the aesthetic realm by means of the expressive pattern of shape, color, movement, etc. into which it is translated. Expression is based on the constellations of forces to be found in all percepts. To see the expression of an object means to see the general dynamic characteristics inherent in its particular appearance. In a functional-looking object, we may see the dynamics of pouring, soaring, containing, receiving, etc. We also see such "character traits" as flexibility, sturdiness, gracefulness, strength, etc., which, just as in a representational work of fine art, are intimately and totally related to the theme: the gracefulness of the spout consists in the graceful pouring it displays visually; the sturdiness of the Doric column consists in its supporting the roof sturdily. Expressive properties are adverbial, not adjectival. They apply to the behavior of things, not to the things themselves.

[4] What has been said about function and its visual counterpart holds also for *structure*, that is, for the nature of the materials and building procedures employed. Just as the forces embodied in function, those embodied in material and construction can be reflected in corresponding expressive patterns of appearance. The knowledge that the object is made of steel or of a soft or light-weight substance or that it is under strong centrifugal pressure or made of a wooden framework fitted together without nails—this knowledge can serve as "subject matter," just as the awareness of function can.

Three properties qualify expression for aesthetic tasks: (a) the generality of the dynamic features perceived in the particular pattern; (b) the capacity of these features to translate spiritual as well as physical behavior into visual dynamics; (c) the fact that visual dynamics is not only received as perceptual information but arouses in the mind the impact, the "experience" of the forces involved. The generality of the expressive features is characteristic of all perception. The extent to which they carry spiritual overtones or stand for spiritual themes varies with the nature of the object and the culture that produces it. Our own technological civilization tends to reduce most implements, including buildings, to their physical function. In this respect there is little difference between our table silver and our surgical instruments. But the notion of the purely practical tool is as much a product of cultural decay as is that of the purposeless work of art for art's sake. Other civilizations have not been impoverished by such a secularization of their tools. They preserve in their activities the ritual aspects of sacrifice, purification, incorporation, aggression, protection, etc., and the implements used in these activities possess the corresponding spiritual overtones. A door is, in many of our modern buildings, nothing better than the hole that will let you in or out. This can be said even of the doors of some modern churches. A true door, however, may embody the architectural gesture of inviting entrance. It translates its physical function into the perceptual expression of openness for reception, and, in a medieval church, is fashioned in such a way that the gesture conveys the experience of spiritual initiation. Thus, the Abbot Suger wrote on the golden portal of St. Denis: "Bright is the noble work; but, being nobly bright, the work should brighten the minds so that they may travel, through the true lights, to the True Light where Christ is the true door. In what manner it be inherent in this world the golden door defines: The dull mind rises to truth, through that which is material, and, in seeing this light, is resurrected from its former submersion" (20, p. 130). In such examples, "function" reveals its true meaning.

Our reminder that applied art is representational art might help to break down the artificial barrier between designers and craftsmen on the one side and painters and sculptors on the other. It is true that the expressive images of physical functions in a building or a water jug may depict simpler states of existence than does a painted scene of human figures. But such a lack of sophistication is compensated by the elementary power of presenting basic forces—a power necessarily diluted by the complexity of human behavior. Just as in music the intricate pattern of a melody may need the simpler substructure of the bass, so does the sacred image on the altar need the simpler sweep of the architectural environment. In daily life, a continuous range of expressive tools, from the knife that cuts the bread to the statue that portrays the thinker, should reflect and shape human existence. This remains a mere desideratum, however, as long as we have to contend with what I called the secularization of the tool, that is, its reduction to purely physical function.

The situation has frustrated craftsmen who are artists and therefore aspire to the status of art for their work. In the past, it was possible to make up for the crippled range of function by the application of pictorial and sculptural elements. But since, for the time being, neither saltcellar nor bed nor lamp base can be draped with ornamental figures, craftsmen have turned for a similar expedient to abstract art. Thus, ceramists will make their pots into abstract sculpture, and, in a recent exhibition of "Woven Forms," a piece of fabric, shaped like a suit of long underpants, but equipped, unanatomically, with a pair of breasts plus a female opening on top of them, was strung up on a line as though for drying. In ceramics, sculptural forms emancipating themselves from the theme represented by the function of the object tend to establish a second theme, incompatible with the first. Thereby, the object is removed to a no man's land, in which references to the one theme discount those to the other, and the result is an unreadable hybrid. In weaving, the dilemma is aggravated by the attempt to obtain sculptural volume from an unsuitable medium.

In architecture, steel and cement have made available for buildings the entire variety of shapes thus far reserved for small objects. At the same time, abstract sculpture has met architecture halfway. We see, on the one hand, buildings so thoroughly devoted to an independent abstract or even representational theme that we are driven to read them as large pieces of sculpture while, on the other hand, sculptors have created environments to be walked through, but not lived in, by the beholder. Here again, confusion can be avoided only by a firm commitment to either a functional or a nonfunctional theme. Thus, the aesthetic evaluation of Jorn Utzon's design for an opera house on a promontory in the harbor of Sydney cannot simply depend on whether it creates a well-proportioned and expressive piece of giant sculpture nor whether its tilted sail shapes go well with its maritime setting (17, p. 3). What counts is, first of all, whether we can perceive these shapes as an expressive pattern congenial to the function of uniting an audience for a performance—as we can when looking at the circular funnel of the amphitheater in the hills of Epidaurus. But more is needed.

Instead of camouflaging a building by a shell of sculpture, the endeavor of an architect and his clients must indeed start with a commitment to the purpose of the building—but not just as a useful object, nor just as an object whose usefulness deserves to be shown, but as an object whose function translated into a corresponding pattern of visible behavior will enhance the spirit of our existence and conduct as human beings. Whether we can hope to reintroduce this commitment to all of our implement-making without first re-establishing meaning in our practical life remains an open question.

REFERENCES

1. Alberti, Leon Battista. Architecture, preface and book 6. In E. G. Holt, *Literary Sources of Art History*. Princeton, N.J.: Princeton Univ. Press, 1947.
2. Arnheim, Rudolf. "The form we seek." This volume, pp. 353–362.
3. Burchard, John E. Symbolism in architecture—the decline of the monumental. In L. Bryson (ed.), *Symbols and Society*. New York, 1955, chap. 12.
4. Frieling, Heinrich, and Auer, Xavier. *Mensch, Farbe, Raum*. Munich: Callwey, 1956.
5. Greenough, Horatio. *Form and Function*. Berkeley and Los Angeles: Univ. of Calif. Press, 1947.
6. Gropius, Walter. *The New Architecture and the Bauhaus*. New York: Museum of Modern Art, 1937.
7. ———. *Scope of Total Architecture*. New York: Harper, 1943.
8. Gutheim, F. (ed.). *Frank Lloyd Wright on Architecture*. New York: Duell, 1941.
9. Hegel, Georg W. F. *Aesthetik*, part 3, section 1: Die Architektur.
10. Köhler, Wolfgang. *Gestalt Psychology*. New York: Liveright, 1947.
11. Loos, Adolf. *Gesammelte Schriften*. Munich: Herold, 1961.
12. Maslow, Abraham H. The expressive component of behavior. *Psychological Review*, 1949, 56, 261–272.
13. ———. *Motivation and Personality*. New York: Harper, 1954, chap. 11.
14. Muller-Munk, Peter. Die Beziehung der Formgebung (industrial design) zum modernen Marketing-Konzept. In Karl Otto (ed.), *Industrielle Formgebung in den USA*. Berlin, 1963.
15. Mumford, Lewis. The case against "modern" architecture. *Architectural Record*, 1962, April.
16. Mumford, Lewis (ed.). *Roots of Contemporary American Architecture*. N.Y.: Grove Press, 1952.

17. Museum of Modern Art Bulletin, XXVI, #2: *Architecture and imagery: four new buildings*. N.Y., 1959.

18. Neutra, Richard. *Survival through Design*. N.Y.: Oxford Univ. Press, 1954.

19. Palladio, Andrea. Four books of architecture, book 4, chapter 2. In E. G. Holt, *Literary Sources of Art History*. Princeton, N.J.: Princeton Univ. Press, 1947.

20. Panofsky, Erwin. *Meaning in the Visual Arts*. Garden City: Doubleday, 1955.

21. Risom, Jens. The purpose of his product. *The Craftsman's World*. 1959.

22. Schopenhauer, Arthur. *Die Welt als Wille und Vorstellung*.

23. Scott, Geoffrey. *The Architecture of Humanism*. Garden City: Doubleday, 1954.

24. *Staatliches Bauhaus Weimar 1919–1923*. Weimar-Munich, n.d.

25. Sullivan, Louis H. *Kindergarten Chats*. N.Y.: Wittenborn, 1947.

26. Valentine, C. W. *The Experimental Psychology of Beauty*. London: Methuen, 1962.

27. Veronesi, Giulia. Una struttura di Pier Luigi Nervi a Parigi. *Zodiac*, I, Milan, n.d.

28. Vitruvius. *The ten books on architecture*, book 1, chap. 1.

29. Zagorski, Edward J. (ed.) *Addresses delivered at the annual meeting of the Industrial Design Education Association*. University of Illinois, 1962.

30. Zucker, Paul. The paradox of architectural theories. *Journal of the Society of Architectural Historians*, 1951, 10, 8–14.

IV. Symbols

ARTISTIC SYMBOLS—
FREUDIAN AND OTHERWISE

The interpretation of art is little more than a suburban area in the vast development of psychoanalysis, and as such has not benefited much from the radical revisions that have brought the theory and practice of Freudian principles into closer contact with reality and with the findings of other psychologists. In the aesthetic suburb, a few specialized devotees, psychiatrists and art theorists, use the orthodox doctrine for the processing of works of painting, sculpture, and literature. Every year, we are presented with still another interpretation of Oedipus and Hamlet. These analyses are obediently swallowed or ignored or laughed off by the rest of the population with very few attempts at constructive discussion. The following sketchy remarks are designed to show the need for such discussion.

Let us assume that someone spoke as follows:

The psychosexual treatment of artistic symbols has prevented us from doing justice to a more adequate method of analysis, which may be termed the psychoculinary approach. This theory asserts, briefly, that artistic symbols must be explained by the artist's preoccupation with food. The precarious economic conditions under which most artists are forced to live are clearly

First published in the *Journal of Aesthetics and Art Criticism*, 1953, 12, 93–97.

expressed in the preference for still lifes found throughout the ages. Vegetarian trends are manifest in landscape painting, while a hunger for proteins is revealed in the frequent representation of animals and the naked human body. The fundamental theme of the concave receptacle, pot, cup, or soup plate, and the actively intruding knife, fork, or spoon is constantly symbolized in the visual arts, notably in architecture with its cubic or cylindrical containers inhabited by the clearly spoon-shaped figures of human beings. Rembrandt's liking for such foods as baked beans and golden mustard is not established by documentary evidence but proved beyond reasonable doubt by conjecture.[1]

Why would such a presentation be considered patently ludicrous by everybody while the identical procedure used by some psychoanalysts is not? In his bewildering treatise, *Der Mensch als Symbol*, Georg Groddeck asserts, for instance, that the attitudes of the figures in Rembrandt's "Anatomy of Dr. Tulp," read from the back of the picture to the front, and those in the marble group of the Laocoön, read from the right to the left, are representations of the male genital in the stages of excitation and slackening. Frederick S. Wight in an article published in 1947 explained the holes in Henry Moore's figures as manifestations of infantile cannibalism (4), and Lionel Goitein in his book on *Art and the Unconscious*, in which he describes Rodin's "Thinker" as "the metaphysician on his privy seat," admonishes his readers: "Not what you see in but what you see into the picture is its importance." (3) These are extreme but not unfairly chosen examples.

The reaction of the average analyst to the kind of resistance implied in my remarks is well known. He will say that my objections contain nothing a good psychoanalysis will not cure. If, in the face of such intimation, we make bold to examine the facts, we notice first of all that the Freudian theory of artistic symbols leaves us with an anticlimactic let-down. Even in cases in which the interpretation does not seem purely arbitrary but is based on some evidence, we feel stopped halfway on the road to the inner sanctum of artistic meaning when someone asserts that the work is only about the desire for a mate, a longing to return to the womb, or a fear of castration. The gain obtained by the beholder from such a communication seems negligible, and one wonders

---

[1] No priority for the "psychoculinary approach" can be claimed here. In the first chapter of his *Varieties of Religious Experience*, William James asserts that "few conceptions are less instructive than this re-interpretation of religion as perverted sexuality" and asked "why not equally call religion an aberration of the digestive function."

why art has been deemed indispensable in every known culture and why it is supposed to offer the deepest insight into life and nature.

Our feeling of disappointment can be accounted for with some precision if the Freudian symbols are examined in the light of traditional logic. In the ancient tree-model of the logician—the tree of Porphyry—a vertical scale leads along the trunk from the most particular sense experiences to the highest universals, while the horizontal branches represent the various levels of abstractness or concreteness. The relation between a symbol and its referent can lie either on the vertical or on a horizontal axis. In the first case, symbol and referent belong to different levels of abstractness and are related to each other as species to genus. For instance, a house may be conceived as a symbol of shelter. In the second case, both are at the same level.

Freudian symbols are of the second kind. Consider the relation between a piece of pottery and the maternal womb. Both are concrete objects, or species of such objects. They both belong to the genus of containers and are distinguished by their differentiae, one of the objects being made of clay, the other, of flesh and blood. Their logical positions are homologous and reversible. But this is not the way the psychoanalyst envisages them. To him, the vase symbolizes the womb. The association based on the common property of the genus "containers" becomes one-sided. Vases, boxes, pockets, caves, rooms, instead of sharing with wombs the property of being containers, are subordinated to one of their kind: they all are wombs.

Logically, this conception has three consequences. It suppresses the homology of position and makes the relation irreversible. It confines the relationship to a horizontal level, thus neglecting the fact that both symbol and referent can be and are perceived as species of a higher genus. It ignores a necessary connection in favor of a merely possible one, for whereas the property of being a container necessarily belongs to any species of the genus, vases or pockets may or may not be associated with wombs. All this seriously limits the validity of the conception and distorts reality.

Analytical theory explains this distortion of reality by two facts. Sexual objects and functions are distinguished by being highly charged with affect. Also the thought of them is repressed into the unconscious. This view is lucidly formulated in Sandor Ferenczi's paper on *The Ontogenesis of Symbols*. He explains that mere analogies on the basis of similarity are not symbols in the psychoanalytic sense. Symbols are formed only when one member of the equation is repressed. Clearly, the vertical dimension of symbolism, that is, the vista of the universals, does not enter his thinking at all.

The orthodox psychoanalytic theory of art is founded on the axiom of the affective and genetic priority of sex. Thus Freud tells us: "I have no doubt that the conception of the 'beautiful' is rooted in the soil of sexual stimulation and signified originally that which is sexually exciting" (2, p. 20). Now it has often been pointed out that this presupposition is hypothetical. At the early stages of mental functioning in man and animal, a fairly large amount of basic drives operate, such as hunger, thirst, self-preservation, maternal behavior, and the need to explore and understand the environment. The dominance of the sex drive over its peers is likely to be a product of special cultural conditions. It occurs when sexual activity is censored and restrained and when an erosion of values has destroyed the top layers of human concerns. But the decisive point to be made here is that if such a priority of sex distorted man's conception of reality in the way described by psychoanalysis, the validity of his artistic and scientific statements would be fatally impaired.

There are artists whose work seems to suggest a preoccupation with sex even when they are concerned with other matters. To cite a recent example, the works of the gifted painter, Max Beckmann, display a somewhat startling array of pointed hats and ears, pine trees, arrows, beaks, daggers, cigarettes, bottles, flutes, guitar necks, trumpets, towers, and so forth. It may be observed in passing that such indirect representation of sexual matters—if that is what we are dealing with in this case—is not necessarily due solely to an unconscious attempt to hide the "real," objectionable subject. In the human mind, different strivings are not completely insulated from each other, and therefore strong preoccupations may be expected to intrude into activities genuinely directed toward other aims.

Now, if the diagnosis is correct, we have found something that might interest the biographer and the student of human motivation. However, the discovery will be in no way sufficient to describe the creative process or to define the content of the work. At best we have discovered one feature, valid if fitted into the context of the whole, but misleading if presented alone. Not only the art theorist but also the psychologist would have to be dissatisfied with a *pars pro toto* procedure because both are concerned with exactly the same processes, and what is wrong for the art theorist is also wrong for the psychologist. Both will have to ask whether or not the sexual overtones suit the theme and plan of the work, whether they enrich it or deviate it into a blind alley. If they had to come to the conclusion that the ultimate aim of a given work were the representation of sexual matters, the art theorist would have to dismiss it as a failure and the psychologist would have to treat it as an atypical specimen. No genuine work of art can ever be limited to sex or love or food or religion or politics or any particular matter at all. It may, however, use any of these things as symbolic material, and their use must be judged by how well they suit the purpose.

If one studies the psychological processes that occur in artistic creation, one finds that no artist who deserves the name indulges in unlimited self-expression. On the contrary, he is most seriously concerned with eliminating, in the course of his work, all features due to accidental experience or preference, and this not in order to cover up objectionable wishes but because he is directed by the demands of his theme. He is most sensitive to the distinction between what belongs and what does not. Thus, some personal characteristics, such as those that constitute his particular style, are enhanced wherever they serve a fresh and pertinent realization of his idea, while the intrusion of subjectively attractive but objectively unsuitable elements is checked by artistic discipline.

In at least one respect, the psychoanalytic approach has done a service to the understanding of art. It has reminded modern man of the fact that in a work of art every element, whether it pertain to perceptual form or to subject matter, is symbolic, that is, represents something beyond its particular self. This fact had been obscured by a school of aesthetics that thought art's purpose was the imitation of nature and that therefore considered symbolic only those works whose manifest content could not be accepted at its face value, such as the story of the unicorn or Titian's "Heavenly and Mundane Love." On the other hand, psychoanalysis has confused the issue by asserting that symbols are an instrument for camouflaging the actual content of a statement. The history of art may contain instances of this kind. But it would take a peculiarly unsubtle and humorless psychology, for example, to assert that the delighted insistence of Renaissance artists upon the adventures of Leda, Danae, Europa, or Io is due to moral censorship. The disguises of Jove do not disguise the sexual appeal of these scenes. They enhance it.

Freud's conception of symbols derives, of course, from his interpretation of dreams. Carl Gustav Jung and other writers, such as Erich Fromm, have opposed his view and pointed out that symbols serve to reveal rather than to hide their referents. We are beginning to understand that during sleep man re-enters into fuller possession of a basic and most valuable capacity of the human mind, which consists in representing abstract states of affairs by striking images. It is this capacity, badly impaired during our waking hours by Western culture, on which the artist also relies. Far from hiding their referent, artistic symbols give tangible appearance to the ideas they represent. They revive and clarify the issues of human existence.

In this connection, attention should be given to the characteristic relationship between universals and particulars in the work of art. The scientist, taking his cues from the observation of particulars, must nevertheless depart further and further from the ground of concretely experienced things as he climbs the tree of Porphyry in quest of the universals. His most comprehensive statements are made, as it were, of the husks of experience. In the work of art, the generalities are not hidden when we contemplate the particulars; nor do we need to abandon the realm of concreteness in order to grasp abstractions. On the contrary, the most abstract affirmations of the artist are the ones most directly received by the eyes of the beholder. Such concepts as large and small, high and low, active and passive, near and far, enclosing and enclosed are immediately perceived as sensory properties whereas the more specific content of subject matter demands recourse to knowledge, learning, memory. The triangle that symbolizes the hierarchic conception inherent in much Renaissance art is directly seen by the eye; but it takes more than vision to recognize a woman, let alone a Madonna.

In conclusion, it is necessary to meet the following possible objection: "You have spoken of the disappointing let-down produced by what the psychoanalyst describes as the ultimate content of art. But what is so enlightening about the general ideas that, in your view, underlie artistic representation? The notions of large and small, high and low, active and passive—aren't they even triter than the Freudian striving for incest or fear of castration?" The objection would be well taken if the artistic statement were confined to a one-way road from the colorful particulars to the pale generalities. But, in the work of art, particulars and universals are simultaneously and immediately present. A given event acquires visual form by a compositional pattern that defines it as an example of a most general kind of event. Raphael's triangular composition not only makes the Madonna and her child visible but also interprets the scene as a situation symmetrically structured around a dominating climax. The indivisible unity of the general and the specific permits and indeed requires the spectator to see the various levels of meaning in constant interaction. These levels remedy each other's deficiencies by exchanging their virtues. The trite emptiness of the general is animated by the liveliness of the specific, and the trite irrelevance of the particular is elevated by the inherent generality of its form.

Thus, the work of art symbolizes all the levels of reality that lie between the phenomenon and the idea. It counteracts the impoverishment of vision that results when any one of these levels is viewed in isolation of the others, and encourages the synthesis of conception that is the mark of wisdom.

REFERENCES

1. Ferenczi, Sandor. *Sex in Psychoanalysis*. New York: Basic Books, 1950.
2. Freud, S. *Three Contributions to the Theory of Sex*. New York, 1930.
3. Goitein, Lionel. *Art and the Unconscious*. New York: United Book Guild, 1948.
4. Wight, Frederick S. Henry Moore: the reclining figure. *Journal of Aesthetics and Art Criticism*, 1947, 6, 95–104.

PERCEPTUAL ANALYSIS
OF A SYMBOL OF INTERACTION

Anthropological and psychiatric observations indicate that basic visual patterns, or kinds of pattern, appear with surprising uniformity in different cultures, different periods, different individuals. Attempts to explain these similarities by migration or other social contacts often fail to fit the facts. The evidence suggests that similar visual conceptions emerge independently from one another. How, then, are we to explain these correspondences?

Symbol and heredity. Carl Gustav Jung, in many of his writings, has suggested that such "motifs and formal elements" of "identical or analogous shape" be derived from what he calls primordial images, dominants, or archetypes. As the principal traits of these motifs, he mentions "chaotic complexity and order, duality, the opposition of light and darkness, above and below, right and left, the unification of opposites in the third, the quaternary (square, cross), the rotation (circle, sphere), and, finally, centricity and radial arrangements organized, as a rule, according to a quaternary system" (7, p. 126). Much of the time, Jung states clearly that he considers the unconscious dispositions

First published in *Confinia Psychiatrica*, 1960, 3, 193–216, and later, condensed and revised, under the title "Perceptual Analysis of a Cosmological Symbol," in the *Journal of Aesthetics and Art Criticism*, 1961, 19, 389–399.

for the production of particular types of shapes to be inherited. It is true that his descriptions of the biological mechanisms he has in mind are limited to curiously Lamarckian hints at "a sort of readiness" created by "deposits of repeated experiences of humanity," by "imprints," "engrams," "precipitates," "condensations," "recapitulations," "heaped-up, or pooled, experiences"; but he explicitly refers to heredity and is willing to count his archetypes among "such patterns of behavior" as "that constitutionally predetermined way in which the chick gets out of the egg, the birds build their nest . . ." (6, p. 54). Since inheritance occurs only through the body, Jung's theory amounts to saying that the germ plasm of every human being carries the mechanisms responsible for the spontaneous production of the visual shapes in question.

The theory has two characteristic implications. First, it assumes the existence of specific hereditary mechanisms geared to furnishing the organism with the pertinent archetypal disposition for, say, the production of centric "mandala" figures. Secondly, the theory need not assume that the organism producing archetypal figures be aware of their symbolic significance, any more than a bird knows why it is building a nest. Hereditary activities do not require understanding. In fact, the theory does not have to presuppose that there exists any inherent kinship—any isomorphism, as the Gestalt psychologists say—among the perceptual characteristics of the visual patterns and the symbolic meaning attributable to them.

Actually, however, Jung does believe that the archetypal patterns are intrinsically related to the meaning for which they stand. He realizes that the symbolic content is perceived directly within the image. Symbols, he says, are "pregnant with meaning," and "image and meaning are identical." Indeed, he might argue that the survival value of archetypes consists precisely in their giving directly perceivable expression to basic patterns of human existence. What he does not seem to realize is that once he admits the perceptual self-evidence of such symbolism there is no need to enlist the services of hypothetical hereditary mechanisms at all.

If every human being's unconscious or conscious mind is capable of spontaneously perceiving certain elementary shapes as images of significant life situations, no genetics is required to explain why these shapes turn up independently in many cases. And since the assumption of spontaneously perceivable symbolism agrees with psychological findings, scientific parsimony bids us to discard, as redundant, a theory based on inherited perceptual matrices.

Inherent expression. Among Jung's many formulations of the problem there are some that do not go well with his notion of inherited archetypes. He will speak paradoxically of "eternally inherited forms" (8, p. 518) or assert that "the archetype did not ever come into existence as a phenomenon of organic life, but entered into the picture with life itself" (8, p. 149). In such statements, he seems to realize intuitively that, as Wolfgang Köhler has put it, "a phenomenon in perception which is unlearned need not, for this reason, depend upon the existence of special histological factors" (9).

The present essay is based on the contention that similar elementary visual symbols appear independently at different times and places because (a) seeing involves perceiving the behavior of configurations of visual forces, and (b) such perceived configurations of forces are viewed spontaneously as images of the behavior of forces in significant life situations. For example, the daily course of the sun is viewed as a symbol of human life because the perceptual aspects of rising, increasing, reaching a climax, and descending are spontaneously perceived as being structurally similar (isomorphic) to the dynamics of birth, growth, mature power, and decline.

Such "identity of image and meaning" may be evident to any intuitive or artistic person but is far from obvious to scholars accustomed to believe that percepts are associated with their meanings by mere convention or past experience. Gestalt psychologists have shown to what large extent the given structure of a "senseless" figure determines the way it is perceived; also, they have pointed informally at the intrinsic similarity of, say, facial expression and the corresponding state of mind. But no concrete analysis of any but the most elementary visual properties (that is, upward and downward, angular and curved) has been presented to demonstrate the correspondences of expressive shape and significant life situations.

A Taoistic symbol. In order to provide such a demonstration, I shall apply the tools of perceptual analysis to the *T'ai-chi tu*, a well-known ancient emblem symbolizing the yin-and-yang principle in Chinese philosophy (Figure 19). The word *T'ai-chi tu* means "the great map of the poles." The visual design and the essence of the thoughts for which the figure stands are simple enough to make a concrete and fairly complete analysis possible; they are, on the other hand, sufficiently rich and subtle to be acceptable as an example of the kind of symbolism psychiatrists, anthropologists, and philosophers are concerned with.

The elements of Taoistic cosmology are familiar to the Western reader. Unceasing change is said to be the character of Nature. The movement of all existence makes for the eternal Return of the Same, which is understood as periodic repetition and, more fundamentally, as the immutable constancy provided by the regularity and evenness of change. This notion of a stationary flux is enlivened by the polarity of the yin and yang, two antagonistic, balanced principles, whose interaction constitutes the duality within the unity, the indivisible, supreme One. The yang is the male principle; it stands for light, warmth, and

FIGURE 19

dryness. The yin is female and represents darkness, cold, moisture. By being opposites, the two principles generate the phenomena of Nature. They are not separate from each other nor do they simply add up to the whole. They represent the constant interaction of everything with everything within the One. When there is harmony, the Way (Tao) of Nature pervades all existence. But harmony is not given automatically. Conduct requires active initiative, which may be in keeping with the Way of Nature or violate it.[1]

[1] I shall use the term "Taoistic philosophy" to designate the actually more complex product of a confluence of Taoism, the Yin-Yang School, certain ele-

Models of interaction. A pictorial representation of the notion of interaction cannot but attract us since the problem of doing justice to this concept is crucial for the science of our time. The notion of interaction appears early in intuitive (perceptual) thinking. In a painting, for example, the interdependence of all parts is evident. Intellectual reasoning, however, comes to face the problem late since reason proceeds by establishing linear connections among elements and recognizes the limitations of this procedure only at an advanced stage of refinement. Even so, all through the history of Western thought, the intuitive recognition of the manner in which true interaction operates in Gestalt contexts has cast disturbing shadows upon the safe rationality of the traditional method, and in our time the attempts to account for interaction with the tools of conceptual theory have increased. Before describing the visual presentation of the phenomenon in the *T'ai-chi tu,* I shall enumerate a few of these conceptual models of interaction under four headings.

1. *Mutual bombardment.* The simplest concept of interaction envisages partners possessing a stable, independent identity. Antagonistic partners, such as darkness and light or good and evil, face each other starkly in static independence. At a more advanced stage of theorizing, the partners afflict each other, but without changing substantially in the process. Interaction is conceived as the superposition of oppositely directed, one-sided actions exchanged among independent partners. ("The earth attracts the moon, *and* the moon attracts the earth"; "the teacher influences the student, but the student *also* influences the teacher.") This model leads eventually to the insoluble puzzle of how to establish, as a point of departure, the identity of any one of the components since the influences caused by the other components must be taken into account from the beginning.[2]

In this most primitive conception of interaction, stable entities merely "do things to each other." They are not in a context determining their very nature. Figure 20, a static forerunner of the *T'ai-chi tu,* may

ments of Confucianism, etc. In order not to burden this paper with citations of Chinese philosophy, I refer the reader to Fung Yu-lan's comprehensive work and the bibliography given therein (4).

[2] John Dewey and Arthur Bentley use the word "interraction" to designate what I call "mutual bombardment": "interaction is inquiry of a type into which events enter under the presumption that they have been adequately described prior to the formulation of inquiry into their connections" (3, p. 122). Their term "transaction" seems to express mainly their concern that the relation of sender and receiver should not be treated as the sum of two separate contributions. The question I am raising is whether the "common system," for which Dewey and Bentley rightly plead, is accessible to exact discursive description.

serve as a pictorial illustration. The two components are fitted into a circle, but whatever mutual influence they display does not interfere with their static, independent completeness. In a more differentiated version, this pattern appears as an image of the yin and yang in the so-called "Diagram of the Supreme Ultimate" drawn by Chou Tun-yi in the eleventh century A.D. (Figure 21). Here the rigidly dividing vertical is preserved, except for the small central disk suggesting oneness by the static device of a piece of common property. Exchange of property is used as a visual demonstration of interdependence and interaction. The multiplication of the circle makes each half contain both whiteness and darkness, with a predominance of white on the left side (yang) and

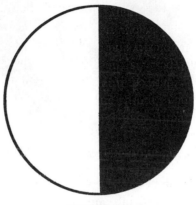

FIGURE 20

darkness on the right (yin). Also the rings of Figure 21 emphasize the unification of the white and the black principles in a common circular shape more efficiently than does the disk of Figure 20, because in a narrow ring the short dividing vertical is much weaker than the unifying double circle of the contour. Thus, the figure hints at the rotation of light and darkness in alternation. Even so, each partner remains essentially confined to its own half of the disk.[3]

[3] Figure 21 has further noteworthy perceptual properties resulting from the ambiguity of the figure-ground situation. For instance, the pattern can be seen as a disk consisting of two unbroken halves (Figure 20), above which are suspended the small central white disk and a ring, white on the yin-side and dark on the yang-side. There is, in other words, an oscillation between the view of two all-embracing principles (unbroken halves) underlying all individualization and that of the particular entities (rings), each of which is shown to be constituted of the same two principles. The interaction of whole and parts is thereby symbolized perceptually.

Other dualistic conceptions belonging under this heading are those in which the conflict between two adversaries is shown to be resolved by reconciliation, unification, or integration. Here, "mutual bombardment" results finally in the abandonment or overcoming of the antagonism. Compare Jung's borrowing of the Renaissance concept *coincidentia oppositorum* (Cusanus, Bruno); the dialectic principle, as used by Hegel and Marx, also offers a pertinent example.

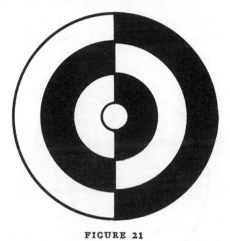

FIGURE 21

2. *Circularity.* In the conceptual model discussed above, the components of the whole are firmly and independently entrenched, like shore batteries firing at each other across the water. This simplification of what happens in true interaction can be avoided, but only at the price of other simplifications. The relationships among the components can be described as a temporal linear sequence of one-sided effects. In our time, the feed-back principle of the physicists has made circularity fashionable among social scientists. Actually, as a device of accounting for interaction conceptually, it is among the most ancient. To use first a modern example, the principle of circularity would describe the interpersonal relations of psychiatrist and patient as follows: Psychiatrist (PS) modifies patient (PA); modified patient (PA′) modifies psychiatrist (PS); modified psychiatrist (PS′) modifies modified patient (PA′); twice-modified patient (PA″) modifies . . . , and so forth in an endless spiral. At any point, any component is but a transitional stage of an ongoing process.

The principle is adequate when the event to be accounted for is in fact a linear temporal sequence, as, for example, in the case of an experimentally created "whisper campaign" carrying a rumor from mouth to mouth or, to use an example from the Taoistic literature, when the yin-yang principle is described as manifesting itself in the circular succession of the seasons. The yang arises between winter and spring, attains its full power in summer, and wanes between summer and autumn, at which time the yin arises to reach its climax in winter and to decline between winter and spring while the yang rises again. Circularity, however, becomes a clumsy expedient when it reduces to a linear relationship the

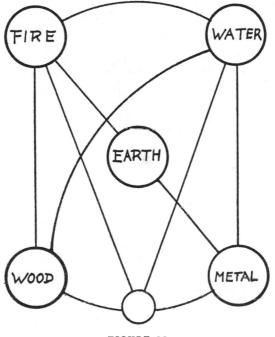

FIGURE 22

interaction of the five elements, which are all differentiations of the yin and yang: Earth is overcome by wood, wood by metal, metal by fire, fire by water, water by earth, etc. The device is equally crude when it is used in our day to describe psychological or physiological processes in which all components interact with each other simultaneously rather than merely acting upon their neighbors in the succession of a linear order.

3. *Network.* Interaction can also be approximated conceptually by a network of one-to-one relations between units or groups of units. Such a network can be illustrated by another section of the already cited "Diagram of the Supreme Ultimate" (Figure 22), depicting the system of

the five elements. The identical principle is applied, for example, in our modern "sociograms," which purport to describe and measure the social structure of a group by determining the relations between any two members separately. Needless to say, the sum of individual influences does not represent the dynamics of the group any more than do the relations between the five elements add up to the physical interaction constituting the Universe. (When I speak of "the interaction of everything with everything," I am using network language, *faute de mieux*.)

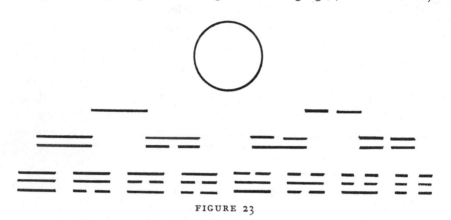

FIGURE 23

Hierarchic differentiation. The interaction between the whole and the parts can be represented by the model of a hierarchic pyramid. For instance, when Gestalt psychologists say that the structure of the whole determines the place and functions of the parts and is, in turn, determined by the parts, they present "the whole" as an additional entity, different from the parts but related to them.[4] A two-way stream of structural influences is conceived of as flowing from the top toward the base and from the base toward the top.[5] In Chinese philosophy, the doctrine of the eight trigrams (*Pa kua*), expounded in the *I Ching* or *Book of Changes,* uses a similar method for a similar purpose (5). Figure 23 shows the Supreme One at the top of the pyramid, or at the root of a genealogical tree. The One differentiates itself into the two principles of

---

[4] In the case of Gestalt psychology, as in some of the other theories discussed, it is necessary to distinguish between the notion of interaction intuitively envisaged and the conceptual models actually presented. The intuitively formed image is indispensable as a beacon, but in order to evaluate the scientific accomplishment of a theory, we must examine the appropriateness of its actual constructs.

[5] Other modern examples of such hypothetical pyramid-tops are the *Zeitgeist,* the "cultural climate," the "group atmosphere," etc.

the yang (one long stick) and the yin (two short sticks), the yang, as usual, representing the male, the yin the female. These two, in turn, combine on the next hierarchic level to four more differentiated forms of offspring, one of which is all male, one all female, while the other two are half male and half female. Another step toward differentiation, and we have the eight trigrams, with masculinity and femininity variously apportioned by thirds. Here again, in order to conceptualize the interaction of whole and parts, the whole is presented as a separate entity, from which the parts spring like children at each level.

The static device of describing each derivate as being made up of the two basic principles is employed in the *Book of Changes* to suggest that the parts are generated and pervaded by the whole, and that, in turn, they constitute the whole. In true interaction, however, the whole is not an entity existing separately from, and prior to, the parts, nor do the parts exist separately from, and prior to, the whole. The two families of vectors, reaching from the whole downward and from the parts upward, are artificially isolated linear relations among separate, static entities.

A perceptual model. None of the conceptual models here examined does justice to interaction. They all fail, not because of individual defects but because the task of describing interaction discursively is insoluble in principle. Conceptual theory can predict the outcome of interaction but it cannot adequately describe the process itself since by its very nature it can account only for linear connections among entities. All language is subject to the same limitation, even that of the poet. When, in Goethe's *Faust*, Mephistopheles exposes the dry enumerations of logic by confronting them with the complexity of genuine thought, he can do no better than use the simile of the weaver:

> Zwar ist's mit der Gedankenfabrik
> Wie mit einem Webermeisterstück,
> Wo *ein* Tritt tausend Fäden regt,
> Die Schifflein herüber, hinüber schiessen,
> Die Fäden ungesehen fliessen,
> *Ein* Schlag tausend Verbindungen schlägt.

But even a web, after all, is only an agglomeration of linear cross-connections.[6]

---

[6] The metaphor of the loom is also used in a similar statement by the "Erdgeist" in the first scene of *Faust*.

Perception accomplishes the feat the intellect fails to describe; for perception *is* interaction. The stimuli received by the brain derive from the isolated pieces of colored matter or sound that constitute paintings or music as physical objects. But, in the brain field, these stimuli arouse patterns of forces that act as components of integrated whole-processes. The resulting field-processes consist of the impact exerted by everything upon everything, and the perceived picture or music is the result of this infinite and incalculable interaction.

However, to achieve interaction is not the same as to demonstrate the nature of the process. Mostly, interaction has already occurred below the threshold of consciousness and everything is "settled" when the percept arises. In order to demonstrate interaction to the senses, it is necessary to look for formative processes occurring while the perceiving is going on, processes, that is, of which the perceiver is aware. If the *T'ai-chi tu* purports to symbolize interaction, it must make use of such processes. What are they, and are they successful?

FIGURE 24

Definition of the test-object. Before analyzing the test-object, we must define what we wish to analyze. What *is* the *T'ai-chi tu?* To this question there are two answers. One is historical. It would be desirable to know the exact shape, spatial orientation, and colors of the object as it appeared in the oriental tradition. The sources I have been able to consult indicate some variety in these respects. However, the shape used in this paper is based on a traditional geometrical construction, and the vertical axis in the spatial orientation I have chosen approaches in many historical examples the position of the yang (*Ch'ien* = heaven = three unbroken lines) and the yin (*Kwun* = earth = three broken lines) symbols when the *T'ai-chi tu* is combined with the trigrams of the *Book of Changes* (for instance, in the arrangement used for the Korean flag, Figure 24). The *T'ai-chi tu* seems to have been established as an image of the yin-yang principle during the Sung dynasty and is likely to be a derivate of the ancient spiral, whorl-circle, and swastika patterns. It appears as a good luck charm on Chinese homes, shops, and schools as well as in jewelry and as a religious symbol on tombs and temples. In 1882, it was adopted as the design of the Korean flag.

The second answer to the question: What is the *T'ai-chi tu?* is psychological. We can investigate the possible variations of the figure and find out what shapes, spatial orientations, colors, etc. produce what perceptual effects, and which of these effects best fit the philosophical doctrine to be symbolized.

After some experimentation I decided to settle for the pattern most easily constructed geometrically. By inscribing in a circle two smaller circles of half of the diameter of the first (Figure 25), one obtains an in-

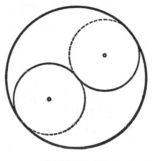

FIGURE 25

ternal S-curve made up of two half-circles. This shape has certain disadvantages. Circular curves are hard and inflexible, which interferes with the dynamics of the patterns that use them.[7] Also, being of constant curvature, they form no apex as, for instance, a parabola would. These possible drawbacks, however, are compensated by the fact that the circular internal shapes reflect the circularity of the total pattern and thereby contribute to the intimate relation of whole and parts, essential to the symbolical meaning of the figure. Furthermore, geometrical simplicity of the stimulus makes for simplicity and clarity of perceptual effect. A geometrically simple stimulus can be assumed to set up a simpler configuration of neural vectors, and it is these neural vectors that

[7] Here, and frequently in the following, I cite perceptual principles without proof or further interpretation. When no other literature is given, the reader is referred to my book on art and visual perception (1) and the bibliography it contains.

create the "expression" of the perceived pattern. Given the purpose of the emblem, its expression should be simple, strong, and clear.

The expression of the *T'ai-chi tu* is influenced by its orientation in space, as will be shown later. The brighter of the two components is placed on top. This is correct historically since the yang stands for the light and the south, and on the ancient Chinese maps the light-giving south appears on top, not at the bottom.[8] The position is also preferable psychologically because, in a figure-ground situation of this kind, the brighter component tends to advance and become figure, and the one placed at the bottom tends to do the same. By holding the lower position, the darker component profits from the prominence of being at the bottom, thus compensating for the prominence of the other's brightness. In this way a desirable equilibrium among the two partners is created. By appearing on top, the brighter component indicates the superiority of the yang without disturbing the balance of the two, which is as essential to the Taoistic doctrine as it is to the perceptual effect.[9]

Expression of the shapes. The choice of the circular shape for a pattern intended to depict the universe is not accidental. The circle (or sphere), the only figure that does not single out any particular direction, is used spontaneously everywhere to depict objects whose shape is uncertain or irrelevant, or to depict something that either has no shape at all, any shape, or all shapes.

As a visual object, such a figure carries two different kinds of expression. (*a*) Seen as a circle, that is, as a one-dimensional figure, it is a line of constant curvature, the track for an endless rotation. In that case it is related to spiral shapes and eddies and well suited to symbolize the oriental conception of time as a constant cyclic Return of the Same (rather than a straight-line progression originating in the past and moving toward an infinitely distant goal in the future). (*b*) Seen as a two-dimensional disk, the figure is a centrically symmetrical area spreading from a center evenly in all directions and hemmed in everywhere, at the same distance from the center, by the barrier of the contour. The barrier generates a family of constrictive vectors moving from the outside toward the center and counteracting the expansive vectors that emanate

---

[8] Traditionally, the top part of the figure is often painted red since red is the yang-color of the south, represented by the firebird. The Korean flag uses this arrangement of colors.

[9] For its proper effect, the *T'ai-chi tu* requires a neutral background, which does not share the color, texture, etc. of either component.

radially from the center (Figure 26). A circular boundary is always under tension like the skin of a balloon, pressed centrifugally from the inside and generating centripetal counterpressure by its resistance to expansion. The symbolic significance of such perceptual dynamics, concerned with activities directed toward, and away from, a center, will occupy us later. I will mention here only that the one-dimensional rotational movement of the circle often symbolizes time, whereas the two-dimensional radial dynamics of the disk denotes spatial relationships, either actual or figurative.

FIGURE 26

Just like the circular boundary, the internal S-curve of the *T'ai-chi Tu* can be perceived either as a line-shaped body or as a contour. If the entire surface of the disk were evenly colored, the internal curve could be easily seen as a serpentine object lying on a disk; thereby the expres-

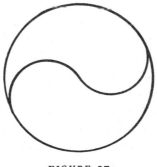

FIGURE 27

sion of the pattern would be changed completely (Figure 27). The different coloring of the two areas transforms the line into a boundary, and the disk splits up into two objects of identical tear-drop shape. In order to have a neutral term, I shall call these tear-drop shapes by their Japanese name, *magatama*. (A *magatama* [Figure 28] is a comma-shaped bead, *maga* meaning "curved" or "bent," *tama* meaning a precious stone or gem. *Magatamas* made of jade or other material and pierced in the center of the circular head are traditional pendants.)

Whenever a pattern is composed of parts, the perceptual effect will depend on how strong the unifying power of the whole is in relation to the self-containedness of the parts. If the whole is simple and well organized and the parts are not, the pattern will appear as a somewhat subdivided whole. In the inverse case, it will be seen as an agglomeration of self-contained units fitting in some sort of whole. In a Taoistic symbol, neither the whole nor the parts must be dominant because the Supreme One is to be understood as identical with the yin and yang

FIGURE 28

composing it, not as superior or inferior to these two principles. In fact, the *T'ai-chi tu* creates such perceptual ambiguity perfectly. Being a circle, that is, an indivisible shape, the outer boundary is as strongly coherent as any contour can be. The two halves, instead of being harshly separated by a diametrical vertical as they are in Figure 20, slip smoothly into each other, thereby reducing the break to a minimum. On the other hand, the *magatamas* maintain their autonomy by being simply shaped and strongly unified. Each of them profits from the isolating power of a semicircular "head." Also, the *magatama* is perceived as a deformation of the simpler symmetrical tear-drop shape (Figure 29). Such potential symmetry adds greatly to the structural sturdiness of a figure. And furthermore, the two *magatamas* are not placed symmetrically to each other, which would promote their fusion and thereby strengthen the whole, but are reversed in such a way that the head of one is next to the tail of the other.

Equal strength of whole and parts creates ambiguity, and ambiguity produces oscillation. The mind cannot hold two different structural organizations of the same pattern at the same time—it can only subordinate the one to the other. Consequently, the mind provides for the necessary hierarchy by alternately giving dominance to either structure. At one moment the whole prevails, at the next, the parts. Such oscillation makes it possible to present identity without losing duality—a feat that, we found earlier, cannot be matched by the conceptual formulations of interaction.

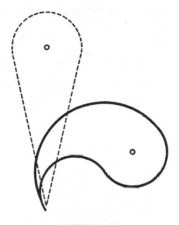

FIGURE 29

The inverted position ("69") characterizes the *magatamas* as antagonists. Through the opposition of two analogous powers, life is created and maintained. The opposition, however, creates productive tension rather than conflict. The two opposing forces, one directed toward the left, the other toward the right, do not clash. They combine in generating a torque and thereby rotation, which stands for the cycle of all existence (Figure 30). Furthermore, by distinguishing the two from each other, the inverted position also furnishes each *magatama* with a degree of individuality. Significantly, these individuals, although complete within themselves, are at the same time mere complements in the context of the whole. They are whole but need each other to attain wholeness. This coincidence of being whole and part simultaneously is another aspect of interaction not representable by discursive formulation. It is accomplished perceptually by the oscillatory alternation of two views: a *magatama* in its own completeness, and the complementarity of the two in the circle, revealing the incompleteness of either.

Figure-and-ground factors. The two partners complement each other at every level of the disk. Wherever one of them is narrow, the other is broad, and so throughout the entire gamut of ratios. The relationship is made even more dramatic by the curvature of the boundary separating the two. The head of the *magatama* is convex, the tail is concave; and where there is convexity in one of the partners, there is concavity in the other. But, while one could almost manage to see both shapes simultaneously if the dividing line were straight (Figure 20), the curve makes this feat quite difficult.

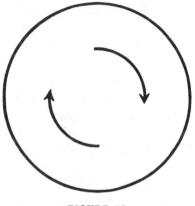

FIGURE 30

At this point, it is necessary to realize that the two *magatamas* not only lie peacefully in the same plane but are also engaged in a struggle for dominance, provoked by a complex figure-ground situation. The Danish psychologist Edgar Rubin, in his fundamental book on the figure-ground phenomenon, speaks of the "complete surprise" experienced when the ground of a pattern is suddenly seen as the figure (10, p. 31 ff.); but he also mentions "reciprocal ornaments," in which both components are of identical shape and therefore can be seen simultaneously. The *T'ai-chi tu* produces the surprise even though the two components are identical. This is owing to two properties of the curved boundary: (*a*) convex shape creates a strong tendency for the area to become figure and to annex the boundary as its own contour, thus transforming the other area into boundless ground; (*b*) the protrusion of convexity is so different from the hollowness of concavity that a sudden change into the very opposite kind of shape is experienced when the figure-ground inversion takes place.

In the *T'ai-chi tu*, the figure-ground situation is most unstable because each *magatama* possesses both convexity and concavity. If one fixates the head of one of them, it will assume figure-character and lie on top; but sliding toward the tail, one is likely to experience an inversion: The tail vanishes in order to become boundless ground, overlapped by the intruding head of the other *magatama*. This internal contradiction induces some observers to see the *T'ai-chi tu* three-dimensionally. It is one of the functions of the third dimension to come to the rescue when things get uncomfortable in the second. In our case also, the contradiction between the spatial locations of the head and the tail in one and the same figure can be mitigated if each *magatama* is seen as tilting forward in space, coming up from behind the head of its partner and surmounting its tail like a breaking wave. This intertwining of two obliquely placed figures is perhaps the most stable organization the *T'ai-chi tu* yields and is, at the same time, a particularly dramatic picture of the two generating powers in interaction.[10]

The over-all result is a protean spectacle. The solidity of a convex object constantly changes into the emptiness of shapeless ground and vice versa. No more impressive perceptual support could be given to the preachings of the Taoists against the short-sighted notion that objects, acts, or events are isolated, self-contained entities in empty space. The *T'ai-chi tu* demonstrates that each fact posits its opposite and complement, and that what looks like mere surroundings from one point of view appears as the central, positive fact from another. Lao-tzu asserted in the Tao Tê Ching that "Being and not-being grow out of one another" and praised emptiness. The reality of the room is the space enclosed by the walls; the utility of the vessel is its hollow (11, chapters 2 and 11). There should be educational value in having a disciple inscribe a *magatama* in a circle and color it, with his mind set on the object he is making, and to have him see the counterobject suddenly and inevitably emerge by itself.

Oscillatory alternation seems to be the most effective way of perceptually symbolizing the interaction of part and part, or part and whole, by which each sharer of the relationship is affecting the others while being affected by them at the same time. Although perceptual oscillation displays alternating views in succession, it is different in principle from the conceptual expedient of describing simultaneously occur-

---

[10] The *T'ai-chi tu* has obvious sexual connotations, and one might speculate that the Yin-Yang dichotomy derives originally from the bipolarity of sex. But to describe the *T'ai-chi tu* as a sexual symbol in the Freudian sense would intolerably limit its significance. Sex is only one of the many antagonistic relationships to which oriental thought applies this cosmological principle (see preceding essay).

ring effects one after the other. When I stated earlier that the views of the *magatamas* are "complementary," I used the term in its traditional meaning of entities completing each other to a whole. Whether both components of the *T'ai-chi tu* really can assume figure-character at the same time and be seen together in one unified percept is debatable. But in addition, or instead, of such peaceful coexistence there surely occurs the oscillation of views that cannot be held together because they exclude each other. In such alternation, the figure-role constantly passes from the one *magatama* to the other while the partner vanishes to become ground. These two views are also complementary but in the modern sense of the term introduced by the physicist Niels Bohr.[11] When the perceptual inversion occurs, a new view presents itself, which is not experienced as a change of conditions in the world of the outer objects but as a changed aspect of the same objective state of affairs. The two conditions contradict each other only as views (perceptual statements) but are experienced as one complex state of the objective situation and therefore as existing together rather than occurring consecutively. In other words, perceptual oscillation performs the paradoxical feat of presenting the components of interaction separately for the purpose of analytical understanding without isolating them from each other.[12]

The restructuring that occurs in inversion makes it possible for the observer actually to perceive an organizational process similar to the kind that generally takes place below the threshold of consciousness before the percept is seen. However, needless to say, even under these conditions we do not actually watch full interaction. The two antagonistic events are experienced as belonging to the same process; but the complex process composed of the two is not directly seen.

Further dynamic properties. In describing perceptual objects and their structural relations, I spoke inevitably of the action of forces rather than of static areas and shapes. The dynamics created by shapes is what

[11] "Information regarding the behavior of an atomic object obtained under definite experimental conditions may, however, be adequately characterized as *complementary* to any information about the same object obtained by some other experimental arrangement excluding the fulfillment of the first conditions. Although such kinds of information cannot be combined in a single picture by means of ordinary concepts, they represent indeed equally essential aspects of any knowledge of the object in question which can be obtained in this domain" (2, p. 26).

[12] According to Derk Bodde (12, p. 21), Chinese philosophy assumes the pattern of the universe to be "consisting either of eternal oscillation between two poles or of cyclical movement within a closed circuit."

perceptual patterns and symbolized life situations have in common. The *T'ai-chi tu* has some further dynamic properties relevant to its philosophical meaning that are worth mentioning here.

Of the two dynamic conceptions of the circle, the rotary and the radial, the *T'ai-chi tu* uses mainly the first. The radial organization would designate the center as a dominant focus—a hierarchic structure, not in keeping with Taoistic thought. The Taoistic cosmos has no focus. In the *T'ai-chi tu*, the central point is acknowledged by the internal contour passing through it, but is unmarked in itself. The radial structure of the disk, however, plays its part in the peculiar dynamics of the *magatama*, which is perceived as the deformation of a symmetrical tear-drop (Figure 29). In consequence, the *magatama* appears either (*a*) as passively pushed out of its natural norm-position and squeezed into the circular enclosure or (*b*) as actively relinquishing its norm in order to adapt itself to the rotational context of the *T'ai-chi tu*. This ambiguity—a property of all perceptual dynamics—is appropriate to the symbolic purpose in that the Way (Tao) of the cosmos not only fits the actions of individuals into its course but also requires that they adopt the proper course by their own choice and initiative. The Taoistic writings abound with descriptions of disasters, both natural and social, provoked by a ruler's unwillingness to tread the Path. The bending of the *magatama* puts the circular boundary under pressure. The serenity of the perfect (circular) shape is not merely the reward of a relaxed abstinence from wilful action but must also be preserved through the constant restraining of constant challenge.[13]

The expression of the *T'ai-chi tu* as a whole and also the expression of each *magatama* in itself derives from the directionless and self-centered shape of a circular disk on the one hand and directed rotational movement on the other. In the case of the *magatama*, the half-circle around the "eye" forms the head, a compact and centered core, giving the figure some self-containedness, which, however, interacts with the directed wedge-shape of the tear-drop tail. Thus, each of the two antago-

---

[13] Since the *T'ai-chi tu* is an ambiguous stimulus, the reactions of perceivers will differ individually. What is known about the whole, detail, and movement responses to the Rorschach blots suggests that the reactions to the structure of the *T'ai-chi tu* will be influenced by personal preferences for wholes or parts, laxity or tension, dominance or submission, activity or passivity, and so forth. However, the *T'ai-chi tu* has more clear-cut structural features of its own than have the Rorschach blots and therefore leads perception in more definite directions.

nists, which together constitute the universe, is shown to have a completeness of its own, modulated, as it were, by its transitory and complementary role in the context of the total system.

The extent to which the *magatama* appears as driven by its own intrinsic initiative depends on the spatial position of two points, namely, the center of gravity and what I shall call the focus. If we assume— admittedly without experimental evidence—that the perceptual and physical centers of gravity coincide, then CG (Figure 31) marks the center of gravity of the *magatama*. The center of the circular "head," emphasized by the "eye," is the focus (F), the point around which the total structure of the *magatama* is organized. That is, each *magatama* is

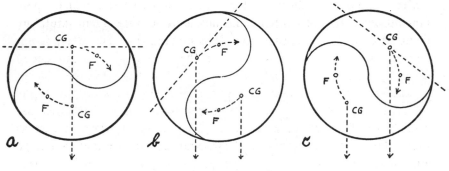

FIGURE 31

a hierarchic pattern and thereby distinguished from the *T'ai-chi tu* as a whole, which disavows these partial hierarchies by demonstrating that in the larger whole they lose their eminence.

In the spatial orientation I have chosen as a standard (Figure 31*a*), the two centers of gravity come to lie on the vertical so that the gravitational weight is equally distributed over both sides. Under these conditions, the emphasis on point F creates a vector, pulling the weight (CG) in the direction of F (see arrows). The *magatamas* are seen as rotating actively "under their own steam."[14]

By comparison, if the *T'ai-chi tu* is oriented in such a way that the two foci come to lie on the vertical (Figure 31*b*), the lower half of each *magatama* is seen as being pulled down by gravity, which stops the initi-

[14] When the two centers of gravity are placed upon the central vertical, they also serve to emphasize the vertical-horizontal framework. Since movement is seen as a deviation from the "zero position" of the basic framework, the rotation of the *magatamas* is more clearly perceived when the figure includes the vertical at least implicitly.

ative of the ascending (left) *magatama* and makes the descending one (right) drop—a passive victim of gravity. Similarly, when the foci are arranged horizontally (Figure 31c), the descending (upper) object is helplessly pulled downward by its own weight while the ascending (lower) one is prevented from rising. Looking back at Figure 31a, we now understand more clearly that in that orientation each *magatama* is seen as moving by its own initiative because its gravitational weight is balanced, the outer attractive power is neutralized, and the internal impulse of the focus alone is responsible for the propulsion. In this way, optimal, internally generated rotation is provided for the perceptual representatives of the yin and yang.

Conclusion. The detailed analysis of the *T'ai-chi tu* has been presented in order to illustrate the visual properties on which spontaneous perception of symbolic meaning is based. One might refute my demonstration on perceptual grounds by proving that the pattern is not seen the way I asserted it is; but once the perceptual facts are agreed upon, the structural similarity of the dynamics perceived in the *T'ai-chi tu* and of the cosmological forces described by Taoistic philosophy should be evident. (The reader is invited to ask himself whether the *T'ai-chi tu* could be an emblem of Christianity or Marxism just as well.) That such isomorphism of appearance and meaning should be able to strike the eyes of the common man— primitive, artist, or psychiatric patient—at any time or place is an assumption hardly beyond what we know about everyday perception. To perceive any object or event means to see it as a configuration of forces, and an awareness of the universality of such configurations is an integral part of all perceptual experience. Metaphors could not be so elementary and widespread a property of languages as they are if, for example, looking into a gorge did not inevitably involve the universal qualities of depth, darkness, and penetration—qualities that permit us to discuss abstractions in words.

Geometrically simple shapes emerge everywhere at an early stage of mental development because they are accessible to the limited organizing powers of a simple mind. They are retained in advanced civilizations for the purpose of schematic, symbolic, or so-called ornamental representations because they provide the most clear-cut images of the basic configurations of forces that continue to underlie man's life, and therefore man's thinking, even in refinement and complexity. Our symbol of interaction is a case in point. Interaction concerned the early philosophers, and it still concerns us today. Given this interest and a pair of reasonably observant eyes, images of interaction can be expected to be spontaneously understood by anybody. They may be sought and discovered by men of any period or country among the stores of simple shapes. And since the possibilities are few, the discoveries will resemble each other.

REFERENCES

1. Arnheim, Rudolf. *Art and Visual Perception.* Berkeley and Los Angeles: Univ. of Calif. Press, 1954.
2. Bohr, Niels. *Atomic Physics and Human Knowledge.* New York: Wiley, 1958.
3. Dewey, John, and Bentley, Arthur F. *Knowing and the Known.* Boston: Beacon, 1960.
4. Fung Yu-lan. *A History of Chinese Philosophy. Princeton,* N.J.: Princeton Univ. Press, 1952.
5. *I Ching, The;* or the Book of Changes. 1950.
6. Jacoby, Jolande. *The Psychology of C. G. Jung.* New Haven: Yale Univ. Press, 1951.
7. Jung, Carl Gustav. *Die Welt der Psyche.* Zurich: Rascher, 1954.
8. ———. *Psychology and Religion: West and East, Collected Works,* vol. 11. New York: Pantheon, 1958.
9. Köhler, Wolfgang. Psychology and evolution. *Acta Psychologica,* 1950, 7, 288–297.
10. Rubin, Edgar. *Visuell wahrgenommene Figuren.* Copenhagen: Gyldendal, 1921.
11. Waley, Arthur. *The Way and Its Power.* New York: Grove Press, 1958.
12. Wright, Arthur F. (ed.) *Studies in Chinese Thought.* Chicago: Univ. of Chicago Press, 1953.

FOUR ANALYSES

The Holes of Henry Moore:
On the Function of Space in Sculpture

In the work of the sculptor Henry Moore, the trunk of the human figure is often pierced and subdivided in such a way that, instead of a compact volume, one sees a configuration of slimmer units. For instance, the chest may be given as a large hole, which is roofed by the shoulders and flanked by the upper arms. What is the artistic purpose of this peculiar procedure?

Reshaping the body. The human figure has always presented the sculptor with a compositional problem. The body consists of a heavy trunk and the much slighter appendices of the arms, the legs, and the head. Since the artist's task is not to copy what he sees but to create a whole pattern of unified form, he must find a way of imposing unity on so heterogeneous an object. How can he organize the trunk and the limbs in one integrated composition?

A valuable monograph could be written on the various ways in which different styles of sculpture have coped with this problem. Some fused trunk and limbs into one volume. Others reduced the trunk to

First published in the *Journal of Aesthetics and Art Criticism*, 1948, 7, 29–38.

stick-like slimness, thus assimilating it to the limbs. Again, limbs could be made short and plump to match the trunk. Intermediate volumes also can be introduced to bridge over the difference between the bulky and the slim. When the artists came to handle the human body more freely, they sometimes eliminated the problem by cutting off the limbs and the head. Henry Moore's solution is of a similarly radical nature. By transforming the heaviest volume, the trunk, into a configuration of narrower shapes, a common denominator has been found for the whole figure. The beam-like or ribbon-shaped units that represent arms and legs differ little from those found in the area of the trunk; and the holes that pierce the body resemble the "legitimate" interstices between the legs or between the arms and the torso. In some of the reclining figures, a surprising symmetry is produced by the correspondence between the frame of the pierced chest and a similar frame formed by the two legs. Ingeniously balanced, the figure reposes on its horizontal base.

Uniformity of the parts is one method among others to accomplish unity. Without ever getting repetitious, Moore stresses uniformity, not only in the roughly equal size and proportion of the units, but also in their shape. More and more he has come to eliminate the distinctive formation and detail of faces, hands, and feet in favor of some over-all shape characteristics. Wherever we look, we notice strongly dynamic form: he avoids the tranquillity of the cylinder, cube, or sphere in favor of conic or pyramidal shapes, which grow smaller or bigger, and egg-shapes, which move in a definite direction. Moore also enhances uniformity and vigorous mobility by avoiding clear delimitation of parts. Although precisely articulated, the units flow into each other. Even the dead ends of the hands and feet are eliminated. They merge with their partners or stream back into the body of the figure, thus permitting the circulation of energy to continue unchecked.

This stress of the interdependence of things, their mutual influence, the indivisible unity of the whole is likely to reflect the artist's conception of the world. But the structural pattern that conveys this meaning is possible only at a high level of formal development. True, no work of art lacks an intimate interdependence of parts, but it is well known that at early levels of conception, for instance in the drawings of young children, the complex patterns of a human figure or an animal are built of geometrically simple units, which are kept apart through explicit outlines. Gradually, these subdivisions disappear and the whole is conceived as one complex unit. Only at a late state of this process of growth, which has a parallel in the developmental laws of human thinking, can the complexity of dynamic interchange be grasped through scientific or artistic patterns. One can also express this by saying that stylistic structures like the one created by Henry Moore approach the representation of the irrational.[1] This is a Romantic tendency, which shies away from the defined and congealed. Moore's Romanticism cherishes the mysterious intangibility of what grows, changes, and interacts. Herbert Read, in his book on the sculptor, has aptly analyzed Moore's equally Romantic attempt to derive an image of man from the organic and inorganic formations of nature (2).

The equalization of the parts, obtained by the breaking-up of the trunk, tends to minimize the biological difference between the limbs as executors of voluntary action and the torso, which is more directly connected with the vegetative, instinctive functions. A uniform, over-all principle of life seems to govern the whole figure in all its parts. This playing down of the late cerebral developments of Homo sapiens in favor of more universal forces of nature is again a Romantic trait of Henry Moore's art. One notes that the horizontal position, which he uses so frequently, devaluates the importance of the head and stresses the abdomen as the compositional center. The heads are small. That is, the role of the brain carrier is reduced. These faceless heads do no thinking or feeling of their own; at most, they occasionally turn around to gaze with the simple steadiness of grazing cattle. Similarly, the tentacles of the hands and feet are planed down, fused, tied together. One has only to think of the alert faces and telling gestures of the terra-cotta figures that recline on Etruscan coffins in almost the same position to realize the difference. The grace and intelligence of Moore's work is all in the form pattern, which characterizes the whole figure with no distinction of any specific part.

Capturing space. Another glance at the holes leads us to notice that they are not merely dead and empty intervals between the material parts of the figure but peculiarly substantial, as though they were filled with denser air. Among the factors that make for this effect, one stands out in particular. The surfaces that delimit the openings are frequently concave, forming hollow containers of space. Striking examples are the spherical holes that pierce the chests of some of the female figures to

---

[1] Rational is what can be related to definable concepts. These concepts can be intellectual as, for instance, when we recognize an object of known nature and function: This is a hand! Or they can be perceptual as, for instance, when the thing we see is relatable to well-defined shapes, colors, directions, etc. Both kinds of attribution, however, are made difficult by Moore's style of form.

indicate the breasts; the circular holes in ring-shaped heads; the dells formed by bent arms. Wherever such concavities dent or perforate the sculptural body, a puddle of air seems to fill them almost tangibly. In observing this phenomenon, the psychologist cannot help thinking of the studies on "figure and ground" started by Edgar Rubin some twenty-five years ago (3). A pattern like the one in Figure 32 is seen by most

FIGURE 32

observers as a circular disk ("figure") in front of a through-going background ("ground"). It is harder to see a white foreground ("figure") pierced by a circular hole, through which part of a dotted background ("ground") appears. Psychological research has discovered some of the conditions on which the figure-and-ground effect depends. (a) The enclosed surface tends to be figure, the enclosing, ground. (b) Inner articulation, such as the dotted texture of the circle, makes for "figure." An empty circle would show the effect less clearly. (c) Convexity makes for figure, concavity for ground. In Figure 33, the second and

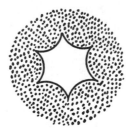

FIGURE 33

third factors are reversed. This time, the internal pattern, in spite of being enclosed, tends to be seen as a hole because it has less texture and a pronouncedly concave contour.[2]

2 Another rule, which I shall not discuss further even though it too has interesting applications to sculpture, indicates that the relatively smaller elements tend to be figure. In Figure 34, the slimmer B-bars are seen as figure more readily than the broader A-rectangles.

In any drawing or painting, figure-ground relationships help create the pictorial space. This is true not only where human bodies, houses, etc. are shown in front of a background, but wherever objects or parts of objects overlap. Generally, a number of figure-ground factors are used simultaneously and for the most part antagonistically. That is, a tree may be made to appear in front of a wall, as figure on ground, while at the same time other factors will check the effect by stressing the figure-character of the wall. The reason for this is that the painter has always to cope with the double task of creating space and "keeping the plane." [3] Even where a human figure is shown in front of a homogeneous background, as in the portraits of Holbein or the Quattrocentisti, the unity of the picture plane can be preserved, for instance, by the amount of space and the color and brightness given to the background.

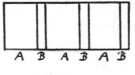

FIGURE 34

Thus far, psychologists have studied the phenomenon of figure and ground only in plane patterns, but their results can be applied to the third dimension. True, there are important differences. Whereas in a two-dimensional drawing, the contour that divides two areas can be observed, the common boundary surface remains hidden when two opaque volumes meet in three-dimensional space. You can see the line that separates Olympia's body from the divan on which it rests, but not the surface that the body and the divan share three-dimensionally. An exception occurs when the outer volume is transparent, as in the case of air enveloping an object. In this case, however, the transparent volume is nonexistent for our eyes to such an extent that one hesitates to speak of a figure-ground relationship at all. It may seem more proper to say that a piece of sculpture is surrounded by empty space than by a substantial "ground."

Within the frame of a painting, every spot is positively present, first as a material part of the paint-covered canvas and secondly as a substan-

[3] Nevertheless, the painter may wish to apply the figure-ground factors in such a way that the intended spatial relationship results clearly. By keeping the effects of antagonistic factors in an unstable balance, one produces the kind of juggler's trick in which Messrs. Dali and Tchelitcheff excel.

tial element of the pictorial construction. In a completed painting, the units of the composition vary as to their apparent density and also as to their spatial position within the figure-ground hierarchy, but none of them may give us the impression of an empty gap, a hole torn in the spatial tissue. This is different in sculpture, where we are used to find all spatial relationships limited to the figure itself. Granted that these relations often reach across a void—and the length of the leap counts compositionally—but they generally do not include these intervals the way they would in a painting.

It seems necessary to state this principle of sculpture so positively even though it does not hold completely. The deviation from it that can be observed in Henry Moore's work has historical antecedents, for example, in Baroque art. For our purpose, however, it suffices to point out the different attitude to space in Moore's work, that is, in the most extreme but at the same time artistically valid example that is available so far.

Mainly through the use of concave forms, many of his figures capture portions of space and make them part of themselves. Much less solid than the wood, stone, or metal on which they border, these air-bodies nevertheless condense into a transparent substance, which mediates between the tangible material of the statue and the surrounding empty space. These statues do not reserve all the perceptual "figure"-factors for themselves. They do have all the textural articulation and are enclosed by the surrounding volume of air; on the other hand they do not consist entirely of bulging convexities, which would invade space aggressively, but reserve an important role to dells and caves and pocket-shaped holes. Whenever convexity is handed over to space, partial "figure"-character is assumed by the enclosed air-bodies, which consequently appear semisubstantial. The "Family Group" (Figure 35) shows a man and a woman sitting next to each other and holding an infant. In most traditional sculpture, the interstice formed by the seated body is essentially delimited by bulging convexities of the chest, the belly, the thighs. Thus, it remains an empty interval. In Moore's family group, hollow abdomens make the two seated figures into one large lap or pocket. In this shadowed cavity, space appears tangible, stagnant, warmed by body heat. In its center, the suspended infant lies safely as though in a womb softly padded with half-solid air.

Since the holes are often shaped according to the same principle, they pierce the body of the statue in a material but not necessarily in a perceptual and artistic sense. In many cases, they do not interrupt the substance of the figure but merely seem to rarify it into a state of transparency. This new function of space offers compositional opportunities.

Sometimes, Moore establishes a contrapuntal correspondence between, say, a protruding head and a hollow of similar spherical shape. These instances prove that almost equal rights are given to hollows and solids.

FIGURE 35. Henry Moore, "Family Group," collection, The Museum of Modern Art, New York

Incidentally, this interpretation also seems to throw light on another disturbing feature of Moore's style, namely, his use of strings and wires. The strings form surfaces that bound transparent bodies consisting of empty space. They too add volumes of rarefied substance to the more solid principal material of the statue. At the same time, the directions of the strings interpret the shape of the volumes they enclose, very much like the lines of the grain Moore uses so deliberately in his wooden and stone figures. Curiously enough, he thus applies the theoretical recipe of another English artist, William Hogarth, who in his *Analysis of Beauty* recommended the interpretation of volumes through similar systems of lines.

The essentially negative role the surrounding air-space has played in sculpture so far is not due simply to its invisibility, but also to the predominance of convex volumes in the figures themselves. Henri Focillon, in his book, *Vie des Formes,* has distinguished two ways of using space in sculpture, namely *l'espace-limite* and *l'espace-milieu* (1, p. 23). "In the first case, space more or less weighs upon form and rigorously confines its expansion, at the same time that form presses against space as the palm of the hand does upon a table or against a sheet of glass. In the second case, space yields freely to the expansion of volumes, which it does not already contain: these move out into space, and there spread forth even as do the forms of life." Since these concepts are intended to apply to traditional sculpture, it seems to me that in the interpretation of *l'espace-limite,* too active a part is granted to the surrounding space. An archaic Greek figure, for instance, does not give me the impression that an inner urge to expand is checked from the outside. The discipline of such a style is all "internal." It is dictated by the law of development, which limits formal complexity at the early stages. There is little capacity or desire to expand beyond the basic block. The function of the surrounding space is almost exclusively negative. The same holds true for *l'espace-milieu.* From the center of the figure, bulging volumes push forward into empty space. Once this principle is stated, a more detailed analysis will trace at the same time admixtures of a third procedure, which one might term *l'espace-partner.* In the later Greek, medieval, and particularly in Baroque sculpture, the use of concavities indicates the possibility of making space an active partner of the figure. In Bernini's horseback-riding Louis XIV, the sweeping locks and folds collect the air in hollow pockets. But even here the concavities are subordinated to the convexity of the whole to such an extent that they contribute no more than a minor enrichment. Among the great sculptors, Henry Moore is the first in whose work the surrounding space is not simply pushed out of the way by the aggressive protrusions of the wood, stone, or metal, but in turn thrusts into the figure from the outside, carving depressions into the yielding matter and adding to its substance. The proper balance and integration of the two antagonistic tendencies is a delicate task for the sculptor, in that the totality of the internal and external pushes must create one consistent unified surface. There are instances in Henry Moore's work where space, as though with a ramming thumb, seems to interrupt the rhythm of the figure by a foreign imprint.

Dissolving the solid. The foregoing examples will have shown that the figure-ground relationship is not simply a static distribution of spatial values but a highly dynamic interplay of forces. This is true even for two-dimensional patterns. The "figure" is distinguished not only by appearing in front of the ground and by its greater density but also by a tendency to expand, to spread over the territory of the ground. In Henry Moore's sculpture, the two-way relationship in which both the statue and the surrounding space assume figure as well as ground functions makes for a dramatic interchange of forces between the two partners. The sculptural body ceases to be a self-contained, neatly circumscribed universe. Its boundary has become penetrable. It has been inserted into a larger context. The masculine aggressiveness of its convexities no longer operates in the void but is countered by positive thrusts from the outside, which force the additional role of feminine passivity on the sculpture. The tendency to avoid isolation and delimitation, to unite parts in an exchange of forces, a tendency we observed within the figure, turns out to be applied also to the relation of figure and environment. This is a daring extension of the sculptural universe, made possible perhaps by an era in which flying has taught us through vivid kinesthetic experience that air is not empty space but a material substance like earth or wood or stone, a medium that carries heavy bodies and pushes them and can be bumped into like a rock.

How valid is this sculptural style artistically? How far can it lead and where? Undoubtedly, it involves problems. Since we are all accustomed to thinking that definite boundaries are needed to determine the structure of a work of art, we notice with apprehension that the inclusion of space removes clearly defined delimitation. These puddles of condensed air that fill holes and depressions have definite contours only where they border upon the body of the figure. For the rest, they seem to dissolve into empty space, leaving the work peculiarly open. True, the Cubist painters, such as Feininger, have dispensed substantial air in crystalline form, but they had the picture-frame to keep all volumes within the bounds of a rectangle. Henry Moore's figures are frequently enveloped by a field of energetic matter, which weakens in power and density with increasing distance from the figure until it finally evaporates. Incidentally, a similar infinity, in the opposite direction, is provided by deep hollows, whose internal end is hidden in the dark. The artistic implications of this style will need to be explored further.

Where will the principle of concavity lead? Its complete realization is known to us only from architectural interiors. But, is there any aesthetic law to prevent the sculptor from creating hollow interiors, works one would have to walk into in order to see? I hesitate to call up the experience of climbing the staircase inside the Statue of Liberty. Even so, the principle deserves a trial. Two settings that have attracted Henry Moore as a draftsman are the hollow tube shelters and the interior of coal mines. His "Helmet" would offer to a mouse-sized visitor the most radical experience so far available of the use of surrounding concavity in sculpture.

What prospects are opened by Moore's attempt to decompose large volumes into configurations of slimmer units freely separated by interstices? [4] Undoubtedly, such a style offers to the spectator a more complete survey of spatial relations. No more than three side-faces of a solid cube can ever be seen from one viewpoint. Looking at an open box, we visualize all six of its planes, some from the inside, some from the outside. The skeleton of a cube built of twelve sticks offers even more complete orientation. This principle applies also to the more complex bodies of sculpture. However, the decomposition of volumes carries the risk of disintegration. I notice a lack of unity in some of Moore's smaller metal compositions. The reclining figures of the deck-chair type are not easily pulled together by the glance. This, however, is merely a matter of artistic accomplishment. There is no reason why even Moore's radical attempt to compose a figure of several entirely separate pieces could not be successful. Perceptual unity does not require physical continuity. Extended beyond the single figure, this principle leads to group compositions, which are indeed a major interest of Moore's. It can readily be seen that this sculptor, by his positive use of intervening space, might be more successful in the combination of separate units than Western sculpture has been traditionally. This may also lead to an extension of subject matter. So far, sculpture has fed almost exclusively on the compact bodies of humans and animals. Some playful experiments in modern sculpture, for instance those by Calder, make me wonder whether

---

[4] A parallel of this development of sculptural style can be found in the breaking-up of the solid cube in modern architecture.

some day a group of twisted tree-trunks, which would delimit and internally organize a volume of essentially empty space, could not become a legitimate subject. Finally, a more dramatic interrelationship of sculpture and architecture could be envisaged, in which the building would be more than an enclosing box, the statue more than an enrichment of walls. Architectural and sculptural forms could unite in the kind of dynamic interplay we observe in Henry Moore's arrangements of separate nonobjective shapes.

Further than this, speculation cannot go, since the art theorist must not trespass upon the land of the prophet. His is a science which allows little prediction. While it seems possible to foresee some of the main directions in which social, scientific, and technical development will move, the road of the arts cannot be traced beyond the next corner.

REFERENCES

1. Focillon, Henri. *The Life of Forms in Art*. New York: Wittenborn, 1948.
2. Read, Herbert. *Henry Moore: Sculpture and Drawings*. London: Lund Humphries, 1944.
3. Rubin, Edgar. *Visuell wahrgenommene Figuren*. Copenhagen: Gyldendal, 1921.

A Note on Monsters

> But if you would consider the true cause
> Why all these fires, why all these gliding ghosts,
> Why birds and beasts from quality and kind,
> Why old men fool and children calculate,
> Why all these things change from their ordinance,
> Their natures and preformed faculties,
> To monstrous quality, why, you shall find
> That heaven hath infused them with these spirits
> To make them instruments of fear and warning
> Unto some monstrous state.
>
> —*Julius Caesar*, Act I, scene 3.

It has always been natural for man to consider monsters as "portentous things unto the climate that they point upon." The birth of a calf with

Preface to a portfolio of drawings by Leo Russell, published in 1949 by Tanagra Publishers in New York.

two heads or of a child without eyeballs was commonly believed to announce upsets, mostly of a catastrophic nature. This was so not only because the world was considered a planned and meaningful whole, in which any impressive event must be expected to cause impressive changes, but also because the monster carries the threatening message that nature can go out of joint.

Disturbances in heaven and on earth are taken to forecast disorder in the state of man. Why is the mere thought of a biological monster so profoundly sickening? So much more than the sight of a mutilated body? In an accident, the organism is hurt by some external force. Foolish mistreatment of what could have been normally shaped organs is responsible for such man-made malformations as protruding paunches or distorted toes. But the birth of a monster is a failure of nature herself and threatens our faith in the basic soundness of what grows.

Portentous things seem to be happening in the arts of our century. Monsters are swarming from the studios of many painters and sculptors. They produce disturbances similar to those aroused by their biological brothers. Not just any deviation from the familiar forms of nature has this effect. Distorted limbs and daring proportions offend; but they are taken merely as violations, committed by seemingly brutal artists, which leave the perfection of the model untouched. Perhaps, Picasso's nudes may be considered a slur upon womanhood, but most of them do not seem to interfere with woman herself. Distortions are comments on nature that may provoke indignation. But the monster creates anxiety because it shows reality itself at fault.

It is true, monsters can be bred the cheap or the hard way. Only a few of them count. The father of the cheap monster is the doodler. It takes only a stroke of the pen to make an arm grow out of a mouth. Unconcerned, or concerned with other things, the doodler exercises his erratic freedom by fitting element to element, since canvas and paper are patient. Only when the desperate awareness of a disfigured world forces the artist to construct a truthful image that reflects the absurd contradictions and dysfunctions from which he and others suffer—only then is a monster bred the hard way.

Monsters have been made in all epochs of art. But there seems to be a difference between the primitive demons of African tribes or the gargoyles of Gothic cathedrals and their modern grandchildren. Our monsters are neither cruel idols calling for sacrifices nor devils of vice who tempt and possess us and must be exorcised. That is, they have ceased to be personifications of hostile elements or externalizations of man's own evil drives. Today, we have been made to recognize evil as a part of our own behavior, and thus the monster has become a portrait of ourselves and of the kind of life we have chosen to lead.

What are the monstrosities reflected in the nightmares of the artist? There is dissolution of the individual, the doubt as to what is mine and thine. Is this my mouth speaking or is it yours? There is the loss of law, balance, and symmetry, an offensive inequality of things that ought to be alike. There is the confusion of man and beast. Also the stable basis of the body has gone and the creature is reduced to a bundle of frantically active organs, which are connected with nothing but each other. Parts lose their inherited places and float around as aimless strangers or are given functions that are not theirs.

Such monsters are not simply manifestations of fear, not mere outgrowths of an allegedly irrational unconscious. When they are valid, they are the findings of precise observation and interpretation—a process in which all instruments of the mind participate: the deep-rooted intuition of primeval symbols as well as the acute insights of reason. Only because the fearful thing is adequately and vigorously presented can it produce the kind of emotional response that counts artistically.

Monsters are not the only means by which the harmful state of human affairs is pictured. Much modern art uses distortion, interference, contradiction, mutilation, crutch, and carcass. It cultivates paradoxical combinations of heterogeneous objects. All these can be interpreted as displays of man-made disorder that could and should be remedied by man. The monster alone, by presenting this same disorder as having grown naturally, calls it the work of superior forces. This leaves man innocent and helpless. The monster affords a comfortable pessimism.

However, there is also a more cheerful note. Disorder can only be shown artistically by means of order. If the artist's visions of monsters were not well organized and balanced, they could not demonstrate the perversity of the disorganized and unbalanced. Compositional order testifies to the functioning of a mind healthy enough to diagnose illness. Here, it would seem, lies our hope.

Picasso's "Nightfishing at Antibes"

Works of art have been investigated mainly in three areas of psychology. The student of motivation asks why the work was made at all, and why in its particular fashion. The social psychologist considers the function and effect of art in its setting. Finally, those of us interested in perception and expression ask why the work looks the way it does and says what it says. I shall try to give a sample of this last approach.

The examination takes the form of a descriptive inventory. We cling as closely as possible to what is directly presented to the eyes, on the assumption that in a successful painting the essential meaning is directly expressed in the properties of the visual form. Picasso's painting (see frontispiece) is composed of three main areas. The vertical panel on the left presents the town and medieval castle of Antibes and continues as a vertical string of rocks, which frame the water of the harbor. There is the central medallion of the two fishermen in their boat, surrounded by lights and fishes. And the panel on the right shows two girls on a stone jetty. In the projective frontal plane of the canvas, the fishermen hold the center of an approximately symmetrical composition. In three-dimensional space, we are led diagonally from the distant castle in the upper left through the fishing scene to the jetty in the foreground, closest to us and directly related to us through the firm foundation of the walls on the base of the frame. After we have traveled through the picture from the left to the right we are caught and held by the company of the girls who, with their bicycle, ice cream cone, and outgoing hair and bosom seem to represent the unconcerned, aesthetically entertained spectators. We ourselves are pointedly characterized by the company we keep. The base of observation in the foreground serves also as a *repoussoir:* it deprives the fishermen in the boat of some of the direct communication with the beholder, which they would have if their central position were as uncontestedly dominant as it is, for example, in Raphael's "Miraculous Draught of Fishes" in the Vatican. Picasso presents the central scene as something looked at rather than as something that is.

First published in the *Journal of Aesthetics and Art Criticism*, 1963, 22, 165–167, as part of a symposium, "One Painting—Three Approaches."

Nevertheless, the theme of the fishermen carries considerable weight, not only because of its size and central position but also by its almost architectural stability, which makes the busy men in the floating boat look, paradoxically, almost more solidly grounded than the stone constructions to their left and right. In the boulder-like shapes of the town, verticals and parallels are avoided: the cubes and pyramids are heaped in emphatic disorder. Similarly, the large cube of the jetty to the right deviates from the stable framework in all three dimensions and tilts obliquely toward the back. In the two girls, the vertical is also underplayed, and crossed by powerful shapes—representing perhaps the play of lights and shadows. In comparison, the central scene has the frontality and flatness of a façade. The upright figure displays its action without impediment, and the crouching man, although somewhat foreshortened, also unfolds freely from the feet to the head. At the same time, this central edifice is, as it were, written on water. Rather than being firmly based on the frame, it floats on the crescent of the boat, surrounded by the immaterial water, like an apparition. This sense of unreality is strengthened by the distribution of the colors. The warm purple shades are reserved mostly for the surroundings while the chill and remoteness of the blues all but monopolize the center.

The strangeness of the apparition is further emphasized and explained when we notice a paradoxical difference between the figures of the two fishermen. The one to the left, bending overboard, stares into the water. Although his stare is intent, he is passive, contemplative. The one to the right is most actively engaged in the spearing of the fish. However, if we now look at the shapes by which the two figures are rendered, we notice that the distribution of motionlessness and motion is reversed. The figure of the standing man is fitted into the most static directions of space: the horizontals of the body and the head, paralleled by the left arm, and the vertical of the leg, right arm, and spear constitute a stable post-and-lintel construction. The balanced spatial orientation of the left arm and the right angle that estranges the arm from the spear deprive the thrust of its power.

On the other hand, the physically inactive partner is alive with the turmoil of active shapes. He is placed upside down, top-heavy, and with his feet sprawling in the air, along an oblique axis, both in the frontal plane and in three-dimensional space. But the axis is not explicitly given. No system of basic lines sustains either the internal skeleton of the figure or its outer contours. The body is broken up into short strongly bent curves, which intercept each other irrationally.

Such a paradoxical contradiction between the nature of the action represented and the dynamics of the shapes representing it is not rare in the arts. It often expresses the contrast between physical behavior and its spiritual meaning. Thus, in Piero della Francesca's "Resurrection," the figure of the rising Christ is fitted to a serene framework of verticals and horizontals in frontal presentation whereas the motionless sleepers are scattered about in the most restless, irrationally overlapping diagonals. For what purpose is this device used in "Nightfishing at Antibes"? It seems legitimate to remember here that the painting was done in August, 1939, when the imminence of World War II darkened the horizon. In this ominous light, the murder of the fishes, portrayed in our painting, acquires a particular meaning. Watched with noncommittal curiosity by the girls, who appear as creatures of pleasure and luxury, the prospect of slaughter looks unreal, paralyzed in its impact by its remoteness, by the incompatibility of violence with the gay setting of the Mediterranean harbor. The apparition on the crescent-shaped boat floats at some distance, flat and cold, separated by a stretch of water from the beholder who is visually connected and thus symbolically associated with the stone jetty, the dwelling place of the gay spectators.

The contemplative companion of the upright fisherman serves as a bridge between the threatening, unreal image and the beholder. Leaning forward, this second man is not contained in the remote frontal plane but sprawls toward us. It is he also whom we meet first as we enter the picture at the lower left corner, stumbling over the crab and the rocks. Whereas the facial features of the upright man are narrowed in restrictive concentration, the leaning man's eyes are open and far apart, and his nose reaches as a probing proboscis down into the water, which looks empty but may hide anything. The pregnancy of water is familiar to the student of dreams, who speaks of water as a maternal symbol. In comparison with the three-dimensionality of the fisherman, who scrutinizes the future helplessly, everything else loses reality. The spearman is stopped in a frozen gesture, the stones of the historical castle recede, the girls flatten out. The foreboding of violent, but unknown things to come emerges as the dominant theme of the painting.

The perceptual features that have been mentioned in this analysis could be spelled out easily in more technical terms. I hope that the quick references I have given sufficiently illustrate the fundamental unity of perception and expression. The meaning of a work of visual art is contained in the properties of its shapes and colors. And there is no sense to those shapes and colors other than the meaning they proclaim.

Concerning the Dance

The artist, his tool, and his work are fused into one physical thing—the human body. Probably, this trait of the dance helps to determine which kind of person chooses this medium. In the other arts, the creator projects his self upon an object outside and tends to vanish behind it; and rightly so because, by drawing attention to himself, a vain artist is likely to obstruct the audience's view of his work. The dancer, however, does not offer his work unless he exhibits himself. The dance is a justification of Narcissus. It involves an interest centered on the self. The dancer does not act upon the world, he behaves in it. And his behavior has meaning only when performed for others. Creative vanity molds the appearance of the self into an image of the world.

One consequence of the peculiar fusion of subject and object is that essentially the dancer does not create in the same medium through which the audience receives his work. The painter looks at the canvas, and so does the spectator. But you cannot see your own dance. The mirror is only a makeshift; in fact, no dancer deals essentially with his visible image. The dance, just as the performance of the actor, is kinesthetic art, art of the muscle sense. This is worth noticing because many have taken it for granted that artistic expression is limited to the higher senses of the eye and the ear. The awareness of tension and relaxation within his own body, the sense of balance that distinguishes the proud stability of the vertical from the risky adventures of thrusting and falling —these are the tools of the dancer. The fortunate correspondence between the dynamic patterns of what the dancer perceives through his kinesthetic nerves and what the spectator is told by his eyes is an example of isomorphism, as modern psychology calls it, that is, the structural similarity of correlated processes occurring in different media. True, the similarity of the dancer's and the spectator's experience is incomplete; particularly, because the distorting factor of self-evaluation is involved. Easily and inadvertently, the presentation of the self shifts from the ruthlessly expressive to the pretty harmony of the normal, and when the dancer's "body-image" does not correspond to his objective appearance,

First published in *Dance Magazine*, August 1946, 20, 20, 38, 39.

a painful discrepancy may result between the choreographic idea and the body that attempts to give it reality on the stage.

All art has to find its place somewhere between two poles: the raw-material of existing things and interpretative form. Music and nonobjective paintings approach the extreme of pure form. The dance is nearer than even the motion picture to the other extreme in that it presents the material body of the dancer, created by nature, not by man. However, in order to be art, the body must become form and be accepted as such. If the spectator views the dancer as belonging to practical reality, he sees something monstrously unnatural, comparable to what we should feel if we met a Picasso figure walking in the public street. Hence Paul Valéry's observation in his dialogue *L'Ame et la Danse:* "The soul has only to stop and to refuse in order no longer to conceive anything but the strangeness and distastefulness of this ridiculous agitation. . . . If you wish, my soul, all this is absurd. —You can, then, depending on your whim, understand or not understand; find beautiful, find ridiculous, at your pleasure?" (3). The dance may acknowledge the "practical" nature of its instrument, the human body, by offering pantomime, illustrating, for instance, the story of a poor cobbler, complete with workshop, boots, and bench. Or it may tend toward pure, nonrepresentational movement. However, the range of its expression is limited by the organic nature of the instrument. Stylized angular movement, for instance, or the camou-flage of the body by inorganic costume easily produces a discord. The painter can be less concerned with this problem because the immaterial image of man on the canvas allows more complete transformation. The expression of the dance, having to rely essentially on the curved and gradually changing movements that fit organic muscle, seems limited to what in music corresponds to the effect of the gradual change of pitch and volume. For similar reasons, the ballet dancer's attempt to ignore gravity—rather than to exploit its symbolic meaning, as the modern dancer does—can hardly overcome a humorous element of visible fail-ure. There is always something pathetic in seeing the contact of man's weighty body with the earth reduced to the pinpoint of the toe, the final barrier to a doomed aspiration. Translated into expression, this physical discrepancy runs the risk of conveying to our modern eyes the embarrass-ing image of a butterfly man, who shuns suffering and struggle.

In daily life, motor behavior is mainly at the service of practical in-tentions or the spontaneous manifestation of emotion. Correspondingly, we watch the behavior of others in order to get some direct or indirect information about their aim or feeling. Appearance serves essentially as a key to the invisible behind it. But, when the body becomes a vehicle of artistic form, it is not an indicator of the other person's hidden soul but is in itself the final object of the spectator's interest. For practical purposes, a trembling mouth may be a sufficient symptom of despondency. However, the dancer's body must not only allow us to *understand* that there is sadness, but make us experience it by movements whose visible dynamic qualities correspond to those of sadness; his whole body may dramatically collapse, head and arms may droop, in order to create visible sadness for our eyes and feelings. Likewise, whereas a quick movement of our eyes suffices for us to shift our attention to a neighbor, the dancer may prefer to turn head and body with an ample gesture, as though his eyes and ears were too dumb to manage with less. Not that dance movement has always to be extensive; but large or small, it must be a translation of its content into visual language.

The necessary transformation of practical behavior into artistic form is illustrated also by the modern dancer's assertion that movements should issue from the center of the body, the torso. This sets a hard task for the beginner, who is accustomed from daily life to meeting most motor demands with localized actions of the head and the limbs. The common voluntary acts do not require the cooperation of the whole body. Artistically, however, such localization is unsatisfactory. In the first place, expression must involve the totality of what is presented. (The reader may recall the ridiculous effect of a well-known piece of sculpture that shows an Indian with his arms raised in ecstatic prayer while the horse on which he sits displays perfect indifference.) Furthermore, the visible image of the human body assigns central importance to the torso, from which head and limbs branch out as mere secondary accessories. The painter or musician is free to invent a compositional pattern that fits a particular subject. The dancer is bound to the given form of the human body and has to derive any composition from it. This given pattern suggests that, as a rule, the central theme be set by the torso and be merely developed in its secondary ramifications by the head, the arms and the legs. One is reminded of Heinrich von Kleist's essay, *Ueber das Mario-nettentheater* (On the Puppet Theater), written in 1810, in which he asserts that a puppet may display perfect grace simply by being propelled at its center of gravity, while the rest of the body follows passively. The line described by the fulcrum is, according to Kleist, "nothing else than the path of the dancer's soul" (1).

This suggestion, however, has important consequences for the spiritual content expressed by the dance. If one asks observers to compare movements issuing from the head or limbs with those springing from the torso, they describe the former as conveying intellectual, conscious action whereas the latter suggest nonconscious, largely emotional behavior. John Martin reports of Isadora Duncan that, "through watching, apparently quite objectively, her emotional and motor impulses and relating them to each other, she discovered to her complete satisfaction that the solar plexus was the bodily habitation of the soul and the center in which inner impulse was translated into movement." This agrees with D. H. Lawrence's curious poetical physiology, according to which the primal affective center of the unconscious is located behind the navel in the solar plexus (2, chapter 3). (It would be tempting to follow up the parallel with sculpture, where the compositional theme is also frequently developed from the center of the body and sometimes limited to a headless, limbless torso.)

Does this mean, then, that in the dance the conception of man is reduced to a biologically lower, precerebral stage? The dancer seems to be faced with the dilemma that functionally the highest, specifically human powers of the nervous system control the organism from the head, while the visible structure of the body suggests as the center an area that typically produces nonreflective action, such as in pain, fear, sex, or the lazy "stretching" of the muscles. If man were shaped like a starfish, with his brain in the center, the dilemma would not exist. It is also true that the above mentioned difficulty of the beginning dancer is connected with the psychological task of having to give up the safe control of reason and modesty in favor of an "indecent" yielding to instinct. This paganism of the dance accounts for its wholesome therapeutic effect on emotionally inhibited people.

True, the dance does tone down the proud acquisitions of reason and conscious discipline. But, on the other hand, a work of art always represents more than the specific subject matter through which it embodies its conception. Though concentrating on man, the dancer, like the sculptor, does not deal with man alone. There is universal significance in the fact that, according to A. Coomaraswamy, the dances of the Indian god Siva manifest the primitive energy of the cosmos. On this plane, the phylogenetically late developments of the organism lose weight. By neglecting a unique attribute of man, the work of art makes his image better suited to reflect the whole of which he is a part.

REFERENCES

1. Kleist, Heinrich von. Essay on the puppet theater. *Partisan Review*, January and February 1947, pp. 67–72.
2. Lawrence, D. H. *Psychoanalysis and the Unconscious*. New York: Viking, 1960.
3. Valéry, Paul. *L'Ame et la dance*. Paris: Gallimard, 1924.

ABSTRACT LANGUAGE AND THE METAPHOR

Artistic representation is frequently considered to be a kind of plastic surgery performed on the raw material of experience. The poet is said merely to omit or add elements, to change or distort, dissociate or re-assemble what he has observed. Such a view neglects the basic distinction between an experience and its representation in an artistic medium. The original vision of, say, the glassy surface-quality of a waterfall may be quite precise as to its perceptual and expressive characteristics. How-ever, such an experience does not consist primarily either of lines or colors that can simply be transferred to canvas or of words that can simply be recorded on paper. Henri Bergson, in his *Introduction to Metaphysics*, has pointed out that there are two profoundly different ways of grasping a thing: we either turn about it or enter into it. The latter method refers to the direct, "intuitive" vision of the nature of the object, whereas the former indicates the often long and laborious task of fitting the experience to the suitable means of representation that are provided by a particular medium, such as the concepts of scientific or literary language. There is no direct transformation of experience into form, but rather a search for equivalents.

The specific characteristics of various artistic media account for the different effects that can be obtained through them. The painter may represent a cemetery by offering an image of its visual appearance. In doing so, he may emphasize specific expressive qualities of the subject, such as its sadness or the peace of the resting-place. The composer Saint-Saëns, in his *Danse Macabre*, imitates some specific acoustical traits, such as the rattle of the bones or the cry of the cock. Apart from these pictorial elements, he renders the morbid rapture of the death-dance through "abstract" sound and rhythm in a way that specifies the expression and feeling-tone of his experience. He does not identify the churchyard, as the painter necessarily would (unless he used "nonobjective" form). The composer portrays no specific thing. At the most, his work permits reference to a range of possible physical or psychological situations that would fit its musical structure. When a writer says "cemetery," he identifies a species of physical place by a group-name, but he specifies neither the perceptual nor the expressive attributes of graveyards. "Darkness" designates a perceptual quality, "fear" a mental reaction. None of these three words, while likely to evoke the kind of content specified by the other two, claims those connotations explicitly. That is, cemetery may be associated with fear but also with serenity; darkness, with a cemetery or a movie theater; fear, with darkness or glaring light. Words, the building stones of language, either designate general attributes without indicating the objects to which these attributes belong or identify individuals or groups of things without specifying their attributes.

The emptiness of concepts permits statements that imply no other characteristics than the few on which the speaker and the listener are agreed. To be able to tell of "a man who showed me to the station" without having to communicate the details of his appearance is helpful in keeping the information to its essentials. If I need to specify, I can do so by using a different term ("bootblack") or by adding one ("an elderly man"). Thus, language fits an important trait of human thinking and behaving: we tend not to specify and differentiate beyond the degree required by the situation. Or, in other words, we keep our concepts, intentions, etc. as abstract as the circumstances permit.

Different needs and interests lead to linguistic differentiation in varying areas. The Eskimos have different words for "snow on the ground," "falling snow," "drifting snow," "a snowdrift" (1, p. 145). An automobile-addict carefully distinguishes Fords, Cadillacs, Chryslers, whereas his neighbor talks of cars. The language of the Klamath Indians connects by a common prefix the names of objects having a common perceptual trait, thus, all round things: circular movements, clouds, stars, hills, fruits, stones, round hats, crowds of animals or people. For us, this common property is of no practical importance. Again, the language of the African Ewe possesses a score of particular words indicating different varieties of gait—one walks leaning forward, or backward; swaying from side to side; slouchingly or smartly; swaggeringly; swinging one's arms, or only one arm; head down or up, or otherwise (5, pp. 153, 165).

Western man does not possess the corresponding specific terms, or, when he does, he uses them rarely because, under the influence of modern natural science, the "physiognomic" qualities of shape, movement, etc. have lost their vital importance for effective dealing with the problems of daily life. For our practical purposes, the significance of a man's walking is largely limited to the mere abstract change of place.

Poetical concreteness. The increasing detachment of modern language from the perceptual appearance of things poses a problem for the poet. It is true that the law of parsimony holds even more severely for poetry than for the loose speech of the streets: specification must not go beyond what is required. However, the poet's task consists not simply in the identification of things and events. He has to convey the vivid experience of the forces that make a phenomenon expressive. These forces are active essentially through the senses. Somebody may tell us correctly but quite unpoetically that the eternal repetition of the seawater's movement suggests a conception of time very different from the one that emerges from the daily strivings of man. T. S. Eliot, in the third of his *Four Quartets,* gives artistic reality to this thought by capturing the movement of the sea in the perceptually effective beat of the bell and by embodying the dynamics of human striving in the image of worrying women:

> The tolling bell
> Measures time not our time, rung by the unhurried
> Ground swell, a time
> Older than the time of chronometers, older
> Than time counted by anxious worried women
> Lying awake, calculating the future,
> Trying to unweave, unwind, unravel . . .

The ways of "practical" language seem to influence early versions of poems. The poet's primary experience may well contain a precise feeling of the perceptual qualities that carry the crucial expression. Yet, as he searches for an equivalent in the medium of words, he will often be inclined at first to use the most abstract practical name, which may call to mind things but not actually convey their characteristics charged with expression. Thus, the following early draft of a passage in Keats' "Hyperion" (Book I, verses 7–9):

> No stir of air was there,
> Not so much life as on a summer's day
> Robs not at all the dandelion's fleece

leads to this final version:

> No stir of air was there,
> Not so much life as on a summer's day
> Robs not one light seed from the feather'd grass.

The precision of the botanist, suggested by practical language ("dandelion"), is given up in favor of a description that omits the identification of the plant but specifies the expressive perceptual features of weight and movement.

Practical language, as we know it in our Western culture, also tends to state the meaning and cause of a phenomenon rather than its mere appearance, because these interpretative factors are valuable for orientation and reaction in life. In a letter dated February 14, 1819, Keats drafts the third stanza of "La Belle Dame Sans Merci" as follows:

> I see death's lilly on thy brow
> With anguish moist and fever dew
> And on thy cheeks death's fading rose
> Withereth too.

This is immediately changed into:

> I see a lilly on thy brow
> With anguish moist and fever dew
> And on thy cheeks a fading rose
> Fast withereth too.

That is, in the final form, the poet omits the diagnosis ("death") but keeps the symptoms. The mere uninterpreted description of the pale face provides the shock of discovery. The draft-version tended to reduce the visible signs to mere factual attributes of death. After the correction, paleness strikes the inner eye as the physical effect of a concrete, though unnamed power.

The transfiguration of the concrete. If it is true that the poet frequently renders an experience by stressing the perceptual features that make it expressive, one may wonder whether such a recourse to concreteness does not interfere with another important task of poetry. As I said before, one of the virtues of language is its abstractness, by which it can limit the description of an event to its essentials and to what is generally valid. In naming an object or happening, language assigns the individual case to a group and by such classification helps man to orient himself in the environment. Art, including poetry, serves the similar function of revealing the general nature of things rather than recording their individual manifestations. If so, is this useful function of art not jeopardized when, in the course of the formative process, the poet presses for the representation of specific characteristics?

This objection would seem to be based on a misunderstanding. Perceptual concreteness does not exclude abstraction in the sense of an emphasis of essentials. The poet does not cite concrete details indiscriminately but stresses the particular features that made the subject artistically pregnant for him. The peculiar ringing of an inner bell indicates to the artist that a particular thing or happening is usable material.   He seems to feel, consciously or unconsciously, that the subject presents or at least suggests a clear-cut, concentrated image of a significant life-situation. Modern man has become capable of thinking in theoretical concepts, but he is still in constant search of perceptual "models" that will allow him to deal with universals in the tangible form of concrete application. Any work of art offers just such a model situation. It stresses and clarifies features that symbolize the general significance of its specific subject matter. An incorporeal transparency distinguishes, for all its vigorous concreteness, the masterpiece from the vulgar, material heaviness of a minor work. The latter does not sufficiently transcend the particular case it presents. The masterwork embraces the whole range of human experience from the sensory perceptions to rarefied ideas. In fact, it often expresses the most abstract meaning through the most elementary stimulation. An example from painting may illustrate this point. In Delacroix' later pictures, the color scheme is reduced to a violent conflict of pure red and deep green. In this way, the appearance of concrete objects—fluttering coats of Arabian horseback riders, bleeding tigers, impenetrable woods, agitated ocean waves—is visibly referred back to the dramatic counterpoint of fiery passion versus the cool succulence of organic substance, that is, to the deep meaning that the painter saw embodied in his romantic subjects. By abstracting natural appearance in the direction of basic expressive values, the artist evokes the universal in the specific.

This transfiguration of the concrete can be observed in the poetical process. The poetry collection of the University of Buffalo possesses the draft of an unpublished poem by Aldous Huxley "about driving a car at night and the symbolic significance of the narrow universe created by the headlights." In the poem, the traces of the scene that, according to the author's comment, inspired it are largely effaced:

> In the chaos of the moon's
> Absence one creative beam
> Shapes the narrow world through which we fly

Of a complex natural situation nothing is kept but the factors that suggest symbolic meaning: the confused darkness in which a searching light discovers comprehensible bits. The adjective "creative" lifts the events expressly to the spiritual level.

The degree to which, in a work of art, the physical situation is dematerialized is an aspect of style, which varies with the author's attitude to reality and that of his period. In any style, the adequate dosage of reality-substance on the one hand and abstracted meaningful features on the other would seem to be one of the secrets of artistic achievement. Marks of the struggle for the right proportion are likely to be found in poets' worksheets. It is a struggle particularly significant for the art of a period in which the attitude toward reality represents a crucial problem.

The practical and the poetical. Aldous Huxley's poem also offers an example of another characteristic difference between practical everyday language and poetical expression. He speaks of animals discovered in the dark by the headlights. The first version reads:

> Calling up the momentary gleam

but the "momentary" is immediately substituted and transferred to the next line:

> Calling up the startled gleam
> Of momentary eyes and passing wing.

This leads to:

> Calling into life the gleam
> Of momentary wing and startled eye.

And finally:

> Calling up from nothingness
> Startled wing and momentary eye.

Probably, several factors are responsible for the changes I am quoting in a somewhat simplified form. One of these factors is particularly interesting for our discussion, namely, the quick shift from objective correctness, which is valuable for practical orientation, to a subjective truth, which may be decisive for the poetical experience. Objectively, there are animals whose existence is momentarily revealed by the beam of light. Subjectively, however, these animals exist only for the short moment during which they are seen. An observer who uses his eyes for the purpose of practical orientation will immediately deduce the objective situation from the subjective sight by means of his past experience. But, for the poet, the dependence of existence on observation is exactly what attracted his attention because that dependence symbolizes an aspect of man's attitude to reality. Therefore the changes from the objectively correct "momentary gleam" to the objectively wrong but subjectively accurate "momentary eyes." Something similar occurs for the expression of alarm, which objectively belongs most directly to the eyes of the animals startled by the light, but is subjectively enhanced by the suddenness of the reflection. Hence the objectively incorrect but poetically fitting "startled gleam." The "startled eye" in the following version represents a regression to the more practical, objective language. (This is an example of the fluctuations that occur in the striving for final expression.) Huxley ends up with "startled wing and momentary eye"—a double deviation from the practically reasonable, designed to intensify the experience the reader is invited to share.

Another illustration of the shift from the practically correct to the poetically relevant is found in one of Stephen Spender's worksheets. Again we can observe how the writer is induced at first by practical thought and language to use a formulation he has to revise in order to do better justice to his subject. A first version:

> What is the use now of meeting and speaking:
> Always when we meet I think of another meeting
> Always when we speak I think of another speaking

is transformed into:

> Oh what is the use now of our meeting and speaking
> Since every meeting is thinking of another meeting
> Since all my speaking is groping for another speaking.

Although the first version makes the situation quite clear, it stresses, in the syntactic structure of its second and third lines, practically relevant aspects instead of the poetically crucial ones. The reader's attention is focused on the mere coincidence in time of two kinds of happening: the physical meeting and speaking on the one hand, the thinking on the other. Similarly, in the first version, the grammatical subjects of the two sentences emphasize the persons involved: when *we* do this, *I* do that. But the practical information about time relations and the persons involved in the situation seems not to have been essential poetically. The poet finds the decisive issue in a paradox, namely, the identity of two contradictory happenings: physical contact and mental aloofness. By reformulating his description in a fashion that is strange to practical usage, the poet achieves a closer correspondence of form and meaning. He transforms the time relation into an equation

$$meeting = thinking\ of\ another\ meeting$$
$$speaking = groping\ for\ another\ speaking$$

and by suppressing the original subjects (we and I), he subordinates the protagonists of the practical scene to those of the poetically relevant happening, namely, the meeting and the thinking, the speaking and the groping, which are now fittingly equated.

Thus, the analysis of poetic manipulation suggests again that linguistic form is not obtained directly from the primary experience but must be considered a re-creation within the medium, subject to the particularities of the medium.[1] The literary medium is influenced by the function served by language in daily life. Similar tendencies to go beyond "practically" important characteristics of things can be observed in the visual arts.

The search for the specific. The indefiniteness of words, to which I referred before, suggests that the literary recording of an experience resembles, in its first stages, trapping an insect with a large net. The worksheets show how the poet gradually closes in on the adequate formulation. As an example, I will quote from Stephen Spender's drafts of a poem, "Abrupt and Charming Mover." The first line, "Like a skater" (quoted on p. 275), read, in an earlier version, "Like dancers." At first, the cold charm of the girl's personality may have seemed fittingly trans-

---

[1] The examples may also serve as modest illustrations of the fact that "poetic" language is not distinguished from practical language by expressing in a deliberately unusual, ornamental manner what we say straight in everyday life, but rather by offering equally straight, adequate formulations of subjects that differ from those with which practical speech is typically concerned. The difference of form springs from a difference of content.

lated into a visible image by dance performances of the ballet-type. But, when the poet made the change, he may have realized that the concept "dancer," in addition to covering the formal entertainment he had in mind, could also refer to the deeply felt compositions of a "modern" dancer—the very opposite of what he was trying to convey. The example shows that whereas logically a concept may possess a constant sum of attributes, psychologically its content varies because the context in which it appears emphasizes some of its aspects while temporarily obscuring others. Max Wertheimer, in his investigation of the syllogism, has shown that productive conclusions occur when the thinker uses his concepts beyond the limitations imposed on them by the primary context (8). Similarly, a writer, confined at first to the specific meaning that suggested the use of a given term, has then to free himself of this limitation in order to examine the additional or different meanings the term may also convey. Failure to consider the "objective" range of words accounts for much unsuccessful writing in poetry and prose.

"Skater" is better than "dancer" because the pirouettes on ice illustrate exactly the lack of emotional involvement for which the poet needed an image. The concept "dancer" turns out to be too large with regard to the pertinent attribute. "Skater" is unambiguous in this respect and therefore renders the comparison with the woman more precise.

A little later in the same draft, Spender wishes to say that the woman, like the skater, somehow attracts the heart but never "can touch beneath the senses' glassy surface." The worksheet reveals how he experimented with various verbs in order to identify the specific kind of effect on the "heart." He tries "tempting," "binding," "drawing," then decides for "enchants the heart." Each of the first three words contains the element of attraction but either leaves out the specific connotation desired or adds unsuitable ones; while "enchants" aptly describes the effect created by a mere spell.

Thus, the primary experience is often matched at first with concepts that belong to the general area of the meaning to be conveyed. These concepts overlap the meaning but do not "pinpoint" it. Which brings us back to our earlier assertion that representation does not consist in the mere selection and combination of reality-elements but rather in the construction of a fitting pattern drawn from a system of pre-existing forms. An experience meets an artistic medium, which possesses specific capacities of expression. The two have to put up with each other as best they can.

Physiognomic qualities. One of the means by which the poet gives concrete expression to ideas or to physical or psychological phenomena is related to what was said earlier about primitive language. The poet is accustomed to rely on perceptual kinships of a kind that until recently had no place in our scientific conception of the world and that are rarely expressed in our practical language. It is true that we speak without hesitation of a "soft tune," thus applying a quality of touch to sounds, or of a "cold color," thus relating temperature to an optical phenomenon. However, we do so not because we consciously acknowledge that there are qualitative similarities among perceptions derived from different senses, but rather because words like "cold," "sharp," "high," "dark" have partially lost their specific perceptual connotation for us and are now used to designate more general expressive values. But, this linguistic phenomenon itself bears witness to the fact that it is natural for man to rely on qualities that different senses have in common. These similarities are fundamental for the primitives' conception of physical relationships. They provide the bases of metaphoric speech in poetry. I quote one of the versions of the Spender passage I have been considering:

> Like a skater
> Who with sweeping silk
> Enchants the heart, but never never
> Can touch beneath the senses' glassy surface,
> So you daily weave
> Over all that's impenetrable, delight.
> For me there's no
> Fulfilment of the ripened luminary,
> Only attraction of the snow.

Silk, glassy, luminary, snow. Later versions contain in addition: "There is no warmth, no kinship" and "No sanguine calm to rest the eyes" or "No mild and sanguine image." Thus, the poet experiments with various perceptual attributes of touch, vision, temperature, and motion in order to express the woman's state of mind.

The scientific explanation of this linguistic usage is still in its earliest stages. Gestalt psychologists have emphasized it as an example of "isomorphism," that is, of structural similarity among phenomena pertaining to different physical or psychological media. The psychological kinship of, say, red wine, velvet, and the sound of a violoncello would be explainable if it could be shown that the physiological stimuli corresponding to these experiences produce effects on the nervous system that resemble each other structurally. Erich von Hornbostel has pointed out in this connection that in simple organisms there is a close unity of various sensory areas, which become differentiated only in more advanced phases of evolution (3). He states that what the senses have in common is more important than their differences. This means that "physiognomic" or expressive qualities, largely independent of the particular medium in which they appear, are probably much more basic in perceptual experience than those that psychologists were accustomed to consider as primary: hue, brightness, pitch, size, shape, etc. The poet, then, in freely connecting phenomena from various areas of experience, relies on a fundamental trait of human perception.

It may be said in passing that the term "pathetic fallacy" implies a painful misunderstanding based on a conception of the world that stresses material differences and neglects structural analogies. When Torquato Tasso relates the wailing of the wind and the dewdrops shed by the stars to the departure of his love, he is not pretending to believe in a fallacious animism, which endows nature with sympathetic feeling, but is using genuine structural similarities of the perceivable behavior of wind and water on the one hand and the experience and expression of grief on the other.

The role of imagination. Schopenhauer, in *Die Welt als Wille und Vorstellung*, praises the abstractness of words because this quality permits the reader through his imagination to supply the missing concrete detail in accordance with his individuality, sphere of knowledge, and personal whim. The opportunity of filling the framework of the literary text with private furniture is supposed to account for the fact that "literature exercises a stronger, deeper, more universal effect than pictures or statues." Schopenhauer defines literature as "the art of calling the imagination into play by means of words" (7, suppl. to Book III, chapter 37). This view tacitly implies the validity of the traditional psychological theory according to which the mind can only hold fully concrete, individual images. If this theory were correct, then, in fact, the abstractness of the contents conveyed through language would require the reader's or listener's imagination to supply the missing details.

However, aesthetic considerations suggest that to enlist the services of this sort of imagination for the appreciation of art is dangerous. It encourages the attitude of the concertgoer who uses the musical sound as a mere starting point from which to float on the stream of consciousness through fanciful landscapes. It justifies the behavior of people who, when viewing a Dutch scene in painting dream back to the sights of their honeymoon trip to Europe. None of us is free of such fancies, but we must realize that they distract our attention from the appreciation of works of art rather than enhance our understanding. This is also true for literature, even though words gain meaning only through the past experience of the reader. In practice, the reactions of readers vary widely in this respect. There are those who visualize the persons and places of a novel with photographic exactness. Others have no imagery at all. They do hardly more than acknowledge the meaning of the words, yet may be vividly touched by the expressive values of the text. The reader who uses the literary text as a mere skeleton that he has to enliven with his own flesh and blood is likely to distort the author's conception. Ample supplementary activity of the imagination is innocuous only if (a) it further develops the content of the text along structural lines set down by the author, and (b) if it does not go beyond the highest degree of concreteness compatible with the style of the particular writing.

The latter point is of importance for our further discussion. Psychological studies have shown that imagination, far from portraying everything with the automatic faithfulness of the camera, may dwell on any level of abstraction (4). Similarly, literary styles are known to vary widely in this respect. The realistic novelist has his theme carried by hundreds of details as though they were so many reflecting facets. The happenings he recounts impart their specific significance only if they are felt to be materially existent. On the other hand, the scarcity of specific characterization in a Boccaccio story or in Voltaire's *Candide* makes for a more rarefied literary climate, in which the characters are to be taken as mere types of human attitude. Their adventures, which might have been distasteful or absurd if the shadows had sipped of the blood of life, are perceived as playful exaggerations. They are but symbols of human aspiration and failure. Obviously, if a reader by means of his imagination endows all the violations of Cunégonde's womanhood with the concreteness of the pain felt by the cat that, in Flaubert's *Bouvard et Pécuchet*, escapes from a kettle of boiling water, he destroys the very substance of the author's conception. Conversely, Flaubert's cat serves its function only if its suffering is experienced as cruelly real.

Metaphor and simile. The search for the adequate level of abstractness is likely to play a role in the poetic process and to be demonstrable in literary worksheets. In this connection, a psychological analysis of the transformations that occur when the poet handles metaphors and similes is particularly promising. The following remarks are intended to offer a theoretical basis for such investigations.

What is the poetic function of metaphors? A glance at recent studies on the subject shows that metaphors are no longer considered mere flourishes designed to make literary statements more colorful and to demonstrate the writer's virtuosity in the discovery of "the similar in the dissimilar." John Middleton Murry describes the metaphor as "the means by which the less familiar is assimilated to the more familiar, the unknown to the known" (6). This use of comparisons would seem to be more didactic than poetic. We find it in scientific exposition, as when atomic structure is described by a reference to the solar system. More frequently, the simile serves to elucidate the essentials of a situation through the example of another one, which is not necessarily better known but is more concrete than the original. Thus, Stephen Spender describes the relatively intangible character of a particular woman by speaking of a skater, of sweeping silk, of glassy surface. Even so, metaphors and similes are not essentially explanatory devices. When, in *Henry V*, it is said of the contending kingdoms of France and England that "their very shores look pale with envy of each other's happiness," the purpose is not to describe the looks of the chalky coasts by a reference to the more familiar paleness of faces; or vice versa. Is this metaphor useless to a reader who, from first-hand experience, knows the Channel coasts and also the paleness of jealous faces? On the contrary, he will find it more powerful.

Later in his essay, Murry calls the poetic metaphor "chiefly a means to excite in us a vague and heightened awareness of qualities we can best call spiritual" and "the analogy by which the human mind explores the universe of quality and charts the non-measurable world." Can the psychology of language account for this effect of the literary device?

A metaphor connects two or more segments of reality, such as the Channel coasts and the pale face. Exactly in what way do these segments coexist in the mind of the reader or listener? Stephen J. Brown asserts that the image is momentarily substituted for the thing or happening it interprets (2). However, if, in the reader's mind, a pale face eclipsed the cliffs of Dover and Calais, the creative merger of the two components would obviously not occur. Brown's contention seems to be based on the above-cited psychological assumption that mental images are possible only in full concreteness; hence more than one of them could not occupy consciousness at the same time. If, however, we remember that mental images admit various levels of abstractness and that, psychologically, the content of a concept depends on the context in which it appears, another explanation suggests itself. When heterogeneous segments of reality are forced into one grammatical whole, a structural conflict results, which must be resolved. Structural unity can be obtained on the basis of certain physiognomic qualities the components have in common. Therefore, the discordant aspects of the components will retreat, the common ones will come to the fore. This does not mean that nothing but the quality of paleness will remain of Shakespeare's line. Little would be gained by that. Rather, I suggest that, negatively, the reality-character of the components is toned down and that, positively, the physiognomic qualities common to the components are vigorously underscored in each. Thus, by their combination, the components are driven to become more abstract; but the abstracted qualities continue to draw life blood from the reality contexts in which they are presented—subdued as these contexts may be.

In the whole-structure created by a metaphor, components that are and remain separate on the reality level unite on the level of physiognomic qualities. The metaphor, then, distills from reality-situations the deeper, underlying aspects of life, for whose sake alone art creates images of reality. This, I believe, is the metaphor's capacity of evoking the "spiritual," of "exploring the universe of quality."

Degrees of metaphoric abstraction. The looser the connection between components, the smaller will be the degree of the resulting abstraction. For instance, in some of Dante's similes in the *Divina Commedia,* an aspect of the story is compared to another situation, which is presented in a small, detailed, self-contained tale tied to the main story by a conjunction: "As sheep come forth from the pen, in ones, in twos, in threes, and the others stand all timid, casting eye and nose to earth, and what the first one doeth, the others do also, huddling up to her if she stand still, silly and quiet, and know not why, so saw I then the head of that happy flock move to come on, modest in countenance, in movement dignified" (*Purgatorio,* III, 79–87, translated by Thomas Okey). The simile vivifies a particular physiognomic quality, but forces little abstraction on the two components. They remain relatively isolated and can therefore retain the realism cherished in the century of Giotto. When, on the other hand, the grammatical construction merges the segments of reality into a strongly unified whole, these segments must lose concreteness. Otherwise, the construction would either split up into incompatible elements or give birth, on the reality level, to a Surrealistic monster. To test this thesis, the reader has only to experiment for a moment with such metaphors as Romeo being stabbed with a white wench's black eye or heaven stopping the nose at the crime ascribed to Desdemona.

The modern metaphor. The comparison provided by metaphor not only emphasizes certain physiognomic qualities in the primary situation, but also imbues it with the flavor of the second situation. That is, by introducing the word "stabbing," Shakespeare not only stresses the aggressiveness that stabbing and the white wench's black eye have in common, but also imports into the love situation the atmosphere of murder.[2] In this particular instance, the connotation of the metaphor obviously exaggerates the ferocity of the attack on Romeo, thus creating a subtly humorous effect. Probably the relations between the "universes," which are joined in the metaphor by the bridge of their common qualities, are a revealing characteristic of an author's literary style. One has only to compare Homer's rose-fingered dawn with Eliot's metaphoric fusion of the divebomber and the dove of the Holy Ghost ("The dove descending breaks the air with flame of incandescent terror," *Four Quartets*) in order to realize that in the first case the two components, the morning sky and the young goddess, are concordant in atmosphere whereas in the modern example the common element of the bird forces the violent contrast of supreme love and supreme murder into a tightly integrated whole. Employed this way, the metaphor becomes a means of expressing comic or tragic or tragicomic contradiction and conflict. (Bad metaphors often unintentionally produce a humorous effect.)

Incompatibility of the components, in addition to making the

---

[2] The metaphors produced in dreams have been interpreted by Freud as disguised presentations of objectionable contents. This theory seems limited because dream symbolism is so universal; it applies to many cases in which no plausible reason for camouflage can be discovered even if one admits that the unconscious censor may be much more prudish than the conscious ego. One might speculate therefore whether, in dreams, imagination does not regress to the primitive perceptual world, to that "universe wherein quality leaps to cohere with quality across the abysms of classification that divide and category the universe of intellectual apprehension" (John Middleton Murry). The symbolic analogies made possible by this evocation of primordial affinities might often serve the purpose that, as I have just described, they do in poetry, namely, they may imbue the primary object with suitable connotations. Thus, if, in a dream, a house substitutes for a woman, this may, in some cases, occur as a disguised allusion to the woman's receptive sexual role but it may further associate her with the qualities of hominess, security, protection, comfort, etc.

metaphor one of the devices by which modern art represents the contradictions of our life, serves also to increase abstractness. This is in keeping
with another trait of modern art, namely, its trend toward the demateri-
alization of reality. For the same purpose, the modern metaphor tends
to eliminate the difference in weight that commonly distinguished the
primary component from the secondary one, called in for comparison. In
our previous example, Romeo's love affair provided a stable basis of fact
even though the metaphor reduced its reality-character. In the passage
from Eliot, the dove and the bomber are more equally weighted so that
the reader, prevented from giving concreteness to the one component at
the expense of the other, is driven to still further abstraction. The fiery
carrier of love and hate as well as the setting in which its descent occurs
are both reduced to a mere shadow of the pertinent reality situations,
which compete on equal terms. Also, in many modern poems, the description of the components becomes fragmentary and there is scant
concrete detail.

An inspection of worksheets will frequently show that such high
degree of abstraction is obtained by a gradual abbreviation and condensation of an originally more concrete form. As an illustration, we may
compare the early draft of the Spender passage quoted above (p. 275)
with the final printed version:

> By night I hold you, but by day
> I watch you weave the silk cocoon
> Of a son's, or a skater's, play:
> We have no meeting place
> Beneath that dancing, glassy surface:
> The outward figure of delight
> Creates no warm and sanguine image
> Answering my language.

The early simile kept the two reality-components of the original experience, the skater and the woman, clearly isolated. The final version fuses
the two motifs to such a degree that the reality-content of the whole is
reduced to a sequence of brief, heterogeneous glimpses. An interesting
short circuit between the "silk" of the first component and the "weaving" of the second has introduced yet another reality-segment, the co-
coon, thus pressing for further abstraction. The early motif of the dancer
reappears, not instead of but together with the skater, and combines
with "glassy surface" in a complicated image. The concreteness of
"skater" is diminished through the introduction of a mysterious "son."

In short, the intimate syntactic connection achieved through subject-predicate relationship, possessive genitive, etc. joins many elements of heterogeneous origin. This confines the experience of the reader forcibly to the physiognomic level, on which the various elements reveal their kinship and hence their capacity of merging in a common whole.[3]

The worksheets also contain cases in which metaphoric reality-elements are eliminated during the process of elaboration because they endanger the unity of the whole. Stephen Spender writes:

The spring like a sea of liquid flame catches the branches

and changes it into:

The spring like a spreading liquid flame hangs to the branches.

In addition to the idea of vastness, the "sea" carries other powerful qualities that seem to be in discord with the physiognomic character of the whole. Probably, the mutual annihilation of water and fire was not introduced intentionally but occurred as an accident. Hence "sea" was replaced by "spreading," a term whose contribution is limited to the one desired quality.

REFERENCES

1. Boas, Franz. *The Mind of Primitive Man*. New York: Macmillan, 1938.
2. Brown, Stephen J. *The World of Imagery*. London, 1927.
3. Hornbostel, Erich M. von. Die Einheit der Sinne. *Melos*, 4, 290–297. (English translation in W. D. Ellis (ed.) *A Source Book of Gestalt Psychology*, 1939, selection 17.)
4. Koffka, Kurt. *Zur Analyse der Vorstellungen und ihrer Gesetze*. Leipzig: Quelle & Meyer, 1912.
5. Lévy-Bruhl, Lucien. *How Natives Think*. London, 1926.
6. Murry, John M. *Countries of the Mind*. 2nd series. Oxford, 1931.
7. Schopenhauer, Arthur. *Die Welt als Wille und Vorstellung*.
8. Wertheimer, Max. Ueber Schlussprozesse im produktiven Denken. In *Drei Abhandlungen zur Gestalttheorie*. Erlangen, 1925. (English translation in Ellis, *loc. cit.*, selection 23.)

[3] Examples like this suggest that the study of worksheets will offer valuable clues to the better understanding of enigmatic modern poetry.

V. Generalities

ON INSPIRATION

Artists have described creative work as an exasperating chore. William Butler Yeats says in "Adam's Curse":

> Better go down upon your marrow-bones
> And scrub a kitchen pavement, or break stones
> Like an old pauper, in all kinds of weather;
> For to articulate sweet sounds together
> Is to work harder than all these. . . .

and Gustave Flaubert, in a letter to a lady-friend and fellow-writer, complained: "You speak of your discouragements: if you could see mine! Sometimes I don't understand why my arms don't drop from my body with fatigue, why my brains don't melt away. I am leading a stern existence, stripped of all external pleasure, and am sustained only by a kind of permanent rage, which sometimes makes me weep tears of impotence but which never abates: I love my work with a love that is frenzied and perverted, as an ascetic loves the hair shirt that scratches his belly" (1).

No wonder that through the ages artists have eagerly tried to unburden themselves at least of the responsibility for choice and judgment. They have looked for means of assuring the power and correctness of what they were saying; and many preferred to think of themselves as the instrument rather than the player.

First published in *Art News*, Summer 1957, 56, 31–33.

Standards were developed so that beauty could be measured with the yardstick. The geometry of perspective substituted compass and ruler for the intuitive comprehension of space, and in our own day, such dogmatic prescriptions as that curved lines are forbidden or compulsory, that the artist must or must not paint women, are used to alleviate the search for the fitting form.

Traditionally, the artist also asks superior powers to assume control or, at least, to strengthen his work and guarantee its value. The Holy Scriptures derive their authority from being inspired by the Spirit. Dante invokes the help of the Muses to "put in verse matters that are hard to think" so that "the saying may not be different from the fact." But, in addition to his pagan and Christian patrons, Dante also calls upon his own mind and genius as distinct from his self, and philologists tell us that invocations to the soul are frequent in writers of antiquity.

It seems safe, however, to assert that even in such intrapersonal appeals, the soul, the genius, or the mind were conceived of as outer and higher powers, as man's part of the Divine Spirit. It took the Romantic movement to introduce the decisive shift that so profoundly affected our modern thinking—inspiration is no longer considered to come from the outside but from the inside, not from above but from below.

In many ways, this development must please the psychologists, who have contributed to putting it on firmer ground. They helped to redefine these fictitious external forces as forces of the human mind itself. They discovered that all human activities, weighty as well as slight, take place only partially in the limelight of consciousness; and they recognized that the gaps in the observable chain of causes and effects are filled by complex thought processes below the level of awareness. Man's creative accomplishments must be attributed to causes inherent somewhere in man himself. (This also holds true for the many instances in which ingenious solutions and inventions occur in a flash, apparently out of the blue, while the conscious mind is occupied with something else or with nothing in particular.) Nowhere are the contributions of the subterranean forces acknowledged more proudly than in the arts, and psychologists agree that probably no work of art that deserves the name has ever been produced, or can ever be produced, entirely at the level of consciousness.

On the other hand, we cannot help being worried by a widespread inclination of modern artists to surrender their conscious initiative, to an extent unknown in the history of art. Creative work tends to be looked upon as something done through the artist rather than by the artist, and what used to be a spiritual activity turns into a spiritualistic one-man séance. A detached observer will seek the cause of this extreme passivity in the nature of our present civilization, while the artist himself is likely to justify his passive attitude by two assumptions: (*a*) that there is a difference in principle between conscious and unconscious forces of the mind and (*b*) that by relying on impulses deriving from "the unconscious," a work of art will acquire significance automatically and infallibly.

We are accustomed to speaking of "the" unconscious as though it were a psychical power. But the unconscious is no power—it is no thing at all. At best, one may call it a place where certain mental processes occur. Even this means using an "architectural" metaphor, that is, thinking of the human mind as a house of many mansions. Strictly speaking, "unconscious" is not a noun, but an attribute of mental phenomena: it simply tells us whether these phenomena are present in consciousness or absent from it. About their nature, it tells us nothing.

Consequently, we must not assume from the outset that unconscious functioning is different in principle from conscious functioning. In fact if, for simplicity's sake, we assume that what we call creativity is a kind of reasoning, and that such reasoning can be either intellectual or perceptual—and, of course, is mostly a combination of both—then we find that intellectual as well as perceptual problem-solving can take place either consciously or unconsciously. (I call "intellectual" the handling of abstract concepts.) There is ample evidence that the mind can work on typically intellectual problems, as for instance, certain types of scientific discovery, below the level of consciousness and have the solution come as a surprise. The psychical mechanisms behind neurotic behavior, so brilliantly reconstructed by Freud, also involve a great deal of intellectual reasoning. Presumably the same holds true for the artist's activities, such as when he passes judgment on the relevance of a theme or subject-matter without consciously knowing why he chose what he did.

By "perceptual reasoning," I mean creative work that involves the handling of relations between sensory qualities, such as size, movement, space, shape, or color. Albert Einstein once described his thinking as a "combinatory play" of "certain signs and more or less clear images," either visual or muscular, the results of which had to be laboriously translated into words and other abstract signs afterward (2, p. 142). Apparently these operations were sometimes quite conscious, sometimes not, for Einstein asserted at the same occasion that "full consciousness is a limit case which can never be fully accomplished." In a similar manner, an artist works out his pictorial compositions essentially through perceptual reasoning, which is steered by processes taking place below the level of consciousness.

If it is true that creative activity operates consciously as well as unconsciously, are there no differences between conscious and unconscious operation? There are; and I have already mentioned one or two of them by implication. Why, for instance, can unconscious reasoning sometimes solve a problem that resisted the most obstinate conscious effort? My guess is that conscious reasoning tends to commit itself rather rigidly to certain patterns, which may exclude the particular connections and separations necessary for the solution of the problem. For reasons we do not know, these preconceived patterns seem to loosen below the threshold of consciousness and thereby permit a freer play of attraction and repulsion among the elements of the problem situation. Unconscious reasoning, however, could not fulfill this liberating function unless the conscious mind had laboriously set the stage before. (Carl Gustav Jung remarks pertinently: "Experience has taught me that some familiarity with the psychology of dreams will often lead people to an exaggerated trust in the unconscious, which impairs the conscious power of decision. The unconscious functions satisfactorily only when the consciousness fulfills its task to the limit of its capacity.")

Another difference between mental operations above and below the threshold of consciousness is illustrated by the artist's incapacity to control the complex interplay of such formal factors as shapes and colors in a pictorial composition by consciously defining the "actions and passions" of each element. To be sure, he senses forces that guide his brush or chisel, but the causes of these impulses lie below the level of consciousness. They derive presumably from the laws of physics, which control equilibrium in the brain fields, and for whose subtle application the conscious mind has no counterpart. The artist profits here from the uncanny capacity of the nervous system to organize a huge number of processes into one integrated activity, as shown, for instance, by the coordination of the hundreds of muscles at play when a person walks or stands.

Perhaps the most important difference lies in the primitivity of unconscious reasoning. For the artist, this primitivity can be a double-edged tool. On the one hand, creative thinking below the level of awareness preserves the primordial unity of thought and image, without which art is impossible. Our civilization promotes a separation of abstract ideas from what the senses perceive, which is fatal for the artist.

In his dreams, the Western adult retains the capacity of children and tribesmen to find symbolic meaning in the outer appearance of our world and to make concepts visible to the eyes. Hence the legitimate interest of artists in dreams. Primitive reasoning also centers forever about the basic concerns with life and death, which must remain the foundation of the work of art lest it lose itself in the shades of private sensitivity. And finally, psychoanalysis has shown that reckless honesty, an indispensable prerequisite of all creative work, is found more nearly in those layers of the human mind most remote from the contaminating influence of our evaluations and conformities.

On the other hand, however, today in both psychology and the arts there is a danger of confusing the elementary with the profound. Cultures in their late, refined stages seem to develop a weakness for primitivism, and one of the forms this inclination takes in our own case is the temptation to believe that the areas of the mind farthest away from consciousness harbor the deepest wisdom. This belief strikes me as a romantic superstition. The elementary or, to use a fashionable term, the archetypal statement has the simple strength of a primitive icon, but in its raw state it is acceptable to the developed mind only as an escape from the confusion of complexity or as a spice for the tired palate. It is a medication rather than a revelation because, in order to meet the requirements of our intricate civilization, the fundamental images of human experience must be modulated by the conditions, traditions, memories, and thoughts that make us what we are. The apparent simplicity of some truly substantial modern art is as deceptive as the apparent substance of some truly simple modern art.

Furthermore, before an artist decides passively to surrender to the spontaneous impulses coming to him from below the threshold, he may wish to remember that such utterances tend to be chaotic. This is known from dreams, which are entangled compounds of many disparate mental processes; it is known from the doodles we produce when our attention is blocked or absorbed elsewhere; or from the automatic writings of the Surrealists. One is reminded of the cryptic wave-patterns recorded when the electrical activities of the brain are caught by a pair of electrodes applied to the skull. What manifests itself on the surface of the skull is the sum total of many different and not necessarily related processes, which can be differentiated only by expert interpretation. What appears spontaneously at the surface of the mind is equally interesting, equally entangled, equally in need of being teased apart by experts, but illegible to the naked eye.

The task of processing the raw material of experience is reserved to the highest functions of the mind. It is the task of finding order in the disorder, of sifting the essential from the accidental, the significant from the private. To renounce this duty is to mistake the obscure for the deep, or, if one wishes to use traditional language, to confuse oracle with prophecy. Both oracle and prophecy can tell the truth. But the oracle, uttered in a state of possession, speaks with inarticulate tongues that need interpretation. The prophet, on the other hand, does not befog his mind with Delphic fumes, the jungle drugs of savages, or strong drink. His method of getting away from "himself" is not that of distraction but profound concentration, which requires severe discipline of all mental powers and gives shape and depth to his pronouncements.

In 1957, the sculptor Jacques Lipchitz exhibited thirty-three pieces, of which he said in the catalogue that they originated "completely automatically in the blind" (3). Nevertheless, he called them "semiautomatics" rather than "automatics" because he had subjected them to a good deal of what the Freudians would call secondary elaboration. He examined the clay figures as to whether they were suitable for bronze and made the necessary adjustments. Furthermore, among the many images suggested to him by any one piece, he chose the predominant one and, from then on, continued consciously until the vision became clarified. Lipchitz also says that during the almost half-century of his work as a sculptor, he noticed that often after periods of tense and controlled work, he felt a strong urge for "a kind of free lyrical expansion" that could not be stopped. He "literally exploded" into the semiautomatics but says now: "I do not intend to turn this process into a durable way of working. I hope with these thirty-three semiautomatics my obsession will have come to an end, having enriched my imagination with more freedom."

Lipchitz's testimony illustrates the place of spontaneity within the context of the creative process. An artist who entirely surrendered to his automatic impulses would be like the aeolian harp, whose strings are randomly put into vibration by the forces of nature. The sounds are charmingly shapeless; but the aeolian harp is a plaything, a kind of musical mobile. The forces of nature produce its sounds but are not portrayed by them. It takes the awake, inspired mind of Orpheus to receive the powers that move all living things, not as their passive victim but as their interpreter who translates the doings of these powers into articulate shapes and thus reveals them to all men.

REFERENCES

1. Flaubert, Gustave. Love, happiness and art. In *Partisan Review*, January–February 1953, p. 92. Letter to Louise Colet of April 24, 1852.
2. Hadamard, Jacques. *The Psychology of Invention in the Mathematical Field*. Princeton, N.J.: Princeton Univ. Press, 1945.
3. Lipchitz, Jacques. *Thirty-three Semi-automatics*. New York: Fine Arts Associates, 1957.

CONTEMPLATION AND CREATIVITY

When we look at simple geometrical figures, we find them to be made up of clearly discernible parts. A square, for instance, is seen as consisting of four edges. These parts allow a variety of groupings. In the square, there are four ways of setting off one edge against the remaining three, and three ways of segregating two edges from the other two; in addition, all four edges can be treated as being equally connected with each other. These groupings, when performed by the eye, are not merely quantitative. They go together with the visual structure of the figure, that is, the position of its axes, its symmetries, and the correspondences of its parts. When the grouping changes, so does the structure.

Gestalt psychologists have shown that not all of the possible combinations of elements are equally welcome to the eye. "Typically," we see the grouping that makes for the simplest available structure and that reduces tension in the visual field to a minimum. The word "typical" is to be understood in two ways. More superficially, it means that behavior in accordance with the "law of the good Gestalt" is typical for people—it will be found statistically in a majority of subjects tested by experiment. More essentially, it means that such behavior is typical for perception: When perception is pure and neutral, uninfluenced by the ex-

First published in *Festschrift Kurt Badt zum Siebzigsten Geburtstage*, edited by Martin Gosebruch, pp. 8–16. Berlin: de Gruyter, 1961.

pectations or needs of the person, the simplest possible structure will prevail.

"Pure perception" is an abstraction, as any scientific concept must be. In daily life, to perceive does not typically mean to scrutinize objects of small interest for the sole purpose of doing some experimental psychologist a favor. However, we cannot hope to learn much about how perception interacts with expectations and needs unless we study first the sensory processes by themselves, that is, in approximate isolation.

Consequently, most of the early Gestalt studies used short exposure times; often the subjects were instructed to rely on their first, fresh impressions rather than brood over what they saw. This procedure was intended to isolate the perceptual process; but there is no denying that it also was in accordance with the demands of a way of life to which Gestalt psychologists were committed, namely, the belief that man is most productively himself when he devotes his powers to the requirements of his tasks rather than to his individual self. Being "stimulus-oriented," this school of psychology by its very nature has been impatient with the subjective and the personal.

A few years ago, a Japanese psychologist, Hitoshi Sakurabayashi, published some simple observations of considerable consequence (4). He found that when the kind of pattern on which the Gestalt studies based their conclusions was subjected to prolonged inspection, fundamental structural changes occurred. The figure spontaneously abandoned its "good Gestalt" and produced other configurations. For example, within ten minutes of inspection Figure 36a presented not only the well-known reversals illustrated by b and c but also break-downs of the circle and of the over-all symmetry. Sometimes, secondary details left their context and became the center of attention, and elements of divergent function combined to paradoxical subwholes. After looking at Figure 37a for a while, subjects could visually isolate the components b and c—a feat that at first was as hard on them as Gestalt psychology predicted.

One could take these findings to mean that the basic Gestalt law of perception holds true only under limited and perhaps artificial conditions and that a much greater variety of responses is characteristic for perception when it is investigated in its proper wide range. The Gestalt thesis, then, would have to give way to a more general formulation, just as, for example, Newton's concept of absolute space was superseded by Einstein's broader theory. However, it is necessary to distinguish between a too narrow view of a large system and an adequate view of a subsystem not yet exposed to influences from beyond its range. In the first case, a correction of the view is needed; in the second, one must learn to tell factors indigenous to the system from external factors and to understand the place and function of the subsystem within the larger whole. I believe that we are dealing here with a situation of the second kind.

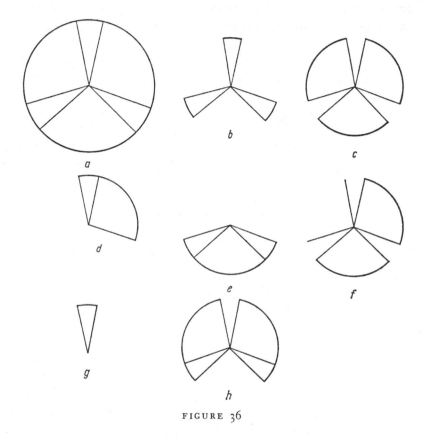

FIGURE 36

The distinction is not always clearly made. For example, in a recent textbook of psychology the authors refer to the principle involved in Sakurabayashi's experiment and, speaking of the familiar reversible figures, note: "The striking thing is that with long enough inspection, the simpler and 'better' figure does transform into the less good figure. We cannot assume that simpler, more symmetrical, and generally 'better' forms will always prevail" (2, p. 107). The statement is correct, but what does it mean to tell the student? Are the authors suggesting that the Gestalt law holds sometimes but not always? Can there be exceptions to a law of nature? Or are the effects of the law in the primary field merely overlaid by its effects in a more comprehensive field?

In my view, the facts here under discussion serve to remind us that perception is a subwhole in need of being considered in its biological context. The Gestalt laws hold without exception as all laws do, but their manifestations are often modified. Traditionally, perception was considered an isolated receptor mechanism. As such, it could be expected to operate the more accurately the longer it was exposed to the

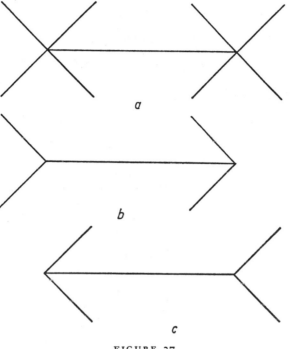

FIGURE 37

stimulus. This, however, we know is not true. Constant sights, noises, or smells drop out of awareness. The electrochemical response of the sensory organ decreases as soon as a stimulus persists unchanged. Optical afterimages demonstrate that the photosensitive substances needed for vision are rapidly exhausted when we stare at an object. When a colored surface is fixated, it soon begins to look pale. These facts go to show that the organism is not equipped to respond to a constant environment, probably because perception has evolved biologically as a means of detecting helpful or harmful events, that is, changes. It is unnecessary and indeed dangerous to spend attention on stimuli that require no reaction.

But a decline of response is not the only reaction to an immobile situation. The lacking excitation can be supplied from the mind's own inner resources. Studies on "satiation" have shown that, when a person is forced to keep up a monotonous occupation, he tries to evade it not only by such devices as inattention or forgetting but by varying the task and by the "dissolution of the whole (of both perceptual and action unities)" (3, p. 254). Sakurabayashi's observations show the ingenuity of the mind in deriving variety from a simple perceptual stimulus. In Figure 36f, for instance, the shape of an incomplete propeller transformed into that of a butterfly, and thereby the pattern changed its axis and the correspondences of all of its parts. Similarly, in Figure 36b, each of the three sectors at one time or another assumed the function of an axial base flanked by two wings. Such restructuring refreshes the perceptual experience and revives attention.

Even in its most elementary functions, the mind refuses to be bored. But its reactions are not mere evasions. By escaping from the satiated view of the "good Gestalt," the mind positively explores secondary structural properties of the stimulus at the same time. Once coerced into viewing the object longer than it would spontaneously, the mind exerts its curiosity and its power of discovering and inventing new patterns. Freed from the tyranny of the dominant structure, the image yields hidden possibilities, aspects out of the ordinary. Original, shocking, paradoxical conceptions appear. In the early stages of the process, the impulses of these changes reside below the level of awareness. The new views present themselves as surprises to the passive observer. But when these spontaneous changes are exhausted and the threat of monotony persists, the response—according to Sakurabayashi's report—rises above the threshold of consciousness and the person finds himself actively exploring and inventing.

No wonder that, in considering his findings, Sakurabayashi was reminded of the creative process. From reports on the working habits of artists such as Cézanne or Rodin, he knew that they often spent a long time looking at their object instead of busying themselves putting down what they saw. What were they doing? Were they perhaps profiting from the Gestalt disintegration brought about by prolonged inspection? After all, was it not the task of the artist to derive "original" patterns from the ordinary view of the world, to loosen conventional connections and replace them by new ones, which the average person found often hard to reconcile with the familiar sight of objects? A tempting idea.

The phenomena of prolonged inspection can be related to creativity either modestly or grandly. It can be thought of merely as a helpful device for facilitating the preparatory stages of creation. Or, more ambitiously, it can be taken as a small-scale model of the whole creative process, displaying under simple conditions the essentials of what happens when the creative thinker, artist or scientist, faces the world. Finally, the transformations caused by prolonged inspection could be considered identical with what is known as creativity. In this case, the actual "work" of the creator would be nothing but a jotting down of the revelations granted him during that inspection.

Undoubtedly, a thorough contemplation of the object to be depicted or interpreted as well as of the work itself at every stage is an essential requisite of all creation, although it is often neglected by beginners, amateurs, and inferior professionals. Even the prototype of all creators routinely paused to survey the day's work and "saw that it was good." It is also evident that such inspection discloses possibilities of structuring and restructuring the total pattern and parts of it. Many relations and groupings or suggestions for such are discovered. These discoveries serve the creative thinker to get away from the "normal" way of viewing the world. In the visual arts, for example, the normal view is determined essentially by four kinds of influence: (a) the law of the good Gestalt imposing the structurally simplest view upon perception; (b) the memory of the "objective" shape, color, proportion, size of things known to the observer from past experience; (c) the conception suggested by the practical functions of the objects; and (d) the manner of seeing and representing that prevails in the culture, especially in its visual arts.

The normal view, although indispensable even to the artist as a basis and standard of operation, cannot prevail if a person is to express with artistic truthfulness what the object means to him. Art educators use their ingenuity to find effective methods of breaking down the familiar norms of perception and representation. Some teachers expel all models from the classroom and studio or show them only briefly; others use blindfolds or dark rooms to exclude the eyes entirely so that the student is guided by memory and motor impulses alone. It seems probable that such methods help to demolish the crust of conventionality, but, in the long run, they are inferior to quiet contemplation—a procedure practiced and advocated, for example, in classical oriental art.

What, however, is contemplation? Its nature is often misinterpreted nowadays in order to make it support certain weaknesses of our civilization. (a) The "consumer-mentality" of our times inclines people toward passivity. The person acts as a receiver, who picks up what he gets and takes dictation from what the world imposes upon him. If changes from the ordinary are needed—for the sake of originality or progress—he tends to wait for such changes to be revealed or donated to him by his outer environment, that is, by the perceived and the social worlds, or furnished by the storehouse of his unconsciously generated inspirations. Given this state of mind, we are inclined to see contemplation as a purely passive activity. (*b*) Since we have learned that success is based on competition, we believe that to be creative is to be different. Originality instead of being understood to mean a manifestation of the innermost sources is perverted into denoting what is externally distinguishable from its competitors. Contemplation thereby becomes a technique for getting hold of deviations from the ordinary. (*c*) A persistent "naïve realism" has led us to believe that dealing with the world consists in recording or manipulating objective data. Learning is understood to mean the accumulation of facts and the tying together of these facts by associations. To think means to change such associations. In the theory of art, we have a long tradition of considering the aesthetic image as a faithful copy of its referent; a selection of parts taken from the referent to satisfy some criterion of taste, beauty, or essentiality; or a reshuffling of all or some of the parts of the referent (1). Therefore, to contemplate the world would be merely to take, select, and rearrange what is given.

In opposition to such views it seems necessary to make the following counterassertions.

(*a*) True contemplation is not mere waiting and gathering; it is essentially active. Even in Sakurabayashi's experiments, the transformations of the stimulus pattern only give the appearance of being changes of the outer world that impinge on a passive observer. Actually, they are the result of defense operations on the part of a mind forced to pay continued attention to an object of small interest; and, in fact, the active attempts to modify the stimulus become conscious to the observer himself as the coercive situation continues. I mentioned this earlier in order to point out that we are dealing with "exploratory behavior." When a person truly contemplates, he questioningly approaches the world, which generally is not simple like an elementary geometrical figure, but invites the mind by its mysterious complexity. The artist looks at his model in search of visible answers to the question: What is the nature of this life? More precisely, he seeks perceivable similes for the constellations and processes of reality. Contemplation does not resemble the attitude of the average "spectator"; it has no answers to offer to a person who does not ask. So many artists and art students are helpless in front of the objects they see and the shapes they make because their desire to be artists does not spring from the profound need to give an account of what it is like to be a human being in this world. On the other hand, contemplation differs from a willful quest in that it is not an interview but an audience granted by the object, which directs the conversation. Only by surrendering to the object will one obtain the answers to the questions that make the object speak.

(*b*) The creative individual has no desire to get away from what is normal and ordinary for the purpose of being different. He is not striving to relinquish the object but to penetrate it according to his own criterion of what looks true. In the course of this penetration he abandons, often unwittingly, the normal view. When Picasso speaks of his work as a "series of destructions," he evidently means the positive destruction required by a search. The desire to be different for the sake of difference is harmful, and the urge to evade the given condition derives from a pathological state of affairs inherent either in the situation, as in Sakurabayashi's experiments, or in the person, as in the "escape mechanism" of neurotics, attributed to artists by the Freudians. Faced with the pregnant sight of reality, the truly creative person does not move away from it but toward and into it. Contemplation enables him to analyze the potentialities of the object for the kind of truth that fits both him and it. "Time and reflection change the sight little by little," writes Cézanne in a letter quoted by Sakurabayashi, "till we come to understand."

(*c*) When the human mind undertakes to give an account of reality, it does not manipulate duplicates of reality. It creates patterns that render certain qualities suggested by the object. A scientific statement, for example, is a model embodying certain properties. Similarly, in the simplest case of a pictorial statement, when we represent a human face by a circle, we are not reproducing the face but are accounting for its roundness by the embodiment of roundness available in the medium of pencil lines. The contemplation of the object therefore is not so much a scrutiny of its constituents and their possible combinations as a trying on of categories derivable from the observer's medium. This aspect of creativity is less evident in the perception of simple geometrical figures, which are preshaped "ready for use," as it were; but it is most prominent when the bewilderingly complex appearance of reality must be fitted to the means of expression at the disposal of the observer.

What I have said has made the nature and function of Gestalt appear in an uncertain light. I cited experiments that seemed to show that, under certain conditions, the good Gestalt disintegrates. Later, I mentioned perception of the simplest over-all structure among the factors that establish the "normal view" and must be overcome by the art student. And when I called the Gestalt approach "stimulus-oriented," did I not accuse it implicitly of the passivity described as an obstacle to creativity?

In order to meet these doubts, it is necessary to mention first of all that Sakurabayashi's observations did not simply demonstrate a breakdown of the Gestalt principle. True, the over-all organization of the patterns, which is normally seen, disintegrated under prolonged inspection. However, if one examines the shapes that emerged instead, one notices that they are not arbitrary combinations of elements but the best possible structures available once the over-all form is blocked. They are structurally simple and are mostly symmetrical figures. In other words, the Gestalt law continues to function within the limits imposed by the situation. We are reminded of what happens under more serious pathological circumstances when the disoriented mind is unable to function as a well-organized whole but assumes nevertheless the best structure available under the stress of the disease.

To comprehend the world according to the simplest possible structure is of the utmost biological importance because the visual form approximates rather closely the physical make-up of most of the things with which we have to deal. The virtue of faithfully doing justice to the object is essential not only to elementary sensory orientation but also to the endeavors of the philosopher, the scientist, and the artist. At the same time, however, even the elementary sensory reactions to the world are bound by the conditions of the receptor mechanisms, and, as we ascend on the organic scale, we are less and less able to ignore the shape of the receptacle that does the receiving. The experiences of the past, the conventional norms and preferences, the beliefs and expectations, wishes and fears—all join in helping to shape the image of the world conceived by the creative mind.

In particular, the encounter of the artist and his world is always charged with high tension because its outcome must satisfy three conditions. It must do justice to the "facts," that is, to the normal view. It must also fit the particular world-view of the creator. And it must present the simplest possible structure obtainable for so complex a set of conditions. Unsatisfactory solutions of this problem are produced every day. In them we either fail to recognize the properties of the objective world,[1] or we find that the conception applied to the world is weak, distorted, or trivial. Or the composition meant to incorporate both demands does not provide the unity, clarity, and intensity needed to make the statement comprehensible and impressive.

The Gestalt structure, far from breaking down when perception is freed from the blinders of the experimental laboratory, is indispensable if the image born of active contemplation and realized in creative work is to have meaning and strength. However, this structure cannot be expected to preserve the monosyllabic simplicity of the geometrical pattern glanced at by a dispassionate observer. When it assumes the task of uniting the complexity of the world with the complexity of the mind, it must attain the higher simplicity of profusion organized by form. This higher simplicity is no mere gift of the senses. It is attained by that blend of freedom and disciplined concentration that the ancient Chinese writers on art liked to describe with the words of Chuang-tzu: "The painter takes off his clothes and sits cross-legged."

REFERENCES

1. Blanshard, Frances B. *Retreat from Likeness in the Theory of Painting.* New York: Columbia Univ. Press, 1945.
2. Krech, David, and Crutchfield, Richard S. *Elements of Psychology.* New York: Knopf, 1958.
3. Lewin, Kurt. *A Dynamic Theory of Personality.* New York: McGraw-Hill, 1935.
4. Sakurabayashi, Hitoshi. Studies in creation IV: The meaning of prolonged inspection from the standpoint of creation. *Japanese Journal of Psychology,* 1953, 23, 207–216, 286–288.

[1] It is perhaps necessary to state explicitly that, in my opinion, properties of the objective world can be rendered not only by images of human figures, trees, or mountains but by "abstract" shapes as well.

EMOTION AND FEELING
IN PSYCHOLOGY AND ART

In many of the more recent writings on art, words like "emotion" and "feeling" have been made to work overtime. The burden of describing the content and function of artistic activity has been carried by them to a considerable degree. Clive Bell asserts that "the starting-point for all systems of aesthetics must be the personal experience of a peculiar emotion," which he calls the "aesthetic emotion" (4, pp. 6, 7). Elsewhere, we read that art expresses and requires emotion and that beauty is an emotional element. There are also emotional aspects of design as well as cosmic emotions; and poetic language is said to express "feeling or emotion presented as the qualitative character of imaginal content" (20, p. 145). When the meaning of such terms is taken for granted, even the kind of sensitive description which aestheticians have given us will not serve to clarify the nature of artistic activity as compared to other activities of the human mind. The implied definitions are either so broad that the statements lose concrete sense, or so narrow that they make art look like an outlet for high-strung ladies.

If the dissatisfied reader turns to the psychology of emotion, he discovers that writers from Descartes to Claparède (21, p. 124) have prefaced their expositions of the subject with the assertion that it makes for the most deficient and confused chapter in the whole field. A few dec-

First published in *Confinia Psychiatrica*, 1958, *1*, 69–88.

ades ago textbook writers were at a loss as to what to say about emotion (21, p. 18). This situation still prevails in academic psychology, which has limited itself to some irritated discussion of whether emotion is to signify everything or nothing and, for the rest, has concentrated on the interesting physiological aspects of the phenomenon. At the same time, clinical psychology, less inhibited by scruples about theory, has set off a veritable inflation, comparable to that in aesthetics. Professionals and laymen speak of "emotional adjustment" and "emotional deprivation," "emotional conflict" and "emotional immaturity," "uncanny emotions" and "emotional disorders." The term covers almost everything not strictly perceptual or intellectual—wishes, attitudes, judgments, reactions, intuitions, opinions, disturbances. I suggest that an appropriate trimming of the term might discipline the thinking of the clinicians, relieve the bad conscience of the theorists, and reopen to scientific research neglected central areas of psychology. I will also examine some of the psychological problems that are hidden in aesthetics by a catch-all jargon in order to illustrate questions still to be answered for psychology in general.

I.

Emotion as a category per se. Most psychologists seem to agree with the layman that there are "emotions," i.e., that among the genera of mental states there is one called "emotion," which is made up of various species. There is no agreement on the number and names of these species. Some authors present lists of "primary emotions," from which an indefinite number of secondary ones are to be derived. Others have sample collections of emotions. R. S. Woodworth (26, p. 410) groups "feelings and emotions" under the following keynotes: pleasure, displeasure, mirth, excitement, calm, expectancy, doubt, surprise, desire, aversion, anger. Robert Leeper (17, p. 16) selects "fear, anger, feelings of guilt, feelings of grief, affection, pride in the doing of good work, enjoyment of beautiful music, and enjoyment of companionship." Here again one notices that the only common denominator is a negative one: "purely" motivational processes, such as instincts, and "purely" perceptual and intellectual ones are excluded. Everything else is stored in the large receptacle for used and discarded matter, labeled emotion. And there it rests.

The term emotion, however, suggests a positive meaning; etymologically it refers to agitation, physical, at first, and also mental, later on. In fact, at an elementary level of psychological theorizing, the term is reserved for states of high-pitched agitation, such as rage and panic. Hence the view that emotion is disruptive by definition. Once theorists look beyond the more patent aspects of the phenomenon, they discover that the spectacular extreme states are nothing but high degrees of the excitation inherent in all mental activity. This point has been made so clearly by several writers that one wonders why it has not yet become a common property of psychological thinking. W. McDougall (18, p. 148) used the swatting of a fly as an example to show that an initially almost neutral activity can work up to a clearly "emotional" state with no other change but the degree of excitement. Similarly, M. F. Meyer (19) and E. Duffy (6; 7; 8; 9) pointed out that emotion is not a particular mode of experience but a component of all experience. Duffy proposed to drop the old term entirely and to speak instead of the degree of excitation, that is, the extent of activation or arousal. To her, this dimension of intensity is one of the two "cross-sectional concepts" that apply to all behavior, the other being a motivational and cognitive one, "goal direction (including responses to relationships)." Compare here also Masserman's energetic statement (22, pp. 40 ff.).

Apparently, this more adequate view is hard to accept, even for psychologists who endorse it in principle. Kurt Koffka, for instance (15, p. 401), cites McDougall with approval, insists that emotion must not be treated as a thing, describes it as a dynamic characteristic applying to "certain psychophysical processes," and continues a few lines later to use the term "emotions." H. Schlosberg (24), in presenting what he calls "the activation theory of emotion," speaks at times as though he recognized intensity as the dimension of human behavior corresponding to what is commonly called emotion ("activation would seem to be a very good name for what emotion does to us") but proceeds to point out "one obvious failing" of his theory: "It deals only with the intensive dimension and takes no account of differentiation among the various emotions."

Emotions as motives or cognitions. Authors who assume that emotions represent a specific category of mental states run into instructive difficulties. Leeper (17), after rejecting disruptiveness and disorganization as differentiating traits of emotion, presents a criterion of his own. He describes emotions as a subclass of motive, distinguished by their complexity from the more elementary "bodily drives or physiological motives such as hunger, thirst, toothache, and craving for salt." When animals become "more complex in their receptor equipment, motor equipment and capacity for learning," they develop fear based on past experience, an interest in their offspring not dependent on physiological impulses, an urge to explore, etc. This is the kind of motive Leeper calls "the emotions." His terminology accomplishes the feat of denying the emotional quality to hunger and toothache and of identifying emotions by means of properties that by no stretch of the term can be described as specifically emotional, namely, the cognitive and motivational capacities for learning, understanding, foresight, interest, curiosity.

Attempts to describe emotions as a subclass of cognition do not seem to fare better. According to C. D. Broad (5), an emotion is a cognition that has an emotional quality. "To be fearing a snake . . . is to be cognising something—correctly or incorrectly—as a snake, and for that cognition to be toned with fearfulness." It will be noticed that, in the example, the cognitive aspect of the reaction is limited to the identification of the snake rather than including, as it surely must, the recognition of its fearsomeness. Once this correction is made, nothing seems to remain of the "emotional quality" but the sheer, unspecific excitement, which accompanies the (cognitive) realization of danger and the (conative) desire to escape. More in general, the reader of Broad's paper finds that the characteristics attributed by the author to the emotions (motivated and unmotivated, misplaced, appropriate and inappropriate, etc.) do not apply to the emotional but to the cognitive aspects of the reactions in question. Therefore it seems hardly justified to call these reactions emotions. On the other hand, calling them cognitions leaves the description clearly incomplete.

A label that stops research. Academic psychology is driven to call certain mental states emotions because it is accustomed to distributing all psychological phenomena into the three compartments of cognition, motivation, and emotion instead of realizing that every mental state has cognitive, motivational, and emotional dimensions and cannot be defined properly by any one of the three. In regard to cognition and motivation, the pigeonholing procedure has had grave consequences for research. Only processes that—without obvious distortion of their nature —can be described as pure percepts, pure acts of thinking or learning, pure motives, etc. are being given more than cursory attention by scientific psychologists. One can strip hunger of its cognitive and emotional aspects and classify it as a motive, and a glance at a blue triangle may not be seriously falsified by being called an act of perception. But the more relevant psychological phenomena resist such treatment. Hope or pride, for instance, do not fit into either box: they inseparably combine certain views of persons and situations with certain needs. They are neither motives nor percepts, and therefore scientific psychologists do not deal with them. Scientific psychologists can speak about sex but have little to say about love because love is not an instinct. Hate, ambition, honesty, grief, trust, happiness, courage, shame, admiration, modesty—stirrings like these have always been considered characteristic of the human mind; but their study has found no place in scientific psychology. It is left to philosophers who still consider the analysis of the mind as their business; to clinicians, who are forced by practical necessity to deal with the essentials of mental life; and to commonsense talk inside and outside of textbooks and lectures. Much of such discussion does not meet scientific standards; but it is also true that scientific standards will have to fit the essential tasks of psychology if we wish to develop a discipline that, by the standards of the great poets and thinkers and by those of the common man, deserves to be called a science of the human mind.

Academic psychologists have not simply overlooked the existence of the salient features of the mind. Since they could not fit them into the two main boxes, motivation and cognition, they put them in the third and called them emotions. The trouble with this third category has been that while there are enough mental states that can be trimmed to look like pure motives or pure percepts, the excitement of emotion is dominant only in rare extremes and even then it is an unspecific by-product of what the person perceives, knows, understands, and desires. Hence the embarrassed searching for something to talk about in the chapters on emotions, and the attempts to equip emotions with cognitive and conative features in order to give them body, variety, and function. Once such essentially perceptual experiences as pleasure and pain, and such complex states as sadness and joy, had been filed under emotion, there was no stopping, so that by now we have the above-cited lists of emotions—which read like the inventory of a storage vault.

We are not dealing here with a matter of mere terminology nor with one of conceptual tidiness alone. By pigeonholing the essential objects of true psychological interest, academic psychologists have removed them from the grasp of research. No better treatment than disorderly enumeration can be given them as long as they remain labeled as emotions, because the emotional component offers no understanding of the processes that cause the excitement. The history of medicine offers useful analogies. In olden days, people fell sick with "the fever." What we recognize now as a symptom was then considered the nature of the illness. Not before the causal processes of infection, etc. became the center of interest was it possible to understand the diseases and to distinguish them adequately from each other. Nowadays, people have "emotional difficulties." But when, for instance, a college student cannot use his intelligence and his interest, does this happen because he is "emotionally upset," or is he upset because such conative factors as thwarted wishes and such cognitive ones as his particular perception of himself and the world around him interfere with his work? And when a person "reacts emotionally," does he replace reason with emotion, or does he rather replace one set of motives and percepts with another, less appropriate one, as for instance, by viewing a controversy as a matter of personal attack? So long as the psychologist thinks and acts as a clinician, the crude labeling by symptom may matter little. Whatever words he uses, he cannot help getting involved with the substance of the problem at hand. For the psychologist as an academic scientist, however, such labeling has the effect of putting the phenomenon on a sidetrack and thus removing it from the work on motivation and cognition, by which alone it can profit and to which, in turn, it gives its *raison d'être*. Something is wrong if the theorist and experimentalist wait for the clinician to figure out, under the pressure of his practical obligations, what "anxiety" is. We must not blame the clinician if our more relevant concepts give off a sickroom smell; he has done more than his share.

Perhaps the academic psychologist will defend himself by saying that scientific virtue requires him to limit himself to simpler problems until he is ready to deal with complex ones. But it is one thing to proceed with caution and another not to envisage the goal. By hiding the central processes under the cloak of emotion we help make ourselves blind to the true object of our science.[1]

Models of the past. The historian will have to tell us who contributed what to this development. Surely it would seem unjust to blame the great thinkers of the seventeenth century for it. It is misleading, although technically correct, for instance, to state that "Descartes specified six primary emotions" (27, p. 27). In Les Passions de l'Âme, Descartes divided the functions of the soul into active and passive ones ("actions" and "passions"). Passions are affections of the soul, caused either by the soul itself or by the body. Those caused by the body are

---

[1] Recent attempts to put the milled-out vitamins back in the bread are thus far conceived as studies of the mutual influence of "motives" and "percepts." It remains to be seen whether this promising development will lead to the exploration of mental states that cannot be reduced either to motives or to percepts but are compounds of motivational, cognitive, and emotional aspects from the outset.

subjectively attributed either to outer objects (seeing the light of a torch) or to the body (feeling hunger or pain), or they seem to be produced by the soul itself. These latter, the sentiments of wonder, love, hatred, desire, joy, and sadness, plus their derivations, are named passions in the more restricted sense. Of them, Descartes says that they may be called perceptions in that they are passive, or "sentiments" in that the soul receives them in the same way as the objects of the outer senses, or, "even better, one may call them emotions of the soul, not only because this name may be given to all changes that come about in the soul . . . but particularly because among all the kinds of activity the soul can have there are none that agitate and shake it so strongly as do these passions" (article 28). "Emotions," then, means "agitations," and the term is used to describe one attribute of the mental reactions Descartes continues to call passions throughout his treatise. In fact, the first and foremost of them, namely wonder, is said to be devoid of emotion because it does not regard good and evil but is merely the surprised attention given to rare objects (articles 70, 71).

Spinoza also keeps the emotional aspect of human reactions in its proper subordinate place. Where Descartes speaks of passions, the *Ethics* uses the term "affectus," meaning on the one hand affections of the body by which the physical power of action in the body is increased or diminished, aided or restrained, and on the other hand, the conscious awareness ("ideae") of these affections (Book III, definition 3). The basic affection is conscious desire ("cupiditas"), which is experienced as pleasure ("laetitia") when it is furthered and as displeasure ("tristitia") when it is hampered in its striving for greater perfection (Book III, proposition 57). From these primary affections, the others derive, all of which are defined in cognitive and motivational terms; for instance, love is pleasure—that is, unhampered stirring—concomitant with the awareness of an external cause (Book III, proposition 13). Primitive though such a definition may be, it invites and permits further investigation, as distinguished from our present conception of love as a kind of nondescript quiver.

Feeling. In the field of aesthetics, the generation of Clive Bell (4) and Roger Fry (11) preferred to speak of emotions, whereas writers such as D. W. Prall and Susanne K. Langer rely heavily on the word "feeling." Prall (20, p. 147) defines aesthetic experience as "the full felt response to what is directly given," and to Langer (16, p. 40) "art is the creation of forms symbolic of human feeling." Psychologists speak of feelings as well as of emotions, but the distinction between the two terms is admittedly unclear. Emotion tends to be used to describe agitation or to designate a state of mind by the agitation it involves. Feeling is used for cognitive reactions that seem to defy further decomposition. Aveling, for instance (21, p. 49), restricts the term feeling to pleasure-unpleasure, because they "seem to be irreducible to any other conscious experience whereas all other 'feelings' can be reduced either to cognitive or to conative processes." McDougall also appears unwilling to treat "pleasant and unpleasant feelings" as compounds of percepts and strivings. He concedes to them the status of one of the "three distinguishable but inseparable aspects of all mental activity"—knowing, striving, and feeling—(18, p. 146), while emotion is considered only the degree of excitement found in any such activity. To Claparède, "feelings are useful in our conduct while emotions serve no purpose" (21, p. 126). He lists as feelings not only such percepts as pain but also such "intellectual feelings" as surprise, curiosity, doubt, that is, the emotionally toned reactions to intellectual or perceptual insight, as well as William James's "feelings of relation" (14, I, p. 245), those seemingly nonintellectual and nonperceptual cognitions to which reference will be made later. Here again psychology hardly can be said to offer much clarification to the theorist of art.

A conceptual framework. The foregoing discussion will have shown that the misuse of the terms emotion and feeling is only a local consequence of a more general defect of psychological reasoning, namely, the habit of defining a mental act by one of its dimensions. To remedy this situation, I suggested that for all but the most elementary purposes a psychological process must be described by *three fundamental aspects: the cognitive, the motivational, and the emotional.* That is, we must be able to tell what objects or actions are observed, what strivings take place in these objects or actions, and how strong are the tensions produced by the strivings. In the following paragraphs, I shall attempt to define, crudely and tentatively, the roles of these three factors in the general framework of mental functioning.

1. All mental events are *perceived*, either consciously or unconsciously. These perceived events fall under two broad categories, which I shall call extracerebral and intracerebral. Extracerebral percepts are directly stimulated by events outside of the brain. Such events may occur outside of my body (I see a running rat) or inside of it (I feel hunger). Intracerebral percepts are stimulated by events confined to the brain, such as thoughts, desires, images. These latter mental processes are generally not considered under the heading of perception; it is essential,

however, that their perceptual aspects not be overlooked. Thoughts and wishes are just as directly perceived as are running rats and hunger.

2. Every mental event presents itself as *directed striving* in two respects: with regard to the observing and to the observed. My perceiving of the rat, of my hunger, of my thought, is purposeful and goal-directed: I am striving to become aware of what is going on. At the same time, the target of this awareness is also animated by directed striving. The rat is running toward a goal; the hunger clamors for satisfaction; the concepts of thought are dynamic in character and interact in the direction of a finding or solution. Psychologists speak of motivation when they wish to describe the strivings of the perceiving self, the eager rat, the hungry stomach, or the searching thought. They speak of expression when they wish to describe the straining of the rat's body, the soaring of a poplar tree or a Gothic arch. They generally fail to see that the intracerebral thought contents also have expression: in concepts such as power, peace, or freedom, expressive qualities of strength, of quietness, of expansiveness are perceived. Also, with regard to the total situation, psychologists neglect the fact that motivation and expression must be treated under one heading as the dynamics of mental contents and events.

3. The cognitive aspect of mental life represents the substratum of all experience: the totality of what mental events are about; and what is being perceived. Within this totality, the dynamic aspect refers to the forces of mental life, to what is going on. Emotion, finally, is the *tension or excitement level*, produced by the interaction of mental forces. In the mechanics of the mind, emotion is the stress caused by the tractions and pressures that constitute mental activity. Thus, emotion does not contribute impulses of its own; it is merely an effect of the play of forces taking place within the mind.

II.

Among the reasons why the words emotion and feeling are frequently chosen to describe the production and reception of art are the following three:

1. Art is said to be made and sought because it gives pleasure; and pleasure is described as an emotion.

2. The particular aspects of reality caught and reproduced by the work of art are said to be accessible neither to sensory perception nor to the intellect but instead to a third cognitive capacity, called feeling.

3. The aspects of reality inherent in the work of art are not only

received as factual information but arouse states of mind that are called emotions or feelings.

Pleasure—an unspecific criterion. Words such as "pleasure," "delight," and "enjoyment" abound in the writings on art; George Santayana, for instance, defines beauty as "pleasure regarded as the quality of a thing" (23, p. 49). Nevertheless, not much needs to be said about the hedonistic theory.

Since little is gained by describing a mental phenomenon as emotion, that is, by its mere tension level, I ask instead: What kind of percept is pleasure? I find it to be an extracerebral percept, a state of well-being, experienced in the body. Typically, the sensation is connected with some directed tension, such as a striving of the self toward the pleasure-giving object, or a tonic expansion of the self, or a positively experienced let-up of pressure. In such a description, nothing can be found that leads to a distinction between pleasure derived from art and pleasure derived from any other source, as, for instance, food. The erroneous impression that there is a specific "aesthetic pleasure" is due to the fact that a given component of a mental state receives, from the total state, modifications that are easily attributed to the nature of the component itself. If the pleasure derived from a piece of sculpture "feels" different than that derived from food, the difference is due to the context, since everything that can be cited to characterize it is a part of the difference between looking at sculpture and tasting food. Pleasure as such is no more specific than the purr of a cat.

Pleasure always indicates that the given situation conforms to some need of the organism—a need for stimulation or distension. But this attribute of pleasure is, again, not distinctive. Therefore, the hedonistic definition, according to which art is what produces pleasure, conveys nothing but the trivial fact that art satisfies some kind of need; it provides a pseudoanswer, which tends to dry up curiosity. Scores of studies in so-called experimental aesthetics have missed their more relevant data by being based on the question: "Do you like it?" rather than: "What do you perceive?"

If we wish to go further, we must move beyond pleasure itself and ask with what kinds of states pleasure is associated in the particular instance of art. Answers can be drawn from the whole range of percepts, extracerebral as well as intracerebral. The harmony of a color-scheme or a musical chord may give pleasure; so may the well-balanced, integrated, and clearly directed movements experienced by a dancer through the muscle tension in his body. Pleasure may derive from Denise Levertov's lines: "Come back, cat. Thrash the silence with your autonomous feather tail," by the articulate dynamics of whipped quietness, the spirit of independence brought to life in animal motion, the urgent appeal of rhythmical "a"-sounds, brightened at the end by the radiant vowel of "tail." Memory may join sensory perception when a pleasurable correspondence is discovered between the configuration of forces observed in a pattern of shapes and colors or words and that inherent in a significant life situation.

These are not attributes but causes of pleasure. By examining the conditions that produce pleasure, art can be distinguished from other sources of satisfaction. It also becomes possible to make inferences about the nature of the specific needs served by art. Such an approach invites research rather than leading it into a dead end.

Feeling as perception and unconscious judgment. It is commonly agreed that art presents sensory patterns, images, and thoughts not for their own sake but as forms capable of transmitting something else. The final content of the work of art is frequently described as emotions or feelings. Thus, Roger Fry calls the work of art "an expression of emotions regarded as ends in themselves" (11, p. 29). In the older writers, assertions of this kind refer mostly to internal states such as fear, joy, and sadness, but more recent writers have broadened the offering. According to Prall, the feelings conveyed by the artist "may range from the hard look of iron machines or polished brass railings to delicate shallows of light among grass stems, from feelings of the lightest gayety to feelings of fate and doom" (20, p. 160).

Art, then, deals with the kind of mental state that, so far, psychology has failed to investigate. It deals also with the external expression of such states. Psychologists have made short shrift of fear, joy, and sadness by filing them away as emotions. And when it came to experimenting with the external expression of these states of mind, that is, with their manifestations in visible or audible patterns (a human face, a piece of music), they did not investigate these manifestations either. They concentrated on finding out what "feelings"—sadness, or calmness, or passion—observers were willing to attribute to the object and to what extent this was done "correctly." But they rarely asked what particular audible or visible features of the object determined the reactions of the observers. The question of how observers accomplished their feats was not made a part of the study, but was taken care of by an untested assumption. The traditional belief, for example, that in such experiments observers rely on associations established in the past, makes it unnecessary to study either the character of the perceived object or the processes taking place in the perceiver—correlations among unknowns will suffice. Aestheticians have hardly done better, except that their answer to the question: How do people do it? tends to be: By feeling! rather than: By association. They prefer to attribute the accomplishments of the artist and his public to a cognitive faculty *sui generis*, neither perceptual nor intellectual.

Suppose now we wished to find out why people see pride in the Napoleonic stance of an actor or a marble figure; and suppose we were unwilling to gloss over the problem by simply relying on the assumption that observers know from past experience how proud people carry themselves. In examining the stimulus, we would notice that the head is raised above the plane of human interaction, that the eyes are closed or looking upward, that the body is stretched to its greatest height, that the chest is ostentatiously presented, that the hands are withholding acceptance and cooperation by hiding between the buttons of the waistcoat or in the trouser pockets. These features will not suggest any kinship with pride as long as pride is simply an uninvestigated "emotion." But, if we tried to do our psychological duty by studying a proud person's state of mind, even the most primitive examination would show that such a person found creatures in the outer world so inferior to his own excellence that they could only be dominated, not dealt with as equals. We would find him striving to tower over them and to impress his superiority upon them. We might also notice emotion, that is, the degree of tension or excitement involved, but it would tell us nothing specific. But the discovery that the forces perceivable in the image of the Napoleonic figure are structurally akin (isomorphic) to the forces operant in the intracerebral attitudes of proud rising, withdrawing, displaying, etc. would be revealing. The obstructive split between outer dynamics and inner dynamics, caused by the separation of perceptual expression from motivation, would be overcome.

Once we examine concretely what people do when they apprehend expression, it becomes apparent that the instrument they use is perception, not some other mysterious cognitive faculty, for which we need the special term feeling. It is perception, not of the static aspects of shape, size, hue, or pitch, which can be measured with some yardstick, but of the directed tensions conveyed by these same stimuli. (Which particular properties of visible and audible patterns contain the dynamic features has been shown elsewhere [2; 3].) And what is decisive for the present discussion is that these directed tensions are as immediately perceptual as are spatial dimensions, quantities, or locations. Owing to a traditional preference for static conceptions, Western theorizing has tended to exclude the dynamic aspects from perception and to assign them either to a kind of internally generated projection or to the special, negatively defined faculty of feeling (2).

The more comprehensive way of perceiving, which stresses directed tensions, is a prerequisite for, but not a monopoly of, the aesthetic attitude. Once it is understood that the capacity to apprehend artistic expression grows out of full, unrestricted everyday observation, an artificial distinction between the two will break down, and research in the general psychology of perception will cross-fertilize with that in the field of art.

My assertion that it is uneconomical and misleading to assume the existence of a special faculty of feeling has been derived so far from a discussion of the relatively simplest processes, namely, the passive apprehension of perceptual patterns. But art involves more than perceiving the dynamic quality of, say, rapid attack in the swoop of a seagull or the argument of a trial lawyer. It requires, for instance, an ability to judge the correctness of a compositional structure, in the visual arts or in music, as to balance, unity, and rhythm. In such tasks, the intellect, which can apply conceptual rules such as those of proportion, plays a part but only a minor one. The judgment of right and wrong is actually performed by mere looking and listening, often without any awareness of the criteria that determine it. It takes a stubborn effort—successful only in the good teacher or critic—to make some such criteria explicit. But again we should be most reluctant to attribute these "intuitive" judgments to a cognitive faculty *sui generis*. What guides the artist or connoisseur turns out to be the same tensions that we have recognized as the very basis of perception. In a successful composition, the forces that make up the pattern are in balance; but, if the work is incomplete or unsuccessful, pushes and pulls within the pattern indicate not only that something is wrong but also where correction should apply and in what directions it should proceed. Here again, artistic "feeling," to the extent to which it is an intuitive response to the given structure, is nothing but ordinary perception. It is a capacity not different in principle from that displayed by a tightrope walker or even a dog who balances a stick in his mouth.

One step further, and we remember that art goes beyond direct perception. Artistic expression has always a semantic function; the painted and carved images stand for referents, and so do the shapes of music and the events and thoughts described by the poet. Therefore, art requires the judging of meaning, relevance, and truth, and again the task is accomplished largely by the mysterious capacity of feeling. Is the artist's presentation relevant for, or true to, the kind of thing for which it stands? Does the particular sunflower that models for the artist or is seen on his canvas by the beholder look the way sunflowers look—to the artist, to the beholder? Does it conform to their conceptions of the nature of flowers in general? Does its dynamic pattern of, say, graceful heaviness capture a way of behavior worth capturing? These judgements are not simply perceptual although ultimately they refer to percepts. They are based on the observer's entire life experience and involve his convictions, values, biases, memories, and preferences. They presuppose translations of intellectual conclusions into perceptual images, and vice versa; and, at the moment at which they take place, they necessarily require a lightning-fast comparison of the given individual object with this complex precipitate of thought and vision.

Here again, feeling is defined merely by what it is not. It describes a cognitive capacity that is neither mere perceiving nor based on conscious logical operations of the intellect. Here, too, there may be no awareness of the guiding criteria at work. How does the human mind perform such feats?

In searching for the answer, the student of art discovers one of the most astonishing gaps in the program of modern psychology. If we remember to how large an extent all human activity, from the driving of a car and the adding up of digits to the dealing with other people and the solution of creative problems in art and science, is done "intuitively" or "mechanically," that is, without conscious awareness of the processes that determine the action, it is hard to understand why psychologists limit their interest in this basic aspect of our unconscious functioning to the special case of "Freudian" repression. The mere fact that so many of our judgments of right and wrong are made before we know why we make them should alert the profession. William James estimated that "a good third of our psychic life consists in these rapid premonitory perspective views of schemes of thought not yet articulate" (14, I, p. 253).

Judging by the accomplishments of these unconscious performances, we must conclude that mental capacities of the highest order are at work: reasoning, selecting, comparing, problem solving by restructuring, etc. But are these processes the same as their counterparts, known from conscious experience? And if so, do they function the same way? What should be made of the ample anecdotal evidence according to which scientific and artistic thinking can solve, under the protective cover of the unconscious, problems whose solutions the conscious mind vainly struggled to find? (12; 13). Is unconscious creation perhaps less subject to sets or other constraints that hamper conscious invention? Psychoanalysis has given illustrations of what distinguishes conscious from unconscious reasoning, but it has also uncovered certain striking similarities. For instance, the dream mechanisms of condensation, fusion, displacement of function, and symbolism (10, chapter 6) closely resemble typical, and often conscious, operations of the artist.

Unless concrete research suggests that the processes involved here are fundamentally different from those operating in conscious experience, there is no reason to imitate Molière's doctoral candidate who explained the sleep-inducing effect of opium by a *virtus dormitiva*.

The aesthetic experience. Up to this point, art has been discussed as though it were only a transmitter of information about visible objects or audible events, subject matter, and the significant patterns of forces inherent in such material. But art not only acknowledges the presence of, say, agitation in a piece of music or bewildered wavering in the thoughts of Hamlet; it makes the artist and his public "feel" these dynamic states as personal "experiences." Tolstoy defined art as "a human activity consisting in this, that one man consciously, by means of certain external signs, hands on to others feelings he has lived through, and that others are infected by these feelings and also experience them" (25, p. 123). What is the nature of such experiences?

In the aesthetic discussion of this question, the use of the word feeling has made for a curious pseudoproblem. The notion was introduced by the theory of empathy, according to which architecture or music owed its expressiveness to past experiences of the observer, projected by him on suitable objects. When the theory was abandoned by those who realized that properties of the perceived objects themselves are responsible for the bulk of expression, the terminology remained, and with it the problem of how a lifeless object could manifest feelings if they were not cast upon it by some "pathetic fallacy." According to Susanne Langer, who entitled a book on aesthetics *Feeling and Form*, "the solution of the difficulty lies . . . in the recognition that what art expresses is *not* actual feeling, but ideas of feeling" (16, p. 59). This formulation hides the problem by the word "expresses"; for either Langer's "ideas" are received, the way ideas usually are, as intellectual information, in which case the difference between an artistic and a purely informative statement is neglected by the formulation; or the ideas are "felt," that is, are "feelings," in which case the dilemma remains what it was.

Once the terminological camouflage is removed, it appears that three different states—or perhaps three degrees of one state—must be distinguished in the phenomenon under discussion.

a) At a first level, the difference between the mere apprehension of information and the fuller artistic "experience" is identical with that between the static and the dynamic properties of percepts. A piece of music can be played or listened to in a way that conveys only an assembly of pitches and durations. The resulting sounds are "dead" because, by lacking dynamics, they lack the main structural quality of life; and they leave the listener indifferent because only by exhibiting patterns of forces it shares with the human mind can music build a connection between two media that otherwise are alien to each other—the extracerebral world of pure sounds and the intracerebral one of human striving. Similarly, so long as Hamlet's monologues are only understood but not dynamically perceived as a zigzag course of motivational vectors, they remain in the domain of the psychologist or historian. So far, then, there is nothing in aesthetic experience that was not discussed in the preceding section as a property of ordinary perception.

b) Dynamic features will enliven not only the percepts of the outer physical world but also sensations received from inside the body, notably the kinesthetic cues of muscular strains and stresses. In particular, the performance of actors and dancers depends mainly on kinesthetic messages. In this sensory area, it is even more evident than in vision or hearing that the percept consists not only of information about muscular displacement, the size and direction of effort, etc., but is itself strongly dynamic, that is, expressive. However, intense though such awareness of the behavior of kinesthetic forces may be, it is not necessarily and, in fact, not commonly experienced as a property of the observer's own self. The actor senses his body assume the stance of a reckless tyrant without "feeling" tyrannical himself. As carriers of expressive kinesthetic patterns, the performer's bodily sensations are detached from his self, which observes and controls them, as a painter observes and controls the visual forces produced by shapes and colors on the canvas. These sensations function as a perceptual object. Animated by their dynamic character, the performance of the actor or dancer looks expressive, as distinguished from a cold display of gestures.

Kinesthetic reactions may also occur in the viewer. Indeed, such reactions may be aroused by the perception of any expressive pattern in any medium, such as the dynamic shapes of music, of architecture, of painting. These kinesthetic responses in the observer have led to the theory of empathy, that is, the notion that expression is nothing but the observer's own (past or present) experience, projected upon the percept. Erroneous though this theory is, it has drawn attention to the bodily resonance effect, which in some persons and at some occasions heightens the artistic experience considerably.

c) A third level is attained when the dynamics of the art product engulfs the self of the performer, creator, or beholder, that is, when the actor *becomes* Othello, when the novelist's body is shaken by the pains that torture his poisoned heroine, or when melancholy music moves the listener to tears. Theorists and practitioners have called such "internalization" of perceived expression artistically inappropriate. "Aesthetic distance" has been described as a prerequisite of the "aesthetic attitude." However, when Tolstoy speaks of the "feelings" by which the reader or listener is "infected," he clearly refers to the flooding of the self with the dynamics of the work of art. So, presumably, does Herbert S. Langfeld when he asserts that both phylogenetically and ontogenetically, "we can trace in the development of aesthetic appreciation a gradual diminution of the emotional response."

A psychology of the self does not yet exist that is subtle enough to describe the precise difference between situations in which the self acts as an autonomous perceiver of a dynamic state and those in which the self is the very center of such a state. The difference between feeling fear within oneself and being afraid is illustrated by the well-known effect of adrenalin injection. Whatever may be the exact psychological nature of the experience when it is driven to its aesthetically suspect climax, there seems to be no reason to assume that it goes beyond the confines of ordinary perception. No additional mental faculty of "feeling" is involved.

The curious, variable relation between perceived dynamic patterns and the perceiver's self plays a role in a number of insufficiently explored mental states, such as pity, sympathy, identification, self-control, self-estrangement, persona, spontaneity, affectation. Here are tasks that will be noticed and approached when "emotions" and "feelings" will have ceased to obstruct the view.

REFERENCES

1. Arnheim, Rudolf. *Art and Visual Perception*. Berkeley and Los Angeles: Univ. of Calif. Press, 1954.

2. ———. The gestalt theory of expression. This volume, pp. 51–73.

3. ———. Perceptual and aesthetic aspects of the movement response. This volume, pp. 74–89.

4. Bell, Clive. *Art*. London: Chatto and Windus, 1931.

5. Broad, C. D. Emotion and sentiment. *Journal of Aesthetics and Art Criticism*, 1954, 13, 203–214.

6. Duffy, Elizabeth. The conceptual categories of psychology: a suggestion for revision. *Psychological Review*, 1941, 48, 177–203.

7. ———. Emotion: an example of the need for reorientation in psychology. *Psychological Review*, 1934, 41, 184–198.

8. ———. An explanation of "emotional" phenomena without the use of the concept "emotion." *Journal of General Psychology*, 1941, 25, 283–293.

9. ———. Leeper's "motivational theory of emotion." *Psychological Review*, 1948, 55, 324–335.

10. Freud, S. *The Interpretation of Dreams*. New York, 1927.

11. Fry, Roger. *Vision and Design*. Harmondsworth: Pelican, 1937.

12. Ghiselin, Brewster (ed.). *The Creative Process*. Berkeley and Los Angeles: Univ. of Calif. Press, 1952.

13. Hadamard, Jacques S. *The Psychology of Invention in the Mathematical Field*. Princeton, N.J.: Princeton Univ. Press, 1945.

14. James, William. *The Principles of Psychology*. New York: Dover, 1950.

15. Koffka, Kurt. *Principles of Gestalt Psychology*. New York: Harcourt, Brace, 1935.

16. Langer, Susanne K. *Feeling and Form*. New York: Scribner, 1953.

17. Leeper, Robert W. A motivational theory of emotion to replace "emotion as disorganized response." *Psychological Review*, 1948, 55, 5–21.

18. McDougall, William. *The Energies of Men*. New York, 1933.

19. Meyer, M. F. That whale among the fishes—the theory of emotions. *Psychological Review*, 1933, 40, 292–300.

20. Prall, D. W. *Aesthetic Analysis*. New York, 1936.

21. Reymert, M. L. (ed.) *Feelings and emotions: the Wittenberg Symposium*. Worcester, Mass., 1928.

22. ———. (ed.) *Feelings and emotions: the Mooseheart Symposium*. New York, 1950.

23. Santayana, George. *The Sense of Beauty*. New York, 1896.

24. Schlosberg, Harold. Three dimensions of emotion. *Psychological Review*, 1954, 61, 81–88.

25. Tolstoy, Leo. *What is Art? and Essays on Art*. New York, 1942.

26. Woodworth, Robert S. *Psychology*. New York: Holt, 1940.

27. Young, Paul T. *Emotion in Man and Animal*. New York, 1943.

THE ROBIN AND THE SAINT

In the garden of my mother's neighbor there is a bird-feeding station. The open box containing the seeds is protected by a wooden gable roof. On a console under the roof stands a small white figure of St. Francis, who thus presides over the feeding operations; and on the rim of the box, there is a life-sized and realistically colored wooden robin, poised to dip into the feed. The feeding station is not a work of art, but it can serve to illustrate some aspects of the question: What is the place of art in the world of things?

A setting of flower beds harmonizes with the modest carpentry work of the neighbor but shows it up as a stranger also. The flowers, too, are in the backyard by the will of man, but they are not his handiwork. They are nature, partially surrendered. They cannot be forced to grow. They cooperate, and while the rectangular beds and the studied arrangements of colors indicate an imposed autocratic order, there is an equally deliberate margin of freedom, a mitigation of the regularity, which is needed if the flowers are to fulfill the function demanded of them by man. Through the partial disorder they are permitted to create, they reveal themselves as being truly grown, and it is this property of growth that makes them precious to man beyond anything of their kind he can fashion with his own hands.

First published in the *Journal of Aesthetics and Art Criticism*, 1959, 18, 68–79.

Man cherishes the perfection of symmetry, pure curve, and clean color because it enables him to identify, relate, and understand what he sees. He himself can quite easily produce objects with such properties, but, although useful, they only mirror the capacities of his own mind and therefore do not offer the comfort of the flowers. The flowers visually testify that order, indispensable for survival, is a principle of natural growth itself and that man, in needing and creating order, does not simply impose an alien demand upon reluctant wilderness. Rather, he reveals his own kinship with nature by insisting upon an inherent property of nature.

Flowers, then, in order to serve as intermediaries between man and nature, must not only display perfection of form but also supply that admixture of irregularity through which growth is made visible. Irregularity, of course, is only a superficial symptom of growth. It is more essential that the appearance of growing things is caused by the forces internally organizing the object. The symmetry of the flower is the outer expression of symmetrically distributed internal forces. The shapes of nature are not form applied to substance; Martin Heidegger has observed that the distinction of substance and form is derived from artifacts and does not hold for nature (3, pp. 16–18).

The generating power of the internal forces, however, cannot be read directly from the surface. A grown flower is hardly distinguishable from a well-made artificial flower. What *can* be seen is an indirect effect of such origin. Molded by a team of internal forces, the natural object is under the influence of other equally local teams of forces, which may constitute neighboring objects. The internally generated shape of a plant shows the interference of other plants, of the wind, or of the dominant position of the sun; and even within one plant, the simple perfection of any leaf or branch is modified by the expansion of its peers. Such approximation and distraction of shape distinguish natural things from manufactured ones since the craftsman can be in complete and exclusive control of the objects he makes. In the artifact, irregularity—that is, modification of the intended shape—appears as a flaw, caused by the technical imperfection of tool or mind. But irregularity may also be understood as a virtue of the artifact when it recalls the diversity of antagonistic forces within the craftsman, who thereby creates in the manner of nature.

There is also a small bridge in the garden, which lets the neighbor walk across the creek. Being made of redwood, it accords with the surrounding plants. But the rectangular shape of the boards is not the natural shape of the wood; it is imposed by the will of man—form imposed upon substance. All straight edges are completely straight, and the curve of the handrails is completely symmetrical. All relations of angle and size conform to one totally realized design. No interference by forces of the environment is discernible.

Even so the bridge is the product of forces outside of itself, and is visibly dedicated to the service of such forces. The meaning of its existence derives entirely from man. The bridge displays itself to the eye as a track and a facility. It is a preserved track of man's crossing the creek—not a passive imprint, however, but a planned facility. Its visible shape incorporates man's presence in the past and in the future: it recounts his crossing in the past and foretells his return. The bridge is a tool of man, and therefore its shape can be understood only by whoever knows about man. In fact, even the very percept of the bridge, in order to be complete and correct, must include the presence of the absent bridge-crosser. Otherwise it is an enigmatic ornament.

The flower also is a tool, but a tool of the plant itself. It is perceived properly only if it is seen as a dispenser and receptor of pollen. Otherwise it, too, is an enigmatic ornament, which is actually what man prefers to see in it. Without blushing he looks at the shamelessly exposed and immodestly colored sexual organ of the plant, and he goes so far in his misinterpretation as to enjoy in the sight of the flower the purity of purposelessness. As a thing of nature, the flower is innocent of man. At best, it tolerates his company. The bridge, being a tool, makes man visible even though he be away. The sight of the bridge is an invitation; that of the flower is more nearly an exclusion.[1]

Now for the bird-feeding station. Built of rectangular redwood boards like the bridge, it presents itself as an artifact. One hesitates, however, to call it a tool since its percept does not include actions of man to be performed by means of it. One part of it, the feed box, can be seen as a tool if man is thought of as feeding the birds; but even the box is more properly an opportunity donated by man for the birds to feed themselves—not a tool of the birds, since they did not make the box as the plant made its flowers, but certainly a party to a transaction with the birds from which man has withdrawn. Whereas the bridge, by being so close to man, is relatively remote from nature, the feeding station joins

---

[1] Bridge and flower may or may not have "valence." Valence means attractiveness. An object may be attractive because or even though it invites us, and it may be unattractive under the same conditions. It may also be attractive or unattractive because or even though it excludes us.

with nature in its independence of man. Even so, it does not entirely ignore its maker: it "faces" man by its frontality.

The "inviting" gesture of this frontality will concern us later. For the moment, we notice in its symmetry the almost harsh intransigence of the man-made, self-contained artifact. More in particular, the triangular gable serves as a protective frame for the small figure of the saint, which, less geometrical and closer to nature, would otherwise be in danger of being taken as a part of nature. Although the little man resembles the shapes of natural things, he clearly takes sides with his encasement. Placed precisely upon the central axis of the feeding station, the figure defines itself as an integral part of the wooden pattern; that is, it declares itself an artifact.[2] In addition, its fully front-face attitude repeats the frontality of the encasement and shuns any interaction with the environment, except for the curious gesture of "exposure," already noticed in the design of the feeding station as a whole.

The wooden robin, perched on the rim of the feed box, resembles the shapes of nature even more strongly than does the figure of the saint. Yet, no attempt is made to protect it from such association. It is not framed by the gable nor does it conform to the symmetry of the construction. The bird is placed off center, which characterizes its present relation to the feeding station as accidental and transitory (1). And instead of facing the beholder frontally, it sits on the box obliquely, ready to take a peck at the feed.

The robin relates to the station as a visiting customer, an emissary of nature. At the very least, it is an intermediary between the solemnly symmetrical artifact and the creatures that come and go and grow about it—not unlike the painted figures of those occasional bystanders in the group compositions of Renaissance or Baroque art who point out the central scene to the public. Whereas, however, the figure of the pointing guide is located on the stage within the picture frame, being itself a part of the presentation it presents, the robin does not share the dwelling place of the saint. The bird is an outsider.

[2] Edward Bullough (7, pp. 646–656) notes that "unification of presentment," by which he means the compositional qualities of symmetry, opposition, proportion, balance, etc., increase "aesthetic distance" by distinguishing the object from the "confused, disjointed and scattered forms of actual experience." It would appear that such distance is not specific to aesthetic or, in fact, man-made objects, but separates typically "natural" things from shapes of high rationality, often associated with artifacts but also found in the "unnatural" orderliness of crystals or radiolaria.

The fundamental difference between the robin and the saint is clearly expressed in their relation to size. We call the robin "just right" in size because, when compared with the norm of the live species, it is neither too large nor too small. The saint, compared with the human species of saints, is much too small, but this standard does not apply. Instead, the saint also may be called "just right," because, given the size of the garden and of the various plants, the little figure occupies just as much space as its function demands. The same figure, however, does not admit a comparison with other physical objects in the garden when it is viewed as a representation of the absent saint. As an image it does not dwell in physical space; it then is not a physical object, and therefore it is neither large nor small. Its relation to the man it represents is purely referential, not spatial.

The curious isolation of the figure is demonstrated when we ask: Is the saint larger or smaller than the robin? Obviously, it is neither. St. Francis in the mural of the Upper Church of Assisi is clearly and significantly taller than his "sisters, the little birds" (*sorores meae aviculae*), to whom he addresses his famous sermon. If we force the neighbor's St. Francis and robin into such a unitary scene, we discover—almost with surprise—that the robin is large enough to serve the saint as a giant eagle or else that the saint is a dwarf. But these percepts are so disturbingly wrong that it is hard for us to produce them at all.

Notice that this perceptual incapacity of ours comes from cultural training. A child or savage would spontaneously see what we can barely force ourselves to see: "The bird looks at the little man!" For us, the two figures are unrelatable. If we look at the sight as a scene of nature, the saint becomes a white puppet. If we look at the saint as a representation, the robin becomes a nonexistent impurity—something like a fly crawling over a painting. The two views exclude each other. We cannot hold them simultaneously.

The isolation of the image of the saint from physical space corresponds to its isolation from time. The robin, as a robin, exists in time as the garden does. It just arrived at the feeding box and will be elsewhere soon. The flowers are a state of transition from the bud to the scattered petals withering on the ground. In the creek flows the Heraclitic water; and even the bridge was once made and is perishable. The saint also has such a past and present—but only as its wooden self. As an image *of* the saint it is outside of time. If the figure is seen as something of a kind with the robin, it looks rigidly arrested, deprived of life. Seen as something of a kind with the saint, the robin drops out of time and becomes a figure, alien to life.

For too long, however, we have treated the wooden robin as though it were a real bird. That, indeed, it is when it deceives us: "Look, there is a robin feeding at the box!" But, although its size, shape, color, and position are such as to make it resemble a real bird as much as possible, it would miss its purpose if it deceived longer than for a moment. Only when the deception is uncovered does it reveal a triumph of human virtuosity. The deceptive bird proves that the human artisan is a match for nature or the divine creator. At the same time, it playfully points out the inferiority of man by the let-down of the discovery that the bird is wooden after all. In short, the robin is "cute"—a useful word of the American vernacular, which means: being amusingly clever beyond one's own standards.

The wooden robin can be said to be an epitome of the work of art as it has been popularly understood since the Renaissance. This concept misinterprets the work of art as a sleight of hand by which man cleverly duplicates nature for the purpose of entertainment. The skill is admirable but not quite serious since its product is dispensable. In this conception, a piece of sculpture or painting replaces the material presence of a natural object by either being like it or existing instead of it. Although identified as a duplicate of the "real thing," it does not serve to inform us about that real thing but is a rival object in its own right. It is an image but it mainly makes its own properties visible. Therefore I shall call it a *self-image*.[3] The wooden bird does not say: Such is a robin! It *is* a robin, although a somewhat incomplete one. It adds a robin to the inventory of nature, just as in Madame Tussaud's Exhibition the uniformed guards, made of wax, are not intended to interpret the nature of their fellow guards but to weirdly increase the staff of the institution.[4]

We call an object a self-image when we find that it visibly expresses its own properties. Its functions derive from the properties it reveals.

---

[3] The term self-image should not be misunderstood to mean an image in which the maker or beholder represents or recognizes his own self.

[4] The same example is used by E. H. Gombrich (8, pp. 209–228), who points out that, "originally," images serve as substitutes. Speaking of portraits, he mentions the "unwarranted assumption: that every image of this kind necessarily refers to something outside itself—be it individual or class. But no such reference need be implied if we point to an image and say 'this is a man.'" Thus, he clearly holds the view I am here adopting. He seems to believe, however, that the "substitute"—which is what I call the self-image—is limited to an early conception, later replaced with the image as a representation of "something outside itself." This "change of function," it seems to me, does not and should not eliminate the earlier conception of the self-image, which continues to operate side by side with what I later call a "likeness."

Being an addition to nature, a work of art of this type is most at home at the places where its prototypes belong. The wooden robin sits on the feed box, the wax guard lounges in a corner of the Exhibition, the still life of fruit and fowl hangs in the dining room. Beautiful women in marble or oil populate the palaces and mansions. They supplement the wealth of their owners by offering the promise and partial fulfillment of actual consumption.

About the year 1570, Paolo Veronese painted on the walls of the Villa Barbaro life-sized children and pages peeping through half-open doors. It is a virtuoso's feat, "cute," done with a smile and presumably as an ironical comment on the eagerness of the period to vie with nature and supplement it. Toward the end of the eighteenth century, Goethe, in his essay *Der Sammler und die Seinigen*, tells of a man who engages several painters to make him meticulously exact copies of birds, flowers, butterflies, and shells. In an upstairs room behind a door, there is a life-sized portrait of the gentleman himself and his wife as they seem to enter the room—frighteningly real, as Goethe puts it, "partly by the circumstances and partly by the art" of the painter. Shortly before his death, the old friend of the arts has a plaster cast made of his face and hands. With the help of a wig and a damask housecoat, a replica is produced, which, mounted on a chair, is kept behind a curtain. The ironical smile which we attributed to Veronese is in this story also, but only in the words of Goethe. It is ominously absent from the mind of the uncanny gentleman he is describing.

Less than a hundred years later, Auguste Rodin conceives the idea —fortunately blocked by the good sense of the burghers of Calais—of having his bronze figures of Eustache de St. Pierre and the six other citizens placed in single file directly on the pavement of the square in front of the Town Hall, as though they were actually on their way to meet the English conqueror. "By almost elbowing them," says Rodin, "the people of Calais of today would have felt more deeply the tradition of solidarity which unites them to these heroes" (6, p. 103).

Such intermingling of art and the traffic of daily life is a vulgar aberration, which proves that the intuitive knowledge of the nature and function of images—a universal possession of the human mind—can be fatally weakened by unfavorable cultural conditions. In the works of Rodin as well as those of other artists of the same historical period this deficiency also manifests itself in the absence of truly interpretative shape. As art degenerates into the material duplication of individual objects, the artifact threatens to invade nature and so causes nightmares of what might be called the Pygmalion complex, traceable in the literature of the period (Wilde's *Portrait of Dorian Gray*, Meyrink's *Golem*, Zola's *L'Oeuvre*, d'Annunzio's *La Gioconda*, Pirandello's *Come Tu Mi Vuoi* and *Sei Persone in Cerca di un Autore*). In these novels and plays, the creations of painting, sculpture, and fiction acquire the physical reality of psychotic hallucinations while at the same time human beings vainly try to attain the perfection and immortality of images.

In a materialistic culture, whose natural sciences are concerned with the exact physical qualities of things and capable of reproducing them faithfully, self-images tend to be accurate and complete. They serve the purposes of material consumption and interaction. A recent newspaper advertisement offered a hot-water bottle in the shape of a well-known movie actress dressed in two bits of bathing suit. Made of pink plastic and presenting the lady in a pose of chaste surrender, the image adds the touch and temperature qualities of the human flesh to the visual resemblance and thereby carries duplication to a new height. Nevertheless, the figure is only twenty-two inches in length—partly, we suppose, for practical reasons but also because the reduced size conceals somewhat the otherwise unveiled obscenity of the bedtime gift, which, in the words of the advertisement, is "guaranteed to bring a smile and warmth to Father, Fiancé, Friend or Foe."

We notice that the deviations from the accuracy of duplication do not necessarily interfere with the functions of the self-image and, in fact, may enhance its suitability. This observation holds for most images. Only under particular cultural conditions must they be deceptive replicas. That a self-image can fulfill its functions without being a strict duplicate is demonstrated by the capacity of children to treat a stick as a horse and a stuffed bag as a baby. These toys have been a puzzle to theorists, who have asserted that the child is capable of creating within himself the "illusion" of dealing with a real horse or baby—an obvious absurdity since such delusions would make it necessary for us to diagnose the child as insane. The theory, a sibling of the naturalistic schools of art, presupposes that identification requires mechanically complete replication.[5] But no conception of identity could mislead the psychologist more than the assumption that two things are either totally identical or not identical at all. The existential uniqueness of the individual object is negligible compared with the fact that all things are experienced as being identical to some extent with all others. Identity, in other words, is a matter of

[5] Here again, compare with Gombrich's enlightening remarks (8).

degree.[6] The stick is a horse because, for the purposes of the play situation, it has enough of the horse's properties. The statements "the stick is a horse" and "the stick is not a horse" do not contradict each other.

The North American Indians who told the ethnologist and painter George Catlin that his portrait sketches of their chiefs were "a little alive" (4, p. 46) asserted correctly that images not only represent, but *are* what they represent. All images tend to be treated as self-images, and, as such, they share some of the powers of their prototypes. A photograph of my father *is*, in a diminished way, my father. To tear it up would be a diminished form of murder. The wooden robin is a gift of real birdiness to the feeding station, and the figure of St. Francis actually spreads peace, sympathy, and the solidarity of the creatures through the garden. A framed caricature of Daumier's on the wall subtly poisons the room by the presence of an ingeniously potent distortion. When these effects are no longer felt, that is, when the image ceases to be perceived as a self-image, art is no longer whole.

The self-image is treated as identical with its prototype when it possesses attributes of the prototype pertinent to the given situation. Its other, deviating attributes may enhance its suitability and power. The golden calf is a calf in spite of being golden, and the shiny rare metal adds powerful splendor to the fetish. The neighbor's St. Francis is painted with white lacquer, which decreases its resemblance to a live Franciscan monk but enhances the purity and unworldliness of the figure; and its smallness is in keeping with the delicacy of its saintliness and the limited function allotted to it in the garden, which is not a place of worship. We note here that the expressive qualities of perceptual appearance—shape, size, color, etc.—serve the self-image to create, define, and enhance the powers it exerts.

But, let us examine the figure of the saint more closely. Earlier, I described the difference between the flowers as things of nature and the bridge as a man-made tool. The flowers were said to be experienced as being grown, existing by themselves, and for their own purpose. The bridge had the appearance of an artifact and of a track and facility of

---

[6] An object or creature, far from being only an exclusive "id-entity," is experienced and treated by us as a syndrome of general properties and categories, partial images of other things or beings, etc. In the extreme case, a person's identity may consist for us in only one general property, as his being a waiter or an intruder.

man. How about the saint? First of all, is the figure perceived as being grown like a flower? It does not deceive us, as the robin might, but on the other hand it does not appear shaped for and by the use of man. Even its frontality, by which it displays itself to the eyes of the beholder, can be perceived as its own initiative, rather than an arrangement made by man for his convenience. The little figure has the independence of a flower: its properties exist for the purpose of its own being. Heidegger remarks that the work of art in its self-sufficient appearance is like the "self-grown and unentreated" things of nature.[7] The figure is even more independent than the flowers because it is completely itself and therefore alone.

However, a thing of nature or an artifact acquires a new dependence upon man when it is treated as an image of a higher order, namely, what I call a *likeness*. It becomes a statement about objects and properties beyond itself. As a self-image, too, the object is a statement, but a statement about its own powers. We say, it expresses itself. When treated as a likeness, the object is made (or found to be) an image of things elsewhere. Its being an image then becomes a means to an end, and only man can make it that. A self-image possesses the properties of other things as parts of its own identity. The golden calf is a calf. It does not point to other calves although we can make it do that by treating it as a likeness, e.g., by putting it in a museum.

Even as a likeness, however, the object is not necessarily a tool although it is used as one—an object is classified as a tool only when its usability is viewed as the cause of its being what it is. A likeness, therefore, is a tool only to the extent to which it appears as having been made for the purpose of being used as a likeness. Thus, the frontality of the saint, which appeared as an accommodating gesture of the figure's own initiative in the self-image, can be perceived as a facility provided by man for his convenience when the figure functions as a likeness. But on the whole, even as a likeness, the object tends to preserve a large measure of that self-sufficiency that distinguishes a flower from a hammer.

A *likeness, then, is an object treated as a statement about other objects, kinds of object, or general properties, which are recognized in the object*. The figure of the saint, in addition to being its own moderately

---

[7] Heidegger (3, p. 18): "Trotzdem gleicht das Kunstwerk in seinem selbstgenügsamen Anwesen eher wieder dem eigenwüchsigen und zu nichts gedrängten blossen Ding."

powerful self, is also a portrait of the son of the merchant Bernardone, who lived in Assisi in the thirteenth century. Looking more closely, we notice that no attempt has been made to render the individual features of the historical Francisco, but that he, in turn, has been used to portray the saintliness of saints. In the last analysis, the figure represents those disembodied qualities of peace, harmony, and love, which we found emanate from it as a self-image.

Now, when the figure is viewed as a likeness and the flowers around it are not, the distinction must be expressed by means such as the symmetrical wooden frame, and the saint appears as a stranger, unrelatable in space and time. As far as he is a self-image, no such estrangement exists. The wooden St. Francis, diminished perhaps, but fully present as a gentle power, dispenses bliss as the flowers spread their scent, and resides as the high-spot of the miniature-Creation in the backyard among and above his minor brothers and sisters. But, removed from them by the wooden frame, he tends to change curiously into a mere transition to something beyond himself.

As the transformation occurs, the perceptual properties of the object change function. In the mere self-image, they serve, we said, to create, define, and enhance the powers exerted by the object. They are, as it were, consumed by the task of creating the nature of the object. The darkness of the thundercloud is absorbed in the "threatening" character of the cloud. The whiteness of the saint is an aspect of his visible saintliness and a source of his beneficial power. Heidegger says about tools: "The stone is used and consumed in the making of the tool, e.g., of the ax. It disappears in the serviceability" (3, p. 34). This relation changes to its opposite when the object is treated as a likeness. Employed to illustrate universal qualities, the object now appears as the vehicle of its properties. The thundercloud presents darkness; the saint becomes the carrier of whiteness.

This prominence of the expressive qualities must not be confused with the separation of percepts from their meaning, often mistakenly described as the aesthetic attitude. The dark mass in the sky can cease to be a thundercloud and become an interestingly shaped patch of blue color harmoniously related to the orange streaks painted around it by the sun. The saint can become a small column of whiteness, a stimulating contrast to the meandering greens around it. This disengagement of vision from its biological duty as a discoverer of meaning—far from being aesthetic—is a serious disease, which can ruin the efficiency and self-respect of whole generations of artists. The view is spread by innocent art educators and has all but succeeded recently in perverting the nature of what is known as abstract art.[8]

It cannot be denied, however, that even by treating objects as pure likenesses we are courting the danger of alienation. Whereas the stoniness of the ax disappears by making the stone ax sharp and hard, stoniness assumes prominence in a statue of Henry Moore when the sculptured block is viewed as a likeness of sharpness and hardness; and since the stone is in addition a likeness of a human being, the qualities portrayed through its being human combine with those of its stoniness in an intriguing counterpoint of forces. As the observer focuses upon this rather abstract contrapuntal pattern, with his eyes adapted, as it were, to infinity, the tangible stone figure all but dissolves.

Undoubtedly, the capacity to see objects as likenesses is a sublimation of vision, a privileged accomplishment of the human species. It enables us to roam beyond the particulars toward the mainsprings of all existence. At the same time, the image becomes ever emptier as we proceed from the individual to the universal. Being a complex, particular creature himself, man recognizes himself only in what is complex and particular, so that in his pursuit of the universal he risks losing either it or himself. Also, since he can only contemplate the universal but not act upon it, he tends to lapse into inactivity, which in turn will distort his contemplation. In the extreme case, a person will perceive all things only as what they stand for, not as what they are, which will transform the world of beings into one of apparitions and destroy his own foothold within the world.

We are driven to the conclusion that full vision requires us to treat the object as a self-image and a likeness at the same time. To deal with the object as nothing but an image of its own self is an elementary form of vision, accessible even to animals. It belongs to the early state of mind in which experiences can be understood only as related to the present and its extensions into the past and future. At that stage, the expressive perceptual qualities of the object appear as its own powers, and it is

---

[8] Genuine abstract art is not a game of shapes and colors. It makes statements just as any other art. It does not represent objects of nature but carries expressive properties, which, in the self-image, endow the abstract piece of sculpture or painting with the powers of harmony, aggressiveness, frivolity, solemnity, or whatever their nature may be. Treated as a likeness, abstract art makes statements about these same qualities as universal forces.

to them that we respond when we interact with the object. Art serves here to make the perceptual properties of the object pure, clear, and intense. It makes the object visibly itself.

To deal with the object as only a likeness is a late development. It occurs when the human mind withdraws from interaction with the here and now and reserves itself for the contemplation of the universals. At that stage, art plays down the material existence of the object and treats it as a mere statement about fundamentals. The expressive qualities are given dominance over the object carrying them.

When in full sight, the object is completely and personally present in the world of the eyewitness. It possesses the powers of its appearance, which are not only visible but affect the witness and must be reacted to by him.[9] At the same time, the powers of the object appear as manifestations of universal forces, so that by dealing with the object the witness deals with existence in general. The savage who treats the object only as itself is as remote from full vision as the critic who only judges it.

What has been said here applies to objects of nature as well as to artifacts. What, then, is art? Art makes the expressive properties of the object perceivable. Nature applies art, and so does man, who is one of nature's products. Originally, nature does not aim at visibility. It achieves it as a by-product through the external manifestation of the generating forces within the object. But visibility provokes the creation of eyes and, with the existence of eyes, nature begins to take account of its visibility. The history of evolution tells us that the flowering plants or angiosperms, inventors of advertising color, develop in correspondence with the kingdom of insects. Color, shape, and behavior of animals are influenced by the visual information they supply or conceal. The same is true for almost anything man does or makes. A recent illustration is the use of color in factories for the purpose of distinguishing objects from the background, classifying machine parts according to their functions, warning of dangerous contact, and also making the workroom a clean-looking and cheerful place.

When living organisms take their visibility into account, they do so as a part of their coping with life in the physical world. Man has invented objects that operate exclusively through being looked at. Many

---

[9] Even though the self-image dwells as an object among objects inside the world of action, all sensible civilizations provide for the distinction between things of nature and effigies, that is, between what is alive physically and what is alive only perceptually. Humans do not intermingle with the images they make but set them off by special appearance, location, or ceremony.

of these objects indicate their function by their "frontality"—sculpture often has a principal view and paintings display their content within the frontal plane. The self-image, by its visual properties, transmits its own powers, which play their part in man's practical life. Note here that although works of visual art acquire their powers exclusively through the sense of vision, they have not always been among the objects made only for the purpose of being seen. The images of gods and rulers were placed in temples, tombs, and palaces in order to exert certain powers, quite regardless of whether they were seen or not; in fact, they were often kept hidden. This is a fundamental difference between much art of the past and our modern paintings and sculpture, which are meant to act only through being seen.

As a pure likeness, the image fulfills its purpose by referring to matters outside of the present situation. For this reason, the purpose of the pure likeness is a puzzle to the innocent. Albert Michotte, asserting that we learn what things are by what they do, reports that one of his children at the age of three or four asked what the paintings on the wall of the living room were for, and after receiving an explanation exclaimed: "Mais alors, les tableaux, ce n'est rien!" (5, p. 3).[10] No such comment is likely to have been elicited by the statue of Pallas Athene in a Greek temple since it was very much of a self-image and as such performed action and was reacted to. The pure likeness, unrelated in space and time to its environment, requires a beholder who is able to cut his own ties to space and time. An observer incapable of full vision corresponds to an object not in full sight. Such alienation is quite different from the attitude of a man who, moved by the course of his life into the presence of an object whose powers answer his demands or destroy his hopes, pauses to contemplate life itself in the image of its pregnant manifestation.

The true work of art, then, is more than a statement floating adrift. It occupies, in the world of action, a place suitable to the exercise of its powers. It cannot be alone. Primitively, it performs only as a thing among other things. At its most human, it rules as an embodied statement over a world in which every tool, every flower, and every rock also speaks as itself and through itself. We find it perhaps in the tea room,

---

[10] The purpose of the pure likeness seems to remain a puzzle to some aestheticians even to our day. "There is nothing one can do *with* a painting," explains Gilson (2, p. 118), except look at it. What distinguishes tools and instruments from a work of art is "that their final cause lies outside themselves. Not one of them is made for its own sake." The work of art allegedly *is* made for its own sake. *Alors, ce n'est rien!*

in the Japanese garden. The backyard of my mother's neighbor, I am afraid, lies somewhat behind.

REFERENCES

1. Arnheim, Rudolf. Accident and the necessity of art. This volume, pp. 162–180.
2. Gilson, Etienne. *Painting and Reality*. New York: Pantheon, 1957.
3. Heidegger, Martin. *Holzwege*. Frankfurt: Klostermann, 1950.
4. Lévy-Bruhl, Lucien. *How Natives Think*. London, 1926.
5. Michotte, A. *La perception de la causalité*. Paris: Vrin, 1946.
6. Rodin, A. *On Art and Artists*. New York, 1957.
7. Weitz, Morris (ed.). *Problems in Aesthetics*. New York: Macmillan, 1959.
8. Whyte, Lancelot (ed.). *Aspects of Form*. Bloomington: Indiana Univ. Press, 1951.

VI. To Teachers and Artists

WHAT KIND OF PSYCHOLOGY?

Wherever there are human beings, there is art, and wherever there is art, there are art teachers. We may think of master painters and sculptors transmitting their skills to the young in the prehistoric caves, in the medieval workshops, and in modern studios and academies. The job has always been more or less the same, but the masters have often changed their views of what an artist is supposed to be.

The art teachers of the twentieth century are working on assumptions that are new in the recent history of the craft. They believe that art is not the privilege of a few people but a natural activity of every human being; that a genuine culture depends less on the rare geniuses than on the creative life of the average citizen; and that art is an indispensable tool in dealing with the tasks of being. Art is considered one of the ways of producing mature, complete, and happy people. This has made the task of the art teacher difficult because it presupposes more than specific skills. It requires some knowledge of the capacities, needs, and development of the human mind. Therefore, the psychologist was called in as a consultant.

What actually happened was that the psychologist said he was sorry

First published in the *College Art Journal*, Winter 1954, 13, 107–112. The paper was prepared as a lecture for the annual meeting of the Committee on Art Education in New York, 1954.

he could not make it, he was busy with other things, so the psychiatrist was asked instead. Throughout the nineteenth century, academic psychology had been concerned primarily with problems that excluded what is nowadays called "personality." It prided itself on being a psychology without the soul. In the laboratories, one measured the thresholds of light or sound stimuli, and when the psychologists of those days dealt with art, as they sometimes did, they were concerned with such problems as how to represent the brightness of sunlight on canvas, what proportions of the rectangle are preferred by a majority of people, or what are the overtones of a given instrumental sound. (This approach survives in much of what is offered as "experimental psychology of aesthetics" today.) In the meantime, dealing with mental patients became a psychological discipline, which required insights psychologists were not prepared to offer. Thus, the psychology of personality had to be created by psychiatrists.

The psychiatric approach to psychology has produced ingenious conceptions, but at the same time it possesses inevitable shortcomings. It is concerned mainly with what is wrong with people and it is mainly based on observations of patients. The resulting one-sidedness showed up even more strongly when simplified versions of psychiatric conceptions were adopted by laymen for practical use in various professions.

Many educators have come to realize that art is an expression and an instrument of the human personality. But, if one looks at what they mean by personality, one finds too often that they take it to be the manifestation of what is wrong with people. They scrutinize the work of their young students for signs of hostility, depression, anxiety, jealousy, and they have surprisingly little trouble in finding them. By personality, they mean, too often, the reactions of individuals to other people's stupidity, selfishness, narrow-mindedness, imbalance, and lack of self-control. Now, there is no doubt that most people, young ones and old ones, suffer from the effects of mistreatment; but in no field of knowledge can one gain much understanding by limiting oneself to the study of aberrations and abnormalities. One would learn very little about the solar system by concentrating on the eclipses of the sun or the moon. These dramatic fits of darkness become explainable only after one has investigated the normal, and perhaps less exciting, rounds of the planets.

Art teaching cannot be effective without an appropriate notion of what art is for and about. Here the psychiatric bias has created a problem by suggesting that art is a substitute for true living. It is said to offer vicarious satisfaction, which replaces what we really want but cannot get or have not the courage to fight for. In other words, art is described as a neurotic escape from life. Of course, it is true that neurotics may use anything from social work to modern dance as devices for not facing the challenges of life. But this should not tempt us to look at human activities in the perspective of the sick room. Genuine artistic activity is neither a substitute nor an escape, but one of the most direct and courageous ways of dealing with the problems of life. To be sure, one can use the peaceful silence of the studio to withdraw from reality; but, similarly, the so-called active life can serve to give protection from the constant exposure to the truth, which hurts like a dangerous radiation.

If art is a way of dealing with life, in what particular fashion does it do so? One of the basic tasks of man, it seems, is to scrutinize and to understand the world, to find order and law outside and within himself. At the early stages of human development, such scrutiny is performed mainly by the senses. The conceptions of children and primitives as to what things are and how they function are derived from the visual world by means of wonderfully fresh and colorful observations. Early thinking is essentially visual thinking.

In the olden days, people used to consider thinking and the activity of the senses as neatly distinct capacities. But all art education, and indeed all art, depends on the fact that there is such a thing as visual thinking. At later stages of human development, abstract conceptions are handled by the intellect. But, wherever human beings deal with reality most effectively, abstract thought remains intimately connected with the search for, and the sensitivity to, the revealing experiences of the senses. In the work of Aristotle, Dante, Leonardo, or Goethe, every idea is clothed with shape and color and every sight is transparent with universal meaning. The most characteristic trait of a genuine culture is the integration of concrete everyday experiences with guiding philosophical ideas. Wherever the simple performances of eating and sleeping, work and love, or the sensations of light and darkness, are spontaneously felt as symbols of the powers that underlie human existence, there we have the foundation of culture and the seeds of art.

During the past decades, psychologists have found out a good deal about perceptual processes, which constitute the language of the arts. Thus far, these findings are not well known among artists, art educators, and art theorists. True, some lip service is paid, for instance, to Gestalt psychology. Even so, present-day writing and teaching largely neglects the modern psychology of visual perception. Outdated theories, which go back to the days of Helmholtz in the nineteenth century, are still taken for granted. Certain aspects of pictorial representation, which nowadays can and should be explained in visual terms, are still considered as manifestations of the intellect, witness the old chestnut that the child draws what he knows rather than what he sees. Also, problems of visual representation are explained away by references to other senses, such as the haptic, or kinesthetic, sense. Or universal characteristics of perception and representation are misinterpreted as expressions of deep-seated individual desires or fears.

It is necessary to stress the cognitive aspects of the artistic process because the one-sided psychological approach to personality that left its mark on art education has led to a peculiar negative attitude toward the representational aspects of art. All through the history of man, art has represented objects—animals, human beings, trees, houses. Again, in most cultures, we find nonrepresentational patterns, notably ornaments and architecture. There are, then, two legitimate means of visual expression; but under the influence of what the psychologists and some modern artists have been saying, there has crept into art education the notion that the drawing or painting of objects is a mechanical reproduction of nature, which prevents the artist, young or grown-up, from expressing his own self. Self-expression is said to be something that occurs only in abstract form. Supposedly, young children turn to the depicting of objects solely under the deplorable influence of grown-ups. Rose Alschuler and La Berta W. Hattwick in their book *Painting and Personality* assert that the average two- or three- or four-year-old "most likely has never thought of his painting as the representation of an object. . . . His painting has come from those depths of his being from which feelings flow outward in generalized, rather than representative, form." And further on in the same book: "Abstract or pre-representative paintings and drawings can be, and often are, more expressive of inner feeling than are representative products because the very process of representation involves a conscious awareness of outside stimuli rather than a direct expression of self" (1, pp. 6 ff).

In particular, abstractions are supposed to be direct and faithful representations of the unconscious, referred to as the true self. To this, the psychologist has to say, first of all, that there can be no such thing as a direct representation of the unconscious because, as Freud has clearly pointed out, the unconscious can manifest itself only indirectly, either by external action or by conscious experience. And, if we look at conscious experiences, in dreaming, thinking, remembering, or observing, we find that they are not concerned with triangles and rectangles but with people and animals, trees, the sun and the moon, or fire. And these contents are far from being mechanical recordings of outside stimuli.

During the past ten years or so, psychology has begun to show concretely that man's way of perceiving and treating outer objects is imbued with personal feelings, needs, and attitudes. It appears that the self expresses itself most clearly through its dealing with the outer world. There is no psychological justification for the separation of the inner self from the reactions to outer reality. This truth was strikingly expressed by Goethe, who in 1823 wrote in one of his essays: "Herewith I confess that I have always been suspicious of the great and high-sounding demand: Know yourself! It is a request that looks to me like a ruse of priests secretly rallied to confound the people by unattainable goals and to lure them away from their activity in the outside-world toward a state of false contemplation. Man knows himself only to the extent to which he knows the world, and he finds the world only in himself, just as he finds himself only in the world. Every new object, well observed, discloses a new organ in ourselves" (2). This is not an antipsychological statement, but simply good psychology.

It is true that the drawings of many older children tend to become less expressive. This happens not because they abandon "abstractions" but because bad training and other deadening effects of their environment press their work into conventional schemata. Similar harmful influences can turn the delightfully spontaneous nonrepresentational patterns of the earlier years into mechanical imitations of modern idioms. It makes no basic difference whether a child, or an adult artist, paints circles and triangles or animals and trees. Both methods represent the inner world and the outer world, and neither psychology nor art separates the two.

If, then, modern psychology is not identical with the narrow view of personality that determines certain trends in art education, what are the nature and function of art in the light of a broader conception?

Educators agree that a person's growth must go beyond the acquisition of facts and skills. If we have to say about someone: "He has studied many things, he has seen the world, he has learned much—but he has not changed, he has remained untouched," we feel that with all his achievements, he is humanly a failure. What exactly is missing in such a person?

Suppose someone has studied certain facts, say, the physics of gravitation. He may have thoroughly understood the theoretical and practical consequences of the phenomenon. One day, suddenly, he is seized by the experience of what gravitation actually does to life and nature. He acknowledges the sensation of being pulled downward and feels the same pull in all the animate and inanimate things about him. Mere information is enriched by the experienced impact of forces. Once the fact has become "real," it also reveals the broad symbolic meaning contained in being tied to the ground and striving to overcome the burden. This sensitivity to the forces that underlie the facts of reality makes the difference between mere existence and true living. Man can achieve no higher goal than to become aware of what it means to be alive. There is no other final achievement to this life, which will be destroyed with all its products sooner or later, either by the slow cosmic forces or by the impatient ingenuity of man. Such sensitivity is closely related to, and perhaps identical with, art. Art goes beyond the making of pictures and statues, symphonies and dances; and art education should go beyond the classes in which these crafts are taught. Art is the quality that makes the difference between merely witnessing or performing things and being touched by them, shaken by them, changed by the forces that are inherent in everything we give and receive.

Art education, then, means making sure that such living awareness results when people paint pictures and play music, and also when they study biology or economics, take a job, fall in love, witness birth and death. Today there is a danger that many persons spend many more years than ever as well-equipped mammals, busy with metabolism and reproduction, but without using their one chance of experiencing what it means to be alive. It is the task of teachers and artists to see to it that the chance is not missed.

REFERENCES
1. Alschuler, Rose H., and Hattwick, La Berta Weiss. *Painting and personality*. Chicago: Univ. of Chicago Press, 1947.
2. Goethe, Johann Wolfgang von. *Bedeutende Förderung durch ein einziges geistreiches Wort*. 1823.

IS MODERN ART NECESSARY?

Now and then in the art magazines a large advertisement appears that sports as a headline the question: "Do you make these common mistakes in painting?" The "mistakes" are illustrated by pictures and captions such as "poor perspective . . . each object seems viewed from a different direction" or "portrait looks flat—lacks form and depth—no light and shade" or "road that will not go back—hangs down picture like necktie" or "relation of pictorial elements to each other—auto and livestock too large for farm buildings." The advertisement comes from an art school and is signed by a number of artists. Among them is Norman Rockwell; but there are also Stuart Davis and Ben Shahn.

Whoever visits the museums of modern art to see the works of Davis and Shahn will also notice paintings by the Cubists, by Matisse, by Cézanne, by Chagall, and it will occur to him that what the two colleagues of these great painters call "mistakes" are some of the traits on which the main contributions to the art of our century are based. Here then we have a symptom of the state of suspension in which art is today. It grows its colorful flowers somewhere high up, sending out aerial roots that barely reach the soil, which is the nutritional base of all growth. There is a gap between art and its natural supporters. On the one side, there are

Unpublished enlarged version of an address presented at the annual meeting of the Western Arts Association in Louisville, Kentucky, in April 1958.

those who create the art of our time, not because they intend to be modern, but because modern art is what they happen to produce when they translate honestly and precisely into pictorial or sculptural shape the impact of the forces that appear to activate our society, our philosophy, our thinking. These artists are joined by a group of sympathizers, people who truly live in the century in which they were born and who find their inner and outer reality accurately reflected and interpreted by the best of our painting or sculpture. They distinguish the few originals from the many fakes and imitations, not because they have been told what is modern but because they are sensitive to what is true, fresh, and profound. On the other side of the gap, there is the vast majority of the artists' fellow citizens, who identify art with the style of the late Renaissance and its descendants. They learn about modern art as they learn about the goings-on in insane asylums. They laugh, they complain, they get irritated, they accuse the artists of cheating and subversion. Or they have reasons to hide their ignorance, in which case they admire and imitate everything they find puzzling or repulsive. Among them are a goodly number of people who spend their days painting pictures, carving marble monuments, welding steel with blowtorches, assembling junk, selling and collecting art objects, or writing reviews and books.

So much confusion, hypocrisy, and bad faith is possible only when the distinctions between true and false, and good and bad, have been obscured. We know that this blindness has developed through the atomization of our culture, in which each occupation threatens to become a reservation of experts. It is for the historian to describe the causes of this disintegration. Our present purpose requires merely that we diagnose it. We realize that we cannot blame the artist for being incomprehensible or the public for not understanding. But we find that the unnatural gap makes for serious deficiencies in both camps. It makes the motor of art run out of gear, fast but idle. It tends to remove the artist's thoughts from the elementary concerns of human life and to limit him to the technicalities and small thrills of the secluded workshop. On the other side of the gap, the public's need for visual enlightenment, stimulation, and spectacle are satisfied not by artists who could give clarity, weight, and depth, but instead by the brutalities of commercial entertainers.

No civilization can survive such a split for long. We teachers know that. We also know that if any single group of citizens can be expected to influence the situation, it is the teachers who must look for remedies.

But we are most uncertain about our qualifications. And there are many problems.

First of all, we can only teach by what we are. Children and adolescents are easily depraved, but hard to fool. A teacher who is uncertain, confused, or unconvinced himself will not make a case for art. A teacher who himself spends his evenings staring at the blue ghosts of television, cannot provide his teen-agers with the counterweight of culture in the morning. A doctor who carries a disease infects the patients he is trying to cure.

But take now the teacher at his best and let him ask: Shall I teach my students modern art? They are growing up as children of this century. Should not the idioms of contemporary art suit them best when they express themselves visually? And will not the use of such modern language help them to get in tune with the spirit of our time, by which those shapes are created? All this may be true. On the other hand, we must keep in mind that modern art is the late product of a long historical evolution and that the awareness of this multiform past participates in its meaning. A child has no such past, no such awareness. Granted, in his own development he may not have to run through all the by-ways of history in order to catch up with the present. But he does have to proceed from the simple to the complex.

The solution of our problem seems to hinge on the question: Is modern art simple? And here we realize that in some of its essential aspects the modern style happens to be closer to the beginnings of all art than any style has ever been throughout our entire culture. When the authors of the unfortunate advertisement I quoted in the beginning enumerate those "common mistakes," they demonstrate not only that they ignore and misunderstand modern art, they do not know—and this is an even more serious handicap for anybody who wants to teach art— that the rules of realistic painting, far from providing the standards of art in general, are as remote from the usual principles of art as any style has ever been. In very few periods of great art, for instance, has it been presumed that all aspects of an object or a pictorial scene should be observed from one constant viewpoint only. Much more often, the picture is a synthesis of what the artist remembers by having watched the things of this world from all sides. It is equally rare for painters to determine the relative size of objects by their actual physical sizes or by the exact optical sizes they assume in projection depending on their distance. And, similarly, it has been the common practice of painters through the ages to translate their observations of nature into the language of the two-dimensional medium, in which the illusions of depth, volume, and lighting and the effects of foreshortening and perspective are quite alien; these devices are sophisticated latecomers without universal artistic validity.

In short, modern art is, among other things, a return to an approach that derives commonly and naturally from the psychology of spontaneous observation and from the inherent conditions of the media. Indeed, it has gone back further. The modern artist's pleasure in primitive daubing, his emphasis on action, his playful experimenting with materials, his preference for elementary shapes and pure colors are typical of the earliest phases of artistic activity. The new appreciation of primitive art and children's art suggests in turn that the modern style has created a favorable climate for art education. No longer are the early attempts of beginners considered worthless crudities to be replaced as fast as possible by remote and highly refined skills. Instead, they are valued as legitimate and often beautiful statements. Painting and sculpture cease to be taught as techniques of mechanical reproduction. They are recognized as essential tools for the tasks of finding one's bearings in this world. From what I have said, it also seems to follow that the young student, in order to arrive at the present forms of art, does not have to make the historical detour via realistic representation. You do not have to have been a small Caravaggio or Monet in order to become a small Matisse or Mondrian. A more direct and continuous evolution can be established from the early daubings of the child to the adult craftsman's highly controlled and significant shapes.

All this looks like an unprecedented boon for the art teacher, and in many ways it is. Other aspects of the situation, however, suggest a great deal of caution. The very similarity of early art and modern art may tempt the teacher to use harmful shortcuts. In order to avoid them, he needs to remember that much modern art is anything but naïve. If in their pictures both the kindergarten child and the abstract painter are far removed from the appearance of nature, they are so for opposite reasons. The faithful realism of the Dutch still-life and genre painters, although technically refined beyond anything a child could attempt, is nevertheless tied to material reality and its sensuous truth in a way that is much closer to the attitude of a youngster than the aloofness of the modern artist. It is true enough that children spontaneously produce what we call abstract designs. They do so because the handling of materials for their own sake and effect is accessible to the growing mind earlier than is the discovery that shapes on paper or in clay can be made to stand for people, animals, or houses. But the step from mere shape to the representational image is short and quick and almost immediate because a healthy child's interest in the world around him is immensely strong and vital. It takes gentle coercion on the part of the progressive teacher to keep him satisfied with the designs and collages and stabiles for any length of time. Even the college student is not easily kept by wire, plaster, and plastics from the ancient and legitimate satisfaction of the Creator who formed man of the dust of the ground.

In a very important sense, then, the similarity of early and late art is deceptive. The beginner uses simple shapes because he has not yet achieved full contact with reality. The modern artist does so because he has gradually withdrawn from reality. His work is abstract because he has abstracted himself. His mind is not a clean slate; it is full of relinquished memories and trained in all the trickeries of the civilized intellect. Simple shapes are a refuge from unmanageable complication and a barbarian refreshment to the tired Alexandrian palate. Furthermore, the artist as a sensitive observer and citizen is subjected to the disorder, violence, and ghostliness of modern life, and his traumas are reflected in his work.

Nothing could be more remote than this attitude from the child's mind or, for that matter, from the attitude a teacher may wish to enhance in his adolescents. The teacher's task is not that of transforming the new crop as fast and completely as possible into the dissatisfied, unfulfilled, disoriented, and frightened creatures that populate our civilization. Rather, he receives every year a number of relatively intact human beings for the purpose of preserving and strengthening their integrity while getting them ready to absorb the kind of life they will have to contend with. This objective of the teacher always involves a notion of completeness: we affirm in the educational manuals that we want to develop the potentialities of the student to the fullest. Which is to say that we ask for full range in the educational program as a whole as well as in any particular area of study.

The art teacher wants to awaken in his student many ways of reacting to the various aspects of life: to the multiformity of its appearance as well as the lawfulness of its principles; to the clarity of its order as well as the mysteries of its dreams. And here the teacher finds himself confronted with another puzzling aspect of our problem, namely, the curious partiality or incompleteness of certain influential forms of modern art. What we encounter here is something more than the necessary privilege of the mature adult, who limits himself to definite positions, views, and purposes. It is also something more than the necessary privilege of every artist, who must say things in his own way. It is rather the fact that so much of what we see in the galleries today is in the nature of partial explorations, restricted both in outlook and in scope. We welcome such experiments as useful stages in the long-range development of art; but we begin to raise questions as soon as we try to evaluate one piece or one artist's total output as a valid encompassment of the reality we know. We also think of the person behind the work and we ask: How rich and substantial is the human experience from which these shapes emanate?

I am not speaking of the few great men. I am speaking of the kind of artistic occupation the teacher has to choose for his students. It seems evident that if the student is forced by decree to adopt modern techniques, art may not help him to recognize himself through his work. Such a procedure will rather alienate him from his work and thereby from himself. Moreover, by forcing him into certain attitudes and preventing him from assuming others, such a drill will impose upon him an artificial one-sidedness. Instead of helping him to become a citizen of his century by inclination and choice, we shall do our share in bringing up another conformist, haunted by the question: Who am I?

What, then, can the art teacher do? It seems to me that he can seize upon the unique opportunities offered him by modern art without surrendering to it unconditionally. He can profit from the new appreciation of spontaneity, the acceptance of simplicity in conception and technique, the freedom from the obligation to acquire the skill of realistic imitation. Such encouragement and freedom, however, should allow the student to grow his own way, to make his own discoveries, and to move in his chosen direction. The teacher cannot be sure that by this procedure he will breed a new partisan of the modern movement; but he will help to bring up an individual who, when he gives his loyalty to a cause, does so by conviction.

So far I have talked about what the presence of modern art does to the work in the art room and the studio. However, we face its presence even more directly and inevitably when we instruct students in what is known as the appreciation of art. Even today, the average student is likely to come to us with the conviction that the more realistically a picture portrays exciting or pretty things, the better it is. To meet this attitude, the teacher must rely on something better than contempt. He must realize that faithful likenesses fulfill a legitimate need even though their connection with art has become tenuous. It is a need that is strong, elementary, and down-to-earth in that it is a part of people's practical intercourse with the things of this world. Norman Rockwell's cover paintings are a useful and pleasant extension of our existence. They mirror by repetition. As such they are easily acceptable. On the other hand, to introduce students to the arts of our century means also to ask them to accept many unpleasant sights. This leads me to one more aspect of our subject.

If you examine what the average person has against many of our painters, sculptors, composers, poets, or architects, you will find that their works seem incomprehensible, violent, full of tension and conflict, frightening, disillusioning, and ugly in form and content. These are qualities from which people always retreat, not only in art. And we have reasons to believe that never in history has there been a similar collective effort to produce distortion, mutilation, dissonance, riddles, and monsters. Shapes previously reserved for portraying devils, demons, and dragons are now presented as the image of man, and scenes of collapse, destruction, and explosion depict our landscapes, cities, and homes.

The bewilderment and repugnance of the man in the street is more honest, appropriate, and perceptive, than, to quote Igor Stravinsky, "the vanity of snobs who boast of an embarrassing familiarity with the world of the incomprehensible and who delightedly confess that they find themselves in good company. It is not music they seek, but rather the effect of shock, the sensation that befuddles understanding." The man in the street correctly recognizes that what he sees and hears is neither easy nor pretty. Only when he demands that easy and pretty is what it ought to be, only then he goes wrong.

Here is one of the greatest obstacles to the understanding and acceptance of modern art. Both, the snob, who uses the anxious visions of his fellowmen as decorations, and the man in the street, who rejects them, are the products of a century-old tradition according to which it is the task of the artist to amuse, to stimulate, and to sweeten the lives of his neighbors. When we examine in a museum the art that developed during the Renaissance or listen to the operas and madrigals, the suites and concerti, we should realize, in the midst of all the beauty: "But these men were interior decorators!" Because that is what they were. They supplied harmony and perfection, a gentle lift and distraction, entertainment and virtuosity. To be sure, every great artist of the period is, by his very nature, an objection to my statement, which he nevertheless confirms. Michelangelo, while trying to accommodate his customers, could not help turning allegories into tragic heroes, just as Rembrandt found the shadows of distress in the official faces of the Dutch gentry.

The same happened to Molière and to Shakespeare, to Monteverdi and to Mozart. Whether their patrons realized it or not, these entertainers and decorators were cheating.

To be sure, the demands of these patrons were unusually one-sided. Granted that art had served everywhere to embellish containers and columns, fabrics and the naked skin, ceilings and canoes; and if the figures of pharaohs, fetishes, and saints were not pleasing to the eye they would hardly be suitable to decorate the living rooms of our own contemporaries, who ignore their meaning. But hardly ever was embellishment the main function. Art served, rather, to make gods visible and rulers immortal, to exert magic powers, to give praise, to tell about the past, or to unite a crowd by a common rhythm.

At the same time, under any condition, art fulfilled its principal, though mostly unacknowledged, function of making the nature and meaning of human existence visible and audible. The greater the art, the more energetically it went beyond its limited social assignments. It showed the perfection of man in the Greek athlete, it made power and striving visible in the cathedrals of the Middle Ages, it sounded the passions of love and hatred for the ladies and gentlemen in the theaters and opera houses. But I venture to say that never before the gradual advent of modern art in the nineteenth century has art professed and practiced this principal function collectively and explicitly as it does now. In men such as Beethoven or Cézanne, Flaubert or Ibsen, one notices something essentially new. These men did not pretend to work for anybody except, possibly, for everybody.

A modern artist may still be able to produce for a market, but he is no longer at the service of anybody's ideas and ideals, save his own. This independence influences the character of his work. I have spoken of the many dissonances and distortions, the images of violence, contradiction, and instability that characterize modern art. Quite plausibly it reflects the conflicts, confusions, and insecurities of our age. Now, granted that life in our century deserves such description; but, as we look back in history do we not find just as much conflict, confusion, and insecurity in the past? And if so, do we find all that tension reflected in the art of those periods? Is oppression by dictatorship conveyed in the serene stone figures of the pharaohs? Do we sense slavery or civil war in the temples of the Acropolis? Is the political climate of Rome or Florence reflected in Raphael's and Leonardo's Madonnas? Or the Thirty-Years War in the still lifes and landscapes of the Dutch? Why, then, must our own art choose to be so painfully symptomatic?

The answer is, of course, that as long as art serves a particular institution, a dynasty, a religion, a community, or a patron, it must embody a particular set of ideas. It cannot freely contemplate the human condition as such. Neither William Blake's description of the city of London nor Dylan Thomas' "The hand that signed the paper felled the city" could have been written by an official, government-employed poet. And not by chance are the modern idioms of painting, sculpture, poetry, and music banned in Soviet Russia. Having nobody's ax to grind, the art of our time is perhaps hardening itself with a hermit's exercises of isolation, starvation, and nightmare for the task of serving a new generation—not as an entertainer and not even as a public relations officer for democracy, but as the indispensable demonstrator of truth.

And here I will come back to the point from which I started and point out that it is not sufficient when the scientist alone holds the mirror up to nature and speaks the truth as an unattached and uncommitted man. The artist must join him, if only because the truth of the scientist has become partial. Not only in the natural sciences do we find the gulf between the abstractness of first principles and the immediacy of experience. Even the social sciences and psychology, fairly young and therefore still fairly close to the tangibles of common sense, are now reaching for remote formulae as they dig through the surface after the roots. In their statements, we seldom encounter the poetic charm that distinguished the writings of the early astronomers or physiologists, or the philosophical explorers of the human soul. Our world threatens to become illegible and inaudible, confusing and opaque.

Our need to be rescued from this predicament is, I believe, the positive reason for the arrival of what sometimes has been called art for art's sake. The painting not commissioned for any wall, the statue without a temple, the music that does not worship and the poem that does not praise—homeless and true like scientific theorems, they are here to guide us when we attempt to reconcile what we know with what we can see and hear.

The fact that the mysterious paintings, poems, and musical compositions of modern artists bewilder and frighten us is often explained by a lack of aesthetic training. To be sure, there is need for better art education; but this can be remedied. However, there is a much greater obstacle: Nothing is so unusual in our lives, nothing so unwelcome, as the request that we look at the truth! We are accustomed to living as consumers and voters, flattered, pampered, misled. We rely on the concerted response to our daily prayer: And lead us on the path of least resistance! The entertainment industry of television, radio, motion picture, and the printed press constantly misuses the artistic media for this purpose. But the artist cannot join in this profitable deception. He can only look at the truth. And we must do the same if we wish to understand what he is after.

THE FORM WE SEEK

Anybody picturing the craftsman as a white-haired, solitary gentleman or lady with an apron, patiently and silently molding, cutting, or combining small pieces of precious material needs only to look at the proceedings of your earlier conventions [1] to realize that there is as much variety among craftsmen as there is in other professions. This makes it all the more difficult for an outsider to say something useful about your business. All he can hope to rely on is the wisdom of innocence. Less distracted by details and complications, he may grasp some of the more general aspects of your condition and localize it in the larger context of the cultural landscape as it presents itself to the distant observer.

Looked at from that distance, the first thing that strikes me is that to be called a craftsman is to receive an honorary title. It is perhaps the most flattering thing that can be said nowadays about a worker in any field. This is remarkable if you remember that traditionally the artisan scored low on the social scale and that, for example, Leonardo da Vinci's strenuous attempts to prove in his writings that painting is as good as, or superior to, the other arts made sense at a time when painting as well as sculpture wished to escape from the inferior company of the mechanical

First published in *Craft Horizons*, 1961, 21, 32–35.
[1] This paper was read as the keynote address at the annual convention of the American Craftsmen's Council in Seattle, Washington.

arts and aspired to the status of the liberal arts, worthy of free men. To remove the stigma from manual labor and to join the ranks of the philosophers, the poets, the musicians, was the craftsman's aspiration in those days.

Things have changed because the craftsman has become the idealized image of a person safe from some fundamental dangers of our society. In a commercialized world, in which millions of people never handle anything more tangible than paper references to actual products, the craftsman enjoys the privilege of being in manual touch with objects of primary value. In an age of mechanized mass production, the craftsman still fashions single, precious things; and while in a factory or business office, every activity is split up into small, partial manipulations, the craftsman is seen as the master in his house, free to do the complete job according to his own standards. Finally, modern science has raised much of our dealing with reality to such a rarefied sphere of abstraction that we view with envy the craftsman's handling of concrete solids as a most desirable remedy for our estrangement.

Only after listening in on the conversations of craftsmen does one realize that, far from being in undisturbed possession of the values of which we feel deprived, they are caught in our society after all, deeply involved in trying to cope with the very troubles from which one fancied them to be the refuge. In fact, the craftsman's puzzling condition is a true reflection of the general state.

What are some of the basic problems? Let me start from the sober and familiar distinction between visual shape and visual form. Shape is described by the spatial boundaries of objects; it is a purely visual property. Form is not purely visual; it is rather the relation between a shape and something it is the shape of. Form is the shape that makes a content visible, and that content in itself may not be visible at all.

However, to distinguish in this way between form and content is risky. The distinction is indicative of the split that has occurred in our culture between the visible and the invisible worlds. We cannot easily tell to what extent this split is progress and to what extent decay. To earlier, simpler cultures, the world, as they conceived of it, was totally visible. The world was made of substances and run by forces that, if not directly given to the eye, were visually imaginable. The infinitely large and the infinitely small were represented by analogy of the conveniently sized environment, the mental appeared in the guise of the physical, and the gods and demons differed from the next man only in the quantity of their powers. From the seed to the mature shape, from raw material to

finished product, from the individual citizen to his community, everything was perfectly visible in principle. Let me add that in such a totally
visible world all shape was form. The notion that something could be
sheer meaningless, unrelated shape, nothing but shape, did not exist.

I had better confess at this point that when I think of art I think of
what makes the nature of things visible. I don't much care whether it is
made by nature or by man, by hand or by machine, intentionally or unintentionally. All that matters is whether or not shape makes my eyes
understand what they see. If it does, I call it art, whether it be a waterfall or a flower, a human face, a spoon, a pair of shoes, a statistical chart,
a pitcher, or a picture. In arriving at this view, I have been greatly helped
by a remark of the philosopher Martin Heidegger, dealing with the well-
known fact that the ancient Greeks used one and the same word,
téchne, to designate art and handicraft. This fact has been misinterpreted to mean that the Greeks thought of the artist as a mere artisan
—a misunderstanding, by the way, favored by some of our artists, who
like to present themselves as manual laborers, rough, tough, illiterate,
and suspicious of the intellect. Here Heidegger asks us to remember that
to equate the artist and the artisan was not to degrade the artist but
rather to exalt the artisan. A *téchnites* was a man who made the world
visible, and this was the business of the shoemaker as well as that of the
architect or sculptor. The shoemaker lets the function of the footwear
assume shape, he brings its nature to light, just as the architect gives appearance to the protective power of shelter, the relationship of carrier to
weight, etc. This is not different in principle from the sculptor's task of
making body and soul visible.

Here, then, we have a formula. "The purpose of art and craft is to
make the world visible." So simple and convincing is this program that
it may tempt us to misjudge our task. The goal, we may say, is evident.
Our problem is how to attain it. The form we seek is simply the shape
that will make the nature of things comprehensible to the eyes. Let us
then discover how to make beautiful, original, practical, economical
shapes—for this is our problem! I hasten to say that I do not see the
situation this way. I believe that we can find the means only by searching for the ends. As we look around in the field of the crafts, we see an
abundance of talent and skill. We notice strikingly original shapes, ever
new ways of using new techniques and materials, and occasionally a delicate sense of order and proportion. If nevertheless the general state of
affairs is not quite satisfactory, it is because of an uncertainty of aims.

In the discussions at your earlier conventions, I found much thought given to such questions as whether to make few things or many, practical ones or useless ones, functional or freely expressive ones. Should the craftsman work by hand or by machine or for the machine? Should he consider the taste of the consumer, and if so, what consumer? It seems to me that, to the extent to which these are aesthetic questions, they can be answered only by a clarification of goals. What are we aiming for?

In the days when I was a student in Germany, shape was supposed to be determined by practical function; and indeed the Bauhaus buildings and chairs and lamps looked thoroughly functional to us. Examine these products today and you may or may not find them practical; but you are certain to discover that their shape was not determined by physical function only. What the Bauhaus group thought and said they were doing was to give each object the appearance directly derived from its practical purpose. Actually they tried to meet two conditions: to make the object useful and to make it assume the geometrical shapes of disk or sphere, rectangle or parabola—a preference of taste that is not surprising if you remember that among the Bauhaus masters there were Kandinsky and Klee, Moholy-Nagy, Feininger, and Schlemmer, but which certainly was not simply demanded by function.

In the meantime, it has become evident that to make an object practically functional is not the same task as to make its function visible. Years ago, you might remember, somebody designed a small coffeepot for cafeterias that was as cubic as a brick so that it could be stacked by the hundreds. The coffee poured from a small hole at one corner, and along the opposite edge was an opening creating a handle. That pot was thoroughly functional. It poured well, it was easy to grip, it stacked, and for good measure it was geometrical. Nevertheless, it was a monster to the eye because its form contradicted its function. The symmetry of the cube created correspondences between parts of the object contrasting with the differences of their functions, and the functional distinctions and relations were not expressed in appearance. And, since coffeepots are an important part of our world, we must insist that rather than make the world visible, this useful object misled the eyes by making them believe that there were no coffeepots around while actually there were.

More and more objects are made nowadays whose shape does not offend the eyes by contradicting their function, but hides their function almost completely. You may hold in your hand an attractively shaped thing, unable to tell whether it is a transistor radio, an electric shaver, or a model of the office building that will perch on the roof of Grand Central Station in New York—surely three objects of different function. Whether or not such hiding of function is acceptable depends on what? It depends on how much the physical nature of things is considered essential to the view of the world. A consumer culture, which fosters the quest for easy satisfaction rather than curiosity, tends to suggest that it is enough for an object to serve its purpose smoothly, never mind how. Hence the streamlined abbreviations of shape.

In the arts and crafts, we have witnessed opinions on this matter change within our lifetime. I remember an exhibition of modern architecture in Stuttgart in the late 'twenties. The first thing you noticed when you entered the front door of one of the homes—I believe it was by Le Corbusier—was the heating system, with its pipes spreading in all directions. Since the furnace was the very heart of the house, it had to be shown first and in the center. And, of course, none of the waterpipes throughout the house were inside the walls. That would have been dishonest. But, even in those days, nobody objected to sculpture showing the female body with lungs and heart and stomach, ovaries and intestine hidden beneath an envelope of external shape—a most unfunctional sight. In fact, the statues in those days of functionalism were less anatomical than usual.

I am trying to demonstrate that what aspects of the world are to be made visible is a matter of philosophical creed. Take another example, closer to the particular concern of the craftsman. I have heard it said that the wooden chairs of the past with their straight backs and seats meeting at right angles are not functional because they do not adapt themselves comfortably to the human body. However, we surely remember that those chairs were not made for our sort of comfort. In those days, for a person to be seated had something of the ceremoniousness we now reserve for judges and presidents, because the daily gatherings around the dinner table or in the livingroom were dignified social occasions with religious overtones. The straightbacked chairs, then, were eminently functional. The human back was supposed to adapt to *them*. If we, on the other hand, enjoy letting our bodies fall into a bag of fabric or leather suspended at four corners, we contribute to making a world visible in which the proper way of meeting one's friends is to drop back into a state of inarticulate inertia—that of the human body before the first craftsman breathed a living soul into it. This sort of modern chair, then, is highly functional in a setting governed mainly by material values and purposes, by relaxed passivity, and by the notion that the smaller the effort, the better the life.

Another typical problem may illustrate my contention that what is commonly considered a question of means is really a question of ends. In an age of machines, should objects be made by hand? I do not see how one can discuss this issue simply as a technical matter, related to the money in the pockets of consumers and producers, the trend on the market, and the personal satisfaction of the craftsman. Looked at in itself, one technique is as good as the other, and no aesthetic choice can be made among them. The situation changes as soon as we remember that the problem is not of recent origin. It came up the first time somebody used a ruler to make a straight line or a compass to draw a circle. The machine raises the ancient and eternal problem of what part perfection should have in an imperfect world. In the days of Pythagoras and Plato, it was assumed that the perfect was the truly real and the truly good, and that the proper way of making the world visible was by numbers and measured shapes. But only a few hundred years later, Hellenistic art delighted in the imperfections of the individual human body, and ever since then our culture has gone back and forth between the Classic norm of perfection and the Romantic need for variety, irregularity, and the imperfection of the individual impulses.

Whenever a craftsman uses the potter's wheel, the saw, or the lathe, he is awakened to the curious fact that the attainment of perfection—in the particular sense in which I am using the word—is not human and that the mechanical tool achieves by its simple nature what man can approach only by an almost superhuman effort to overcome or go beyond his humanity. The straight cut, the simple curve, the flawless symmetry can be achieved only by the application of simple forces. The mechanical tool is simple-minded, and therefore its product is perfect. Man, on the other hand, is the most complex organization of forces in existence.

Now, among us mortals, complexity blocks perfection, but it makes for intelligence, and we have it from the Greek philosopher Anaxagoras that man is the most intelligent of all creatures because he has hands. Aristotle, commenting on this remark, thought that more probably man was endowed with hands because he is the most intelligent being. The same observation occurs, perhaps independently, more than two thousand years later, in the *Anthropology* of Immanuel Kant, and since I am speaking to the aristocrats of the hand, I will translate the little-known passage for you: "The characterization of man as a rational animal is found even in the shape and organization of his hand, his fingers and the tips of his fingers. It is through their build and tender sensitivity that nature has equipped him, not for just one manner of handling things, but unspecifically for all of them, which is to say, nature has equipped him for the employment of reason and thereby designated the technical capacity of his species as that of a rational animal."

By means of what the human hand creates, nature's way of making things reaches into our culture. Granted that the product of the hand is the product of reason, as the philosophers said, but it is reason as the supreme accomplishment of nature. Like the leaves of the tree, hand-made things aspire to some norm of perfection, yet play around that norm in innumerable and unpredictable variations because every producing agent of nature is constantly influenced by the shifting constellations of the moment. Thus, the handmade object we cherish is the reminder and promise of inexhaustible and unpredictable variety; and to make things by hand is almost indispensable for a person in order to contemplate the image of his own individuality, without which he loses his place in the world of the humans.

This, however, is only half of the story and makes no sense without the other half. We must add that the striving for what I have called perfection is as much a part of us as our imperfection. Although the hand cannot attain the perfect, it often attempts to make it, and it seeks help from tools. For the perfect is not only the simple product of the simple-minded tool, it is also the pure case, the liberation from accident. Perfect shape makes for a simple constellation of forces and therefore, in practical matters, it fits things together and holds them in balance and keeps them constant and makes them move with a minimum of friction. This is why builders and engineers need it. In matters of the mind, perfect shape makes our concepts visible. In the pure curves of a vase thrown on the wheel, we see the forces of weight and striving, of containing and receiving depicted in their essence without the distractions of accidental individuality. It is for this realization of the perfect that man has always sought the assistance of the simple-minded tool, and what we now call the machine is nothing worse or better than the latest in the ancient family of instruments, of the wheels and the saws and the lathes. Just as handmade things are the emissaries of nature in the land of reason, so the tool-made things are the emissaries of reason in the land of nature.

The problem we are facing here in our search for form is primarily neither technical nor economical. It is the question where the world we have to make visible should take its place on the scale between the two extremes of rustic clumsiness on the one side and of the Mondrianish nightmare of a life drawn by the ruler on the other. Once we face this problem, we shall see no contradiction between the handmade piece of jewelry and the machine-made safety-pin; nor shall we succumb to the temptation of producing the one by the method that suits the other. For while there is no point in trying to obtain by a laborious discipline of eyes and hands the perfection that the machine can give us faster and better, it is vulgar to imitate by machine the traces of the human impulse. Once these principles are clear, the craftsman will contribute to the image of our world those handmade shapes that are the indispensable manifestation of man as a child of nature; and with equally good conscience will he design for the machine, the way a musical composer designs for the violin or the trombone. Once we envisage the world to which we must give shape, we shall know which objects can and should be made in numbers and which must be unique. We will develop a language by which the craftsman or designer—and I know of no essential difference between the two—can explain himself concretely to the manufacturer, and the manufacturer can speak to the designer. Only when our goals are clarified, will our teachers in the public schools, the colleges, and the art schools be able to talk sense with conviction and begin to educate the population, of whose standards of taste the market is a mere secondary reflection.

The gist of my suggestions is that the search for form can be successful only if it is conducted as a search for content. How to make the world visible is so much of a problem today because that world, being the world of man, must necessarily be one of ideas. Ideas, however, are precariously weak in a culture given essentially to the amusement of the body and the distraction of the mind. If you look around at what is being produced in the performing arts and in the fine arts, you will find that a good deal of it—whether in television or in abstract expressionism —serves, in fact, at different social levels, to amuse the body and to distract the mind. But there is a hitch in this smooth correspondence of demand and supply. Human beings cannot live below their level of capacity without disturbance. You may call it a matter of conscience; for conscience is the instinct of self-preservation applied to the mind. Thus, we observe the rebellion of the few and the indifference of the many, the discontent and spite and touchiness in our painters and sculptors. Compared with them, the craftsmen are a wholesome race, and for good reasons. The practicality of the objects they make used to be considered an obstacle to artistic value by a perverted aesthetics, of which we are the heirs. Actually this orientation toward the practical is today the most promising road to a recovery of the arts. If a man who designs and makes leather sandals is likely to be in a better frame of mind than his friend who paints abstractions, it is because the sandal-maker has a sensible goal by which to determine the choice of his shapes whereas the painter, more often than not, cannot discover what his shapes are for and therefore can judge them only by whether they titillate the sensory organs of the body, or content himself with the precipitation of his gestures on canvas. In fact, if any prediction can be made about the future of painting and sculpture, it must be based, I believe, on the observation that an isolated pattern of abstract shapes, beautiful and ingenious though it may be, falls short of meaning and that, in consequence, abstract painting and sculpture, by a healthy instinct, are moving toward becoming a part of architecture, interior design, and craft work. In other words, I hope and foresee that the harmful distinction of fine arts and applied arts will be overcome by a general movement of the fine arts toward application.

You craftsmen, who have been making abstractions since the dawn of our civilization, know that all shape must be determined by being the form of something, be it the realization of a practical object, or a portrait of a thing of nature, or a message transmitted through the visual language of shapes and colors. But form it must be or else it will degenerate into chaos or a mere tickle of the senses. Now, the making of practical objects would seem to be the most promising way of gradually restoring a loss of meaning in the arts. For the demands and creations of the spirit have always developed from the needs of practical living, and correspondingly, all art has developed from objects of material use to objects of spiritual use. Honest craftsmanship, therefore, has a chance of easing us into a renaissance of significant form.

This aim, however, is not achieved by mere practicality while you wait until the philosophers figure out what sort of a world the craftsman should make visible. The quest for ideas must always take place on all fronts of human capacity, and, in fact, we have reason to believe that human beings think primarily and most effectively by means of what the senses explore and control, that is, by action and by the sort of tangible object you, the craftsmen, make. As a modern example, I remind you only of the fruitful interplay between architecture and social philosophy in our times. But this example shows also that such visual thinking will occur only if the mind is geared to ideas; which makes me suggest that in the life of a craftsman the contemplation of the world at large and a thoughtful reading of the philosophers, poets, and newspapers should probably have priority over the perusal of the latest techniques and market surveys.

For ideas will metabolize into potential shapes, calling on you to be given material existence. And it is this call of the unborn shapes that will lead you to the form we seek.

INDEX

Abstract art, 10 39, 48, 115, 189, 210, 266, 331, 346, 361
Abstraction
    language, 266–282
    shape, 27–50, 86, 301, 340, 346, 361
Accident, 76, 133, 162–180
Actor, 317
Adam, L., 46
Aesthetic
    attitude, 330
    distance, 318, 323
Alberti, Leone Battista, 197
Alschuler, Rose, 340
Ambiguity, 91, 94, 124, 153, 158, 236
Ames, Adalbert, Jr., 138, 157
Ammanati, Bartolomeo, 126
Ananke, 168
Anaxagoras, 358
Angelico, Fra, 164
Antonioni, Michelangelo, 188
Apollo of Belvedere, 203
Archetypes, 177, 222
Architecture, 102–119, 128, 174, 192–212, 361
Aristotle, 358
Art, 163, 189, 355

artistic type, 138
for art's sake, 351
    history, 19, 151–161
Art education, 13, 37, 136, 297, 337–342, 343–352
Asch, Solomon E., 63
Associationism, 56, 75
Attneave, Fred, 171
Autokinetic effect, 74, 75
Automatism, 162, 290

Bahnsen, Paul, 100
Balance, 21, 44, 76, 83, 103, 114, 234, 257
Baroque, 79, 176, 202, 250, 252
Basho, 134
Bauhaus, 193, 196, 200, 356
Beardsley, Aubrey, 47
Beauty, 105, 192, 197, 218
Beckmann, Max, 218
Behrendt, Walter Curt, 196
Bell, Clive, 14, 16, 302, 308
Bentley, Arthur, 226
Bergson, Henri, 266
Berkeley, George, 56
Binney, Jane, 70
Blake, William, 351

Blindness, 68
Boccaccio, Giovanni, 277
Boboli gardens, 126
Bodde, Derk, 240
Bohr, Niels, 240
Book of Changes, 230
Bowie, Henry P., 60
Brain-injured, 39
Breton, André, 176
Britsch, Gustaf, 36
Broad, C. D., 305
Brown, J. F., 22
Brown, Stephen J., 278
Bruegel, Peter, 80
Buhler, Charlotte, 59
Bullough, Edward, 323
Bunim, Miriam S., 38
Burchard, John E., 200
Byzantine art, 164

Cabinet of Dr. Caligari, The, 185
Calder, Alexander, 254
Cannon, Walter B., 45
Cantril, Hadley, 139
Caplan, Ralph, 206
Caricature, 153, 159
Catlin, George, 328
Causality, perception of, 143
Ceramists, 210
Cézanne, Paul, 11, 156, 174, 296, 299
Chance. *See* Accident
Chaplin, Charles, 185
Chardin, Jean Baptiste Siméon, 175
Chesterton, George K., 20
Children, 30, 56, 59
    and art, 29, 34, 36, 45, 46, 115,
    155, 246, 340
Chimpanzees, 30
Chinese philosophy, 224
Chou Tun-yi, 227
Christianity, 126
    art, 44, 201
Chuang-tzu, 301
Circle, 28, 60, 234
Circularity, 238
Claparède, Edouard, 302, 309
Classicism, 124

Color, 22, 54, 117, 332
Communication, 21
Complementarity, 237, 240
Complexity, 46, 48, 91, 115, 123–135,
    140, 163, 183
Composition, 20, 76, 110, 114, 116,
    220
Concavity, 238, 248
Concentration, 178
Concept, 27–50, 142, 217, 267–282
Conceptual art, 155
Concreteness, 27, 28, 268
Constable, John, 34, 152
Consumer, 7–16, 297, 357
Contemplation, 292–301
Content, 13
Continuity, 98
Convexity, 238, 248
Coomaraswamy, Ananda K., 45, 264
Coordination, 130
Correspondence, 96, 131
Cosmology, 224
Craftsmen, 209, 353–362
Creativity, 292–301
Critical attitude, 15
Cubism, 48, 155, 168, 196, 253

Dallapiccola, Luigi, 172
D'Amico, Fedele, 172
Dance, 69–72, 127, 261–265
Dante Alighieri, 32, 279, 286
Darwin, Charles, 56, 59, 63, 69
Darwinism, 144, 195, 332
Decorative art, 47
Definition of shape, 127
Degas, Edgar, 166
Delacroix, Eugène, 270
Depth perception, 22, 80, 99, 239
Descartes, René, 302, 307
De Sica, Vittorio, 188
Design, 197, 206, 360
Detachment, 46
Dewey, John, 226
Diagram of the Supreme Ultimate, 227
Diderot, Denis, 175
Differentiation, 174
Disorder, 125, 128, 169, 182, 256

Donatello, 154
Doodles, 47, 178, 256
Dreams, 176, 219, 288
Dubuffet, Jean, 190
Duffy, Elizabeth, 304
Duncan, Isadora, 264
Duncker, Karl, 22
Dürer, Albrecht, 39
Dynamics, visual, 45, 53, 62, 74, 75, 98, 104, 133, 154, 235, 240, 246, 310

Economy. See Parsimony
Education, 146. See also Art Education
Efron, David, 70
Egyptian art, 106, 155
Einstein, Albert, 146, 287
El Greco, 81
Eliot, T. S., 188, 268, 280
Emotion, 21, 302–319
Empathy, 53, 57, 66, 83, 108, 316
Empiricism, 75, 138, 157
Emptiness, 239, 250
English gardens, 125
Entropy, 21, 172
Epidaurus, 211
Equilibrium. See Balance
Evolution, 144, 195, 332
Expression, visual, 22, 37, 51–73, 82, 100, 153, 160, 192–212, 224, 234, 263, 275, 310, 313
Extracerebral perception, 309
Extroversion, 138
Eye movements, 80

Fechner, Gustav Theodor, 17, 117, 128
Feeling, 302–319
Feininger, Lyonel, 253
Ferenczi, Sandor, 217
Fibonacci series, 106
Figure and ground, 22, 99, 130, 234, 237, 248
Film, 22, 127, 154, 181–191
Fitness of design, 192–212. See also Functionalism
Flaubert, Gustave, 277, 285
Flowers, 320

Focillon, Henri, 252
Forces. See Dynamics, visual
Form, 7–16, 40, 94, 143, 353–362
Formalism, 8, 47
French gardens, 125, 127, 128
Frenkel-Brunswik, Else, 103
Freud, Sigmund, 176, 215–221, 280, 287. See also Psychoanalysis
Fromm, Erich, 219
Frontality, 323
Fry, Roger, 7, 8, 9, 13, 308, 312
Functionalism, 108, 192–212, 356

Gardens, 123–135, 320–334
Gellermann, Louis W., 30
Generality of percepts, 27–50, 142, 163, 217, 220, 270–282
Géricault, Théodore, 77
Gestalt psychology, 21, 30, 31, 36, 44, 45, 51–73, 82, 87, 92, 104, 143–147, 157, 158, 223, 224, 230, 275, 292–301
Gesture, 59, 70
Gibson, James J., 22, 143, 145
Gide, André, 14
Gilson, Etienne, 333
Giotto, 154
Goethe, Johann Wolfgang von, 22, 159, 176, 231, 326, 341
Goitein, Lionel, 216
Golden section, 103, 128
Goldstein, Kurt, 39
Goldwater, Robert, 34
Gombrich, E. H., 139, 152–161, 325, 327
Goodenough, Florence L., 29
Gotshalk, Dilman W., 64
Gottlieb, Carla, 15
Gottschaldt, Kurt, 96, 143
Gravity, 242, 263, 342
Greek art, 79, 152, 252, 355
    architecture, 114, 201
Greenough, Horatio, 195
Groddeck, Georg, 216
Grouping, perceptual, 92
Growth, mental, 37
Gsell, Paul, 80

Hadamard, Jacques, 145
Hadrian's villa, 130
Hand, 358
Handwriting, 60
Hanslick, Eduard, 9, 14
Haptic art, 30, 145
Harmony, 105
Harnett, William M., 169
Hattwick, LaBerta W., 340
Hedonism, 20, 311
Hegel, Georg W. F., 200
Heidegger, Martin, 321, 329, 355
Herder, Johann Gottfried von, 140
Hierarchy, 116, 132, 174, 220, 230
Hirschfeld, Christian C., 131
Hogarth, William, 252
Homeostasis, 21, 45
Homogeneity, 129
Horizontals, 117
Hornbostel, Erich Maria von, 276
Horse, galloping, 77
Hull, Clark L., 145
Human body, 105, 106, 115, 118, 203, 245, 256, 261–264, 357
Humboldt, Wilhelm von, 140
Huxley, Aldous, 271

I Ching, 230
Identity, 328
Ideoplastic art, 29, 38
Illusion, optical, 74–76
Illusionism, 139, 151–156, 326
Illustrations, 40, 148
Images, mental, 277
Imagination, 83, 86, 156, 276
Imitation of nature, 152, 169, 326
Impressionism, 48, 189
Indeterminacy, 184
Induction, 170
Information theory, 171
Inspiration, 285–291
Integrative levels, 113
Intellect, 104, 110, 138, 231
Intellectualistic theory, 29, 31, 38, 145, 155
Interaction, 104, 124, 143, 222–244, 321

Intracerebral perception, 309
Introversion, 85, 138, 152
Intuition, 104, 110, 193, 266, 314
Invention, 145
Irrational shape, 128, 182, 247
Isomorphism, 36, 58–63, 223, 261, 275, 313
Ittelson, William H., 139

James, William, 68, 216, 309, 315
Japanese gardens, 126–135
    painting, 60
Johnson, Samuel, 31
Jung, Carl Gustav, 177, 219, 222, 288
Justi, Carl, 77

Kainz, Friedrich, 44
Kandinsky, Wassily, 22, 156
Kant, Immanuel, 33, 358
Keaton, Buster, 185
Keats, John, 269
Kinesthesis, 253
    response to vision, 67, 83
    dance, 261, 317
Klein, Abraham, 90
Kleist, Heinrich von, 263
Koffka, Kurt, 22, 30, 59, 304
Köhler, Wolfgang, 59, 62, 64, 145, 199, 224
Kopfermann, Hertha, 22
Korean flag, 232
Kracauer, Siegfried, 181–191
Kühn, Herbert, 43

Landscape design, 123–135
Langer, Susanne K., 308, 316
Langfeld, Herbert S., 318
Language, 139–142, 146, 266–282
Laocoön, 216
Lawfulness, 116, 123, 138, 162
Lawrence, D. H., 264
Learning, 145
Le Corbusier, 105–112, 357
Leeper, Robert, 303, 304
Le Nôtre, André, 127
Leonardo da Vinci, 8, 9, 175, 353
Lessing, Gotthold Ephraim, 77
Leveling, 95

Levertov, Denise, 312
Lighting 117
Likeness, 329–334
Linguistics, 139
Lipchitz, Jacques, 290
Lipps, Theodor, 57, 66
Locomotion, 74, 76
Loos, Adolf, 192, 200
Löwenfeld, Viktor, 30
Lundholm, H., 70
Lynch, Kevin, 174

McDougall, William, 304, 309
Machines, 358
Magatama, 236
Martin, John, 264
Maslow, Abraham H., 199
Mass production, 106
Masserman, J. H., 304
Mathematics, 105, 145
Matter, 113
Meaning, 258
Measurement, 104, 110
Medium, 36, 183
Melancholy, 187
Memory, 29, 143, 157
Metaphor, 243, 266–282
Meyer, Hannes, 193
Meyer, Max F., 304
Michelangelo, 164
Michotte, Albert, 143, 333
Mimesis, 154
Modern art, 343–352
Modigliani, Amedeo, 81
Modulor, 106–113
Molecular structure, 113
Momentary phase, 76, 77
Mondrian, Piet, 186
Monet, Claude, 189
Monsters, 255–257
Moore, Henry, 216, 245–255, 331
Motion picture. See Film
Motivation, 20, 310
Movement, 98, 184
    response, 74–89, 90
Mozart, Wolfgang Amadeus, 11, 67
Müller, Georg Elias, 144

Muller-Munk, Peter, 206
Mumford, Lewis, 196
Munro, Thomas, 3, 185
Murry, John Middleton, 278, 280
Mursell, James L., 23
Muscle sense. See Kinesthesis
Music, 9, 10, 22, 64, 70, 105, 110, 162, 267
Muybridge, Eadweard, 77, 80

Nanzenji garden, 134
Naturalism, 8, 29, 38, 42, 46, 152, 163, 189
Nature, 109, 117, 124, 139, 159, 194, 225, 321
Necessity, 76, 162–180
Nervi, Pier Luigi, 205
Neurotics, 339
Neutra, Richard, 195
Nightfishing at Antibes, 258–260
Nonobjective art. See Abstract art
Normal view, 297
Novikoff, A. B., 113

Olivier, Sir Lawrence, 184
Oracle, 290
Order, 113, 123–135, 163, 257
Organization, visual, 21, 31, 40, 44, 87, 92, 141, 147, 257
Originality, 298
Ornament, 44
Oscillation, 236

Palladio, Andrea, 200, 202
Panofsky, Erwin, 45, 111
Parabola, 60
Parrhasios, 154
Parsimony, 47, 100, 172
Past experience, 66, 81, 82, 139, 145
Pathetic fallacy, 53, 64, 276, 316
Pavlov, Ivan P., 137, 144
Perception, visual, 21, 157, 292, 309, 339
    categories, 32, 35
    causality, 143
    See also Depth perception; Organization, visual

Perspective, 22, 158
Photography, 40, 48, 55, 77, 127, 146, 170, 182
Physiognomic qualities, 63, 275. *See also* Expression
Physioplastic art, 38
Picasso, Pablo, 13, 45, 256, 258–260, 299
Piero della Francesca, 260
Plato, 168, 186
Pleasure, 20, 137, 311
Poetry, 268–282
Pointillism, 179
Pollock, Jackson, 172
Porphyry, tree of, 217
Post-and-lintel, 205
Poussin, Nicolas, 8, 9, 14, 15, 175
Prall, D. W., 308, 312
Pregnant moment, 77
Primitive art, 28, 36, 39, 41–43, 145
    language, 267
Projection, 35, 51, 54, 153, 156. *See also* Rorschach
Prophecy, 290
Proportion, 20, 102–119, 128, 152
Psychoanalysis, 21, 176, 177, 215–221, 239, 280, 287–290, 316, 338
Psychology, 198, 337
    of art, 2, 17–23
Psychosomatics, 69
Pygmalion, 154, 327
Pythagoras, 105

Quantification, 19

Random patterns, 170
Rapaport, David, 83, 86
Raphael, 220, 258
Rationality, 106, 111, 127, 247
Read, Herbert, 176
Realism. *See* Naturalism
Reality, 183
    level, 185
Rectangle, 103, 117
Reflection, 140
Rembrandt, 164, 216
Renaissance, 79, 105, 203

Representation, 34, 152
Resnais, Alain, 185
Resonance, 69, 85
Ricci, Leonardo, 141
Right and wrong, 102, 193, 314
Risom, Jens, 197
Ritual, 209
Rockwell, Norman, 349
Rodin, Auguste, 80, 216, 296, 326
Roman architecture, 106
Romanticism, 18, 108, 124, 166, 176, 183, 247, 286, 289
Rorschach, 35, 54, 74–101, 241
Rubens, Peter Paul, 175
Rubin, Edgar. *See* Figure and ground
Ruskin, John, 152
Ryoanji garden, 131

St. Denis, 209
St. Francis, 320–334
Sakurabayashi, Hitoshi, 293–301
Santayana, George, 311
Sapir, Edward, 140
Satiation, 296
Schachtel, Ernest G., 54
Schaefer-Simmern, Henry, 36
Schiller, Friedrich von, 159, 163, 176
Schizophrenic art, 49
Schlosberg, Harold, 304
Schopenhauer, Arthur, 193, 203, 276
Science, 33, 163
Scott, Geoffrey, 117, 204
Sculpture, 210, 245–255, 263, 264
Self-image, 325–334
Semanticism, 142
Seurat, Georges, 179
Sex, 217, 239
Shakespeare, William, 280
Shape. *See* Form
Sharpening, 95
Similarity, 96
Simplicity, 21, 30, 44, 100, 103, 104, 114, 158, 163, 187, 345
Size, 170, 324
Skeleton, structural, 95
Space, 102–119, 245–255
Spender, Stephen, 272, 278, 281

Spinoza, Baruch, 151, 308
Spontaneity, 174, 290
Standardization, 106
Stereotypes, 57, 72
Stimulus, 32
    equivalence, 144
Stravinsky, Igor, 349
Structure, 95, 113, 208
Style, 11, 118
Subdivision, 92, 112, 236, 246
Subjectivity, 91
Suger, Abbot, 209
Sullivan, Louis H., 194, 203
Surrealism, 158, 162, 176, 279, 289
Symbol, 12, 44, 200, 215–221, 222–244, 257, 260
Symmetry, 88, 93, 124, 132, 165, 194, 321, 323
Szondi test, 55

T'ai-chi tu, 224–244
Taoism, 126, 224
Tasso, Torquato, 276
Television, 15, 16, 148
Tension. See Dynamics, visual
Texture, 129, 172, 189, 248
Theater, 127
Thinking, 142
    visual, 145
Thomas, Dylan, 351
Thomas Aquinas, 45
Thompson, D'Arcy, 113
Time, 324
Tintoretto, 166
Titian, 175
Tobey, Mark, 172
Toepffer, Rodolphe, 159
Tolman, Edward C., 82
Tolstoy, Leo, 316, 318
Transactionism, 138, 226
Trompe l'oeil, 169
Tussaud, Madame, 325

Unconscious, 176, 286, 315, 340
Universals. See Generality

Utility, 193–211, 353–362
Utzon, Jorn, 210

Valence, 322
Valentine, C. W., 198
Valéry, Paul, 48, 262
Van Gogh, Vincent, 35, 65
Vasari, Giorgio, 175
Veronese, Paul, 326
Versailles gardens, 127
Verticals, 117
Verworn, Max, 29, 38
Villey, Pierre, 68
Visibility, 202, 332, 355, 357
Visual education, 37, 146
Vitruvius, 105, 111, 197
Volavka, Vojtěch
Voltaire, 277

Waddington, C. H., 113
Wallach, Hans, 62
Watteau, Antoine, 80
Weaving, 210
Werner, Heinz, 63
Wertheimer, Max, 21, 44, 62, 96
Whistler, James A. McNeill, 34
Whorf, Benjamin Lee, 140
Wight, Frederick S., 216
Willmann, R. R., 70
Witkin, Herman A., 86
Wittgenstein, Ludwig, 146
Wölfflin, Heinrich, 79, 188
Woodworth, Robert S., 303
Wright, Frank Lloyd, 193
Wulf, Friedrich, 95

Yeats, William Butler, 285
Yin and yang, 225

Zen Buddhism, 178
    gardens, 126
Zeuxis, 154